Visual Modeling Technique

Object Technology
Using Visual Programming

Visual Modeling Technique

Object Technology Using Visual Programming

Daniel Tkach
Object Technology Practice Leader
IBM Consulting Group
San Jose, California

Walter Fang
Senior Object Technology Consultant
IBM ITSO
San Jose, California

Andrew So
Object Technology Managing Consultant
IBM Consulting Group
Hong Kong

 **ADDISON-WESLEY**

An imprint of Addison Wesley Longman, Inc.

Menlo Park, California • Reading, Massachusetts • Harlow, England
Berkeley, California • Don Mills, Ontario • Sydney • Bonn • Amsterdam • Tokyo • Mexico City

Senior Acquisitions Editor: J. Carter Shanklin
Editorial Assistant: Angela Buenning
Senior Production Editor: Teri Hyde
Manufacturing Supervisor: Janet Weaver
Composition and Film Supervisor: Vivian McDougal
Cover Design: Yvo Riezebos

Text Design: David Healy, First Image; Fog Press
Copyeditor: Barbara Conway
Proofreader: Holly McLean-Aldis
Composition: Fog Press
Indexer: Nancy Kopper
Illustrations: Ben Turner Graphics

Many of the designations used by the manufacturers and sellers to distinguish their products are claimed as trademarks. Where those designations appear in this book, and Addison Wesley Longman was aware of a trademark claim, the designations have been printed in initial caps or all caps.

The following terms, denoted by an asterisk (*) in this publication, are trademarks of the IBM Corporation in the United States and/or other countries: IBM; APPC; AS/400; BookMaster; CICS ECI; CICS OS/2; C Set++; CUA; DataAtlas; DB2/2; DRDA; ECI; MVS/ESA; OS/2; RISC System/6000; SAA; System/390; TeamConnection; VisualAge; VisualGen

The following terms, denoted by a double asterisk (**) in this publication, are trademarks of other companies: CommonView—Glockenspiel; ENVY—Object Technology International, Inc; Excelerator II—Intersolv; GemStone—Servio Corporation; MacApp—Apple Computer, Inc.; Objectivity/DB—Objectivity, Inc.; ObjectStore—Object Design International; ObjectWindows—Borland; Ontos—Ontos Corporation; OMTool—GE Advanced Concept Center; OpenODB—Hewlett-Packard Corporation; Visual Basic—Microsoft Corporation; Visual C++—Microsoft Corporation; VXRexx**—WATCOM; Powerbuilder—Powersoft; VisualWorks—ParcPlace; Enfin—Easel; PARTS Workbench—Digitalk; Windows—Microsoft Corporation

This document is intended to provide the customer with an introduction to the concepts, terminology, and practical issues related to the use of visual modeling technique in an application development environment.

The information in this document is not intended as a specification of the interfaces that are provided by any of the products mentioned in this publication.

Printed in the United States of America.

Library of Congress Cataloging-in-Publication Data
Tkach, Daniel.
Visual modeling technique : object technology using visual programming / Daniel Tkach, Walter Fang, Andrew So.
    p.   cm.
Includes bibliographical references and index.
ISBN 0–8053–2574–3
1. Visual programming (Computer science)   2. Object-oriented programming (Computer science)
I. Fang, Walter. II. So, Andrew. III. Title.
QA76.65.T54   1996
005. 1' 2--dc20

96–2842
CIP

1 2 3 4 5 6 7 8 9 10 MA 00 99 98 97 96

Addison Wesley Longman
2725 Sand Hill Road
Menlo Park, CA 94025

Dedications

To my beloved family:
My dear wife Susy and my sweet children
Karen Elizabeth and Lauren Lee

Daniel S. Tkach

To my mother, who brought me up to be what I am,
and in memory of my father, who taught me, among other
things, how to read, think, and write.
To my family, Susan, Jennifer, and Christine, for their love
and support.

F. Walter Fang

To my father and mother who worked so hard
to support my education.
To my family, Maria, Jonathan and Adam, who give me
unconditional love and support. I love you all.

Andrew C. So

Foreword

Application development efforts in today's corporations can be greatly enhanced by choosing the right development tools and a suitable application development methodology. Tools and methodology must complement each other: The tools must support the use of the methodology, and the methodology must help harness the power of the tools.

The development of object-oriented applications received a productivity boost with the advent of visual programming tools such as the IBM VisualAge tools family. However, sound methodologies are needed to fully capture the power of building applications from components, as in object-oriented visual programming.

The Visual Modeling Technique (VMT) methodology described in this book introduces very significant contributions to object-oriented application development for both stand-alone and distributed applications,

The authors have improved the approach to requirements modeling by using the IBM VisualAge Requirements Tool to capture essential business knowledge, not only from use-cases and problem statements, but also from the business rules that govern the life of a corporation. By fully exploiting the power of visual programming, the authors have assigned VisualAge development products a key role to play in prototyping, modeling, and testing activities.

The authors also expand the scope of object-oriented application development by integrating business process re-engineering with object technology. Thus they provide clear meaning to the assertion that object technology models the real world—the world of corporate business processes after reengineering. The IBM ProModeler tool is shown to be an invaluable visual tool for supporting this integration.

The VMT methodology developed by IBM has been proven, in many client engagements, to be sound and complete. It has been selected as the methodology of choice for the IBM VisualAge family of application development products: Smalltalk, C++, and Object-Oriented Cobol.

The solid background and extensive experience of the authors are evident in this book. They have created the VMT methodology and enriched it through their frequent interactions with clients, students, IBM Software Laboratories, practitioners, and academicians. Their contribution to the maturity of object technology is worthy of acknowledgment.

— Steve Mills
General Manager
IBM Software Solutions Division

Preface

"If I have seen further than other men,
it is by standing on the shoulders of giants."
— Sir Isaac Newton

The IBM Almaden Research Center, south of San Jose, CA, is in an area of great natural beauty. Considering the process of Object Technology development in this setting brings to mind a simple analogy. Taming the West was an incremental process. First, the pioneers opened trails into the wilderness and marked the way to go. They mapped the mountain peaks and the waterholes, the peaceful meadows and the treacherous quicksands. And once the territory was open, safe, and growing, immigrants came from everywhere, attracted by the new opportunities.

Now, everyone wants to live in the new territory. New vehicles cruise the region faster, but the pioneer trails are narrow; some must be expanded, some combined, and some replaced with streets with pavements, sidewalks, and stores, so the dwellers can travel efficiently as well as shop. It is time for highway builders as well as for masons and plumbers to go to work resolving some of these problems.

Object-oriented technology and its applications went through a process very much like that new territory. First came the programmers, the language definers, and the compiler builders for Simula, Smalltalk, C++, Clos, Eiffel—too many to name. Hackers played with messages, discussed encapsulation, and dreamed about "software integrated circuits." Everyone agreed that the new approach offered a lot of potential to enforce well-known principles of software engineering that most were too lazy to apply, but nobody was sure how to realize the potential in a systematic way.

The designers then showed how object-oriented code had to be planned and built. Approaches such as those described in the first Grady Booch book, Object-Oriented Analysis and Design with Applications, the CRC technique, and Responsibility-Driven Design, became popular. In the meantime, the theorists established a framework of respectability for object technology through discussion of issues such as the implications of inheritance and polymorphism, relationships with formal language theory, and the differences between classes and types.

The last to arrive on the scene were the analysts, who reminded everyone that, in the end, it was all about solving real-world business problems. Object modeling transformed approaches into methodologies and gave object technology the respectability it needed to attract the MIS crowd. Starting from data modeling, the new methods evolved by including the dynamic aspects of the real world that data modeling ignored. OMT, OOSE, and the Booch Method provided a pathway between business requirements and the resulting application code. Meanwhile, theory and design evolved accordingly, with Design by Contract and Syntropy leading the way toward formality in object-oriented design.

All these efforts notwithstanding, there is a long way to go from attraction to acceptance, and an even longer one from acceptance to embracing. Languages and methodologies are not enough; the corporate world demands productivity, which translated to application development means that tools are needed to support every aspect of development. For instance, modeling can be successful only if the proper modeling tool is used, especially when iterations are encouraged. Also, application development from components entails the use of tools to construct, store, browse, retrieve, and assemble components with others from a components repository.

In 1991, when IBM started to build what is now known as IBM VisualAge for Smalltalk, it became obvious to the authors that existing object-oriented methodologies were inadequate to harness the power of visual programming. The dominant view at the time was that visual programming was to be used mainly for GUI building. We saw an opportunity to enhance the productivity of the development of the whole application, but we also saw a need to integrate visual development into the application development life cycle, from requirements to code. To that end we developed Visual Modeling Technique (VMT), the methodology we describe in this book.

When we developed VMT, we decided not to reinvent the wheel but to take from existing methodologies the elements proven to be successful, combine them to meet our needs, and add components to address the specific needs of visual programming. We were strongly influenced by a memorable panel session at OOPSLA 93 called "Shootout at the OO Corral," where the pioneers in object-oriented methodologies explained clearly the weak and strong points of their methodologies, and what each would like to adopt from the work of their fellows and why. We decided to build into VMT the enhancements that were pointed out at that session.

VMT covers a larger span in the application development life cycle than most methodologies. The statement that "object technology models the real world" was immediately challenged by the question "which real world?" We adhered to Hammer's thoughts about business process reengineering in "Reengineering the Corporation," {Ham 95} but we needed a visual way to express the processes of an enterprise and the changes the reengineering activity would produce. We postulated that the real world we want to model resides in the reengineered enterprise, described through its processes rather than through its organization; the VMT methodology should thus be applied to support a process architecture that adds value to the corporation and enhances customer satisfaction.

Fortunately, the Line of Visibility Enterprise Modeling (LoVEM) that IBM Canada (reengineering consulting practice) has developed provides an excellent reengineering approach based on graphical descriptions of the enterprise processes as they are today ("as-is" processes), and as they will be after the reengineering effort ("to-be" processes). This graphical description is supported by a flexible tool developed by IBM Boeblingen Lab called Business Process Modeler (BPM), which makes process charting easy and allowed us to integrate business process reengineering with object application development to build automation support for the reengineered ("to-be") real world.

Once the relationships were established among the processes and the objects used by the supporting automation systems, we were able to define and build a blueprint for creating very rich and descriptive enterprise architectures based on the enterprise processes and objects. This architecture can be customized to a particular corporation or abstracted to an industry level, describing the fundamental processes and objects of a given industry.

The work on business process reengineering led us to the need for capturing the business rules that govern both the essence and the details of a business. To that end, we augmented the use case paradigm by splitting each use case into its component input and output transactions, and making explicit the business rules that govern the outcome of each transaction. This powerful approach would have been very difficult to handle in any practical way without the support of a good development tool. We found an excellent visual tool for handling business requirements, including transactions and rules, at the IBM Santa Teresa Laboratory in San Jose, California. This tool facilitates our use case decomposition and augmenting approach.

This book is directed to people who are already familiar with object-oriented technology and want to put the technology in place so it can live up to its promises. The content of this book will appeal to MIS managers, object architects, modelers, designers, programmers, and anyone who is involved in developing real-life object-oriented applications. It will also be useful to business process engineers and consultants involved in business process modeling and automation.

How This Book Is Organized

Part 1 of the book describes the VMT methodology and its application. Chapter 1 sets the stage for the description of the VMT methodology. It discusses the contents of an object methodology and the importance of modern visual programming tools in the application development process. The chapter also describes the object-oriented application development process and the methodologies that had an influence in the building of VMT. Chapter 2 introduces the VMT methodology and describes the way it approaches object-oriented analysis. Chapter 3 demonstrates the application of VMT analysis techniques to a case study based on a real-life foreign currency exchange (FCE) application. Chapter 4 introduces the use of relational databases to store persistent objects. Chapter 5 looks at the VMT design phase. Chapter 6 describes the transition from the model step by step and shows how designing by contract can be used to leverage object-oriented visual programming. Chapter 7 applies the design techniques to the FCE application modeled in Chapter 4.

Part 2 of the book extends VMT to the design of distributed object-oriented systems. Chapter 8 introduces the subject. Chapter 9 explains designing distributed object applications with VMT. Chapter 10 returns to the case study of Chapter 4, looking at distributed objects.

Part 3 of the book examines the project management aspects of using VMT in developing applications to meet business needs resulting from reengineering. Chapter 11 discusses the various project management issues, such as staffing and training, project estimation, etc. Chapter 12 discusses testing and documentation considerations.

Part 4 of the book discusses the integration of VMT with business processing engineering. Chapter 13 describes business processing engineering and the Line of Visibility Enterprise Modeling (LOVEM) method. Chapter 14 discusses integrating VMT with business process reengineering based on LOVEM. Chapter 15 discusses augmenting VMT requirements modeling with business rules and transactions. Chapter 16 provides perspectives in object technology development trends and concluding remarks.

Acknowledgments

The VMT methodology was created in 1993 and has evolved greatly since. Its creation and current shape were influenced by our exchange of ideas with many individuals, to whom we are grateful.

We thank the many specialists who came from IBM locations worldwide to ITSO San Jose, California to work on the projects that documented, tested, and enhanced aspects of the methodology—their contributions to the IBM redbooks: GG24–4227, SG24–4390, SG24–4521 have been valuable to our task in developing VMT and this book.

Paul Webb of the IBM Canada LoVEM Business Process Reengineering practice helped us to understand the nature of business processes and discussed with us their relationship to the object technology concepts, allowing us to integrate in both a clear and logical way. Dr. Paul Luker, Head of the Computer Science Department at De Montfort University in Leicester, UK, encouraged us to continue our work and provided us with academic feedback about the validity and correctness of our approaches. Dr. Carlos Goti, creator of IBM VisualAge Requirements Tool, discussed the world of business rules with us, provided us with beta versions of the tool, helped us in developing the enhanced VMT requirement modeling approach by augmenting the use cases with business rules and transactions, and implemented some of our requests in the VisualAge Requirements Tool.

No methodology is really sound unless it has been used productively in real business environments. We are thankful to the CIOs, development managers, and developers in businesses worldwide, who have used this methodology in their projects and given us highly useful feedback. In IBM, Skip McGaughey championed our VMT initiative. IBM Software Solutions has chosen VMT for the IBM VisualAge Developer Certification program in Smalltalk, C++, and object-oriented COBOL, and we are grateful to Michael Ha and Oma Sewhdat for their support of that choice, to Marc Carrel (IBM ITSO–San Jose) and Peter Jakab (IBM Toronto Lab) who used VMT in C++ environments, and Joe DeCarlo (IBM ITSO–San Jose) who ran projects using VMT with object-oriented COBOL.

This book would not have been possible without the support of Jens Tiedemann, IBM ITSO–San Jose Center Manager, who provided us with the needed resources. Barbara Isa, at the IBM Santa Teresa Lab, gave us invaluable support to overcome the unavoidable legal and contractual hurdles involved in publishing.

Books are written by the authors, but are made legible by editors. We want to recognize Maggie Cutler, ITSO-San Jose Center editor, and Barbara Conway, copyeditor, for helping us to express our thoughts in a clear and concise style. And thanks to Carter Shanklin, Senior Acquisitions Editor and Teri Hyde, Senior Production Editor, and the rest of the Addison-Wesley staff for their key roles in the success of this book.

California, April, 1996

D. S. T

F. W. F

A. S.

Contents

Visual Modeling Technique

1

Introduction: Why VMT?

Visual programming has an impact on all phases of application development: requirements gathering, analysis, design, coding, and testing. The activities of these phases, when carried out in an environment with visual development facilities, change their flavor and sequence.

The development process actually begins long before the requirements specification. It is first necessary to determine which business processes exist in the corporation, and then which of those business processes will benefit from automation given the current or near-future state of the art in computing. In this book, we show how visual modeling techniques can be applied to the automation of process reengineering and requirements gathering phases, hence the name Visual Modeling Technique, or VMT. This book covers all the application development phases, including analysis, design and coding.

Many mature object-oriented methodologies are available, but integrating visual programming into the application development process adds some special requirements to the application development life cycle that have not been addressed before. VMT was created to address them. In addition, it is commonly said that object-oriented analysis models the "real world." However, there is the real world of the enterprise as it is today (that is, where the customer is serviced through the current enterprise processes), and there is the real world as it will be after reengineering and streamlining the current

2

processes. In VMT, we have extended the realm of a methodology to include integration with business process reengineering in order to be able to develop systems for the reengineered real world "to be" while maintaining the capabilities to model the real world "as is."

Another key contribution of VMT is explicitly integrating GUI building and prototyping into the modeling process. Because these activities are critical to reaping the benefits of a visual programming tool, we developed a new approach to provide a systematic way of building object-oriented applications in a visual programming tool environment.

VMT thus represents a new synthesis of proven techniques. It explicitly integrates object application development with business process reengineering and provides a solid foundation for capturing requirements through the use of business rules and prototyping.

VMT is a third-generation methodology created to address the need to integrate visual environments into mainstream object development. It is the object-oriented methodology chosen by IBM Software Solutions for the IBM VisualAge Developer Certification Program and has been used in large IBM client projects worldwide.

1.1 Contents of an Object Methodology

The term *object methodology* is a shortened form of *object-oriented application development methodology.* The goal of an object methodology is to use object technology to guide the development of a computer-based application. Object technology provides the basis for describing a problem and building a solution by using object models, thus ensuring a better understanding of the problem and faster development of a robust and flexible solution with significantly less maintenance cost.

A technically good solution, however, is not necessarily the right solution, that is, the solution that enables a software developer to achieve his or her goals. The right solution has two main facets: solving the right problem and providing the usability required to achieve a high level of user satisfaction. Object technology is only an enabler—a guide in the selection, specification, and development of the right set of applications.

Modeling the problem domain through object-oriented analysis immediately raises the question of which domain is to be modeled. Is it the domain defined by the reality of today (the *as-is* domain) or the new reality that arises from process reengineering (the *to-be* domain)? This question threatens the stability of the problem domain which, as part of the real world, is supposed to be inherently stable. For example, we expect accounts, cashiers, and bank reserves to be part of the banking application domain today and tomorrow. However, if reengineering of the bank's processes leads to closing a branch and replacing it with automated teller machines (ATMs), the cashier and bank reserve of that branch are no longer relevant to customer relations. Such objects therefore are not part of the problem domain and will not be part of the solution. If the bank also finds that foreign currency exchange services are not profitable in most small towns, the ATMs that will replace the branch offices probably will not provide those services. Foreign currency is then part of the as-is domain but not the to-be domain.

This example highlights the need to integrate process reengineering methodologies, which help transform a business, with object methodologies, which guide the development of applications that support business processes.

Usability is the second main facet of a right solution. The application should provide the required function; in addition, it should attend to the nonfunctional requirements that will guarantee user acceptance. Some nonfunctional requirements are basically domain independent: It should make no difference to response time or font size specifications whether the application supports inventory management or order entry.[1] The nonfunctional requirements depend on the way the application is used, however. If the requirements are not satisfied (as when response time at a bank teller's station is 20 minutes), the application is totally unusable, even if it is functionally correct.

An application is usable, therefore, only when it complies with both the functional and nonfunctional requirements. Functional requirements are derived, in principle, from domain knowledge and requirement statements, such as a client's request for proposals (RFP). Nonfunctional requirements are derived primarily from the interaction between user and expert. Oral descriptions and screen paintings do not yield a full understanding of the user's needs; more powerful techniques, such as prototyping, provide the user with the look and feel of the application and help the modeler capture the real needs of the user.

Although nonfunctional requirements are not related to the problem domain, understanding the user's interaction with the system can modify the domain to some degree. For instance, an application to support credit card validation may be developed on the basis of the customer's Social Security number. The user may point out that frequently a customer's mother's maiden name is used for validation, so this information should be recorded and displayed. This request expands the original domain.

Users who are domain experts or business professionals are accustomed to thinking in *business terms.* They know about processes, tasks, business rules, and real-world objects. Such users will probably describe their requirements more accurately in business terms than in newly acquired computer-related constructs. Bank officers, for instance, will feel comfortable describing loan processes, accounts, deposits, and transfers; it is harder for them to describe

---

1   Even though the response time required for a real-time rocket control system may differ from the response time required for a customer billing application, the difference is not related to fuel, steel alloys, or O-rings.

the responsibilities of a transaction class, which is a convenient abstraction for the application developer.

Information technology can bridge the gap between users and analysts with new approaches to modeling user requirements and transforming them into program specifications. One approach is to prototype the function as well as the look and feel of the application in an iterative fashion, interacting with the user in each iteration, until the user is thoroughly satisfied. For this approach to be practical, it must be supported by tools that allow rapid prototyping and graphical user interface (GUI) building.

This prototyping approach leads to the design of basic GUIs. More important, from an object-oriented point of view, it leads to an early determination of a key subset of the object model. To be productive, however, the prototyping approach requires fast turnaround. Early techniques for prototyping included the use of screen painters and storyboards (with no basic logic except that implied by the screen sequence) and database-oriented fourth-generation languages. Both techniques were unproductive, however, for object-oriented development, which had to rely on the skills of "language wizards" who made good use of the model-view separation allowed by object-oriented languages such as Smalltalk.

The breakthrough in improving application development and understanding user requirements came with the implementation of visual programming: the use of graphical representations to specify to a computer what it is to do. Visual programming relies on visual programming languages designed to handle visual information, support visual interaction, and enable programming with visual expressions.

In a visual programming language, the language primitives (for example, icons, lines, arrows, and form constructs) have well-defined syntax and semantics. The "sentences" expressed in these languages (for example, icons connected by arrows) can be parsed and interpreted and therefore translated to, for instance, Smalltalk, C++, or Object COBOL.

Tools that implement visual programming, such as IBM VisualAge family products, facilitate both rapid prototyping and solid object-oriented programming while reducing the training and skill prerequisites for these tasks. Visual programming is therefore a key instrument in understanding, recording, and filling user needs, resulting in improved application usability.

Object-oriented methodologies have initially been built as part of the evolution of work previously done by their authors in a particular field. This is recognizable in the aspects of requirements gathering that the methodologies emphasize. Authors who have been working on data modeling tend to emphasize the static (structural) aspects of the requirements, while those who have worked with real-time systems emphasize the dynamic (behavioral) aspects. Object modeling, however, must address both the static and dynamic characteristics of objects with the same care. In other words, some objects have to be modeled because of their importance in the description of a problem, as stated in an RFP or problem statement that describes mainly the static aspects of the problem. Other objects, however, whose behavior is significant, are found by the modeler when describing the interaction between users and the system. These objects are derived from the input provided by users and domain experts. VMT combines both aspects of requirements gathering through a systematic modeling process, supported by the visual development environment.

1.2 Visual Programming

Visual programming, a major breakthrough in tools technology, uses the power of meaningful graphical representations to specify what we want a computer to do. Visual programming environments provide a mechanism for the computer to understand graphical representations and transform user interactions with a pointing device such as a mouse into components of source code. In this way, they establish an environment for code execution, testing, and debugging. Additional components may represent modules of executable code, databases, and other application elements. These elements can be composed through graphical operations, such as point-and-click or drag-and-drop, to produce business applications.

1.2.1 Visual Programming Tools

A visual programming tool enables users to specify programs interactively, in a highly graphical manner. Routines, programs, and data have graphical representations, such as metaphors and icons. Relationships among those components are depicted graphically as well. Programs themselves are constructed graphically: The programmer manipulates and articulates graphical representations of components to create an application.

Visual programming tools differ significantly from tools used for program visualization. In program visualization, programs are written with traditional techniques; the tools merely show a graphical view of them. Program visualization tools use graphics only to illustrate aspects of a program or its execution. Such tools are commonly used for debugging and teaching.

1.2.2 Current Tools

Current visual programming tools avoid the shortcomings of earlier tools in the following ways:

- Improved ease of use
- Extensibility through support of a scripting language
- Robust capabilities and increased productivity beyond GUI building
- Capability for reuse with existing legacy applications

- Access to off-the-shelf software
- Adherence to industry standards
- Support of client/server computing
- Support of team programming and software configuration management

The ability to support a scripting language is an important advance. Visual programming has limitations and requires a language environment to provide completeness. The second-generation tools approach is to build a development environment around visual programming techniques and explicitly couple it with a complete language environment.

With visual programming tools such as VisualAge, developers specify as much of an application as possible in the visual environment. When they believe that the visual environment is inadequate to complete a job, they can switch to the language environment to finish it. The visual environment provides productivity; the language environment provides completeness.

There are many visual programming tools on the market. Not all of them are based on object-oriented technology, however; some have hybrid implementations, and others have only object-based user interfaces.

Object-oriented visual programming tools differ from other visual programming tools in that they are based on object technology and integrated with a complete object-oriented application development environment. These tools provide a comprehensive and consistent approach to application development; all components (user interface, business, and computing entities) at every stage of development are objects. Thus there is no need to map from the conceptual view of the problem to structured representations.

The trend in visual programming development tools is to provide a complete application development environment that allows the use of applications with both object-oriented and client/server technologies. VisualAge for Smalltalk and VisualAge for C++ from IBM provide such capabilities.

1.2.3 Construction from Parts

Construction from parts is an application development paradigm in which applications are assembled from reusable software components, or parts. A part is a software object with several external features that allow it to be connected to other parts to implement an application. A part can be primitive, or it can consist of many interacting subparts. The construction-from-parts paradigm is analogous to building a house with prefabricated building blocks, such as doors, window frames, and cabinets.

Although construction-from-parts concepts are new to software development, they are not new to the computer industry or to manufacturing. However, the success of the construction-from-parts paradigm in software development depends on several factors. First, interactive tools for visual construction must be available, and the tools must integrate with a development platform to design and build parts and frameworks. Second, interfaces and messaging protocols must be specified and supported by an architecture for interoperability of tools and component parts. Third, a set of standard parts must be available, and the software providers must move toward the building of components.

Among the foreseeable effects of the construction-from-parts paradigm and the adoption of visual programming tools are changes in the application development community. New roles will also be identified because the new tools address nonprogrammers as well as programmers.

Currently in application development, a boundary line exists between software developers and users. On one side of the line are computer professionals who know programming languages and can write applications. On the other side are application users. Most likely such users know what applications should do, but they do not know how to develop applications and cannot afford to learn complex programming languages and techniques that are beyond the scope of their responsibilities.

Object-oriented technology alone certainly increases the productivity of application developers and, if properly applied, gives users better and more timely results, but it does not change the position of the boundary line. The advent of visual programming in object-oriented environments, however, helps move the boundary line to increase the number of people who can assemble and customize their own applications. People without sophisticated programming skills will be able to assemble applications. For instance, analysts, user interface specialists, and individuals within MIS departments that support users will be able to build prototypes by using existing parts. In such an environment, high-level programming skills will be required only for the fabricators of parts.

1.3 Application Development Phases

Application development tasks are grouped into *development phases*. The definition and number of these phases in the literature vary. In this text, we refer to the following phases:

- Requirements specification
- Analysis
- Design
- Implementation
- Testing
- Maintenance

The purpose of the application is defined in the requirements specification phase. *Requirements* are "the conditions or capabilities needed by a user to solve a problem or achieve an objective" (IEEE Standard 729). These requirements can be satisfied in many ways, not all of which use a computer. The same business process, such as a customer financial transaction, can be defined as "high tech," providing a banking self-service kiosk, or "high touch," where a bank employee (who may be supported by a computer system) interacts with the customer. The requirements include a specification, as complete as possible, of the desired external behavior of the software system to be built. This is also called a *functional description* or *functional requirements.*

The objective of the *analysis phase* is to understand the problem that the software must solve in order to comply with the requirements. It describes *what* the software must do without saying *how* it will do it. The requirements focused on during the analysis phase are those of the software rather than the user; however, the perspective is always from the business or problem domain, not toward implementation.

The *design phase* deals with the task of *how* to satisfy the software specifications defined in the analysis phase, that is, how to build the software. The design phase includes system design and application design.

System design starts with the overall structure of the system—the system architecture—and includes the following steps:

1. Determine the application, support, and services subsystems and their relationship. The application subsystem is the software implementation of functional specifications, such as scheduling the shipment of goods or evaluating the risk of a loan. Support subsystems provide support related to the application logic, such as the database subsystem. Service subsystems, such as the communications subsystem, are transparent to the logic of the application.

   Subsystems are usually represented as layers, indicating that there is a defined interface among them. The system architecture defines the layers, their responsibilities and relationships, and their distribution in the network. In a distributed system, the architecture defines the relationships between corresponding layers in different nodes, for example, between the client and the server application layers. The relationship between adjacent layers is usually defined by the software products, for example, between the Smalltalk application and the DB2 database shown in the figure below.

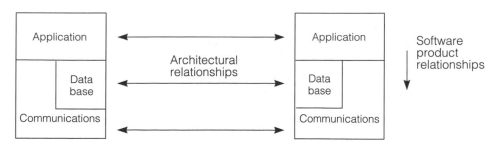

2. Allocate the subsystems to different resources, such as network nodes and processors in each node. A subsystem may be defined as a client or server subsystem. Many factors affect subsystem allocation, including task concurrency, network traffic, common use of functions, processor capability, and user access requirements.

3. Determine how data is managed, which includes defining the database paradigm (relational, hierarchical, or object oriented), distributing data in the network, warehousing and replicating the data, and defining transactions and commit points.

4. Define priorities and trade-offs between desirable characteristics.

Application design starts by dividing the application into subsystems and defining the application architecture. The criteria for dividing the application into subsystems are related to software engineering principles such as modularity, cohesiveness of the components of each subsystem, low coupling among subsystems, and system design decisions such as client and server considerations. Once the application has been divided into subsystems, those subsystems must be defined. In an object-oriented design application subsystem, definition involves establishing the responsibilities of each object and how it works with other objects, specifying the algorithms of the methods, designing the relationships or associations among objects (for instance, by using dictionary classes, arrays, or hash tables), handling external events, and using design patterns and optimization considerations.

The *implementation phase* covers the coding of the application. The structures and algorithms defined during the application design phase are translated into a programming language. This can be done in a textual, visual, or mixed fashion. It also includes the "building" of the applications, that is, the integration of the different application subsystems into a working unit.

The *testing phase* comprises unit testing and integration testing. Unit testing, also called *functional testing,* ensures that each coded module behaves according to its specification [DAV93]. Integration testing first tests the interconnection of sets from the previously tested modules and then tests the full application to ensure that it responds to the specifications based on the user requirements.

After an application is delivered to the user, it enters the *maintenance* phase, which includes error detection and correction and the addition of enhancements required to adapt it to a new environment or meet requirements that were not initially specified. The maintenance phase is not a true phase; it is a full path through the application development life cycle: Introducing an enhancement requires an understanding of the requirement, defining what it entails, how to do it, and how to integrate, test, and maintain it.

1.4 The Application Development Process

A *process* is an operation that transforms the nature, status, or composition of a defined input to produce an output following certain rules and policies. A *process path* is defined by the flow and relationship of tasks and information that complete a cycle of the process. At the end of a cycle, the defined output is delivered. Both the process and its component tasks are guided by a *process plan,* which is the basis for progress monitoring and is used to allocate resources and help decide what to do in the case of deviations from the plan.

1.4.1 Application Development Process Models

An application development process model, often called a *life cycle model,* characterizes the tasks of producing a software product, the relationships of the tasks and their sequence, their inputs and outputs, the resources available for each task, and the policies, measurements, disciplines, and plans used to manage the process.[2]

Among the many approaches to the life cycle model, the main difference is in the role, importance, and sequence of the process tasks. Each approach provides a set of prescriptive guidelines, stages, and phases for software engineers and application developers to follow. The goal of an application development process model is to establish tasks according to software engineering principles and practices. A process model is therefore a schema of how to lay out tasks, such as analyzing, designing, programming, and testing, that occur at different stages of an application development project.

In general, development processes can be classified as either *sequential* or *iterative.* In a purely sequential development process, once a task is completed, the process path never goes back to that task or any previous task. In an iterative process, the process path can return to a previously completed task, at which point changes are introduced, and the effects of those changes are propagated forward in the process path.

A third possibility is an incremental approach that combines aspects of both sequential and iterative models. Together, the iterative and incremental process models form a spiral model.

Sequential Process Model

MIS managers generally prefer a sequential development process model because of the control it provides over the process. It allows for streamlined plans and precise estimates of resources and durations. Therefore, user requirements must be (1) clearly and completely understood and (2) stable over the development period. Those two conditions, particularly the second, are frequently not true for business application development processes.

---

2 A *software product* in this context is application software that solves a set of business problems; it is not a "shrink-wrapped" commercial software product.

The waterfall approach to application development has been very popular among structural analysis and design and information engineering practitioners. It requires a formal signoff for each phase before work commences on the next phase. Once a phase is completed, it is not normally revisited.

The waterfall approach (see Figure 1) has several appealing properties: the project's status or percentage of completeness can be easily established, each phase is performed by using the information developed during the previous phase, and the order in which tasks are performed is easy to determine [RUM92].

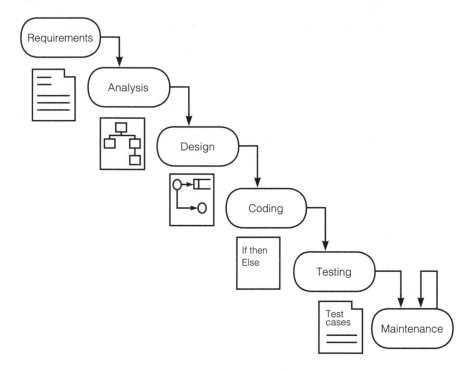

Figure 1. Sequential process model: the waterfall approach

The waterfall approach may be adequate when there is a complete understanding of user requirements and the analysis and design are performed by highly skilled people. However, the lack of flexibility in this approach may cause problems. For instance, when the user first uses the application, it is usually in the last stage of the development process. If the user does not like the result or if the requirements change, a major rework would be required to accommodate any modifications.

Iterative Process Model

The main advantage of an iterative process model is the ability to feed changes and corrections found necessary in one phase back to an earlier phase. These changes are applied and propagated forward, thus maintaining the traceability of the changes and providing an application that meets user requirements (see Figure 2). In a fully iterative process model, the feedback loop has no limitations; it can go from any task to any other task. Generally, the object-oriented paradigm benefits from an iterative approach, although an object-oriented application can be developed through a sequential development process.

The disadvantage of an iterative process model is that the feedback loop can be difficult to control. Therefore both a minimum and maximum number of iterations must be established. Most practitioners favor a minimum of three iterations. A typical iterative development approach, such as the Iterative Development Process described in [LOR92], consists of a set of iterations, each of which has *planning, producing,* and *assessing* periods (see Figure 2).

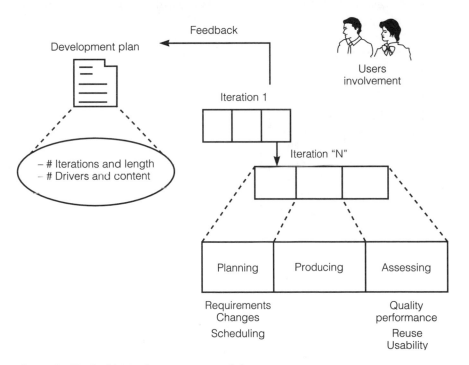

Figure 2. Typical iterative process model

The planning period in each iteration is the time allotted for dealing with new or modified requirements. The planning period should include activities such as prioritizing all known requirements, documenting all external dependencies and deliverables, determining specific goals for each iteration, establishing a schedule, and planning for the assessing period of each iteration.

The producing period is devoted to the design and implementation of what has been scheduled for the iteration, and the assessing period evaluates the product that results from the producing period. The assessing period of an iteration provides input to the planning period of the subsequent iteration. Some factors to consider during the assessing period are conformance to customer requirements, usability, performance, extensibility, and reusability.

Incremental Process Model

The incremental process model of software development (see Figure 3) uses the same development phases as the other approaches but differs in both the scope of the phases and the management of the project. The incremental process delivers a reduced set of functions, which is then enhanced in each iteration. In addition, iterations can occur between steps, as indicated in Figure 3.

The incremental approach to application development starts to deliver limited function earlier than other approaches, with a corresponding faster return on investment. However, it requires careful planning and very tight management control.

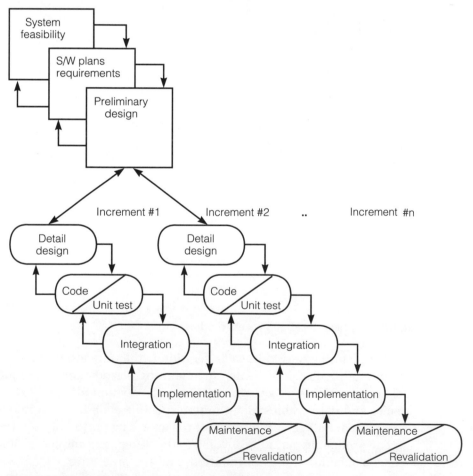

Figure 3. Typical incremental process model

Spiral Process Models

The iterative and incremental processes combine to form the spiral process. The spiral process model (see Figure 4) prescribes building several levels of prototypes and performing risk analysis at each level. The spiral process consists of six steps:

1. Plan the initial or next iteration of the problem solution.
2. Determine the objectives, alternatives, and constraints.
3. Perform a risk analysis.
4. Produce a prototype solution.
5. Validate the prototype against the current objectives.
6. Perform the whole process again until a product, capable of being implemented, has been produced.

Step 1 is analogous to the requirements specification phase of the waterfall process model, Steps 2 and 3 represent the analysis and design phases, and Steps 4 and 5 correspond to the implementation and testing phases.

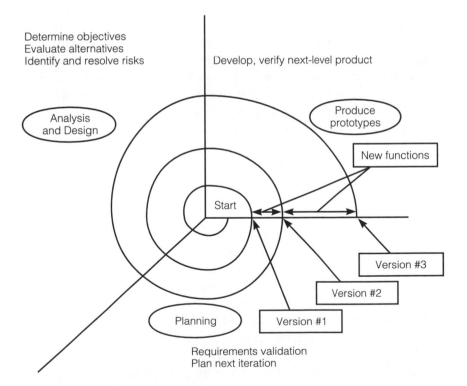

Figure 4. Typical spiral process model

The spiral process model's dynamic approach to application development is good for medium to large projects in which

- The total problem to be solved is not fully understood.
- The real world can be expected to change during the development.
- The solution itself might have an unknown effect on the real world.
- Management focus is on quality and function rather than financial controls.

The spiral process model is described in [BOE88]. Use of the spiral approach in object-oriented application development is described in [WAS91].

1.5 Process Models and Methodologies

The traditional software development process is a sequential process best represented by the waterfall approach. Such an approach has advantages when applied to project management and project status and resource control. It is also good for problem domains where the requirements are well-defined and static.

Software requirements are seldom well defined and immune from changes, however, so a sequential process is inappropriate. It simply cannot respond to the dynamic nature of software requirements. The iterative development approach is better as it builds the software one iteration after another until the requirements are met. Such an approach accommodates frequent user feedback and continuous refinement of the software throughout the development cycle.

Object methodology covers the process from modeling to programming. However, there is no direct dependency between a process model and a methodology. Any object methodology could be used with any process model. This is clearly discussed in [YOU92], where all the process models are described as variants of the waterfall approach, with different grades of overlap among the phases.

1.5.1 The VMT Development Process Schema

VMT does not prescribe a particular life cycle model. The choice of a life cycle model depends on the type of applications, the development tool and facilities used, the development team dynamics, and the characteristics of the delivery of the application. Regardless which life cycle model is chosen, however, the development productivity will be higher if it includes prototyping, iterations, and incremental construction.

We can describe a generic process schema for application development using VMT, as shown in Figure 5 on page 17. When an enterprise decides that it needs to develop a certain application, this decision may be the result of an urgent operational need, but more frequently, in a mature organization, it will be the result of a strategic planning activity that has to include the modeling of

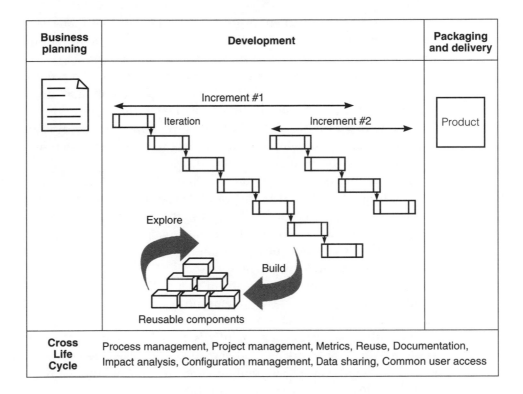

Figure 5. Development life cycle

an organization's business processes within and across business areas to provide the right computer services.

Strategic planning and business modeling normally result in an identification and prioritization of a number of application development projects. Sometimes, however, a request to solve an identified business problem that may or may not be a result of the business modeling effort can also initiate an application development project. In our schema, we will call the application to be developed the *product* of the development process. The process to build this product in this schema has three stages: business planning, development, and packaging and delivery.

Several iterations are expected to occur within the development stage of a product's life cycle. These iterations include a planning period for this iteration, followed by a producing period and an assessing period. (In this schema, we include under the term *development* the analysis, design, coding, and testing activities.)

Because the development team learns about the proposed solution and the product characteristics from each iteration, the scope of each iteration changes over time. The extent of each activity during each iteration varies depending on both the size of the project and the iteration objectives. Early iterations focus on the analysis of the problem, followed by iterations that focus on design and coding. The last iterations involve performance tuning and final testing to get ready for packaging and delivering of the developed product.

An iterative approach requires planned reworking of a fixed set of functions, while an incremental approach divides application functions into a number of increments to be developed and delivered in stages.

For large projects involving several development teams, it is also possible to have concurrent development iterations carried out by different teams, each responsible for the development of part of the target application.

Prototyping is part of the development process. Analysis prototyping is used to solicit user feedback and validate user requirements. Design or development prototyping is used to build a partial working solution and evolve it into a final product. Visual programming tools provide a seamless way to keep evolving the design and code at various levels, such as object classes, subsystems (categories), frameworks, and so on.

Reuse of components is a natural part of the development process. Early iterations of the product development life cycle involve finding, matching, and customizing components from reuse repositories. The planning process also includes the "harvesting" of potentially reusable components. These components will be later "hardened," that is, fully debugged, generalized, and documented. The harvested components are then stored and cataloged into the repository for later use in current or future projects.

1.6 Object Methodologies

Once the sequence of steps that leads from user requirements to software building has been established, we have to define what to do in each step and determine which deliverables from one step are to be used in the next and which are to be fed back to a previous step. We also have to define a starting point and a route, both of which depend on the software-building paradigm. For instance, information engineering has a top-down approach, which starts with an executive vision of the enterprise and goes down the hierarchy to the business areas, data models, and information processes. Object technology has a middle-up approach, which starts with a real-world model, goes up to the enterprise level, and down to the program level. The process path and activities are usually prescribed by a methodology.

A methodology defines the instructions, guidelines, and heuristics of a process. It defines a series of steps and the techniques and notations associated with each step [RUM91]. One problem with object technology is that often the methodology is confused with the notation it prescribes.

Another issue that must be considered is the extent of the methodology. Object technology practitioners usually limit the scope of their methodologies to finding objects and their relationships and implementing them in code. Consulting firms may broaden the scope of their methodologies to include the relationship with the client's business processes, the roles of management and teams, infrastructure, metrics, and deliverables. Advanced object methodologies also define the complete development and reuse environment, including criteria for parts certification, retrieval, and reuse.

As illustrated in Figure 6 below, an object methodology usually comprises a modeling process (strategies and steps for creating a model of the objects both in the problem and the solution domain), notations and representations. It may be supported by one or more development tools and techniques. Most methodologies define a core set of deliverables, each with a specific notation but similar semantics. However, for the same problem domain, two similar deliverables (say, object models) can have different contents. For instance, the object model in a methodology that emphasizes the dynamic aspects of the problem domain, such as events or user interactions, will contain objects that are different from those that were obtained through static or data-driven modeling, such as transforming an entity-relationship model into an object model by changing entities into classes.

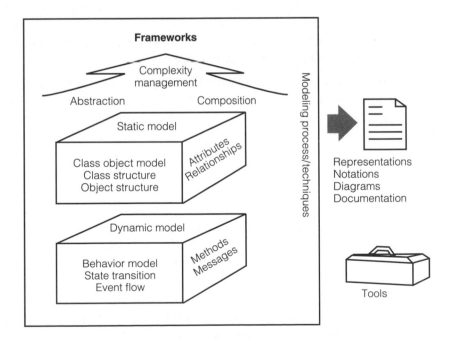

Figure 6. Key elements in an object-oriented methodology

The most current object-oriented methodologies in use today are the Object Modeling Technique, Object-Oriented Software Engineering, Responsibility-Driven Design, and the Booch Method.

1.6.1 The Object Modeling Technique

The Object Modeling Technique (OMT), developed by [RUM91], covers analysis, design, and implementation phases of application development.

Analysis

The analysis phase concentrates on understanding and modeling the application and the domain within which it operates. The analysis results in a generic definition of the system. Objects, relationships, event flows, and functions are detailed. The analysis phase produces three models: the object model, the dynamic model, and the function model. Together they provide three complementary views of a system:

- The *object model* captures the static view of the problem to be addressed. It represents the static object structure, which shows the objects in the system, the relationships among objects, and the attributes and operations that characterize each class of object. OMT suggests that the object model can be built from the elements of the problem statement: Nouns are potential objects, and verbs indicate potential operations or relationships.

- The *dynamic model* represents the temporal, behavioral, and control aspects of the system, including the sequences of events, states, and operations that occur within the system of objects. OMT uses scenarios to describe interaction sequences between objects. Events contracted and created by objects are stored in event diagrams. The dynamic model is represented graphically with state diagrams. Each state diagram shows the state and event sequences permitted in a system for an object class.

- The *functional model*[3] specifies the meaning of the operations of the objects as defined by actions in the dynamic model. The functional model is represented by data flow diagrams.

Design

There are two design phases: *system design* and *object design*. System design results in an architecture for the system in which subsystems are defined and allocated. Object design results in a detailed definition of the model objects.

---

3 Functional modeling is not used in VMT for application modeling. Eventually, DFDs can be used to describe the algorithms for the methods of objects, if their complexity merits the effort.

The three models from the analysis phase are refined in the object design phase, mapping the problem (business) domain to the solution (computer) domain.

Implementation

Implementation details are mapped to the target environment, but new models are not produced during the implementation phase.

OMT is considered a static methodology because the objects are derived from analysis of the problem statement (that is, domain knowledge) rather than from interactions between the user and the objects.

OMT Notation

The OMT notation for object models is shown in Figure 7 and those for dynamic models in Figure 8.

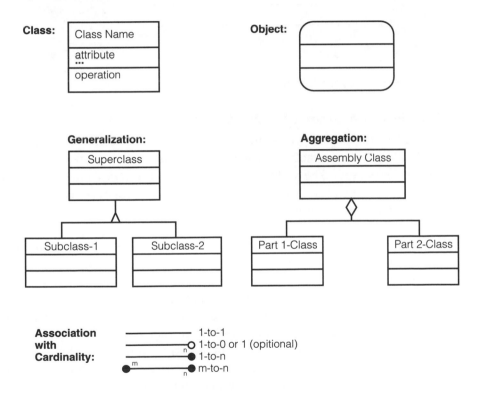

Figure 7. OMT object model notation

1.6.2 Modeling with OMT: A Loan Risk Evaluation System

In this section we present an example for applying the OMT methodology to model a banking application. The example illustrates the OMT modeling techniques explained earlier in this chapter.

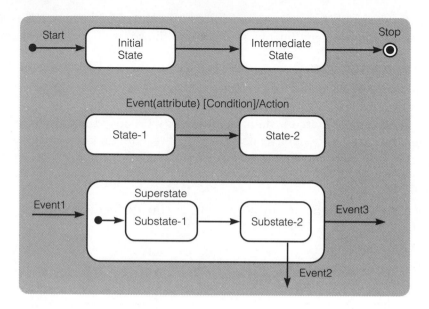

Figure 8. OMT dynamic model notation

Problem Statement for Modeling

As part of its loan approval process, a bank wants to implement a loan risk evaluation system to achieve consistent results from its loan analysts, whether rookies or experts. The system will be used by employees handling retail banking. The output of the evaluation and approval processes will be displayed online as well as printed.

The evaluation process for this type of loan is based on customer-related information gathered in a customer dossier, which includes market positioning and conditions as well as information on revenue, profit, and assets and liabilities. It also includes the customer's performance history (such as bounced checks, bankruptcy filing), enterprise character evaluation (such as dynamic, static, or centralized), and data related to the present managers and owners. The impressions of an on-site evaluation by bank officials are also included in the dossier.

After evaluating the dossier data and applying certain heuristic (expert) evaluation rules, the bank evaluates the loan as a high, medium, or low risk. The decision to grant the loan is based on that risk evaluation and on some factors unrelated to the customer (for example, bank policies, and the availability of federal- or state-supported credit lines).

Object Modeling

Producing the object model is a three-step process:

1. Identify object classes (nouns). The following classes are initially identified: Bank, Loan, Loan risk evaluation system, Loan analyst, User,

Bank officer, Loan type, Evaluation, Displayed output, Printed output, Customer, Customer dossier, Market positioning, Market conditions, Revenue, Profit, Assets, Liabilities, Business performing history, Managers' and owners' data, On-site evaluation, Bank officials (performance evaluation), Heuristics, Risk, Granting the loan, Approval process, External factors, Bank policies.

2. Discard unnecessary and incorrect classes. In this step, we discard redundant classes such as Loan analyst, User, and Bank officer, which are all replaced by the more descriptive term *Analyst*. Discardable classes include those that are irrelevant or vague classes, classes that are really attributes of another class, class names that describe operations, and so on. Implementation constructs should be pointed out; for instance, in Heuristic expert evaluation rules, *rules* is an implementation construct. Since other constructs are possible, it is represented by a class just called Heuristics.

    After pruning and consolidating, these classes remained:

    BANK, ANALYST, LOAN, S&M_ENTERPRISE_LOAN, CUSTOMER, CUSTOMER_DOSSIER, RISK_ EVALUATION, LOAN_GRANT, MARKETING_INFO, FINANCIAL_INFO, CHARACTER_INFO, ONSITE_EVAL, HEURISTICS, RISK, REPORT

3. Identify attributes. Some of the main attributes of the most important objects were identified from the problem statement, but many were identified from the domain knowledge (such as Name and Address of Customer and Name of Analyst).

Figure 9 on page 24 shows the object model derived from this process. Rectangles represent classes, links represent associations, small triangles indicate inheritance (Is-A) relations, small diamonds indicate aggregation (Has-part) relations, and small black circles indicate "zero or more" multiplicity relations.

Dynamic Modeling

Dynamic modeling uses state diagrams, scenarios, and event traces to describe object behavior. Dynamic modeling helps in deriving the operations (methods) that apply to objects. The following scenario was developed for a loan risk evaluation system using the class model names:

1. Customer asks for an S&M_Enterprise_Loan

2. Bank requests data (assume application data entry separate from analysis)

3. Customer forwards data to Customer_Dossier

4. Risk_ Evaluation assesses Risk

5. Loan_Grant determines Decision

6. S&M_Enterprise_Loan is granted (normal)

7. S&M_Enterprise_Loan is denied (exception)

8. Collateral is required (exception)

This scenario is usually translated into an event flow diagram. In addition, object state diagrams are drawn at this stage.

Operations can be derived from the object model as implied by the presence of the attributes (read and write attribute values and associations) and from event-based behavior, as described by the dynamic model. In our case, when the customer asks for a loan (that is, creates a new operation), one step in the risk evaluation will be to get dossier data. A process description can help identify other operations such as print and display for the report class.

In addition, methods are required for the application of heuristics for the risk evaluation and loan grant decision processes.

The modeling process is refined in successive iterations of the analysis and design stages. Then coding of the prototype is usually straightforward. The pro-

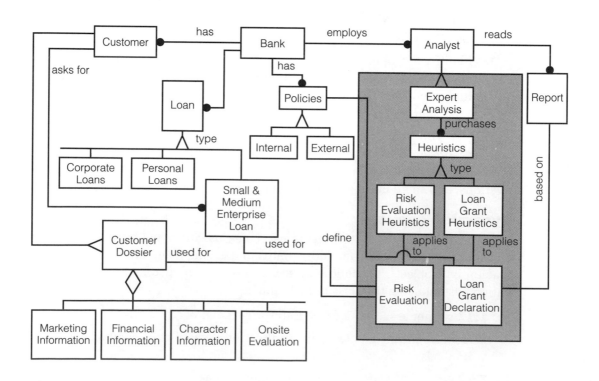

Figure 9. Object model

totype is shown to the user, thus starting a spiral application development life cycle that ends only when full production status is achieved. Class definitions, at the proper abstraction level, can be reused in further applications.

1.6.3 Object-Oriented Software Engineering

Object-Oriented Software Engineering (OOSE) is a use-case-driven methodology (see Figure 10). A use case represents a dialog between a user and the system. The practice of use case analysis was first formalized by [JAC92], who defines a use case as "a particular form or pattern or example of usage, a scenario that begins with some user of the system initiating some transaction or sequence of interrelated events."

Use cases fit naturally into the scheme of object-oriented analysis and design because they portray real-world user-system interactions.

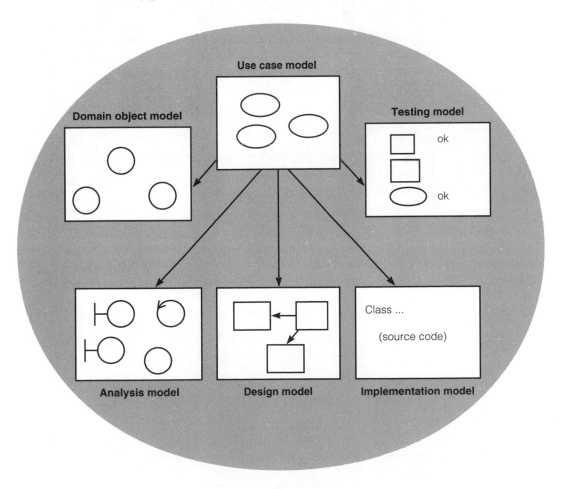

Figure 10. OOSE: a use-case-driven approach

As illustrated in Figure 11, OOSE is divided into three phases:

1. Analysis: The analysis phase involves examining requirements and robustness and produces a requirements model and an analysis model. The requirements model consists of a use case model, interface description, and a problem domain model.

2. Construction: The construction phase includes the design and production processes and results in both a design model and an implementation model.

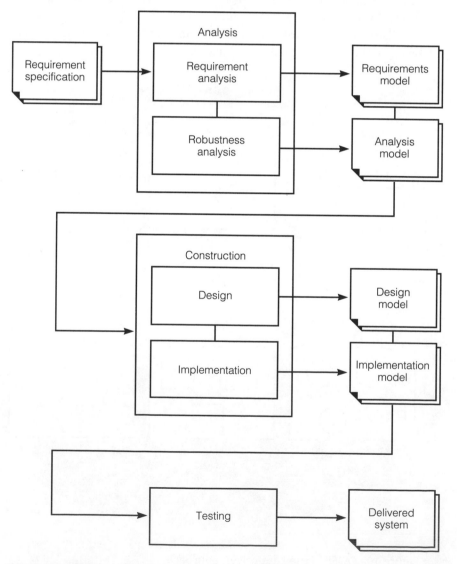

Figure 11. OOSE modeling process

3. Testing: The testing phase covers unit testing, integration testing, and system testing and produces a test model.

1.6.4 Responsibility-Driven Design

Responsibility-Driven Design (RDD) is a dynamic methodology that emphasizes object behavior (responsibilities) and relationships with other objects (collaborations) [WIR90]. RDD is a dynamic methodology because it finds the model objects on the basis of their behavior.

RDD is an anthropomorphic approach that requires the analyst to think of objects as collaborating agents with responsibilities. Each collaborating object assumes the role of either a client or a server. A client requests the server object to perform services, and a server provides a set of services based on those requests. The requests a server can support and the client can make are defined and grouped into contracts that are specified in terms of protocols for each operation of a service.[4] Subsystems are introduced to group classes to provide higher levels of functional abstraction.

The RDD modeling process includes two phases:

1. Exploratory: The exploratory phase has three goals—finding the classes, determining responsibilities, and identifying collaborations—through the following steps:

   a. Read the specifications.

   b. Walk through scenarios and write design cards.

   c. Create class cards and look for nouns in the requirements specification.

   d. Define responsibilities. Look for services for the clients of a class, and look at **is_a** (specialization), **has_a** (attributes), and **is_analogous_to** relationships.

   e. Identify collaborators: Look for class-to-class collaboration to fulfill the responsibilities identified and thus define the architectural interfaces between classes and subsystems.

2. Analysis: The analysis phase involves refining the object's behavior and the service definitions specified in the exploratory phase. These activities include defining interfaces (protocols) and constructing implementation specifications for each class. The work involved includes class refinement and specifications, class polymorphism definitions, and service specifications. The analysis phase produces

---

4 Although Rebecca Wirfs-Brock has dropped *contracts* from the latest version of her methodology, we find that there is still a need to formalize the protocols of the interaction among objects.

- A hierarchy graph, by placing classes in the inheritance hierarchy
- Abstractions, by looking for abstract classes to facilitate sharing common services and attributes
- Contracts, by looking for logical groupings of responsibilities
- Subsystems, by grouping tightly coupled classes into subsystems
- Collaboration graphs, by identifying class relationships and collaborations within and between subsystems
- Protocols (specifications for message formats), by providing textual supplemental information on subsystem, contract, and class cards

Wirfs-Brock's RDD approach uses Class-Responsibility-Collaboration (CRC) cards to identify class responsibilities and their collaborators. (CRC cards are discussed further in Chapter 3.) Venn diagrams, subsystem graphs, and contract specifications are other key techniques used with RDD.

The suggested development process is very flexible and works well on a small project, but more work is required for large-scale projects.

Mark Lorentz created a derivative of the RDD methodology [LOR93]. He extended RDD to cover a broader perspective in the application development life cycle, defining an iterative development process (IDP), which includes the following phases:

- Business planning
- Analysis
- Design and testing
- Packaging

1.6.5 The Booch Method

Booch's earlier work concentrates on design rather than on the full application development life cycle [BOO94]. Although Booch recommends steps, from identifying the object classes to implementing the classes, and discusses design techniques and heuristics, his methodology cannot be divided into clear development phases. In the first edition of his book, the process is described as a "round-trip gestalt design." This is essentially another version of the spiral approach, similar to what has been described as an "analyze a little, design a little, implement a little, and test a little" approach.

In the second edition of his book, Booch distinguishes the micro and macro elements of the development process. The micro development process serves as a framework for an iterative and incremental approach. The macro development process serves as the controlling framework for the micro process.

The Micro Development Process

The micro process of object-oriented development is largely driven by the stream of scenarios and architectural products that emerge from and are successively refined by the macro development process. To a large extent, the micro development process represents the daily activities of an individual developer or a small team of developers.

The micro process comprises the following tasks (see Figure 12):

1. Identify the classes and objects at a given level of abstraction.

2. Identify the semantics of classes and objects.

3. Identify the relationships among classes and objects.

4. Specify the interface and the implementation of classes and objects.

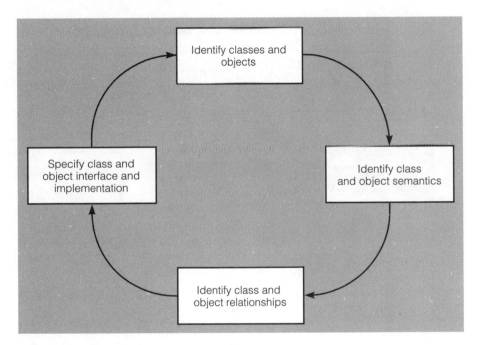

Figure 12. Micro development process

The Macro Development Process

The macro development process serves as the controlling framework for the micro development process. This broader process dictates a number of measurable products and activities that permit the development team to assess risk meaningfully and make early corrections to the micro development process.

The macro development process is primarily the concern of the development team's technical manager. Thus it focuses on risk and architectural vision, the two manageable elements that have the greatest impact on schedules, quality, and completeness.

The macro development process comprises the following phases (see Figure 13):

1. Conceptualization, in which requirements are established

2. Analysis, in which a model of the desired behavior is developed

3. Design, in which an architecture of the system is developed

4. Evolution, in which the implementation in the design phase is refined

5. Maintenance, in which post-delivery evolution takes place

The Booch method does not have a distinct specification phase. Specification occurs in the design phase, along with implementation.

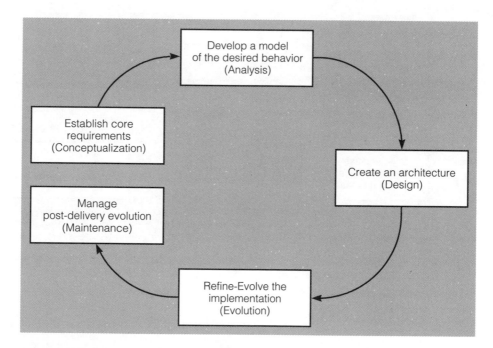

Figure 13. Macro development process

1.7 VMT: A Complementary Approach

VMT methodically and in a novel way combines techniques that have proven productive in other object methodologies.

We selected OMT as our backbone methodology and use its notation throughout. However, although OMT works well when the requirements are presented as a problem statement, as in an RFP, it does not provide a mechanism for capturing user interactions in the requirement phase of the application development cycle. Therefore, in VMT we apply use case analysis to identify user requirements, the activities the user performs, and the services the system must provide for the user. This approach should lead to a better understanding of the interactions between the user and the system to be built. The OOSE use case requirement modeling technique has the advantage of capturing the many modes of user interaction and is particularly well suited to formalizing results obtained by prototyping. A set of reusable GUI prototypes is also a byproduct of the prototyping activity.

OMT starts the modeling process by identifying object classes from the application problem statements. It does this through language-syntax-related procedures, such as noun, verb, and adjective analysis. In the VMT analysis process, the mechanism used to identify relevant objects in use case analysis is similar. When building the domain object model, we use the union of classes and relationships found in both use case analysis and problem statement analysis because the classes derived from both sources usually represent different, albeit complementary, aspects of the application domain. The justification for this approach is that we expect to better capture the user requirements by focusing concurrently on both the static and the dynamic aspects of the problem domain.

We have incorporated RDD techniques into VMT because once classes and relationships are found, the distribution of responsibilities among the classes must be established. We also incorporated CRC cards into VMT. We use them primarily to define object class responsibilities and collaborations, not to find classes. (CRC is most effective for identifying object responsibilities and collaborations after the initial OMT object model has been built.) Eventually, new collaborations may become apparent when class responsibilities are changed.

We apply a concept similar to the concept of *subsystems* defined in OMT, RDD, and OOSE to map subsystems to programming constructs that the development environment can handle.[5]

The next step in VMT, following OMT, is to use event trace diagrams and Harel state charts to model the interactions between objects and the changes of object states. The event traces define the messages among objects and, therefore, the methods to be invoked. The changes of state help us identify and understand the characteristics of the variables (attributes) affected by the methods.

The functions that the methods implement are then defined by preconditions and postconditions, which are related to events. For example, given certain preconditions, an event can change the state of an object; the method invoked to produce this change of state should provide a function that will leave the object in a new state in which the defined postconditions are met.

---

5 For instance, in the team programming environment of IBM VisualAge for Smalltalk, the unit of development is called an *application.* In VisualAge application development, subsystems are mapped to Smalltalk applications.

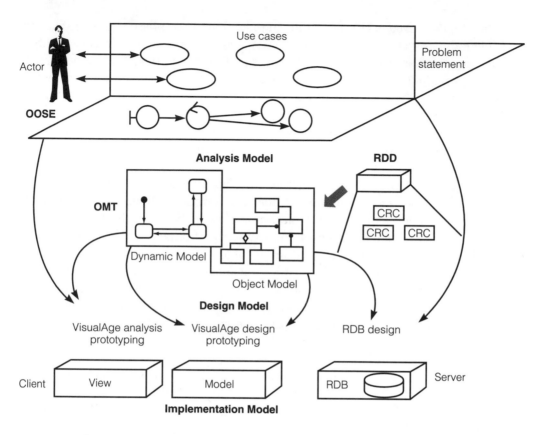

Figure 14. VMT models: analysis, design, and implementation

Figure 14 depicts a high-level scheme of the VMT modeling process and its relationship to the analysis, design, and implementation phases. VMT is a highly productive application development process that integrates visual programming and can be extended to distributed object application development. Through VMT we have augmented the concept of use cases to include the business rules that govern user transactions and have provided a practical and seamless integration to business process reengineering, as described in Part 4 of this book.

1.7.1 Objects, Processes, and Rules

To integrate the work done in the reengineering of the business processes of an enterprise with the modeling efforts of the object-oriented application development, we look at the need to support the new streamlined business processes, which define new job descriptions. These job descriptions give us an initial picture of the interaction of the user with the system; they can therefore be used as an input for the use case analysis of the system to support the to-be processes. The definition of these to-be processes provides the problem statements that integrate the requirements model of the to-be enterprise world.

The business processes and the job descriptions, and therefore the problem statements and the use cases, have implicitly defined business rules. For instance, when a customer wants to withdraw money from an account, whether through an ATM or interacting with a teller, and the account balance is zero, business rules established by the bank decide if the customer gets money and pays interest on the overdraft or if the customer withdrawal is denied. The explicit statement of these business rules is a powerful instrument both in the process reengineering activity and in the analysis of the use cases that are part of the system requirements. Advanced techniques in VMT show how to augment the use case definitions using business rules, thus providing a clear understanding of the user transactions, their outcomes, and the handling of exceptions.

1.8 Summary

Object technology has gained widespread interest among software developers because of its faster and more productive development capabilities, reusable components, and better handling of multimedia data types.

For many programmers, working with textual object-oriented languages has proven too complex. To encourage acceptance of object-oriented programming languages such as C++ and Smalltalk, object-oriented visual programming tools have emerged that enable programmers with varying levels of expertise to take advantage of working with objects. Visual programming enables nonexpert programmers to create whole or partial applications using a graphical approach rather than traditional text-based programming languages. Visual programming also enables users who are not programmers but are specialists in their own professions to assemble their applications from reusable components or create their own custom components.

Visual programming simplifies programming efforts, particularly the building of a GUI, by hiding the programming complexity within the tool. Most visual programming tools also provide frameworks with libraries of reusable system components. In addition, visual programming facilitates the rapid customizing and building of reusable components.

Visual programming thus eases the transition from a traditional to an object-oriented programming environment. One major hurdle that object technology presents is the steep learning curve required for object-oriented programming, even for simple projects. Visual programming's ease of use and higher level of abstraction make it easier to learn. Therefore, a business can take advantage of visual programming to move into object technology and thus increase the productivity of its programmers. The VMT methodology produces a productive framework for object-oriented application development, establishing a consistent and clearly defined role for visual programming.

2

The VMT Analysis Phase

The analysis phase of the application development life cycle structures and formalizes the user requirements. The work products of this phase describe what the system to be built should do, without specifying how to do it. In Object Technology, the work products of the analysis phase are models, and the phase is usually called the Modeling Phase.

2.1 Modeling

Some authors consider application requirements gathering to be part of the analysis phase, and others consider it a separate phase. The deliverable of this phase is a requirements model that includes problem statements, use cases, and GUI prototypes. Starting from the requirements model, during the analysis phase we create a set of object models and dynamic models (including event trace diagrams and state diagrams). The models describe *what* the system must do but not *how* it should be done.

Object-oriented software can be thought of as a collection of objects that interact with each other to provide the required services. Object models describe these objects and their relationships.

Object modeling is done during both the analysis and design phases of application development. The analysis models represent the problem domain; no implementation details are considered. The design models represent the solution domain: they evolve from the analysis models and describe *how* the system will be built. Figure 15 on page 35 illustrates the problem and solution domains.

34

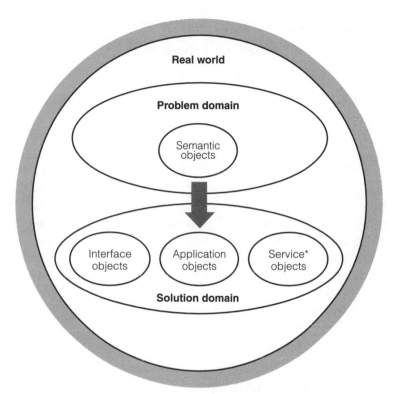

*Service objects here is a generic term for implementation objects, factoring
 objects, utility objects, etc.

Figure 15. Problem and solution domains

We call the objects identified during analysis *semantic objects* because these
are the objects that have meaning from a business domain point of view.

The semantic objects identified in analysis are refined during design. New
objects that are solution oriented are found during design and added to the
model. Solution-domain objects include application objects that represent the
implementation of the semantic objects, interface objects, and service objects (a
generic term for objects that have no business meaning but help implement
relationships, interface to databases, and so on).

2.2 Object-Oriented Analysis

Object-oriented analysis covers the following activities in most methodologies,
although the approaches, sequences, and techniques used to carry out these
activities may differ:

- Understanding the problem
- Finding the objects
- Classifying objects into classes

- Establishing class relationships
- Defining class properties and behaviors
- Modeling object interactions
- Studying object state changes

Object models are generally built using class abstractions, not objects, which are understood here as class instances. Therefore, we can say that the goal of object-oriented analysis is to build a model based on user, expert, and enterprise requirements. The model should include the classes needed to provide the required application behavior and depict the relationships among the classes, the knowledge each class must have of other classes, the services each class must provide, and the description of how external events activate object interactions.

To provide a proper description of what the application does, object analysis must address both the static class structure, which is described in an object model, and the dynamic object behavior, which is described in a dynamic model.

The static class structure and dynamic object behavior of an object-oriented application are tightly connected because they show two different aspects of the same application. Therefore, integrity rules must be applied during the development process to ensure that both models are consistent.

2.3 Requirements Modeling

The goal of requirements modeling is to express explicitly the application specifications to be satisfied when building the system.

Requirements modeling should always be done using concepts and terms related to the business domain, not to the computer implementation. Both users and domain experts participate in the process of developing the requirements model, together with the object modelers (analysts). The main deliverables of this activity are the problem statement and the use case model, although GUI sketches and nonfunctional requirements such as response time and security may be included.

The problem statement is usually defined as part of an information technology planning process and is usually the starting point for application development. The use case model has to be built, determining the (main) actors, their roles, and their transactions with the system.

To build a a use case model we start by drawing the boundary of the proposed system. Then we determine the actors of each use case.

An actor is a role played by an outside entity when interacting with the system. Once an actor has been determined, we develop a set of use cases by prototyping and recording the interactions of the user with the system in an actor's role.[6]

---

6 The same users play different roles at different points. For instance, they play one role when they deposit money in an account and another when they withdraw it. They are therefore represented by different actors.

At a different level of abstraction, we can define relationships among use cases: for instance, all account-related transactions make use of a sequence consisting of introducing a card and entering a personal identification number (PIN) at the system prompt. This small sequence of transactions can be considered a use case in its own right, albeit auxiliary, and can be related to the main use cases. Therefore it can be productive to define relationships among use cases.

Actors are active entities; their behaviors are not predefined and they can be considered sources of events to which the system must react. Actors can also be external systems or machines. The fact that actors can be external systems enables us to model the interaction of our application with existing conventional systems, often referred to as *legacy systems,* or with other object systems.

Finding actors helps us determine what is inside and outside the system, that is, to identify the system boundaries. Because use cases are sequences of transactions between an actor and the system aimed at obtaining some application service, describing use cases helps us to identify not only how actors will use the system but also the services the system must provide.

In Figure 16, the rectangle represents the system, and its borders represent the system boundary. The use cases are represented by ovals placed inside the rectangle, and the actors are depicted as human or system figures outside the rectangle.

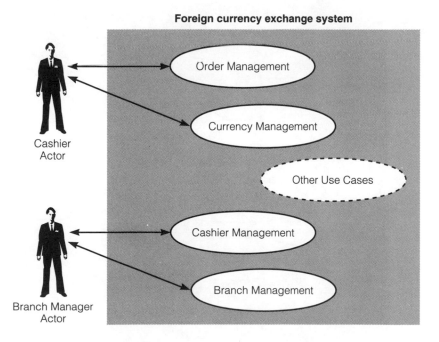

Figure 16. Use case model

2.3.1 Relationships Among Use Cases

Two major relationships can be defined among use cases: *use* and *extend* [JAC92]. Drawing use cases with their relationships helps to portray the system use case structure. Some common and mandatory actor-system interactions can be extracted and placed in separate use cases. All of those use cases can then employ this use case structure with the common sequence of interactions.

If a common sequence of actor-system interactions needed to complete use cases B and C is described in use case A, then use cases B and C *use* the use case A. For example, an ATM money withdrawal use case can *use* a PIN validation use case.

Some extra and optional actor-system interactions of a use case can be modeled by extending other use cases. Use case B *extends* use case A if it can be built starting from A and adding details of the base interactions; case B then *extends* the description of use case A. This extension allows for changes and additions of the use case functionality. For example, an ATM use case reflecting the user's access to an account can be extended by use cases describing the user's access to a checking account and to a savings account. Use cases, and use case relationships, are shown in Figure 17.

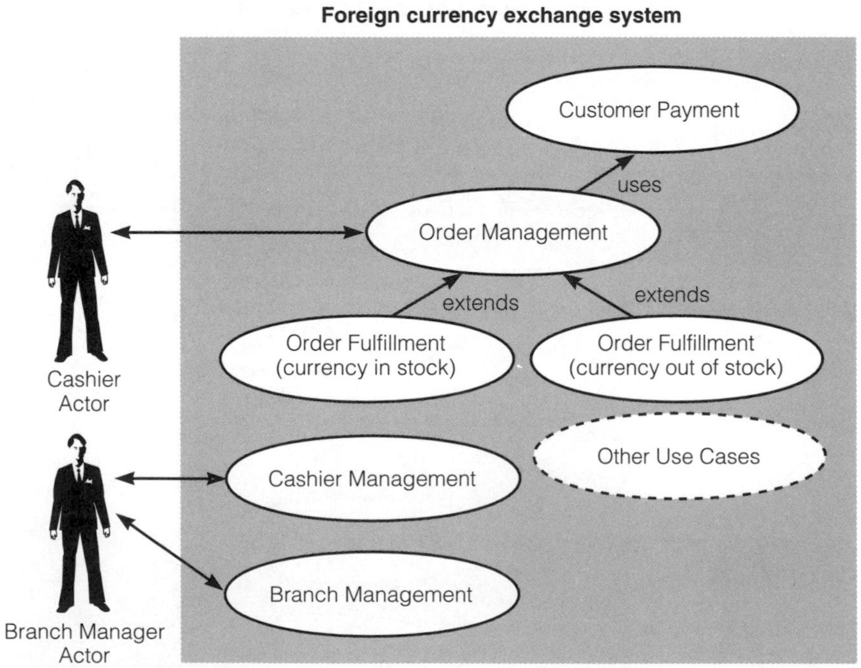

Foreign currency exchange system

Figure 17. Expanded use case model

2.3.2 Level of Detail in Use Case Models

Use cases can be described with different levels of detail. For example, in the case of a bank application in which the cashier creates an order, the use case could be stated as

1. The cashier creates a new order.
2. The cashier enters the order details.

or as

1. The cashier logs on to his or her workstation.
2. The cashier selects New from the menu.
3. The cashier enters the customer name.

The correct level of detail depends on an optimum balance between two contrasting goals: gathering enough information (which calls for a more detailed description) and not committing too early to a specific solution (which calls for a higher-level description).

When starting use case modeling, it is more important to identify all of the different use cases and outline their primary courses of behavior than to describe details of all the variant courses. It is practical to proceed top down for a *use case refinement,* initially sketching a very high-level picture of the system services needed and then extending them with more significant variants.

The object modeler and the target users of the application can jointly develop use cases to reach a common understanding and a common vocabulary for the problem domain. This is particularly valid when the user is familiar with the application aspects. If there is, however, a major change in the application due to process reengineering, or if it is really a new application the user is not familiar with, the use cases have to be developed jointly with domain experts and user professionals for functionality. In a later stage, the user input is required to address usability issues.

It is important that the use cases reflect a level of abstraction of the interactions between the actor and the system. One of the common errors in use case analysis is to include in the domain models the use case instances instead of the use cases. Making explicit the business rules that govern each transaction in the use case is a very effective way to build meaningful use cases.

2.3.3 Limitations of Use Cases

Use cases are effective for modeling the external view of *how* the system is to be used. However, there are limitations in terms of what can be modeled [JAC95b]:

- System internal communications or interactions cannot be modeled. A use case model does not describe the interactions between objects inside the system.

- Conflicts among use case instances cannot be modeled. Conflicting exceptional scenarios of a use case cannot be modeled.

- Concurrency cannot be modeled. Use cases are atomic and serial in nature; they cannot model a concurrency situation in a system.

These limitations can be overcome by taking advantage of scenarios and business rules.

2.4 Analysis Prototyping

To better understand user needs, sketches of the user interface should be developed during requirements modeling. The user interface sketches help to portray the actor-system interactions during use case development. They also help to identify the metaphors that should be used later in the user interface design.

After the user interface sketches have evolved and become stable [JAC94c], prototypes can be developed to represent the initial user views of the target system. We call this activity *analysis prototyping.* The intent is to develop a proof-of-concept of the user requirements. A visual programming tool, such as IBM VisualAge, provides practical prototyping capabilities that can be used to assist in this effort.

The analysis work discussed so far can be related to similar activities involved in object-oriented user interface design. Following [COL95], three elements make up the analysis prototype:

- The use case model: This is a transaction model that shows how the user can interact with objects in the system to accomplish goals and tasks.

- The object model: This is a static system model of the objects and their relationships.

- Possible usage metaphors: These can be identified from user interface sketches and the prototyping of the user preferred modes of interaction. Adequate metaphors allow users to apply their knowledge about the things represented by the metaphor, for instance, an icon of a file cabinet, to understand rapidly how to obtain the desired system behavior, such as searching in a file system.

2.5 Building an Object Model

The object model provides a description of the application object structure, including

- The object classes that make up the application
- The relationship among classes

- The information that each class maintains (its attributes)
- The services that each class provides (its public methods)

The object model is the primary source of information about the results of the analysis work and the starting point for the design and implementation efforts. We adopted the OMT notation (see Figure 7 on page 21) for the description of object models.

2.5.1 Finding Objects

To build an object model, we start by identifying potential objects (that will later be abstracted into classes) from the problem statement of the application and the initial use cases.

The objects found describe the problem domain and are the building blocks of the application. They account for the information held in the system and for its global behavior.

Our approach for finding objects is to perform a syntactic analysis on both the use cases and the problem statement. Nouns or noun phrases are candidate objects, verbs are candidate services provided by objects, and adjectives identify possible different types of the same object (subclasses). Since natural language can be ambiguous, some further analysis, or pruning, is required:

- Two nouns can refer to the same thing (synonyms), so a single name must be found.

- Nouns can refer to things that are not relevant to the problem.

- A noun can refer to something that is better modeled as an attribute. For example, the noun *amount* in the sentence "the total amount of cash held in a cashier's drawer" is better modeled as an attribute of the cashier's drawer than as an object.

- A noun can refer to something that is better modeled as a service. For example, the noun *withdrawal* in the sentence "the cashier makes a withdrawal from the customer's account" is better modeled as a "withdrawal" service provided by the account than as an object.

2.5.2 Identifying Class Relationships

There are three main relationships among the object classes:

- Generalization
- Association
- Aggregation

The following subsections illustrate these relationships.

Generalization

A generalization is the taxonomic relationship between a superclass and its subclasses. A subclass inherits all attributes, operations, and associations from its superclass, and from the superclass of its superclass, all the way up the inheritance hierarchy.

The notation for generalization is shown in Figure 18.

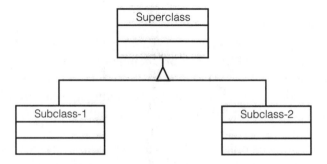

Figure 18. Generalization

Association

An association represents a structural relationship between two classes. Each instance of an association is a *link*—a physical or conceptual connection between two (or more) objects of a single class or of different classes. Each link is a tuple of object references. An association is not always bidirectional. Each end of an association is a role that shows how its class is viewed by the other class.

Multiplicity *Multiplicity* specifies how many instances of one class can relate to a single instance of an associated class. Multiplicity is often described as being "one" or "many," but more generally it is a (possibly infinite) subset of the nonnegative integers [RUM91].

The OMT notation for association with multiplicity (cardinality) is shown in Figure 19.

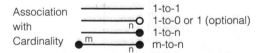

Figure 19. Associations notation

An association can exist between a class and itself; that is, the class participates twice in the relationship, but in each case with a different role. It is always good practice to specify the role names for an association, particularly for a self-referenced association, because without the role names, it is difficult to interpret the meaning of the relationship.

In Figure 20, the relationship indicating that the employee(s) work for a company is depicted by the *work for* association between the classes Employee and Company, indicating the respective *employee* and *employer* role names. The figure also shows an example of an association of a class to itself. The Employee class associates with itself, indicating that an employee in the role of a manager manages an employee in the role of a worker.

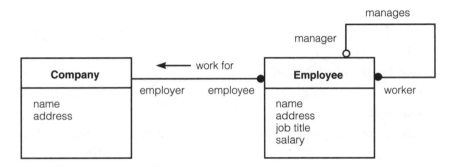

Figure 20. Associations and roles

Modeling an Association as a Class If there are attributes that do not belong to any of the classes related by an association but belong instead to the association itself, we model the association as a class. In Figure 21, the employment position and the salary of an employee within a company are not attributes of the employee nor of the company but of their association. We make this association a class called Employment with the attributes *position* and *salary*.

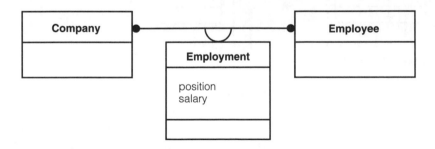

Figure 21. Modeling an association as a class

Qualified Association A qualified association relates two classes and a qualifier. The qualifier is a special attribute that is used to qualify the association. Thus it reduces the multiplicity of the association.

In Figure 22 on page 44, the bank issues a number of bank cards to its customers. Each bank card has a unique number. Using the card number as a qualifier effectively reduces the association between the bank and the bank card from a 1-to-many to a 1-to-1 association. Similarly, the account number is used as a qualifier to model the qualified association between the bank and the account.

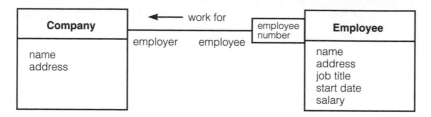

Figure 22. Qualified associations

Aggregation

Aggregation is a special form of a whole-to-part association, in which the components are part of the aggregate or whole (see Figure 23).

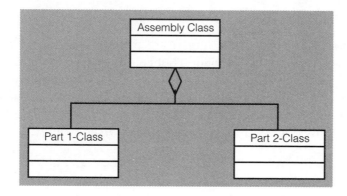

Figure 23. Aggregation

Note that the phrase *part of* has different meanings. For example, the engine and wheels are *part of* a car. When we drive a car, its engine and wheels must be part of the car. If the car is in a garage being repaired, however, its engine and wheels do not have to be part of the car. In an ordinary aggregation, there is no such semantic differentiation.

In visual programming, the construction-from-parts paradigm requires a more crisp semantic definition of a composite object.

A composite object is an extended form of aggregation in which the composite object contains (refers to) all its parts. The composite object is a higher level of abstraction than its parts, although a composite object and its parts can coexist at run time.

We use composite objects to show the structural (configurational) relationship, with a semantic implication of physical togetherness of the composite object and its components (parts). However, in most object-oriented languages, a composite object contains references (object IDs) to the contained objects rather than containing the objects themselves.

In the 1995 OMT notation, a composite object is shown as a heavy box surrounding the components.

Abstraction in Object Modeling

Object technology offers a seamless transition from analysis to design, with a separation line that tends to blur as the iterations proceed. It is important, however, to maintain the conceptual difference between the problem solved in each development phase by using the proper level of abstraction when building an object model. During analysis, the object model represents only business objects. Solution domain or implementation objects (wrappers, dictionary classes representing associations, devices, and so on) should not be present. In other words, the object model should capture the essential structure of the application domain objects, including

- Attributes that actually define the object status, but not, for example, derived attributes, such as the result of a calculation

- Services that actually define the object responsibilities, that is, the object interface but not, for example, the algorithm of the methods or functions that implement services

The inheritance hierarchy should not be detailed early during analysis unless a clear difference in behavior is apparent between different subclasses of a class. Such a level of detail can limit the flexibility of the design work that follows.

2.5.3 Constraints

[RUM91] defines *constraints* as functional relationships between entities of an object model. The entities here may include objects, classes, roles, attributes, links, and associations. A constraint restricts the values that the entities can assume.

General constraints are specified as text within braces. Constraints can also be specified on association link values or association paths.

Figure 24 on page 46 shows a constraint between associations. The constraint *subset* indicates that a subset of the employees of the company are stockholders of the company.

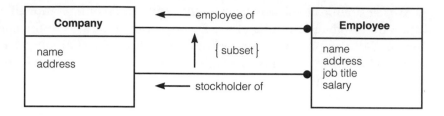

Figure 24. Constraint on associations

Figure 25 shows a constraint on the paths to be traversed in an association. The constraint in this example states that the managers and workers must work for the same company.

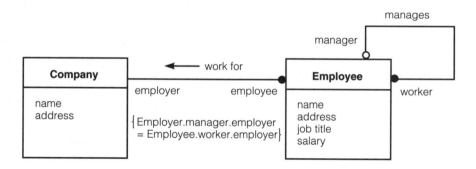

Figure 25. Constraint on association paths

2.6 The Model Dictionary

The model dictionary includes precise descriptions of each class.[7] These descriptions help us understand the purpose and definition of a class. For example, the scope of a class—the assumptions or restrictions on its use in the problem domain—should be clearly documented. Attributes, operations, and associations for the class should also be included.

Creation of the model dictionary can start as soon as classes are identified. The responsibilities of the classes evolve during the modeling and design phases. Therefore, updating the model dictionary to revise or refine the definitions of the classes is a standard activity in the modeling effort. It is recommended that a standard template be established for each type of entry in the model dictionary and used throughout the project.

---

7   The model dictionary is called a *data dictionary* in OMT.

2.7 **Analyzing Object Responsibilities**

[BEC93] makes the observation that finding objects is not the hard part of design; the hard part is distributing behaviors among objects. Distribution of behaviors is the next step in the object modeling phase in VMT.

Once we have created an initial object model, we can start to look at the classes with close scrutiny in terms of the roles they play in the object model. During initial object modeling, we focused on identifying the object classes, their attributes, and the relationships among them. This is still very much a datacentric view. Often the services or operations provided by most classes in an initial object model are still vaguely defined.

We believe that responsibility-driven analysis is a good way to tackle the problem of determining what services the objects are supposed to provide, which in turn defines their public interfaces. Such analysis makes an effective transition to the design activities.

Responsibility analysis is based on two concepts:

- An object has certain responsibilities in the system, such as maintaining certain knowledge (responsibilities for knowing) and providing certain services to other objects (responsibilities for doing).

- An object provides requested services by collaborating with other objects.

Modeling an object's responsibilities and collaborators helps define the distribution of attributes, services, and associations among the classes. For instance, in a relationship linking two classes, defining who does what determines the placement of attributes and methods. This approach suggests a high-level, anthropomorphic view of object interactions, which is quite healthy during application analysis.

Class responsibilities can be derived from use cases. To that end, we define system responsibilities implied by the use cases, and then we distribute responsibilities among all the classes in the system.

Consider the following use case: A cashier fills out an order form, adding requested currencies. If some currency is not available in the stock, the system notifies the cashier. An initial object model of this scenario is shown in Figure 26 on page 48.

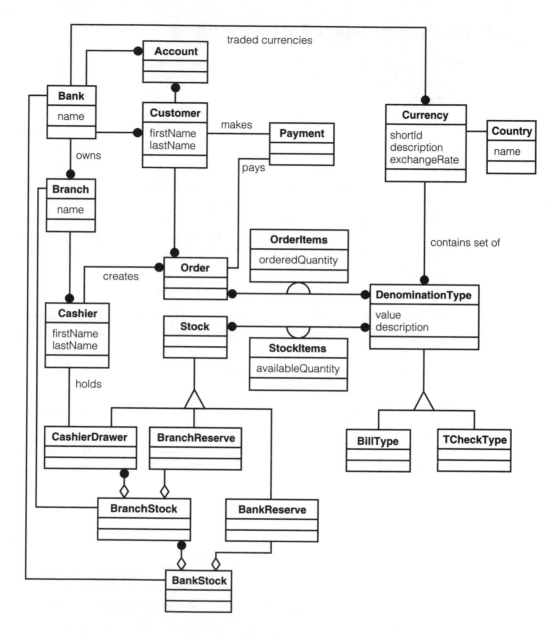

Figure 26. Initial object model for the foreign currency exchange system

This simple scenario highlights some system responsibilities:

- Knowing the currencies requested in an order and allowing the cashier to change them

- Knowing the availability of different types of currency in stock, checking the availability of currency in stock, and so forth

Here *knowing* means being able to retrieve and modify the value of an attribute.

We then assign the following responsibilities to the Order and Stock classes:

- Order should know about ordered currencies.
- Order should be able to accept currency requests.
- Stock should know about currency availability.
- Order should check currency availability before accepting a currency request.

Collaborators are then identified for each class responsibility by verifying whether an object of that class has all the required information to fulfill its responsibility. If this is not the case, collaborators must be identified to provide the required information.

We find that the order object does not know about currency availability and must somehow collaborate with the stock object to get the information. In the object model shown in Figure 26 on page 48 we can see that the order object cannot collaborate with the stock object because no relationship exists between them. This forces us to perform further analysis: We could discover a new relationship (showing that the order must be filled from stock) or extend the collaboration pattern (for example, the order could ask the cashier which stock is to be used and then ask the stock object to fill the order).

Responsibility analysis focuses on the purposes of an object in terms of

- Why a class exists in the object model
- What the class is supposed to do and know
- How the class collaborates with others to fulfill its responsibilities

The event trace diagrams or object interaction diagrams used in dynamic modeling, which we discuss in the next section, help us understand *how* the objects interact with each other. The focus is on the protocol, including event flows or message passing between objects. This contrasts with the responsibility analysis, which focuses on *why* a class has to interact with other classes.

A useful technique for responsibility analysis is CRC. The CRC technique was first proposed by Cunningham and Beck as a tool for teaching object-oriented programming [BEC89]. CRC cards, which are similar to index cards (Figure 27 on page 50) have proven to be useful development tools that facilitate brainstorming and enhance communication among developers.

For each class we create a CRC card that includes the class name, a list of class responsibilities, and a description of the collaborators needed to fulfill each responsibility. Optionally, the superclass and components can also be listed on the card. The back of the CRC card can be used to describe the class definitions and other specifications that later can be transcribed to the model dictionary.

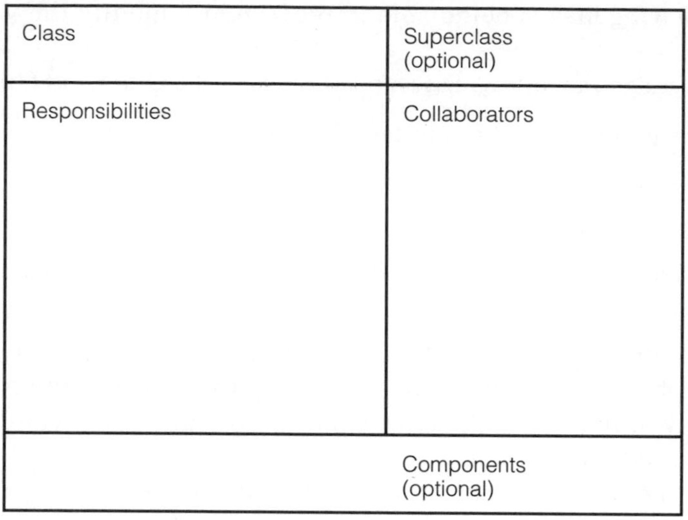

Class	Superclass (optional)
Responsibilities	Collaborators
	Components (optional)

Figure 27. CRC card

CRC cards provide an anthropomorphic view of objects: We think of them as active, living beings that will be responsible for carrying out their duties. During a CRC exercise, we often assume the identity of the objects to identify their responsibilities and collaborators. Collaborator objects are called on for their services to allow an object to fulfill a particular responsibility. In summary, the information gathered during responsibility analysis allows us to

- Define object services
- Refine attributes
- Verify and refine classes and their relationships
- Discover new classes

The result is a refined initial object model that facilitates the analysis of object behavior in terms of the interobject interactions.

There are limitations to the CRC cards technique. For example, CRC cards offer no help in distinguishing the responsibilities of a class from the responsibilities of the instances of a class. Thus we must later scrutinize the responsibilities distribution between the class and its instances.

Also, although CRC cards are effective as an informal tool, they do not provide much help in dealing with complex systems or large problem domains. Thus we must use a more formal technique, such as object interaction diagrams, to document the interactions involving many objects.

2.8 Dynamic Modeling

[RUM91] defines the purpose of a dynamic model as describing those aspects of a system concerned with time and the sequencing of operations—events that mark changes, the sequence of events, states that define the context for events, and the organization of events and states. The dynamic model provides a description of an application's dynamic behavior using event trace diagrams, which describe the flow of events in the application and specifying object state changes using state diagrams known as Harel state charts to show how the state of each object is modified under certain conditions by the events.

State diagrams can be used to describe the dynamic behavior of an individual class or collaborations of classes. At the class level, each state diagram shows the state changes and event sequences permitted in a system for one class of objects. An event trace diagram shows the interactions among objects and with the external actors.

Not every class has significant event-related behavior, so we draw state diagrams only for those classes where it makes sense to use them.

2.8.1 Event Trace Diagrams

An event trace diagram, as shown in Figure 28 on page 52, provides good insight into an application's behavior, information that is valuable for specifying the services that each object should provide.

Events are defined as any communication of information to an object. Such communication occurs when the user requests a service, an object requests a service from another object, and an object returns information on the completion of the requested service. Events can be generated outside the system, such as a message that arrives from the network, or inside it, such as time-generated events.

Event trace diagrams can be developed from use cases. To that end, we derive use scenarios from each use case. A use scenario is an instance of the corresponding use case. We then identify the events, including external events from actors, and the flow of events across the system boundary that were described in the use scenarios.

In an event trace diagram, objects requesting or providing services are shown as vertical bars; events (stimuli) are shown as directed segments from the client object to the server object. The sequence of events is shown proceeding from top to bottom.

Level of Detail in Event Trace Diagrams

An event trace diagram can be drawn at many levels of detail, from very high-level service requests, which are identified during the analysis phase, to the actual (Smalltalk) message passing, which is the level we may want to reach during detailed design.

During analysis, we use event traces to define and depict the high-level object responsibilities, that is, to define the role an object plays in the system. We also concentrate on the event flows (external events) that trigger the system interactions. Detailed event flows inside the system are dealt with during the design phase.

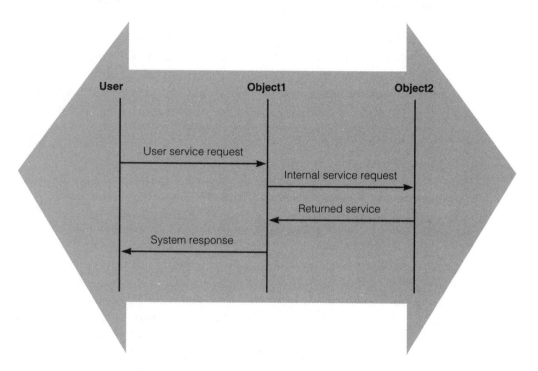

Figure 28. Sample event trace diagram

The sample event trace in Figure 28 shows the following sequence of events:

1. The user requests a service from the system; the service is provided by Object1.

2. Object1, in order to fulfill the service request, in turn requests a service from Object2; thus Object2 collaborates with Object1.

3. Object2 returns the requested service to Object1.

4. Object1 returns the user-requested service to the user (system response).

During analysis, the event trace diagram does not show internal details of objects, only their roles in the application (the events that they service and the events they produce). For example, the work that Object1 undertakes before sending its service request to Object2 is not shown. The set of events serviced or received by an object represents its responsibility in the system.

Sometimes it is obvious that a service request has a corresponding response event from the server object, and it is not necessary to show it. This is valid only if the mechanism of service request from a client to a server has a synchronous (call-like) semantic. However, if message passing is asynchronous, Object1 continues its work after having sent the service request to Object2 and must be able to intercept the completion event.

2.8.2 Interaction Diagrams

An interaction diagram (Figure 29) depicts information similar to that of an event trace diagram but has a more formalized notation. The Booch Method and OOSE use this notation to describe object interactions or communications. The objects requesting and/or providing services are shown as vertical bars, and events are shown as directed segments from the client object to the server; the sequence of events is shown proceeding from top to bottom. Scripts (text description) describe complex scenarios that may involve conditions or iterations. The system boundary and external events from actor(s) are also included.

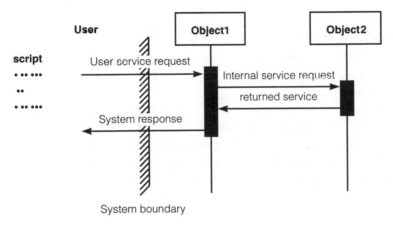

Figure 29. Sample interaction diagram

2.8.3 Object Interaction Diagrams

Both event trace diagrams and interaction diagrams are one-dimensional time-sequencing diagrams. A typical system involves a large number of objects, so a one-dimensional event trace or interaction diagram could become very complex and difficult to create.

The second-generation OMT uses a two-dimensional object interaction diagram (OID), as shown in Figure 30 on page 54. An object is drawn as a solid box, with the object name and its class separated by a colon (:). The stimuli or messages are shown as numbered labels, with optional parameters enclosed in parentheses, each with an arrow showing the direction of the flow of messages (stimuli).

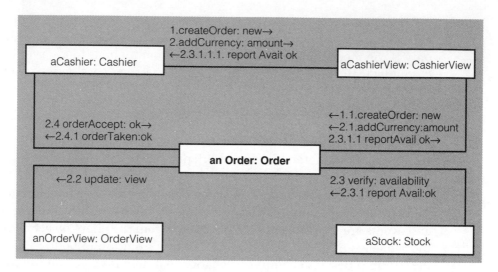

Figure 30. Sample object interaction diagram

2.8.4 State Diagrams

Object behavior can change over time in response to events. For example, an order just created accepts modifications from the user, but an accepted order cannot be modified.

Usually, we can account for the differences in object behavior by introducing the concept of a *state.* The state of an object is defined by the values of its attributes or internal variables. For example, an order just created is in a draft state, and an order accepted is in an accepted state, where draft and accepted are possible values of the attribute status of the object.

In object state diagrams represented using Harel state charts, a bubble represents each state. Inside the state, we can represent the activities that the object performs while it is in the state (and the services it requests other objects to perform). A labeled arrow (transition) exiting from a state indicates an accepted event (a request that can be serviced) while the object is in the state; the label is the name of the event accepted. The arrow points to another state if servicing the request implies a status change. The arrow points to the same state if servicing the request does not imply a state change (see Figure 8 on page 22)

The dynamic model of an application is a collection of state diagrams that interact with each other through shared events. The top half of Figure 8 on page 22 shows the first creation of a state diagram from an event trace, and the bottom half shows the integration of a second event trace in the same state diagram.

In business applications, event trace diagrams are used more frequently than state diagrams because the business application objects rarely exhibit very complex dynamic behavior.

2.9 Validating and Refining Analysis Models

When the analysis models are finished, they must be systematically examined for correctness and completeness. One technique is to walk through the scenarios of the use cases to ensure that the models demonstrate the appropriate properties and behavior in all cases. As each scenario is carried out by the classes in the models, the collaborations provided to the required services to fulfill each operation are examined.

During a walk-through, the CRC cards used to assign responsibilities and define collaborations can be used to check consistency in the object and dynamic models, using the following criteria:

Checking the Object Model

- Each class maps to a CRC card.
- Each role name maps to a CRC collaborator.
- Each method name maps to a CRC responsibility.

Checking the Dynamic Model

- Each class maps to a CRC card.
- Each message from object A to B <—> the CRC card for A declares B as collaborator.
- Each message from object A to B <—> the CRC card for B declares that B has the responsibility to service messages from A.

New modeling tools are appearing in the marketplace that can animate an object model. With the aid of such a modeling tool, the walk-through becomes very productive: Analysts can visually and interactively develop the application object model and validate the required application behavior.

2.10 Summary

The VMT modeling process, as shown in Figure 31 on page 57, consists of the following steps:

1. Define a problem statement based on an initial requirements document.
2. Define an initial set of actors and use cases based on the problem statement and user and expert input.
3. Build a basic functional prototype using a visual programming tool such as IBM VisualAge, with simple GUIs, to understand the user interaction and complete the use case model.

4. From both the problem statement and the use case model, build the initial object model, using syntactical analysis. This object model provides an overview of the classes that describe the problem domain[8] of the application, and the relationships and primary attributes of those classes.

5. As another input to the modeling process, add generic domain knowledge, which can be acquired from the literature. Domain knowledge sheds light on many aspects of the problem; however, it must be used in conjunction with the problem statement to be practical.[9]

6. Use the initial object model, the use cases, and the GUI prototype together to represent the requirements model for the application to be developed. The requirements model also defines the system boundary and external interface.

7. Create CRC cards to define class responsibilities and collaborators. From the class responsibilities, determine the services and attributes in the object model.

8. Redistribute class responsibilities until the object model is stabilized. From the collaboration patterns, redefine the classes and their relationships to obtain a refined object model.

9. From the use case model and the required services for each class, build event trace diagrams and state diagrams showing the dynamic behavior of the system.

10. Iterate through the requirements gathering and modeling processes to achieve an acceptable level of completeness and integrity of the models.

---

8 We distinguish between business classes, which pertain to the problem domain, and development classes, which pertain to the solution domain and include implementation constructs.

9 A type of domain knowledge that can be readily put to use is that provided by industry architectures, which offer a business-oriented framework to model the whole enterprise, including the problem at hand.

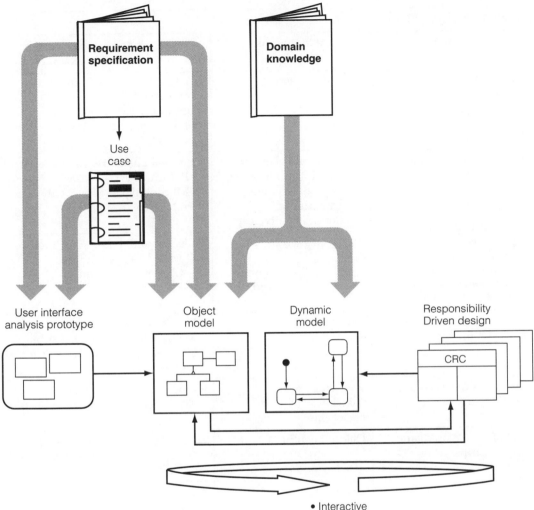

Figure 31. VMT modeling process

Table 1 summarizes the tasks of the VMT object-oriented modeling phase.

The main work products or deliverables produced from the analysis phase are

- Use case model, which consists of a set of
  —Actors
  —Use cases
- Object model
- Model dictionary
- CRC cards
- Dynamic model, which contains
  —Event trace diagrams and object interaction diagrams
  —State diagrams
- Analysis prototype

Table 1. Analysis Phase

Input	Activities and techniques	Work Products— Where to find examples
Requirements specification Potential user roles Problem Statement User input	Use case gathering	• Actor(s)—See "Defining Actors" on page 62 • Initial use case model—See "Identifying Initial Use Cases" on page 62.
Initial use case model User input	User interface sketches —Analysis prototyping —For requirements gathering —For proof of concepts	• Refined model use case—See "Refining the Use Cases" on page 64. • GUI prototype—See "Analysis Prototyping" on page 70.
Application requirements —Problem statement —Domain description —Refined model use case	Syntactic analysis —Underlining nouns —Underlining verbs	• List of candidates—See "Finding Objects" on page 71. —Classes and attributes —Relations
List of candidates classes and relationships	Pruning	• List of good classes and relationships—See "Discarding Unnecessary and Incorrect Classes" on page 72.
List of good classes and relationships	Preparing precise description of each object class	• Model dictionary—See 2.6, "The Model Dictionary" on page 46.
List of good classes and relationships	Object modeling	• Object model (first cut)—See "Creating an Initial Object Model" on page 73.
Initial object model	CRC cards —Class roles and responsibilities —Collaborations	• Object model (first iteration) —Class services and interfaces —Additional attributes —Additional or new classes • Initial CRC cards—See 3.6 "Initial CRC Cards" on page 76.
Object model (first iteration) Use cases model (refined)	Dynamic modeling —Develop use scenarios from use cases	• Event-trace diagrams or state diagrams—See 2.8, "Dynamic Modeling" on page 51. —Pre and post-conditions of event-class interactions
Object model Dynamic model CRC cards Model dictionary	Validate, iterate, and refine . . .	• Object model (refined—not shown in the example) • Dynamic model (refined—not shown in the example) • CRC cards (refined—not shown in the example) • Model dictionary (refined)

3

Case Study: The Foreign Currency Exchange System— Analysis Phase

We present a case study based on a foreign currency exchange (FCE) application.[10] The primary goal of the case study is to illustrate how VMT is used in the application development process from requirements gathering through implementation.

It is important to realize that the application development process is more than building a set of models by using prescribed techniques. It is a continuous process in which each phase has its own specific role and serves as a basis for subsequent phases.

The FCE application described in this chapter is used to show how to

- Detail the business application requirements and use VMT to model the problem and design the solution

- Establish the mapping between the object model and application implementation in VisualAge, and to illustrate the construction of an application from parts

---

10 This chapter covers the analysis phase of the FCE case study. Chapter 7 describes the design and implementation of the same case study.

3.1 Problem Statement

The case study features a bank with a number of worldwide distributed branches (see Figure 32). The bank provides its customers with various banking services, such as automated teller machines, credit cards, and foreign currency exchange.

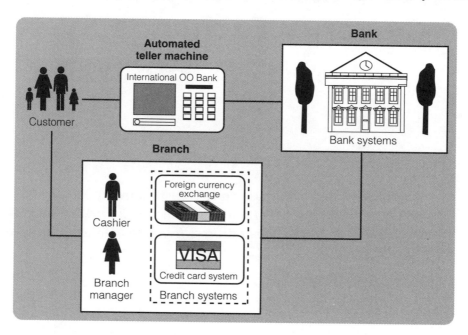

Figure 32. Case study bank environment

The FCE application supports foreign cash and traveler's check trading services to customers based on current exchange rates. Customers who have an account in a bank branch are considered bank customers. Customers who do not have an account in any bank branches are considered general customers. Both bank customers and general customers can use the exchange services.

The FCE application manages information about customers, foreign currencies, orders and payments, and stock availability. Branch cashiers are provided with country information, including country currency name, denominations of both cash and traveler's checks, and foreign country currency restrictions. Cashiers get customer information, create an order, and receive an immediate response regarding the requested stock availability in their drawers and in the local branches. Customer orders can be pending, in process, or completed. An order becomes pending only if sufficient stock is not available in the cashier's drawer or in the local branch.

Appendix A describes the complete requirements specifications of the FCE application.

3.2 Project Iterations

For illustration purposes, we will consider that the modeling of the case study application is done in three iterations. The first iteration focuses on

- Understanding the problem domain by developing use cases
- Identifying and defining candidate objects
- Modeling relationships among objects
- Building a limited function prototype

In the first iteration, more time is spent in planning and understanding the problem than in producing a prototype.

The second iteration uses the knowledge gained from the first iteration and focuses on

- Refining an object model and assigning responsibilities to objects
- Looking for class structures and potential reuse
- Building an expanded function prototype
- Looking at systems architecture solutions

During the second iteration, some time is spent in planning, but we also start to produce a design prototype. Object models, use cases, preliminary object responsibilities, and a limited function prototype are the expected output from this iteration.

The third iteration uses the knowledge gained from the first two iterations and focuses on

- Designing a system architecture
- Designing the object model
- Designing application class structures
- Designing the application

Later iterations focus on refining the design to improve the quality of the application.

3.3 Analysis

From the requirements specifications, we first develop the use case model.

The use case model allows the software engineer and the potential user of the system to analyze the problem domain At the same time, it provides a first look at the user-system interaction that will be maintained throughout the whole process of application development. Thus it is important to preserve the language of the problem domain while introducing the sequences of actor-system interactions.

The following sections summarize the process of developing the use case model of the FCE application.

3.3.1   Defining the Boundary of the System

The FCE application handles the foreign currency exchange services of the bank. Other major banking services, such as ATMs and credit card management, are beyond the scope of this case study project. Some of the foreign currency management activities, such as foreign currency trading and customer use of credit cards for payment, are also outside the scope of the project.

3.3.2   Defining Actors

The primary actor is the cashier. The secondary actor is the branch manager. The branch manager is defined as a secondary actor because he or she uses the support functions of the FCE system only to allow the cashiers to perform the regular functions.

Customers deal with the cashier and do not interact directly with the FCE system. A customer is therefore not an actor.

3.3.3   Identifying Initial Use Cases

We started with high-level user-system interactions to identify the following main task flows:

Order Entry—Currency in Stock

1. Cashier creates new order.
2. System prints tab.
3. Cashier completes order.

Order Entry—Currency Out of Stock

1. Cashier creates new order.
2. System informs cashier of stock availability—out of stock.
3. Cashier places out-of-stock order.
4. System forwards order to the bank.
5. Bank handles order—points to another use case.
6. Cashier handles customer payment—points to another use case.

Customer Selling

1. Cashier creates sell order.
2. System prints tab for customer and bank receipt.
3. Cashier accepts order.

Customer Buying

1. Cashier creates buy order.
2. System prints tab for customer and bank receipt.
3. Cashier accepts order.

Replenishing Stock

1. Branch manager creates a consolidated order to the bank for replenishing or returning stock.
2. Branch manager forwards order to the bank.

Managing Stock—Reconciliation Required

1. Cashier checks stock in the drawer.
2. Cashier verifies stock in the drawer with stock in the system—stocks balanced.
3. Cashier raises compensating accounting entries for loss and gain.
4. Cashier orders replenishment stock.
5. Cashier sends excess stock to the center.

Managing Stock—No Reconciliation Required

1. Cashier checks stock in the drawer.
2. Cashier verifies stock in the drawer with stock in the system—stocks balanced.
3. Cashier orders replenishment stock.
4. Cashier sends excess stock to the center.

Canceling Order

1. Cashier identifies order to be canceled (when customer cancels order to buy or sell currency).
2. System displays the selected order.
3. Cashier cancels order.
4. System confirms that order is canceled.

3.3.4 Exceptions

The initial use cases usually reveal only basic actions in the sequences that require further elaboration. Some refinements deal with exceptions in the normal flow of the use case. For example, in our use cases, a customer can reject the prepared order for buying or selling currency, in which case a cashier must cancel the order. A cashier can reject buying currency if he or she discovers a forgery, in which case the order must be canceled. (The need to cancel can be avoided by putting the inspection of the currency at the beginning of the Customer Buying use case.)

Extensions can be used to model optional or alternative courses that seldom occur, such as a customer's rejection of an already prepared foreign currency exchange receipt, or a cashier's rejection of a foreign currency purchase because of forged bills or traveler's checks. (Also, extensions can be executed in certain cases; sometimes they are used to insert special use cases.)

3.3.5 Considering Generalizations and Abstractions

While building a use case model, it is important to identify similar use cases or the similar parts in use cases. Both are good candidates for abstract use cases, which are not instantiated on their own but rather describe the common parts of other concrete use cases.

Among the use cases for the FCE application, we can find several candidates for abstraction. Both Customer and Cashier can reject buying currency for certain reasons. Order Entry—In Stock and Order Entry—Out of Stock use cases have a lot of commonality. We can create abstract Cancel and Order use cases, respectively, and then create the concrete use cases based on the abstractions.

3.3.6 Refining the Use Cases

After some refinement and considerations mentioned in the previous sections, we can develop the refined use cases as follows:

Customer Purchase Order—In Stock (Normal Course of Events)

1. Cashier creates new order.

2. Cashier fills in order: currency type, amount, amount type: cash or check, type of payment, customer information.

3. System gives cashier information about currency or check: exchange rate, country restrictions, forgery information, and so on.

   System internal interactions not described in the use case:[11]

   • System determines currency type based on country.

   • Order can include a variety of currencies and checks, singly and in combination.

   • System determines country restrictions.

4. System informs cashier: stock availability—in stock.

---

11 The use case describes the interaction between the user and the system. What happens inside the system is either described in the problem statement or must be elicited from the user or expert knowledge.

5. System determines payment and exchange rate.

6. System prints tab.

7. Cashier notifies system: customer accepts (signed) order.

8. Cashier handles customer payment—points to another use case.

   System internal interactions not described in the use case:

   • System reduces stock level of currency type and amount of order.

   • System generates accounting entry.

9. System prints tab.

10. Cashier completes order.

11. System informs cashier: order in Completed Orders.

Customer Purchase Order—In Stock (Alternative Course of Events)

1. Cashier notifies system: customer cancels order.

2. Cashier cancels order.

3. System informs cashier: order in Canceled Orders.

Country Restriction Query

1. Cashier asks system about country restrictions on selling particular foreign currency.

2. System gives requested information to cashier.

3. Cashier creates customer purchase order—points to Customer Purchase Order use case.

Customer Purchase Order—Out of Stock (Normal Course of Events)

1. Cashier creates new order.

2. Cashier fills in order: currency type, amount, amount type: cash or check, type of payment, customer information.

3. System gives cashier information about currency or check: exchange rate, country restrictions, forgery information.

   System internal interactions not described in the use case:

   • System determines currency type based on country.

   • Order includes multiple currencies and checks.

   • System determines country restrictions.

4. System informs cashier: stock availability—out of stock.

5. Cashier marks order out of stock.

> *System internal interactions* not described in the use case:

- System determines payment and exchange rate.

6. System prints tab.

7. Cashier notifies system: customer accepts (signed) order (deposit taken).

> *System internal interactions* not described in the use case:

- System forwards order to the bank.
- System passes accounting entries to the bank.
- Bank handles order—points to another use case.

8. Cashier completes order.

9. System informs cashier: order in Pending Status.

Customer Purchase Order—Out of Stock (Alternative Course of Events)

1. Cashier notifies system: customer rejects order.

2. Cashier cancels order.

3. System informs cashier: order in Canceled Orders.

Order Fulfillment—In Stock, Pending Order (Normal Course of Events)

1. Cashier asks system to find the pending order for the customer.

2. System gives cashier information about the pending order for the customer.

3. System prints tab.

4. Cashier notifies system: customer accepts order.

5. Cashier handles customer payment—points to another use case.

6. Cashier completes order.

7. System informs cashier: order in Completed Orders.

Order Fulfillment—In Stock, Pending Order (Alternative Course of Events)

1. Cashier notifies system: customer cancels order.

2. Cashier cancels order.

3. System informs cashier: order in Canceled Orders.

Customer Selling Order

1. Cashier creates sell order.
2. Cashier fills in order: currency type, amount, denomination, customer information.
3. System gives cashier information about currency: country, denomination, description of currency, common forgery errors.

   System internal interactions not described in the use case:
   - System determines exchange rate, payment.
4. Systems prints tab for customer and bank receipt.
5. Cashier examines currency.
6. Cashier accepts order.

   System internal interactions not described in the use case:
   - System adds stock to stock totals.
   - System passes accounting entries to the branch or bank.

Forgery Handling (Normal Course for Customer Selling Order)

1. Cashier asks system about forgery information for a particular foreign currency.
2. System gives requested information to cashier.
3. Cashier creates customer selling order—points to Customer Selling Order use case.

Forgery Handling (Alternative Course of Events)

1. Cashier notifies the system: forged currency.
2. Cashier cancels the order.
3. System informs cashier: order in Canceled Orders.

Customer Management: Enter New Customer

1. Cashier requests to perform customer management function.
2. System provides form for the cashier to fill in.
3. Cashier completes customer information form.
4. Cashier requests system to perform the create job.
5. System performs the customer create job.
6. System notifies cashier: job is successfully completed.

Customer Management: Update Customer

1. Cashier requests to perform customer management function.
2. System provides list of customers to the cashier.
3. Cashier identifies customer to update.
4. System acknowledges cashier-selected customer.
5. Cashier requests to perform customer update function on the selected customer.
6. System provides cashier with customer detail information.
7. Cashier modifies form with new information.
8. Cashier requests system to perform the update.
9. System performs customer update job.
10. System notifies cashier: job is successfully completed.

Customer Management: Delete Customer

1. Cashier requests to perform customer management function.
2. System provides list of customers to the cashier.
3. Cashier chooses customer to delete.
4. System indicates to cashier the customer has been selected.
5. Cashier confirms to system to delete the selected customer.
6. System deletes customer.
7. System notifies cashier: job is successfully completed.

Branch Stock Replenishment

1. Branch manager consolidates cashier requests (for stock replenishment orders or requests to return excess stock).
2. Branch manager creates consolidated order to replenish or return stock.
3. Branch manager forwards the order to the bank.

The actor for this use case is the branch manager, or this could be a batch function initiated at a predetermined time during the day.

Cashier Drawer Management—Reconciliation Required

1. Cashier checks stock in drawer.

   System internal interactions not described in the use case:

   • System obtains exchange rate for each currency.

2. System displays each total for currency and checks and local currency equivalent.

3. System displays each currency or check denomination totals and local currency equivalent.

4. Cashier verifies stock in the drawer with stock in the system—stocks balanced.

5. Cashier raises compensating accounting entries for loss and gain.

> *System internal interactions* not described in the use case:

- System amends stock accordingly.
- System archives reconciliation records.

6. System verifies and informs cashier if minimum stock quantity reached.

7. Cashier informs system: transactions confirmed by the branch manager.

8. Cashier orders replenishment stock.

9. System informs cashier if maximum stock quantity exceeded.

10. System verifies and informs cashier whether the maximum stock quantity has been exceeded.

11. Cashier sends excess stock to center.

12. System displays total local currency equivalent in stock.

Cashier Drawer Management—No Reconciliation Required

1. Cashier checks stock in drawer.

> *System internal interactions* not described in the use case:

- System obtains exchange rate for each currency.

2. System displays each currency, check totals, and local currency equivalent.

3. System displays each currency or check denomination totals and local currency equivalent.

4. Cashier verifies stock in the drawer with stock in the system—stocks balanced.

5. System verifies and informs cashier if minimum stock quantity reached.

6. Cashier informs system: transactions confirmed by the branch manager.

7. Cashier orders replenishment stock.

8. System verifies and informs cashier if maximum stock quantity exceeded.

9. Cashier sends excess stock to center.

10. System displays total local currency equivalent in stock.

The initial use case model is shown in Figure 16 on page 37. The refined use case model is shown in Figure 33.

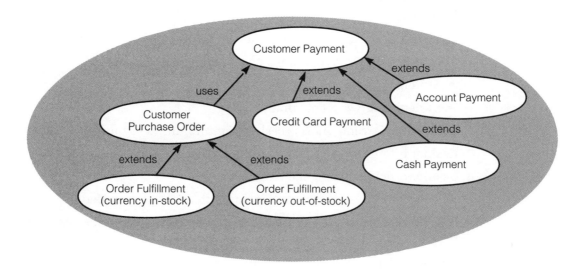

Figure 33. Part of the use case model for the FCE application

3.3.7 Analysis Prototyping

Analysis prototyping serves the purpose to better understand the user needs. The analysis prototype could be simple sketches, just to help portray the actor-system interactions described in the use case, and as a proof-of-concept of the user requirements. These sketches can also be used later in the user interface design.

As an example, a sketch of the user interface for *Customer Purchase Order—In Stock* is shown in Figure 34.

3.4 Object Modeling

Object modeling starts with identifying potential object classes. From the use cases and the problem specifications, we conduct systemic analysis to find potential objects. Reading the use cases, the nouns or noun phrases represent candidates for object classes.

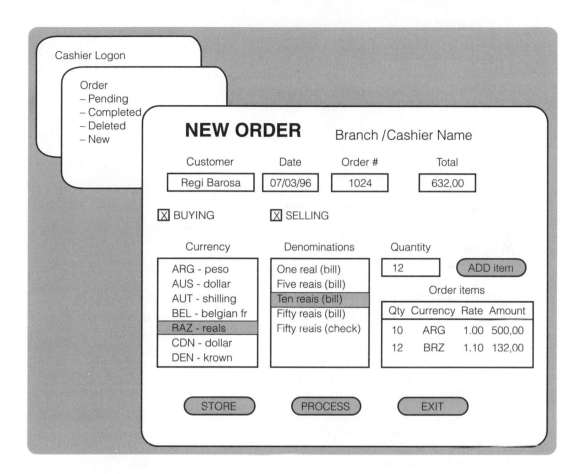

Figure 34. Analysis Prototype for Customer Purchase Order-In Stock

3.4.1 Finding Objects

Table 2 shows the potential object classes found in the *Customer Purchase Order—In Stock* use case. We identify more potential object classes from other use cases using the same process.

Note that many candidate object classes will be discarded later. Also additional classes that do not directly appear in the use cases can be identified from the knowledge of the problem domain, or are implied in the problem statement, like *order item.*

use case

Table 2. Potential Object Classes for Customer Purchase Order—In Stock		
Cashier	System	Customer
Order	Cashier information	Stock level
Currency type	Currency	Amount of order
Amount	Exchange Rate	Accounting entry
Amount Type	Country restrictions	Order in Completed Orders
Cash	Forgery information	Order in Canceled Orders
Check	Stock availability—in stock	Requested information
Type of Payment	Payment	Customer purchase order
Customer information	Tab	

3.4.2 Discarding Unnecessary and Incorrect Classes

Many candidate object classes will be discarded because they are redundant, not important; are actually class attributes; are class methods; or because they reflect the roles of the object classes. Some examples are listed below:

1. Redundant Classes: we choose the name that better describes the object class, and eliminate redundancies.

   For example, *Cashier information* and *Cashier, Customer information* and *Customer*. We will keep *Cashier* and *Customer*.

2. Irrelevant Classes: classes that have nothing to do with the problem domain must be eliminated.

   For example, *form* and *job* noun in the use case of *Customer Management: Enter New Customer*. Form and job are not really part of the problem domain.

3. Vague Classes: classes that are not specific or have a broad scope.

   For example, *System* is too broad in scope.

4. Class Attributes: some potential class objects are attributes and not classes themselves.

   For example, *Exchange Rate* will be an attribute of the class Currency. *Stock availability—in stock,* it will be an attribute of Stock, etc. . . .

5. Class Methods: some noun phrases sometimes are methods and must be discarded.

   For example, *create customer job* in the use case *Customer Management: Enter New Customer* is more likely a method of some class.

6. Roles: the class cannot reflect a role it plays in an association.

   For example, *Country restrictions* is a role to be played by some class, but we will not consider it as an object class.

7. Implementation Construct: things that are not part of the real-world problem domain but has to do with how the problem is solved should not be a part of the selected objects.

   After some pruning, some final candidate object classes include: Bank, Branch, Cashier, Customer, Order, and Stock.

Please note that we have identified cashier as a required object class for the object model. Cashier is an actor which is an entity outside of the FCE system. So why is it a class inside the FCE system? Sometimes, we need to have a class representing the actor in the system. In this case, the Cashier class in the system contains and encapsulates the information about a cashier actor, such as the name, cashier ID, etc., for the purpose of tracking the creation of orders, and managing cashier stock in the cashiers drawer belonging to a cashier.

3.4.3 Creating an Initial Object Model

We have identified the good candidate object classes, their attributes, and their relationships. At this point, we use a case tool to document the initial model as shown in Figure 35 on page 74.

3.5 Model Dictionary

We identified the following descriptions for the object classes in the context of the FCE application:

- Account: An account in a bank against which credit or debit transactions can be applied. A customer who owns an account in the bank can deposit into and make payment from the account to pay for the foreign currency purchase orders.

- Bank: A financial institution that holds accounts for customers and holds the stock of foreign currencies for the purpose of providing foreign currency exchange services to customers.

- Branch: An establishment of a bank that provides foreign currency exchange services to bank customers.

- Cashier: An employee of a bank, working in a branch, who is authorized to create customer orders for purchasing foreign currencies and accept customer deposits and order payments.

- BankReserve: An inventory of foreign currencies in the bank saved for future use in the foreign currency exchange service.

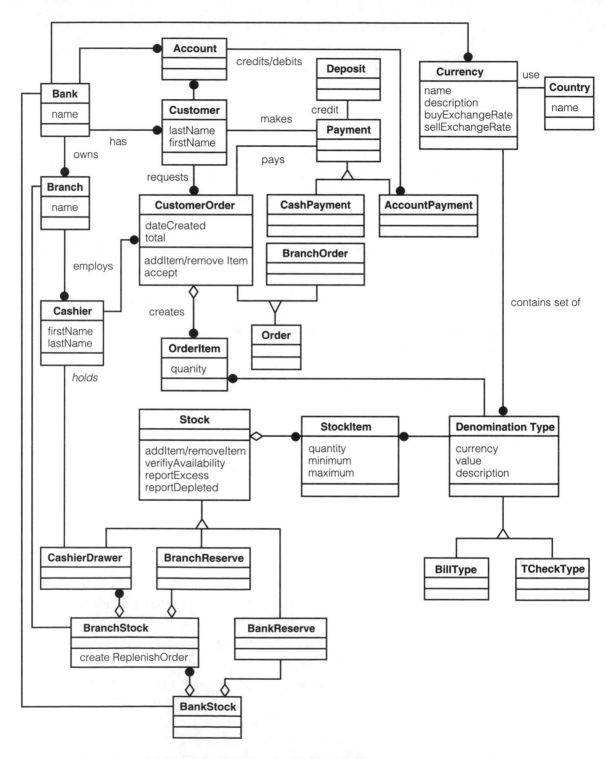

Figure 35. Initial object model for the FCE application

- BankStock: An inventory of foreign currencies in the bank, including both the portion in circulation and the portion saved for future use in the foreign currency exchange service.
- BillType: A unique type of currency that has a specific value.
- BranchReserve: An inventory of foreign currencies in the branch saved for future use in the foreign currency exchange service.
- BranchStock: An inventory of foreign currencies in the branch, including both the portion in circulation and the portion saved for future use in the foreign currency exchange service.
- CashierDrawer: A temporary storage containing foreign currencies used by a cashier to conduct foreign currency exchange business.
- Country: A state or nation that has its own currency. A country may have restrictions or policies in the amount of currency a traveler can get.
- Currency: Money in circulation as a medium of exchange, acceptance, and general use. A country has its own currency, which consists of a set of denominations. In the context of this application, currency includes bills and traveler's checks.
- Customer: A client who has an account with the bank to purchase foreign currencies.
- DenominationType: A unique type of value in the currency system.
- Order: A request for purchasing or supplying an amount of foreign currencies with itemized specifications. An order can be a customer order or a branch order.
- CustomerOrder: An order requested by a customer for purchasing or selling an amount of foreign currencies with itemized specifications.
- BranchOrder: An internal order requested by a branch for transferring (replenshing or supplying) an amount of foreign currencies with itemized specifications.
- OrderItem: An item in the order.
- Payment: A transaction to pay for a foreign currency order.
- TCheckType: A unique type of traveler's check.
- Stock: The supply of foreign currencies kept on hand by a financial institution (bank) or an establishment (branch) to conduct foreign currency exchange business.
- StockItem: An item in the stock that represents a specific type and amount of the supply in foreign currencies.

3.6 Initial CRC Cards

The following are the initial results of applying the CRC technique.

Class: Customer	
Responsibilities	**Collaborator**
Answers name, ID, phones, address	
Knows account	Account
Checks account balance	Account

Class: Order	
Responsibilities	**Collaborator**
Answers type of order (customer or branch)	
Knows and can modify currency, check, and amount requested	
Knows status (new, pending, completed, canceled)	
Calculates payment amount	Currency (exchange rate), Denomination (amount), Branch (commission)
Checks country restrictions	Country

Class: CustomerOrder	
Responsibilities	**Collaborator**
Answers date created	
Answers order number	
Changes and answers order status	
Knows customer information	Customer
Answers foreign total	
Calculates and answers local total	
Calculates account total	

Class: OrderItem	
Responsibilities	**Collaborator**
Knows currency and denomination	Currency, Denomination Type
Answers local and foreign amount	

Class: Country	
Responsibilities	**Collaborator**
Knows restrictions	
Knows currency to use	Currency
Identifies currency type	Currency

Class: Currency	
Responsibilities	**Collaborator**
Contains set of denomination type	DenominationType
Answers name, denomination, description, exchange rate, ID	
Knows country using it	Country

Class: Bill Type	
Responsibilities	**Collaborator**
Knows its value	
Knows currency type	Currency

Class: Tchecktype	
Responsibilities	**Collaborator**
Knows its value	
Knows currency type	Currency

Class: Denomination	
Responsibilities	**Collaborator**
Answers description	Currency
Answers value and type	Currency
Knows currency	
Calculates local currency equivalent	

Class: Cashier	
Responsibilities	**Collaborator**
Answers name, ID, branch	Branch
Manages list of all orders	Order
Manages list of pending and completed orders	Order
Checks stock and stock level	Stock

Class: Branch	
Responsibilities	**Collaborator**
Answers name	
Knows bank	Bank
Knows cashiers in branch	Cashier
Knows branch stock	BranchStock

Class: Bank	
Responsibilities	**Collaborator**
Answers name	
Changes and answers list of branches	Branch
Changes and answers list of currencies	Currency
Changes and answers list of bank customers	Customer
Changes bank stock	Stock

Class: CashierDrawer	
Responsibilities	**Collaborator**
Answers list of bank currencies	Bank
Answers list of available currencies	
Adds additional currency (checks/bill)	
Calculates total availability of currency	
Manages a list of depleted stock items (quantity < minimum)	
Manages a list of excess stock items (quantity > maximum)	
Knows minimum/maximum quantity per currency	
Calculates local equivalent in U.S. denominations	

Class: BranchStock	
Responsibilities	**Collaborator**
Answers list of cashier drawers	CashierDrawer
Answers branch reserve	BranchReserve
Answers current level of stock	BranchStock, BankReserve
Manages replenishment of currencies	CashierDrawer, BranchReserve, Bank
Manages transfer of currencies	CashierDrawer, BranchReserve, Bank

Class: BranchReserve	
Responsibilities	**Collaborator**
Answers list of bank currencies	
Answers list of available currencies	
Adds and removes additional currency (checks/bill)	
Calculates total availability of the currency	
Manages list of depleted stock items (quantity < minimum)	
Manages list of excess stock items (quantity > maximum)	
Calculates local equivalent in U.S. denominations	

Class: Account	
Responsibilities	**Collaborator**
Answers account number and description	
Answers branch ID	Branch
Credits/debits account balance	Payment, Deposit
Answers account balance	

Class: StockItem	
Responsibilities	**Collaborator**
Answers currency and denomination	Currency, Denomination Type
Changes and answers quantity	
Answers state (depleted or in excess)	Stock
Answers local currency value	
Answers availability of currency against requested quantity	Stock

Class: BankReserve	
Responsibilities	**Collaborator**
Answers bank reserve stock	

Class: BankStock	
Responsibilities	**Collaborator**
Answers available stock of the bank	Bank

Class: Payment	
Responsibilities	**Collaborator**
Accepts deposits	Deposit
Pays customer who purchased order	CustomerOrder

Class: CashPayment	
Responsibilities	**Collaborator**
Holds cash deposit for nonaccount customer	

Class: AccountPayment	
Responsibilities	**Collaborator**
Credits account with deposit	Account
Debits account with payment	Account

3.7 Dynamic Model

The dynamic model comprises object interaction (event trace) diagrams and state diagrams. The object interaction diagrams for order entry of in-stock and out-of-stock scenarios are shown in Figures 36 and 37, respectively.

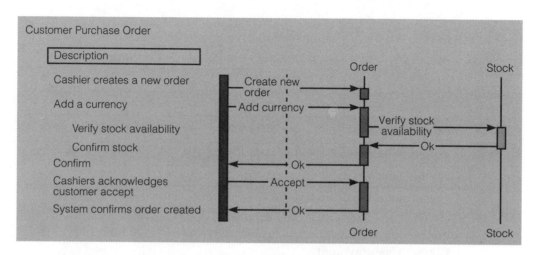

Figure 36. Object interaction diagram for order entry (in-stock scenario)

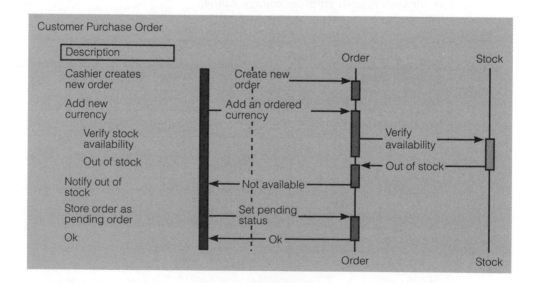

Figure 37. Object interaction diagram for order entry (out-of-stock scenario)

The initial state diagram for the order class is shown in Figure 38 on page 83.

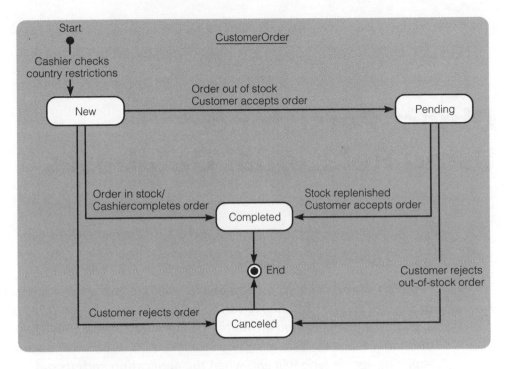

Figure 38. Initial state diagram for the order object

3.8 **Summary**

The requirement gathering and modeling phases are extremely important in object-oriented application development. Failing to recognize this fact and concentrating mostly on design and coding presents the risk of developing "a brilliant solution to the wrong problem." Both phases are intimately related; iterating one will usually affect the other.

The analysis phase produces a set of work products that can be reused in future developments. The work products of the analysis phase include

- Use cases
- Graphical user interface prototype
- CRC cards
- Model dictionary
- Object model
- Dynamic model

4

Object Persistence Using Relational Databases

The life cycle of an object in most application run-time environments is similar to the life cycle of a dynamic variable: Objects are created (that is, space is allocated in storage), and attributes are initialized as required. Objects can be deleted later, thus reclaiming the storage used. If an object is not deleted explicitly, its life cycle will end when the application ends its run.

When the value of a variable in a program must be kept until the program's next execution, it is stored in a nonvolatile medium, usually external to the program, where it can be retrieved when needed. The organization of the external storage depends on the way the data is used. It can be a flat file or it can be a database structured according to the hierarchical, network, or relational paradigms.

The same approach is valid for objects. If an object will be needed in a future execution of the program, it must be stored in a permanent medium, which may be organized in different ways. Those objects are called *persistent objects.*

This chapter deals with the storage and retrieval of persistent object data using relational database technology. It also covers the design process of encapsulating the database access logic in database broker subsystems.

4.1 Persistent Objects

Designers are faced with several options for storage and retrieval of objects that must last longer than the execution time of the program that invokes them. Each option has advantages and disadvantages.

Smalltalk enables the designer to save a complete image of the application's current state, including the values for all the variables in the application's objects. When the system is restarted, the internal state of the objects is restored. Smalltalk systems also provide facilities to write an object into a file as a string from which the object can be reconstructed.

These alternatives are not adequate for a multiuser environment. Such an environment requires data uniqueness, security, and integrity, which only database management systems (DBMSs) can provide.

Several types of DBMSs can be used. We discuss the use of two: object-oriented databases and relational databases.

4.1.1 Object-Oriented Databases

The most straightforward approach to persistent objects is to use an object-oriented DBMS, which is designed to store and share objects. An object-oriented DBMS has a data definition language (DDL) and a data manipulation language (DML), both of which can be defined as extensions of the application programming language or as built-in languages inherent to the DBMS. However, if a DBMS requires a language for database access that is different from the application programming languages, a significant amount of execution time can be wasted copying data from the database language format to the programming language format and back again [CAT91]; this is called the *impedance mismatch*. Moreover, if the DDL and DML are extensions of a particular language, such as C++, the database is not directly accessible to a program written in another language, such as Smalltalk. A built-in database language can provide a canonical way to deal with persistent objects independent of the language in which they were originally defined.

Objects consist not only of data but also of access methods, which are handled in different ways in different object-oriented DBMSs. Some systems store methods in the database; others keep them in external files. In the latter case, when a class is updated in the database, there can also be a requirement to update the methods in the external file.

The main drawback to the use of object-oriented databases to store persistent objects is the need to use two separate database systems when data access is heavy, particularly from legacy applications. Object-oriented databases do not support set operations, and usually a relational database is also needed.

4.1.2 Relational Databases

The widespread use of relational databases has prompted many organizations to look for a transition path to object technology that does not require a major conversion of their existing data repositories [TKA96]. A relational database can be used successfully to dematerialize objects, that is, to store their attribute values in the cells of relational tables and later retrieve the object data to recreate, or materialize, the object. As we see later in this chapter, there are several ways to perform this operation, and there are many performance implications in the choices that are made. Relational databases, however, offer a feasible and compatible solution, particularly for commercial business applications.

Relational database technology has many advantages. It provides a simple data model based on the use of tables, their columns and rows, integrity constraints, and so forth. It also provides a structured query language (SQL), which allows the user to specify what to retrieve but not how to do it; navigation through the database is not necessary.

Relational databases, however, do not provide a full solution to object persistence. In addition to handling only simple data structures, such as integer, real, blob, and string, the relational model does not support complex nested data. Only one data value is allowed per table cell, and cells cannot be navigated through memory pointers. In addition, relational database management systems (RDBMSs) are designed to handle only short transactions. Managing long transactions that involve handling temporal data, history, and data versions is beyond the scope of these systems. When such features are not required, however, RDBMSs are an excellent solution for supporting object persistence.

4.2 Basic Concepts of Relational Databases

This section presents an overview of the basic concepts and rules of relational databases. It provides the foundation to understanding the use of RDBMSs to store persistent object data. Although the use of object-oriented databases remains the most straightforward for object persistence, it is hard to expect that it will eventually prevail.

4.2.1 The Three-Schema Architecture

Databases always provide some level of data abstraction by hiding details of data storage not needed by the user [ELM93]. This is provided through a data model, which is a set of concepts that can be used to describe the data types, relationships, and constraints that should hold on the data—that is, the structure of the database. Most data models also include a set of operations for database retrieval and update.

To understand a data model, we must differentiate between the description of the database and the database itself. The description of a database is called the *database schema,* which is specified during the design of the database and is not expected to change frequently.

The currently accepted description of an RDBMS adheres to the ANSI-defined three-schema architecture (see Figure 39 on page 88), which was designed to separate the user application from the physical database (thus fostering the independence of programs and data). In this architecture, schemas can be defined at three levels:

- The external schema level, also called the view level, comprises a number of external schemas known as *user views.* Each user view describes a view of the database by a certain group of users.

- The conceptual schema level consists of a conceptual schema that describes the structure of the database, hiding the details of physical storage structure and focusing on entities, data types, relationships, and constraints. The conceptual schema can be obtained by integrating the external schemas of the system and by analyzing the problem statement in a way that is similar to finding objects during object modeling. From a business point of view, the conceptual schema can be considered a database design.

- The internal schema level describes the organization of data on the physical storage medium, including available access paths (links and indexes). The internal schema describes the physical implementation of the conceptual schema, and it is usually expressed in terms of the DDL of the database management system.

The internal schema therefore describes a specific DBMS, and the DBMS must transform a request to the external schema into a request to the conceptual schema, which gets translated as a request to the internal schema to be processed on the physical database. If the request is for data retrieval, the data extracted from the database will be formatted to match the external schema in order to be presented to the user.

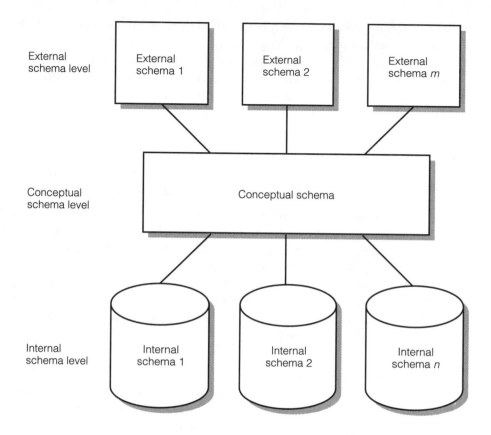

Figure 39. Three-schema architecture for relational databases

As it is described in this chapter, object modeling is useful for designing both the external and conceptual schema of an application system.

4.2.2 Data Independence

An important property of an RDBMS is data independence. It allows changes in data organization without changing application programs. Data independence can be physical or logical:

- Physical data independence: The internal organization of data, such as indexes and record layout, can be changed without modifying any application. Physical data independence therefore means that the internal and conceptual levels are independent.

- Logical data independence: The conceptual schema can be changed without modifying applications, for example, when adding relations or attributes. Logical data independence therefore means that the conceptual and external levels are independent.

4.2.3 Tables

The fundamental structure in a relational system is the relation, which is a two-dimensional matrix consisting of columns and rows of data elements. An instance (or occurrence) of a relation in the database system is called a *table*. *Field* is a general database term used to refer to the basic unit of data found in the database. A field represents one data fact. A table must consist only of atomic (indivisible) fields of data, such as numbers or character strings.

The following general information applies to tables:

- Each table has a unique name.
- Every column in a table has a descriptive label that indicates what the entity represents.
- Every table column contains atomic values of the same data type. Each atomic value is an attribute value drawn from the set of possible values that is the domain of that column.
- Each table consists of zero or more rows of attribute values (tuples), and each value is a data fact.
- The order of the columns is not significant and can be changed without changing the meaning of a tuple.
- Every table row represents one object or relationship. The order of the rows is not significant. A row's identity is determined by its unique content, not by its location.
- No duplicate rows are allowed. (Primary keys are unique.)
- Any column in the entire database can be referred to by a unique pairing of the table name with the column label. By referring to each field in this way, the user does not have to care about any ordering dependencies.
- If the value of a particular field is unknown or does not apply, the relational model marks that attribute with a null value.
- The domain of every attribute must consist of atomic values. There are no repeating groups. All tables must be in first normal form, as described in Section 4.2.7.

4.2.4 Candidate, Primary, and Foreign Keys

Tables contain information about entities or the relationships among entities. Each tuple refers to a different entity instance, and each attribute value in that tuple supplies information about one characteristic of that instance. Each table must have a column or group of columns that uniquely identifies the tuple.

Any set of attributes that ensures the uniqueness of every tuple is called a *candidate key*. A sample of a candidate key would be the set of all attributes in a relation, because each tuple must be distinct. A relation can have multiple candidate keys, but one must be designated as the primary key.

Foreign keys define a link to another table. A foreign key is a key taken from another table to create a linking value that serves as a means of navigating from one table to another. A table can contain as many foreign keys as needed to relate it to other tables.

4.2.5 Relational Integrity

There are two types of relational integrity:

- Entity integrity means that primary key attribute values cannot be null. To ensure key integrity, the column values in the primary key must uniquely identify the subject to which the tuple refers.

- Referential integrity means that every foreign key in a table must refer to an existing key in the related table, or it must be null, which means that it does not refer to any key in any table.

In general, RDBMSs support the declaration of primary keys in their relational language.

4.2.6 Functional Dependencies

A functional dependency is the reliance of an attribute or group of attributes on another attribute or group of attributes for its value. For any given instance of a relation, a dependent attribute can have only one value for a certain value of the attributes on which it depends.

For example, in a relation with the following schema:

```
PART (PartNumber, PartName, Description, SizeXYZ)
```

the value of the PartName attribute is dependent on PartNumber. The PartName attribute is functionally dependent on PartNumber, and PartNumber functionally determines PartName. Therefore,

```
PARTNAME = f(PARTNUMBER)
```

4.2.7 Normalization

The process of determining the correct location and function for each attribute to minimize redundancies is called *normalization.* Generally, normalization decomposes relations that are incorrectly constructed into multiple correctly normalized relations. There are a number of classes of normalization, the three most important of which are first normal form (1NF), second normal form (2NF), and third normal form (3NF), as described below.

First Normal Form

To be in first normal form, a relation must have domains consisting only of atomic values for each attribute. Repeating sets of attributes and multivalued attributes are not allowed. For example, consider a car relation with the following schema:

```
CAR (Car#, CarName, Year)
```

A part relation might have the schema

```
PART (Part#, PartName, Weight, RespName, RespPhone, {Cars})
```

where the attribute Cars is intended to be a multivalued field containing the car numbers for each part. This is not in first normal form.

The same problem might also have been conceived as containing a series of repeating fields of the same type:

```
PART (Part#, PartName, Weight, RespName, RespPhone, Car1,
Car2, Car3)
```

Again, this is not in first normal form. Here an attribute type is repeated (Car1, Car2, Car3) in an attempt to store a data element that has multiple occurrences for a part. If a part is used in more than three cars, there will be a problem, and if the part is used in fewer than three cars, some default value must be defined.

Transforming this schema into first normal form results in the following schema:

```
PART (Part#, Name, Weight, RespName, RespPhone, Car)
```

which repeats the part information for each car in which the part is used. This approach still has problems, however. If a part changes (for instance, its weight increases), all the part tuples must be found and updated. Also, if a part is not used in any car, all the part information will be lost.

Higher forms of normalization help solve these problems.

Second Normal Form

To be in second normal form a relation must

- Already be in first normal form
- Have all its nonkey attributes fully functionally dependent on the primary key

This means that all functional dependencies should be noted, and each nonkey attribute must be functionally dependent on all the attributes that make up the primary key. Any attributes that do not meet these criteria must be moved out of the relation and put into another relation.

For instance, starting with the previous example, in which the schema is in the first normal form and Part# is the primary key, there are multiple values for Car for each Part# value. This means that Car is not functionally dependent on the primary key and therefore this relation is not in second normal form.

To get the relation into second normal form, it is necessary to decompose the part schema into two tables with the following schemas:

```
PART (Part#, Name, Weight, RespName, RespPhone)
USAGE (Car#, Part#)
```

Third Normal Form

A relation is in third normal form, if it

- Already is in second normal form

- Contains no transitive dependencies

This means that each nonkey attribute must depend on the primary key, the entire primary key, and nothing but the primary key. There are no hidden dependencies in which nonkey attributes depend not only on the primary key but also on other nonkey attributes.

In the second normal form example, the RespPhone (the phone number of the responsible person for that part) is functionally dependent on the RespName attribute. Because the RespName attribute is nonprime, this is a violation of third normal form.

The solution is to move the attribute RespPhone out of the part relation:

```
CAR (Car#, Name, Year)
PART (Part#, Name, Weight, RespName)
USED (Car#, Part#)
RESPPHONE (RespName, RespPhone)
```

The relational model requires that all tables be at least in first normal form. Second and third normal forms are optional. Higher normal forms do exist and can be useful, but generally it is sufficient to normalize relations to third normal form.

4.3 Mapping Objects to Relational Schemas

To store an object that must persist in a relational database (RDB), we map the object to one or more relational constructs. Each attribute of the object must map to a table element. To that end, the base types of object attributes should be supported by the relational database. If so, we can dematerialize the object, storing each of its attributes in an RDB cell.

The main mapping constraints are given by the materialization process, reconstructing the original object from the stored data. The constraints arise because objects have an identity within the context of the object-oriented application run-time environment; therefore we must be able to map the right data to the attributes of an object of a given identity.

This section explains the principles of mapping object models produced from object-oriented application development techniques to relational database technology. We follow the general approach to mapping described in

[RUM91]. Figure 40 on page 94 shows the data mapping process within the three-level architecture of an RDBMS.

One of the deliverables of object-oriented analysis is an object model. This model relates mainly to the conceptual schema of the three-level RDBMS architecture. Each object model must be translated to a conceptual schema and then to tables.

Views and interface programs connect external schemas to the conceptual schema, which then converts to the internal schema (tables). The object model defined by the VMT methodology subsumes the external object models that map in [RUM91] to the external schemas because it includes the objects derived from the use cases.

Object models consist of classes, associations, generalizations, and attributes. We need to define the mapping that will allow us to translate from an object model to the conceptual schema and then to the internal schema (tables) in a proper way. We can use several mapping alternatives. Also, some details that are not mentioned in object modeling, such as the primary key and candidate keys for each table, must be supplied.

4.4 Object Identifiers

Within an object-oriented environment, every instance of a class (that is, any object), has an object ID (OID), although this OID is internal and not usually accessible. Without an OID it is not possible to refer to a specific object within a program.

From an application and object persistence point of view, every object has an ID that is unique and public. For instance, a car type (such as convertible or sedan) can be identified within an application by its name. Therefore its name has to be unique. Otherwise there could be two car types with the same name, which would make it impossible to distinguish them.

Let us assume that the car type's name is unique. This car might be referenced by many other objects. Referencing could be done by name because of the uniqueness of the car type's name.

When a specific car type changes its name (for instance, because convertibles have to be divided into two groups), all references to the previous car type must be updated because they refer to a nonexistent object.

In real-world applications, this problem led to the use of unique ID numbers. In our example, a car type would get a unique ID number. All references to that specific car type would use this car type ID number instead of the name. Thus the name of a car type could be changed without updating all the references.

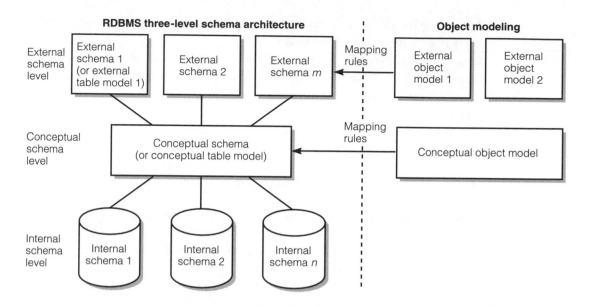

Figure 40. Mapping the object model to the relational architecture (the mapping rules describe mapping between the object model and the table model)

If an application still requires identification by name, a secondary index can be defined to enforce uniqueness among names. Nevertheless, all references to the object would use its OID. OIDs are artificial; they do not have counterparts in the real world. They are used only for convenience and performance reasons within an RDBMS.

The problem we had with names could also arise with OIDs if they could be changed as well. Therefore we must use OIDs that never have to be changed. Because OIDs are artificial constructs, they are usually implemented as unique integers. They are also transient, existing only while a system or application is alive.

If OIDs were persistent, the problem would be what to do with the OIDs of deleted objects (that is, whether to use them again or not) and how to find a free OID. Smalltalk environments therefore do not provide access to OIDs, which are only used internally.

One property common to an environment OID and to a persistent object ID is that both identify an object uniquely. However one is persistent and the other is not. Although the OID is unique within the whole object-oriented environment (that is, within all existing objects or, from the database point of view, within the whole database), the application or persistent object ID is unique only within one class or table (in our example, the class containing the car types).

The ID of an object, both from the application and the persistent object points of view, survives the end of an application. This ID might be shared with many applications, even applications running in different environments. Thus this type of ID is persistent; that is, it is the same if an application is started again or another application wants to access the object.

While the unique key technique of an RDBMS enforces uniqueness only within one table, an object-oriented system enforces uniqueness of the OID within the whole object-oriented system. The ID chosen for persistence will normally be one of the object attributes, but it may be a direct attribute (such as a Social Security number) or an artificial attribute generated by the application.

In the sections that follow, to avoid confusion between an OID and an application ID, we talk about the primary key of an object rather than about the ID of an object when designing for object persistence.

4.4.1 Mapping to Tables

Both a class and an association can be mapped into one table. Each class-derived table has a primary key as the unique identifier of the objects stored in the table. A combination of the primary keys of the associated tables forms the primary key of an association-derived table. This strategy is compatible with the object-oriented language notation in which an object has an identity apart from its properties.

The primary key does not have to be an artificially generated numeric ID; it can be a name, a date, or another data type. In some applications it is convenient to use artificial IDs instead of attribute IDs. The benefit of using artificial IDs is that they are immutable and completely independent of changes in data value and physical location. The stability of IDs is particularly important for associations because they refer to objects. In contrast, referring to objects by name makes it necessary to update many associations if a name changes. Unique IDs provide a uniform mechanism for referencing objects.

Artificial IDs have disadvantages, however. Generating IDs is a nuisance, for which RDBMSs provide no inherent support. For example, it is awkward to track previously allocated IDs and reclaim deleted IDs for reuse. In addition, RDBMS theory emphasizes that data is located and manipulated according to attribute values. While it is permissible to define IDs as attributes and adopt a protocol for handling them, an ID is not a value; it is an implementation artifact that RDBMSs are trying to eliminate.

The use of artificial IDs must therefore be carefully considered in every case, although an artificial ID will be defined and used often as the primary key of a table.

4.5 Mapping Object Classes to Tables

A table can correspond to a class, a subset of a class, or more than one class. A rule for mapping object classes to tables is that each class maps to one or more tables. However, because an object should have knowledge only about itself and nothing else, it is usually mapped into one table. Any association to other objects is implemented by defining additional attributes within the objects at the end of both sides of the association. Those additional attributes reference the associated objects by their IDs. No further attributes of the associated objects are contained within the referencing object. Even if it made sense to store within an object some attributes that are derived from other objects, it is not recommended. The difficulty arises when the original attribute changes. The difficulty is avoided by defining an association attribute that references the corresponding object.

A class can be partitioned *horizontally* or *vertically* to improve application performance. In horizontal partitioning, some rows go into one table and some into another. For instance, in a catalog of car parts, some part types might be accessed frequently and others rarely, so that it might be useful to partition the class into two tables by row. In vertical partitioning, a table is divided into two (or even more) tables by column. For instance, if one group of applications accesses only the Name and Description columns of a part type table, and another group of applications refers only to the size and material attributes, it might be useful to partition the table into two tables by column.

To benefit from horizontal or vertical partitioning, an application needs instructions as to which table to use.

4.6 Mapping Associations and Aggregations to Tables

In general, associations can be binary or *n*-ary (where *n*>2). An *n*-ary association maps to a separate table (or sometimes multiple tables to maintain key integrity). In the sections that follow, we cover binary associations only.

A binary association may or may not map to a table. Mapping depends on the type and multiplicity of the association and the database designer's preference in terms of extensibility, number of tables, and performance trade-offs.

The following rules can be established for mapping associations to tables [RUM91]:

- Each many-to-many association maps to a distinct table.
- Each one-to-many association maps to a distinct table or can be buried as a foreign key in the table for the "many" classes.
- Each one-to-one association maps to a distinct table or may be buried as a foreign key in the table of either class.
- Role names are incorporated as part of the foreign key attribute name.

- A qualified association maps to a distinct table with at least three attributes: the primary key of each related class and the qualifier.

The mapping of the three types of binary associations to tables is described below. Since aggregations are special cases of associations, the same mapping rules apply.

4.6.1 One-to-One Associations

A one-to-one association can be mapped to a separate table. Therefore, each class and its association maps to a separate table. Another approach is to store both objects and the association in one table for performance reasons. Usually this second approach is preferred. The first approach makes sense only when the association is extended to a one-to-many or many-to-many association.

Merging a one-to-one association into a single table improves performance and reduces database storage at the cost of less extensibility and possible violation of the third normal form. (The merged associated attributes can be dependent not only on the primary key of the merged table but also on some nonkey attributes.)

An example of mapping object classes and associations to tables in a one-to-one association is shown in Figure 41 on page 98.

4.6.2 One-to-Many Associations

There are two common approaches to mapping a one-to-many association to a table. A separate table can be created for the association, or a foreign key can be inserted into the table representing the class of the "many" side of the association. The approach taken depends on both the needs of the application and performance considerations.

The advantage of merging an association to a class is that developers have to deal with fewer tables, which, in addition, ensures better system performance. The disadvantage is that design rigor is reduced.

In general, it seems inappropriate to contaminate objects with knowledge of other objects (this would break encapsulation). Reduced extensibility is an additional problem. It is difficult to expand a one-to-many association to a many-to-many association.

In a merged association, we deal with greater complexity because an asymmetrical representation of the association complicates search and update. Theoretically, a one-to-many association, together with both classes, can be mapped to one table. However, this mapping is not desirable and can violate second normal form requirements.

4.6.3 Many-to-Many Associations

A many-to-many association always maps into a separate table. This schema satisfies the requirements of third normal form.

The primary key of the many-to-many association table is a concatenation of the primary keys of the two associated tables. The association table also contains any attribute of the link. Each primary key of the association tables is referred to by the definition of a foreign key.

In general, an association can be used from either class. The foreign key clause of the SQL code indicates that each tuple of the association table must reference an entry in both related tables. An association table always sets the foreign keys from the related objects to not null. This is necessary because, by definition, a link between two objects requires that both objects exist. On the other hand, if a given pair of objects have no link, no entry is made in the association table.

Figure 42 on page 99 shows the mapping to tables of a complex relationship including associations and aggregations.

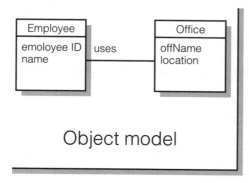

Many class tables approach

Attribute name	Nulls?	Domain
employeeID	N	ID
Name	N	name

Table for employee class

Attribute name	Nulls?	Domain
offName	N	name
location	N	location

Table for office class

Object model

Single class table approach

Attribute name	Nulls?	Domain
employee ID	N	ID
name	N	name
offName	N	name
location	N	location

Attribute name	Nulls?	Domain
employeeID	N	ID
offName	N	name

Table for association

Table model

Figure 41. Mapping to tables: one-to-one association

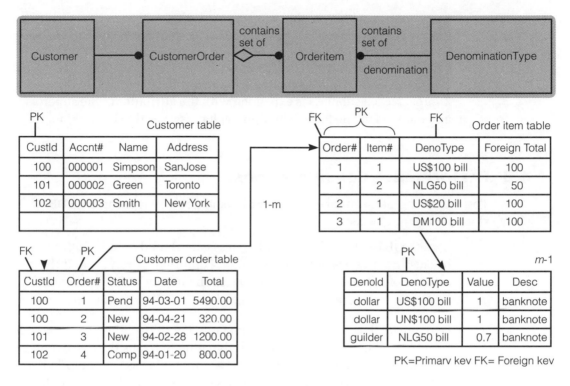

Figure 42. Mapping classes and associations to tables

4.7 **Mapping Generalizations to Tables**

In general, there are two types of generalizations: single inheritance, in which a subclass inherits from one superclass, and multiple inheritance, in which a subclass inherits from more than one superclass. Therefore there are many ways of mapping generalizations to tables.

For single inheritance generalizations, there are three mapping alternatives [RUM91], as depicted in Figure 43 on page 101.

- Build just one superclass table: In this alternative, the attributes of the subclasses are "exploded" in the superclass, and this construct is mapped to a table. This approach is not frequently used, and it may violate third normal form because nonkey attributes may depend not only on the primary key but also on other attributes.

- Build one table for the superclass and one for each subclass: This is the standard approach. The superclass table and each subclass table have the same defined attribute as the primary key: the ID. If necessary, an object can be stored in the superclass table and the appropriate subclass tables using the same ID.

One problem with this kind of mapping is that SQL permits storing an entry with the same ID in each subclass. Special application code must be written to enforce the generalization mapping.

- Build one table for each subclass but not for the superclass: In this approach each subclass is expanded with the attributes of the superclass and mapped to one table. This approach preserves third normal form.

4.8 Performance Considerations

The following performance considerations apply when using an RDBMS to store persistent objects:

- Static SQL has the advantage of being faster than dynamic SQL, because queries are not interpreted, or compiled, at run time. If the amount of data processed in relation to the number of queries made is large, however, the speed advantage of static SQL is negligible.

- Dynamic SQL is more flexible than static SQL, thus allowing for a wide variety of ad hoc queries. However, dynamic SQL has the disadvantage of being slower than static SQL. The fact that queries are compiled at run time can result in speed improvements, because the query optimizer uses the current database state. Improved speed is especially noted in highly volatile databases. The flexibility of dynamic SQL can also reduce the amount of code that must be written for object-to-database mapping, because all the information necessary for building a select statement can be defined at run time. If the amount of data processed in relation to queries made is small, the speed disadvantage of dynamic SQL is large. Object queries, when defined by the user at run time, can almost always be managed with reasonable programming effort when dynamic SQL is used.

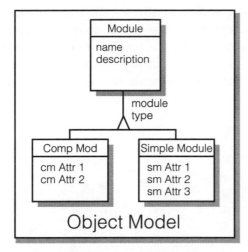

Object Model

One superclass many subclass tables approach

Attribute name	Nulls?	Domain
modID	N	ID
name	N	name
description	Y	description

Table for subclass

Attribute name	Nulls?	Domain
modID	N	ID
cm Attr 1	N	domain 1
cm Attr 2	Y	domain 2

Table for subclass

Attribute name	Nulls?	Domain
modID	N	ID
sm Attr 1	N	domain 3
sm Attr 2	Y	domain 4
sm Attr 3	Y	domain 5

Table for subclass

Many subclass tables approach

Attribute name	Nulls?	Domain
modID	N	ID
name	N	name
description	Y	description
cm Attr 1	N	domain 1
cm Attr 2	Y	domain 2

Table for subclass

Attribute name	Nulls?	Domain
modID	N	ID
name	N	name
description	Y	description
sm Attr 1	N	domain 3
sm Attr 2	Y	domain 4
sm Attr 3	Y	domain 5

Table for subclass

One superclass table approach

Attribute name	Nulls?	Domain
modID	N	ID
sm Attr 1	N	domain 3
sm Attr 2	Y	domain 4
sm Attr 3	Y	domain 5
sm Attr 1	N	domain 1
sm Attr 2	Y	domain 2

Table for subclass

Table Model

Figure 43. Three mapping alternatives for single inheritance

4.9 Summary

Despite their many shortcomings, such as impedance mismatch, using relational databases for object persistence is a popular approach. The object model, which is not intended for a relational environment, requires additional details for the mapping, such as primary keys and candidate keys for each table. The complete mapping process involves mapping of object classes and object relations (including associations, aggregations, and generalizations).

A major defect of such mapping is the inability of relational databases to represent the behavior of objects. Therefore, the use of object-oriented databases remains the most straightforward approach for object persistence and is expected to gain wider dominance with the advances in object-oriented database technology and the development and acceptance of industry standards for object-oriented databases by various database vendors.

5

The VMT Design Phase

The purpose of design is first to devise solution strategies and create an over-all architecture as the base for implementing the solution, and then to explore means and make tactical decisions that translate design criteria into the ele-ments of the solution.

It is logical for object-oriented design to follow object-oriented analysis. After modeling the problem domain for an application, we proceed with designing and building a solution for it. However, after a while, design and analysis become part of a continuum, and it is hard to separate them. Because the dis-tinction between analysis and design is extremely useful, we should keep it in mind. Before making a decision we should ask ourselves, Is the decision related to the business domain, or is it an implementation issue? The answer to that question helps us make the right decision and maintain traceability from requirements specification to implementation in the application development life cycle.

The VMT design phase covers *system design, object design,* and *designing for object persistence.*

System design involves, but is not limited to, making high-level system decisions, determining the basic software architecture, and structuring a solu-tion system.

Object design involves refining the analysis model, adapting to an actual implementation environment, identifying additional (solution domain) object classes, fleshing out object details, looking for design patterns and reusable components (from class libraries and frameworks), and building the design model (design modeling).

More specifically, the process of object design involves the following steps:

1. Map the semantic classes identified in the analysis object model to application classes. This entails transforming the classes that have a purely business-oriented meaning into implementation constructs while maintaining traceability to the problem (business) domain.

2. Model the object behavior and properties details, as well as produce refined class structures involving additional solution domain classes.

3. Design the service classes, which are domain-independent classes used for system-related functions, such as database access, communication interfaces, and so on.

Analysis of the application should be independent of implementation characteristics, such as the programming language and the run-time platform, but reality shows that object design is dependent on the language construct. Also, system design must always consider the target implementation environment.

To illustrate the VMT design approach, we use IBM VisualAge as the implementing environment, although the design process can be generalized to other implementation environments. The following steps are based on the characteristics of the IBM VisualAge products family:

1. Design the details of the VisualAge nonvisual classes,[12] which include

   - The nonvisual classes' public interfaces (attributes, actions, events) and methods.

   - Nonvisual classes' instance methods and variables.

   - The preconditions and postconditions for each service a class provides. Preconditions are to be met before a service can be requested; postconditions are guaranteed as the result of a service being successfully executed.

   - Derived attribute policies.

2. Design the details of the VisualAge visual classes (that is, build the GUI of the application), which include

   - The elementary visual class for each application class

   - Additional composite visual classes as required

   - Input data validation

   - Deferred updates

3. Perform iterative design prototyping.

---

12 These classes are implemented in the language chosen—Smalltalk, C++, or OO Cobol.

Designing for object persistence can be undertaken when the object design shows an acceptable degree of functionality. It involves modeling and designing server databases[13] and defining the interactions between database access objects and model objects, the distribution of objects in users' run-time images, and access policies for retrieving or updating shared data.

5.1 System Design

System design is the design of a high-level architecture for a proposed solution. A *system architecture* defines the major system building blocks and their high-level connectivity. The building blocks reflect system functions, as opposed to hardware or software products. An *application architecture* organizes the solution into subsystems for allocation to the system building blocks.

There are three levels of detail—conceptual, logical, and physical—for both the system architecture and the application architecture.

We start designing with a conceptual view of the solution architecture, which is being formulated as we complete the analysis of the problem. The use case model, the object model, and the dynamic model provide the basis for the conceptual architecture of the desired solution.

The system design initially concentrates on the logical design of the solution architecture. But as part of system design, we need to make the necessary design decisions for the placement of data and processing, and select the system platforms to implement the solution. Taking into consideration the available information technology and the current environment, such as existing legacy systems, design decisions are made to select the enabling technology and products for implementing the major system building blocks.

Eventually, the designer will need to produce the physical architecture that shows the allocation of logical system and application components in the solution to the implementing platforms as well as the programming modules.

The main input, activities, and work products of the system design stage are shown in Table 2.

---

13 This work includes the mapping from object schemas (classes) to database schemas (tables); therefore, it requires a "schema mapper" artifact.

Table 2. Design phase: system design overview

Input	Activities and techniques	Work Products
Object model, Dynamic model Event trace diagrams	System partitioning	High-level system architecture • Subsystems • Subsystems interaction diagram
Object model subsystems	Mapping	VisualAge applications and subapplications
Subsystems Common data access requirements Considerations in criteria for: Performance Concurrency Data Integrity Security Replication Backup and recovery Legacy system	Designing end-to-end system	System platforms selection and design decisions for • Object placement (object-oriented client) • Data/function placement (non-object-oriented server)

5.1.1 Decomposing the Object Model into Subsystems

The term *subsystem* is used in OMT[14], OOSE, and RDD to refer to a group of tightly coupled classes. There are many reasons to split the object model into subsystems:

- Managing the complexity of the design effort (divide and conquer)
- Splitting the design effort among the developers or among several teams
- Isolating specific design decisions that the designer believes can be changed later
- Distinguishing different levels of abstraction in the services provided
- Allocating units for distribution (for distributed object application)

The first goal can be successfully met if a subsystem provides some useful abstraction that makes the structure of the application more understandable. The second goal can be successfully met if the dependencies among design teams are loose (that is, they do not depend too much on each other's design decisions). This can be achieved only if the message flow among all subsystems is much simpler than the message flow within each subsystem.

---

14 The "unified method" [RUM95] calls the subsystems *categories*.

One guideline to follow in decomposing an application's object model into subsystems is to decompose in such a way that the message flow among subsystems is minimized.

The following is a sample metric for good subsystem selection:

MsgSent   is a set of messages with senders in a class of
                     a subsystem

MsgGoingOut   is a subset of MsgSent with implementers in
                     another subsystem

MsgStayIn   is a subset of MsgSent with implementers in the
                     same subsystem

The subsystem has been well selected if **MsgStayIn >> msgGoingOut.**

A heuristic to finding a good set of initial candidate subsystems is a responsibility-driven approach: Decompose in such a way that a well-defined subset of the application responsibilities can be assigned to each subsystem.

Partitioned and Layered Application Architecture

A subsystem can contain subsystems, that is, subsystems can be recursive.

Initially, we divide the application into *vertical* subsystems. These subsystems (categories) provide the basis for application partitioning based on functionality. In other words, the subsystems can be categorized based on their particular roles and responsibilities, which translate to well-defined interface.

Many well-engineered systems are built in layers. "A layered system is an ordered set of virtual worlds, each built in terms of the one below it and providing the basis of implementation for the ones above it" [RUM91].

Applications can be built with layered *horizontal* subsystems. A subsystem knows about and depends on the layers below it and provide services to the layers above it. A layered application architecture helps to produce a cleaner and more portable design. This is particularly important in a visual programming environment, such as VisualAge. By dividing the application into layers, we can

- Avoid "visual spaghetti" programming
- Enhance application portability
- Facilitate object distribution (for distributed object applications)

A layered application architecture can be either open or closed. The distinction is that in an open architecture, a layer can use the services of any lower layers, while in a closed one, a layer is built only in terms of its immediate lower layer. The choice for an open or closed architecture often is a trade-off between efficiency and modularity.

View-Model-Data Segmentation

Figure 44 shows the view-model-data layered structure that maps to the logical three-tier architecture for a generic client/server application.

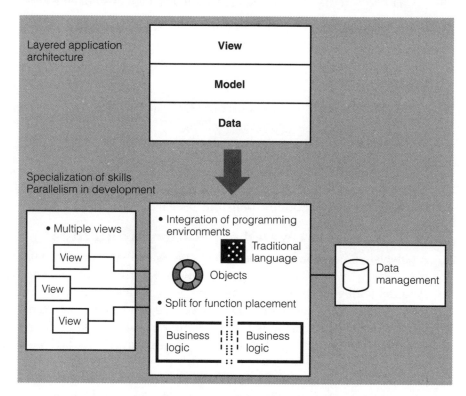

Figure 44. View-model-data layered application architecture

The view layer defines how the user and the system interact. It represents the user interface responsible for presenting information to the user and accepting input from the user on behalf of the model.

The model layer consists primarily of the application objects, which implement real-world objects of the application. The model defines the behaviors of these application objects without considering how users interact with them. It corresponds to the business logic of the application.

The data layer provides data access functions. From the application developer's perspective, it can be viewed as an extension of the model. It deals with the object persistence issues.

The view layer is made up primarily of interface objects, the model layer contains the application objects and service objects, and the data (access) layer consists of service objects.

Layering the application this way helps to separate the *models* from the *views.* Thus we can connect multiple views to the same model. When we implement the solution in VisualAge, we can build views from interface parts and application parts, and we can build models with application parts and services parts. This separation helps to reduce the visual complexity in building the VisualAge applications. By separating the portable and platform-specific layers, we also enhance the portability of the application.

In designing the application structure, we use both the partitioning and layering techniques. We divide the application object model into subsystems, and each subsystem can then be organized in layered subsystems. A layer can also be further divided into partitions. We could also group similar layers in various partitions into a "common" support layer to support all these partitions. The result is generally a partitioned and layered application architecture (see Figure 91 on page 165 for an example).

Subsystem Notation

The subsystems are represented as rectangles; there is notation for the abstract view and the detail view. Arrows denote dependency between subsystems. Figure 45 shows the foreign currency subsystems as an example.

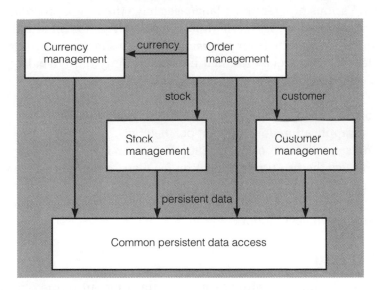

Figure 45. Sample foreign currency exchange subsystems

5.1.2 Selecting the Implementation Platform

For the application solution to work, we must first select the system platforms and infrastructure required to implement the application design. In other words, the logical system architecture must be mapped to the implementing system environment. A physical system architecture shows the actual hardware- and software-implementing platforms for the proposed solution.

Choosing Client/Server-Enabling Technology

Implementing the design as a client/server solution in a heterogeneous environment requires the selection of a variety of client/server enabling technologies. Depending on the client/server computing style, different middleware can be used to implement the solution design. The persistent object design process involves refining the application's object design to include distributed objects in multiple processes or platforms. This includes designing the interface between business application objects and the client/server wrappers, such as the ones provided by VisualAge.

For the case studies in this book, the implementing platform is assumed to be VisualAge running in an OS/2 DB/2 2 LAN environment. The enabling technology and component selections for our system building blocks were predetermined by the available supporting platforms of VisualAge at the time of our project.

5.1.3 Mapping Subsystems to VisualAge Applications

The identified subsystems must be mapped to program modules for implementation. Various programming languages have their own programming constructs that represent program modules. In VisualAge for Smalltalk, the term *application* is used in the team programming environment as a containment of related classes, with a class defined in one and only one VisualAge application. In VisualAge for C++, we normally use a .VBB file to contain all related parts. We will loosely refer to this .VBB file as the equivalent of a VisualAge application, even though there is no such term in C++.

From an application development perspective, a VisualAge application can be viewed as a collection of parts that can be managed as a whole and packaged to produce the run-time application for distribution to end users.

Although *VisualAge application* does not have the same exact semantics as *subsystem,* we define the VisualAge applications based on the subsystems derived from the object model.

5.2 Object Design

Object design includes a refinement and a fleshing out of the object details. The main input, activities, and work products during object design are described in Table 3.

The subsystems derived from application partitioning during system design also serve as the units for development work assignment among developers. Because of the way the subsystems are selected, it is practical for the developers to work on their assigned subsystems independently until the system integration stage.

During analysis, for each class in the object model, we defined the attributes (the knowledge that the object is responsible for maintaining) and the services the

Table 3. Design phase: object design overview		
Input	**Activities and techniques**	**Work Products**
Object model (classes)	Designing classes Mapping semantic classes to VisualAge nonvisual classes Adding interface and service classes	VisualAge nonvisual classes
Object model (services and attributes)	Designing public interface for VisualAge nonvisual classes	VisualAge public interfaces (attributes, events, and actions)
Object model (associations), VisualAge nonvisual classes	Designing association implementation	• Refined VisualAge public interfaces (more attributes) • Smalltalk or C++ implementation collection classes
Base classes, GUI prototype	Designing elementary GUI components	VisualAge elementary visual classes
Base classes, VisualAge elementary visual classes	Designing composite GUI components	VisualAge composite visual classes
Use cases, GUI prototype, VisualAge elementary and composite visual classes	Building application GUI	VisualAge end-user visual classes

object must provide to other classes. The object model also shows associations among classes (that is, the knowledge that classes of objects have of each other).

From this information we proceed with the effort of designing the required solution domain classes: determining the solution classes and fleshing out the details of these classes for each subsystem. These are the subjects of the following sections.

5.2.1 Designing Solution-Domain Classes

The set of object classes that make up a running application is usually much larger than the set of classes identified during the analysis phase. The initial set of semantic application classes identified in the analysis object model represents only the core business behavior of the application. Other solution-domain classes must be designed to provide the concrete functions of the application. Classes that represent the user interface and service classes that provide service functions, such as input data validation, database access, and interface with communications framework, are examples of additional classes required for the implementation of the application. In practice, the designer may invent some of these solution classes and may recover others from the reuse class library.

The design of solution-domain classes is, like everything else in object-oriented development, iterative. We suggest the following design steps when using IBM VisualAge:

1. Map the semantic application classes, identified in the object model from analysis, to VisualAge nonvisual classes; this is fairly straightforward.

2. Add interface and service classes[15] to provide user interface and additional functions, as explained below.

For each application class in the analysis model, an elementary user interface is added to display its content and to verify its function. The elementary user interface classes can be constructed with VisualAge as potentially reusable view classes to form more sophisticated composite views. Additional views may be required to satisfy the various needs in designing the solution.

The result of these design activities lead to additional solution domain classes, including

- Interface classes, to provide user access and interface[16]
- Service classes, to provide database access, system control and service functions, and other operations.

5.2.2 Modeling in Object Design

When building a house, we draw a blueprint before we actually carry out the construction. Similarly, modeling is a way to help us design the object classes for the solution before we actually perform code construction. We refer to the modeling activities during object design as *design modeling*.

We apply the same modeling techniques we used during analysis to conduct design modeling. These techniques include the RDD or CRC exercise, event trace diagramming and state diagramming, as well as object modeling. However, levels of detail may change as the focus also switches from the problem to the solution. To distinguish these design modeling activities and techniques from their counterparts in analysis, we refer to them here as design CRC, design event trace diagrams, design object models, and so on.

---

15 Jacobson's OOSE suggests three kinds of objects: entity objects, interface objects, and control objects. We use these three categories to assist in identifying the additional solution classes. One benefit of distinguishing among the three kinds of object classes is that it helps to enhance the robustness of the design. However, our interface objects refer to the user interface objects, while OOSE interface objects include both user and system interface objects. We include the system interface objects and control objects in the service classes category.

---

16 The interface classes will evolve to become the VisualAge visual parts.

5.2.3 Design CRC

As we introduce the new solution classes during the design process, these new classes participate in the collaboration and interactions with the domain classes we identified earlier. Quite often we need to conduct additional CRC exercises for these new classes.

CRC is an effective design technique for validating a proposed grouping of functionalities into objects by reviewing the responsibilities and dependencies of each object via a role-playing process. Using CRC as an informal technique, we first try to make good design decisions about object responsibilities without the burden of an equally important task of designing the method interfaces. The goal is to come up with the right responsibility distribution among the object classes first. We can then design the message passing, using event trace diagrams (or object interaction diagrams) to specify the object interactions and interfaces.

Starting with the CRC cards we kept from the analysis stage, we create additional CRC cards for the new classes we designed, assigning responsibilities to the new classes and reallocate responsibilities among the classes. In general, we follow the principle of evenly distributing responsibilities among objects [WIR90]. We try to avoid introducing specialized control objects to keep the solution robust and flexible.

Some modelers use an extended or modified form of CRC cards to design parts on paper, indicating the required attributes, actions, and events, which make up the public interface for each VisualAge part [LIN95]. Others record the class of the requesters in addition to that of the collaborators, in the design CRC cards. The extent of CRC card usage is determined by the designer's preference. Nevertheless, building these paper parts and playing them out first allow us to achieve well-balanced responsibility design before actual prototyping.

The CRC cards also provide a convenient way to record the attributes, object messages, and methods during design, until the design is more refined. We then transcribe the design decisions to a more formal documentation, such as class specifications in the model dictionary.

5.2.4 Design Event Trace Diagrams

Design event trace (or interaction) diagrams are useful for designing the message passing between objects and their operations.

In doing the CRC exercise, we define the roles and responsibilities of the classes involved in the solution. The responsibilities of an object class are expressed in terms of the services it can provide to other objects in the system. As an object class offers the services through its operations, to design the operations is to further define the services an object class provides. The definition should include a description of the semantics of the operation, that is, what the operation does, and a specification of the signature of the operation, that is, how the operation can be invoked. An operation's signature consists of the name of the operation, as well as the input and output parameters and their types, that must be supplied to invoke the operation. An operation is implemented as a method (in Smalltalk) or a member function (in C++).

During analysis, we focused on the external events generated by actors (stimuli), describing their interaction with the system. As a result, the event trace diagrams in the analysis stage do not involve many objects internal to the system and do not involve the solution objects.

During design, we now focus on the events and object interactions within the system. The objective is to devise the message-passing details among the solution-domain objects.

In addition, we refine use cases and use scenarios, and consider secondary or exceptional cases. We consider what object interactions are required to carry out the scenario, involving additional solution domain (interface and service) objects and internal events as necessary to support the scenario and to invoke the operation of the receiving object. This entails identifying message passing between the objects. We then draw more detailed event trace diagrams, design the message format, consider the input and output parameters and their data types, and walk through the scenario, simulating method invocation and message passing as part of the validation process.[17]

5.2.5 Design Object Interaction Diagrams

As explained earlier, an object interaction diagram basically depicts the same object interaction information as an event trace (or interaction) diagram in a different format. A sample design-level object interaction diagram is shown in Figure 46.

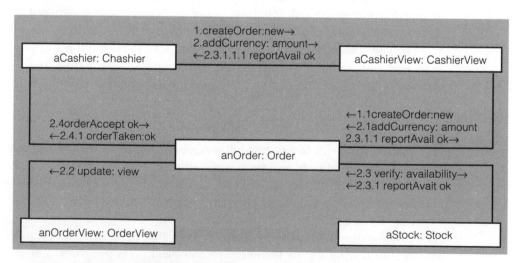

Figure 46. Sample design-level object interaction diagram

---

17 This is usually done with paper and pencil. However, advanced object development systems provide executable models and animation facilities which highly improve the productivity of scenario walkthroughs.

5.2.6 Design State Diagrams

During the design phase, the state diagrams focus on local object-state changes, rather than on the global states that were the focus in the analysis phase.

5.2.7 Design Object Model

The object model developed in the analysis phase is refined here. Refinement may include

- Adding and removing classes. Obviously, the design-level object model will include additional solution-domain classes. But some of the domain classes identified during analysis may turn out to be inappropriate; they will be removed. Superclasses or abstract classes may be created to abstract common properties and behavior for generalization or reuse.
- Adjusting the inheritance hierarchy.
- Defining the types, range of values, and initial values for the attributes. To prepare for implementation, we need to define the data types for the attributes, their initial values, and the ranges for their possible values.
- Adding attributes for association traversal or object visibility purpose.
- Refining class relationships.
- Specifying multiplicities for the associations.

5.2.8 Expanding the Model Dictionary

During analysis, the model dictionary contains a brief description for each class. In the design phase, the entries in the model dictionary are expanded to include the detailed specifications for each class:

- For all attributes, specify
    - Public/private/protected
    - Data types
    - Value ranges and initial values
    - Constraints and invariants for the attributes
- For all operations, specify
    - Public/private
    - Pre- and postconditions
    - Algorithms
    - Description of the semantics and the signature for the operation

5.2.9   Refining and Validating the Design Model

The result of design-level modeling is captured in the design object model and the design-level dynamic model, which includes event trace diagrams and state diagrams at the design level.

The "correct" design model is not derived in a single iteration; mistakes happen. Some design errors will not be discovered until we have done some prototyping. In practice, design modeling and prototyping tasks are carried out in iterations, until we reach a satisfactory design.

To achieve a better design, we often identify and use documented design patterns. The use of frameworks also affects the design. These are the subjects of Section 5.2.10.

5.2.10 Design Patterns and Frameworks

"Design patterns capture solutions that have developed and evolved over time. They reflect the untold redesign and recoding as developers have struggled for greater reuse and flexibility in their software. . . . Design patterns capture these solutions in a succinct and easily applied form" [GAM95].

A framework is a set of collaborating classes that work together to provide a reusable software design to suit a specific purpose. A framework has a pre-defined flow of control. We use the main body of a framework and add only customized code. This is often referred to as the *Hollywood principle:* "Don't call me, I'll call you."

Patterns and frameworks have some similarities, but they are different in three ways [GAM95]:

- Design patterns are more abstract than frameworks.
- Design patterns are smaller architectural elements than frameworks.
- Design patterns are less specialized than frameworks.[18]

Many useful design patterns can be found in [GAM95], [COA95]. Let us look at the model/view/controller (MVC) pattern, and see how it relates to design patterns and frameworks.

The MVC Design Pattern

MVC was first introduced in Smalltalk-80 for building a user interface. The MVC triad consists of three kinds of objects: The model consists of the application objects; the view is the information presentation user interface window; and the controller defines the way the user interface reacts to user inputs.

The main idea of MVC is to separate model (application) objects that closely relate to the business domain from the view (interface) objects that are for information presentation, using a controller to manage the user interactions and to

---

18 Frameworks are usually domain-oriented, while design patterns are domain-independent.

mediate between the interface objects and the model object. As explained earlier, one of the main reasons for this model-view separation is that while the model objects are relatively stable, the views could change often as a result of changes in user preferences and requirements. Also, one model object can be associated with many views.

Systems that support the MVC application structure must provide some kind of notification framework that plays the controller role to facilitate communication between views and models. The name of the notification framework[19] and its implementation details may differ in each system, but the general concepts remain the same. We will describe the VisualAge Notification Framework in the following section.

The VisualAge Notification Framework

IBM VisualAge provides a notification framework that contains *notifiers* and *observers* (the INotifier and IObserver abstract classes in VisualAge C++, respectively).

A *notifier* maintains a list of objects that depend on the occurrence of specific events. It provides a set of interfaces to enable other objects to register their dependency on an event, or to rescind their dependency from it. To register itself to a notifier, an object adds an *observer* to the notifier's list. An object can then signal the occurrence of each of its events to the notifier. The notifier is responsible for publishing its supported notification events and managing the list of observers when an event occurs. The notifier indicates the notification events that it supports by providing a series of unique identifiers in its interface.

Whenever an event occurs, the notifier searches its lists and forwards the notification to all dependent observers. It is the responsibility of the observer to handle or ignore a notification.

Figure 47 shows how this notification framework works as the controller for the model and views in a VisualAge environment.

---

19 Sometimes this is called a *dependency manager* or a *notification channel.*

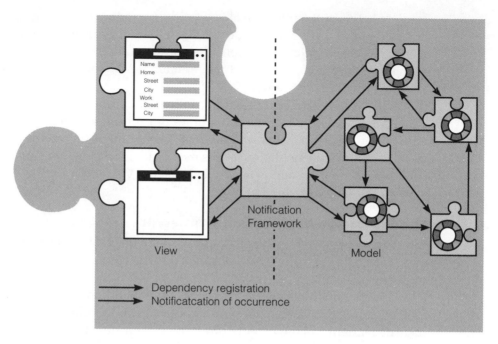

Figure 47. VisualAge notification framework

Control Objects

Earlier we mentioned Jacobson's use of the three kinds of objects: interface objects, entity objects, and control objects. They provide some guidelines for us to design our solution objects. But what is the role of control objects?

Extending the MVC design pattern to a higher level of abstraction than the original MVC triad used in Smalltalk-80, we find that control objects can be used to maintain the control or navigation logic for the scenarios described in a use case. The use of control objects is not always necessary. As Jacobson points out, in most cases, the flow of a use case can be satisfied with the behavior of the required interface objects and entity objects. Only in some complex use cases, when some behaviors remain that cannot naturally be placed in either the interface objects or the entity objects, do we consider creating control objects. Typically, functionalities placed in the control objects are transaction-related behavior, such as an update that should be completed either as a unit of work or not at all, or control sequences specific to one or a few use cases. The control objects tie together a course of events and communicate with other objects [JAC92].

There is a tension between the use of control objects and decentralized control, in which we distribute the control logic over a number of application (entity) objects. The best control strategy is the one that will localize and minimize subsequent changes.

5.3 **Object Persistence Design**

Design for object persistence involves many considerations, including the following:

- Data retrieval requirements
- Object and data placement
- Designing for client/server enabling
- Object replication synchronization (data integrity for replication)
- Object materialization strategies (when to bring in objects from persistent media)
- Mapping of objects to relational databases

Although this is by no means a complete list, these issues provide a good picture of the tasks related to object persistence design.

5.3.1 **Data Retrieval Techniques**

There are various techniques for retrieving the data stored in a database. Depending on the type of application and the amount of data to be processed, any or all of the techniques presented below can be used. Questions that must be answered include how to commit and update data that has been retrieved from the database for processing and how to handle references made to objects not currently instantiated by the application. In a multiuser environment, control can be placed at the database level, using a time stamp or similar concept, so that multiple updates are not allowed unless the data involved has not been altered since it was initially read by the updating process.

Retrieval on Initialization

When small amounts of data are involved and the data is infrequently updated, the application can retrieve everything necessary at initialization, thus avoiding the overhead of database access while the user is working.

Much depends on the efficiency of data retrieval in the target environment. If data access is relatively slow, initial caching of data can contribute to significant increases in performance. If data access is quick, the all-at-once method is probably not beneficial. Ideally, in a multitasking system, the initial data access as well as all other accesses run concurrently with the user interface portion of the application, thus hiding the amount of access time involved.

In the case of multiuser systems, data updating must be controlled. In a sense, the facilities provided by the database management system are rendered inoperative by the use of local copies of data. In that case, a plan for managing access is implemented at the application level, something that should be avoided if at all possible.

Retrieval in Chunks

Chunks of data can be brought in (similar to bringing in pages of data when a single item is requested) in an attempt to anticipate the user's next request. For example, if the user requested a particular object, the application could also bring in other objects either of the same class or of another class related to the first one through a frequently traversed association.

To implement this technique successfully, the application must be tuned to typical use cases so that it brings in useful data in the majority of cases. The penalty for bringing in the wrong data is that the system becomes sluggish and sometimes more difficult to use because it is burdened by excess data.

Retrieval on Demand

Retrieving only instantiated objects that have been specifically requested avoids long initial startup periods and makes data retrieval flexible. If a database is constantly accessed for information, however, the retrieval-on-demand technique can adversely affect the performance of the system.

As each object is requested, the application checks whether the object is available. If it is not, it can be requested from the database. At this point the application could also request all associated objects. (Whether this is desirable or not depends on how efficiently the application deals with a batched request for data, as opposed to many single requests.)

The on-demand technique has the advantages of making costly data accesses only when necessary and reducing the problem of outdated data. The technique could be extended by providing a mechanism to hide from the application whether or not an object is already in memory (this is discussed in Section 5.3.4).

5.3.2 Object and Data Placement

The initial decisions for object and data placement are made during system design. These decisions are reassessed during object design. Data retrieval and update requirements affect data placement. In general, data should be placed close to its source and to where it will be used. In deciding data placement, the design consideration is also to avoid data replication and duplication if possible.

There are three general design steps:

1. Map objects to processors: Identify which objects each user will need to be instantiated on his or her machine.

2. Map object replicas: Identify objects that need to be present at the same time in different images.

3. Design and build an appropriate application or DBMS mechanism to keep replicas congruent from an application logic and database perspective.

5.3.3 **Synchronization of Object Replicas**

Managing different replicas of objects poses many problems. We can classify these problems as logical problems and physical problems.

Let us look first at the logical problems. A multiuser application may require that an object be replicated in all user images. The problem is that each object has an identity, and at a given moment each user may or may not have a copy of that object, thus affecting the requirement for object synchronization. We need to review the object model and use test cases to see which objects are needed to run the application.

The policies regarding when to read replicated object data are as follows:

- Read data when object is instantiated
- Read data when object is queried
- Read data when object is requested

The policies regarding when to write (update) data are as follows:

- Update data whenever an update is indicated
- Update data when requested (foreground or background)
- Cannot update data.

Figure 48 illustrates these policies.

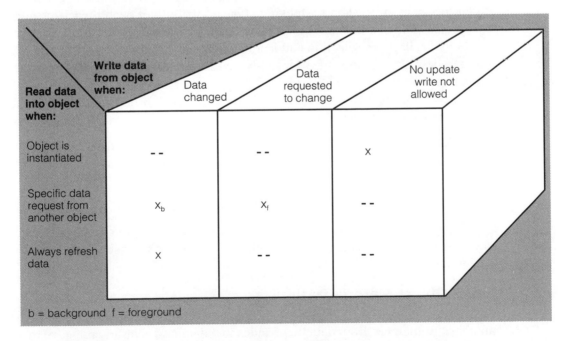

Figure 48. Overall policies regarding object and foreign data retrieval

Policies for mapping objects to foreign data need to address two levels: the object level (where do we store an object as such) and the attribute level (where do we store an attribute for a given object). The data policies are summarized in Figure 49.

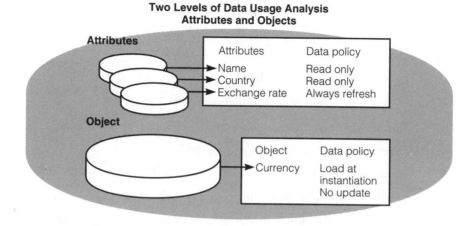

Figure 49. Data policies for mapping objects to foreign data

In a complex implementation environment, it is useful to build a matrix of data access per subsystem by looking at each attribute of each object in each subsystem. This matrix is used for reviewing data and message flows. It ensures a coherent subsystem selection and facilitates the normalization of the design of the database. It is also useful for analyzing the patterns of data access and update.

To select among the placement alternatives, we can define the data and process placement of each object as follows:

- Close to the location of use (the locality-of-reference/distributed-database design rule can be applied to data and process placement)

- Where hardware support is reliable, redundant, and scalable

- Where software will provide application performance and data integrity

Object data policies give data element groupings, data reference patterns, and ideas on performance requirements to help the database administrator design the database.

5.3.4 Object Materialization

As it was described in Chapter 4, object materialization is a method of creating an object in memory from data that resides in a database. The advantage of this method is that an application can simply send a message to an object and know that the object will either process it immediately if it exists in memory or be created and then it will process the message.

By creating an object of references, such as an object of the dictionary class in Smalltalk or the map class in C++, which can be initialized with references to all the objects that could be materialized when the user requests a particular instance, the application can locate that instance by searching the dictionary (or the map) based on the identification of the object.

Materialization involves the following steps:

1. An object wants to send a message to another object.

2. The sending object gets the ID of the receiver through the reference object.

3. The sender sends the message to the ID.

4. If the receiver is in memory, the message is accepted and processed. If not, a message is sent to the database to get the data of the object being referenced, which is then reconstructed.

5.4 Database Access Design

Earlier in this chapter we mentioned that a layered application architecture can be open or closed. In a layered view-model-data application structure, we could choose an open architecture, in which the views use the database access services of the data layer. This architecture is well suited for some decision-support systems that do not involve complex application logic; there, the user interface logic and data access logic are the primary parts of the application.

In applications where business logic is dominant over data access logic, an open architecture is less appropriate. In this case, a closed view-model-data application architecture leverages the full benefits of a more modular design. Some of these benefits are

- More resilient application model

- Dynamic application behavior

- Application component reuse

- Application extensibility and adaptability

Object And Data Responsibilities This view-model-data segregation design approach also facilitates the integration of database access into an application. With this approach, application prototype code requires virtually no modification to integrate with database access. Let's examine this approach in more detail.

In Figure 50, we see that the application view is supported by test instance data. The application model contains logic to request and access the data, which is initialized at application startup, and to return the data. The view requests the data from the model and has no knowledge of the data access process, which is controlled by the model.

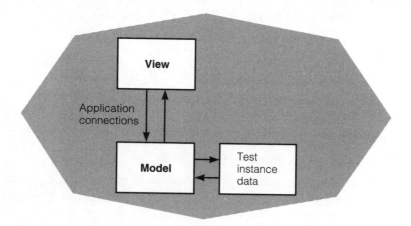

Figure 50. View-model and test instance data

Figure 51 shows that the model's data access class issues requests for data from the VisualAge portfolio of wrapper classes, that is, service classes that provide an object interface to the database.

As noted, the view is isolated from data access. The model contains the data access class that requests data services. These services are provided by the wrapper classes. The model also becomes partially isolated from data access. The data access class is the only model object that provides and requests services from the database.

We assign responsibilities to the objects in the object model data access class. The responsibilities of these objects are as follows:

- Know the table and row of all data items.

- Apply changes to the table(s).

- Commit changes to the table(s).

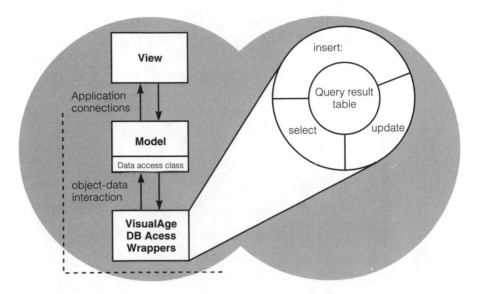

Figure 51. View and model isolation from data access

Object Instantiation Responsibilities Object data must be brought into memory (instantiated) from persistent storage before it can be used. The responsibility for bringing object data into memory is assigned following the "knows-of" hierarchy of the object model. For example, Stock knows its stock items; therefore, we assign to Stock the responsibility to bring stock items into memory when needed. Stock is thus the control object for the operations on stock items.

Objects are brought into memory from persistent storage following different data policies. The control objects know and enforce these policies.

As most model (entity) classes need to be persistent, we could define a persistent class for each model class in our solution. This assists the application developer by keeping persistent and nonpersistent object behaviors separate and distinct. In this way different persistent object implementations can be used with minimal impact on overall application behavior.

In the following sections, we explore the three commonly used techniques for designing the persistent data access class: by the use of class specialization (inheritance), object composition (aggregation), and delegation or use (association).

5.4.1 Using Inheritance

Using class specialization seems to be the most obvious way to design the data access for the persistence class, since most object-oriented programming languages provide the inheritance mechanism.

Figure 52 shows the inheritance hierarchy for the FCE Currency subsystem.

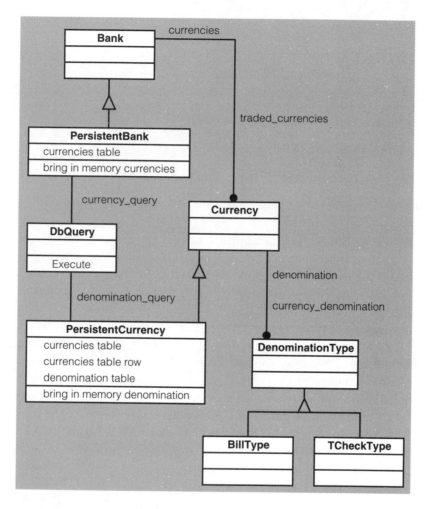

Figure 52. Persistent classes hierarchy

Using inheritance to implement the persistent data access class has some merits. For example, the class hierarchy is defined statically at development or compile time and is straightforward to use. However, there are disadvantages in this approach. First, because inheritance exposes the subclass to the details of the superclass's implementation, inheritance breaks encapsulation and creates implementation dependencies of the persisting class on the model class. Also, when data access is supplied by the visual programming tool, such as the VisualAge C++ Data Access Builder (DACS), this approach may not be feasible because the DACS class inherits from the IPersistence class, and we cannot make it inherit from the desired business part.

Data Access Builder in VisualAge C++ provides a class library and parts to access database. To provide persistence to the business part, we can choose either the aggregation or the association option.

5.4.2 Using Aggregation

We could create a composite object containing the model object and the persistent object. In other words, we aggregate the business and persistent parts in one VisualAge nonvisual part and promote the relevant features. The composite object then contains both the business and persistence behavior and can be used for visual programming connections in creating the views directly.

Figure 53 shows how this can be done using VisualAge C++ Visual Builder (similar approach also applies for VisualAge for Smalltalk). We create a composite object with classname FCECustomerObject, which is an aggregate of the business object busCustomer and a persistant object DAXCustomer.

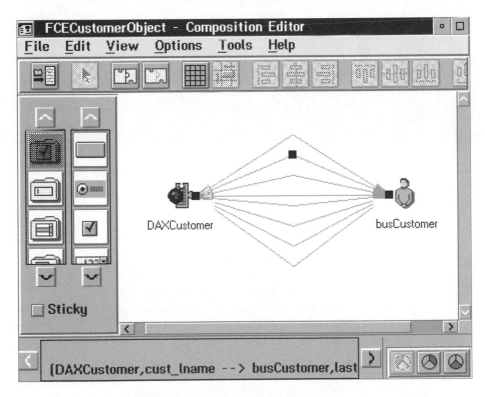

Figure 53. Composite object with persistence

Figure 54 illustrates how this composite object can be used to create a Customer view. In the figure, compositeCust is of the type of FCECustomerObject.

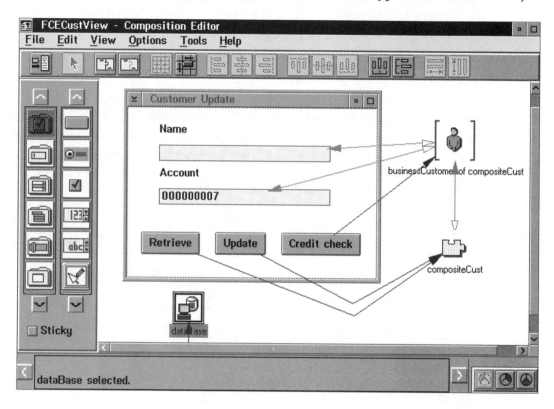

Figure 54. Using a composite object for persistence in a view

The advantages of this approach are many. The composite object contains and encapsulates the model class and persistence class behavior, which makes the visual programming for the views much simpler, as there are fewer connections when using the part. It does not create inheritance dependency between the model class and the persistence class. However, it does present a tight coupling of the business part and the persistent part with no inheritance relationship. Also, the persistence class is instantiated every time the composite object is referenced, which may cause some performance concerns. Since we need only one instance for the persistence class to do the job, we should try to make the persistence class a *singleton* class. In the extended FCE case study, only one instance of the persistence class is instantiated and used subsequently by any instances of the composite object.

5.4.3 Using Associations

Another approach is simply to let the model class use or delegate the persistence class. The model class and the persistence classes are loosely coupled via an association. We can separately use both the business part and the associated persistent part. The persistent part holds the methods to access the database, and the business part holds the other methods required for providing the business function-related behavior. The attributes of the business part are not persistent. The advantage of this approach is that there is minimum dependency between the persistence class and the model class. The loose coupling between the two parts provides more flexibility when building the business part. The disadvantage of this approach is that we need to use the model object and persistence object together for the views. This causes the visual programming connections to be more complex, which in turn makes the maintenance of the visual application more difficult, as use of the part entails more connections.

5.5 Summary

The design phase in VMT bridges the analysis of the business problem to the implementation of its solution as a computer application. This phase is of critical importance to object-oriented application development since it defines the way the application will comply with both the functional and non-functional requirements.

The VMT design phase covers system design, object design, and object persistence design. The system design defines the overall system architecture for implementing the target solution, as well as the application architecture including the definition of subsystems, service layers, and partitions. Object design translates the object model built in the analysis phase into an implementable construct. To that end, the semantic classes with business meaning are fully designed, and new service and implementation classes are added. Object persistence design provides an efficient solution to storing and retrieving objects that have to last after the execution of the application program has ended, and include the definition of mapping schemas and the placement and retrieval of data within a multiuser network.

The design process is summarized in Figure 55.

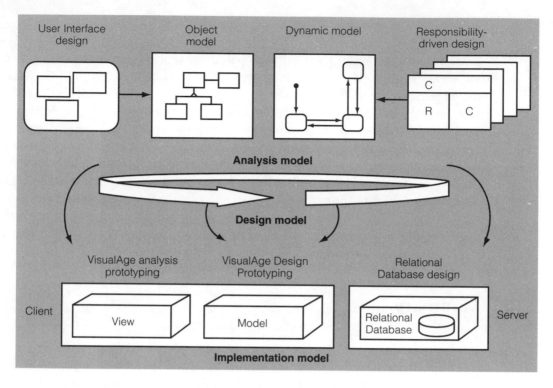

Figure 55. VMT design process

6

Implementation with VMT: From Model to Code

This chapter discusses the mapping process for translating an object design model into an implementation of the solution and the productivity increments that derive from using a visual programming environment to build object applications.

Two approaches are used in VMT in the mapping process from design to implementation: a class-oriented approach and a part- or component-oriented approach. In the latter case, we show how applying a *programming-by-contract* [MEY88] discipline when building software from components can provide an effective and systematic approach to software developments.

We use IBM VisualAge to provide examples of implementing the solution code. (In this book, the name VisualAge refers to both the VisualAge for Smalltalk and VisualAge for C++ products. When it is necessary to distinguish between the two, we use VisualAge Smalltalk or VisualAge C++ specifically. To that end, we provide an introduction to the VisualAge Development Environment and explain some terminology for those readers who are not familiar with VisualAge. We chose the Currency Management subsystem from the FCE application to illustrate how the process works.

6.1 The VisualAge Development Environment

VisualAge is a visual programming tool with facilities to compose and customize parts and assemble applications in a visual way by using its visual builder (also known as composition editor). By allowing us to combine parts visually, without writing code, the visual tools eliminate much of the tedium and error-prone detail from application programming, especially user interface programming, so we can concentrate on the essential business logics of the application.

6.1.1 VisualAge Parts

In VisualAge, a part is a class with a well-defined public interface, which supports a simple and architecture-based messaging protocol. The term *subpart* refers to a part taken from the palette and used to build a composite part.

Parts range from simple to highly sophisticated and provide a wide range of functions, as shown in Figure 56. They can be as simple as a text-entry field or a default window. More complex parts are often composed of several interacting subparts, such as a personnel view that may include multiple text-entry fields for names and telephone numbers and, possibly, views for addresses, a mail system, or a protocol-independent client/server component. VisualAge Smalltalk parts can also represent (wrap) programs written in COBOL or C language, thus allowing the reuse of existing code in a construction-from-parts paradigm.

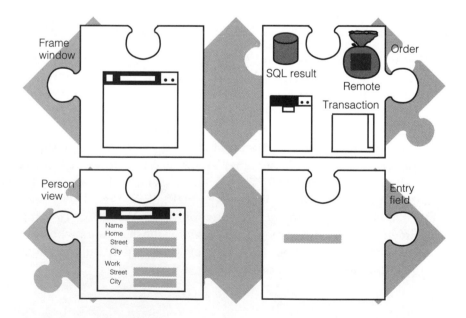

Figure 56. Examples of parts

Parts

As shown in Figure 57, parts can be categorized as composite parts and primitive parts. Composite parts are composed from primitive and other composite parts. The parts can be grouped further into two major types: visual and nonvisual. The major difference between them is the capability of visual parts to present a graphical view to the end user at run time, such as a list box, a window, a view of an address or person, and so on. A visual part can also contain nonvisual parts to form a composite part.

Nonvisual parts usually do not have a run-time view. Examples are business logic objects, such as an address or a person, or parts that represent generic database queries or generic DLLs. Currently, a VisualAge C++ application must have at least one view.

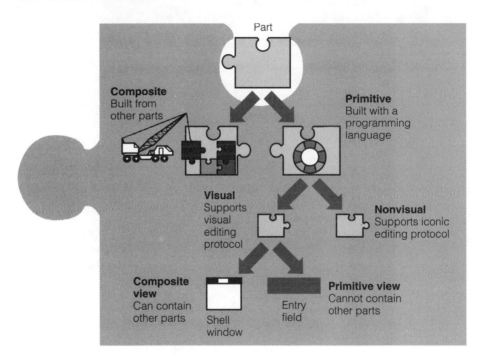

Figure 57. Various types of parts

Public Interface of Parts

The *public interface* of parts refers to the features used to connect parts, as shown in Figure 58.

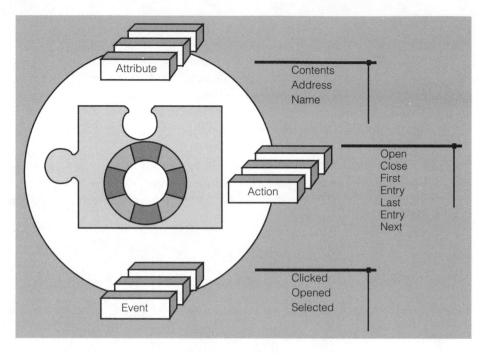

Figure 58. Public interface of parts

To specify the public interface of parts, VisualAge introduces three clearly defined features that correspond to a natural way of seeing parts and objects in general and express the possible interactions among objects:

- Attributes, which are the logical properties of a part. At a conceptual level, attributes are an important and integral aspect of an object's semantic definition. Attributes are objects that the part can return or set on request.

- Actions, which are the behaviors of the part, that is, the services or operations the part may be requested to perform.

- Events, which provide a notification mechanism, signaling that something has happened to the part. For user interface parts, events are often related to some user interaction, such as the clicking of the mouse, the selection of a check box, and so on. Events are used to trigger some action.

The term *application* commonly refers to a collection of software components used to perform user-oriented tasks on a computer. VisualAge supports applications from a development perspective. Therefore in VisualAge, an application is a collection of parts that can be managed as a whole and packaged to produce the run-time application for distribution to end users.

6.2 The Mapping Process

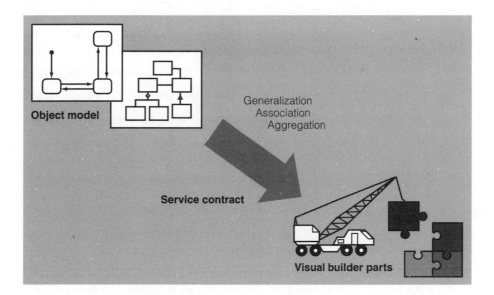

Figure 59. Mapping process

Implementation is the process of translating the design object model into code, such as VisualAge parts. The application is then constructed from these parts. This mapping process involves several activities (see Figure 59). The activities normally do not have to be done in a rigid sequence, but the following sequence is most common:

1. Define the VisualAge applications.

   a. Map each subsystem in the object model to a VisualAge Smalltalk application, or to a .VBB file in VisualAge C++.

   b. A VisualAge Smalltalk application represents a program module in which closely related classes are defined. In VisualAge C++, all related parts within a subsystem can be placed in the same .VBB file.

2. Develop the VisualAge nonvisual parts.

   a. Map the object model classes to VisualAge nonvisual parts.

   b. Define the nonvisual classes (the public interface) with their required attributes, actions, and events.

   c. Map the object model class relationships and define them in VisualAge. Relationships include generalization, aggregation, and association.

    d. Implement the methods for the required actions or services, including Smalltalk methods, instance variables, and service contracts between parts.

3. Develop the VisualAge visual parts to provide the necessary user interface or views.

    a. Build an elementary view for each concrete nonvisual part.

    b. Build a create or edit view or both for each concrete nonvisual part.

    c. Build a list or summary view for each concrete nonvisual part.

    d. Assemble composite views to match to the eventual user interface specifications.

4. Implement the object persistence design.

    a. Map the classes to relation tables.

    b. Map the relationships to relation tables.

    c. Build database access persistence parts.

The mapping process applies to both VisualAge for Smalltalk and VisualAge for C++. For easy reference, Table 4 compares the terms used in Smalltalk and C++.[20]

Table 4. Smalltalk and C++ terminology equivalents

Smalltalk	C++
Superclass	Base class
Subclass	Derived class/subclass
Method	Member function
Instance method	Member function
Class method	Static member function
Message	Member function call
Attribute	Attribute
Instance variable	Attribute
Class variable	Static attribute
Signal/event	Event

The following sections provide more details on the mapping process except for step 4, which is discussed in Chapter 4 and will be illustrated in Chapter 7. We use the Currency Management subsystem from the FCE application to illustrate the process. A fragment of the object model is shown in Figure 60 on page 137.

---

20 This comparison is not a fully rigorous one; it rather provides a practical equivalence of terms functionally similar.

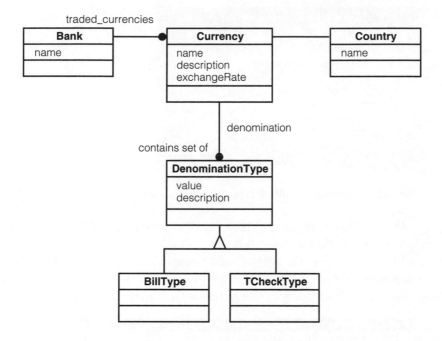

Figure 60. Fragment of the object model for the Currency Management subsystem

6.2.1 Defining VisualAge Applications

We use the term *VisualAge application* to refer to a programming unit for the software configuration or packaging of a subsystem. Each subsystem defined in the design model is a candidate for a VisualAge Smalltalk application, which is then the basis for software configuration and packaging.

Figure 61 shows the screen used to create an application. By simply typing the name of the designed subsystem into the application name box and pressing Enter, we can create a VisualAge Smalltalk application with the given name.

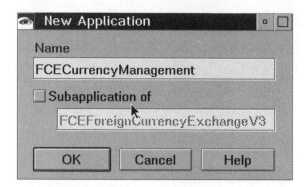

Figure 61. VisualAge Smalltalk New Application screen

When implementing in VisualAge C++, we use a .VBB file to group all the related parts within a subsystem.

Figure 62 shows the screen used to create a new part that will be contained in the specified .VBB file. In this example, the .VBB file named CurrencyManagementV3 is to contain all the parts for the Currency Management subsystem.

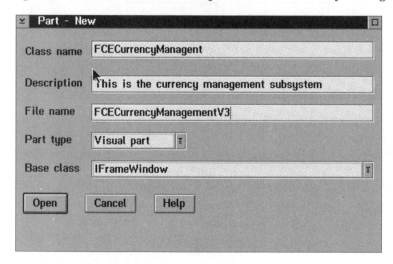

Figure 62. VisualAge C++ Part-New screen

6.2.2 Developing the VisualAge Nonvisual Parts

The following subsections describe the steps to implementing the solution-domain classes.

Mapping to a Nonvisual Part

Each class in the design object model becomes a class in the VisualAge environment. This is a one-to-one mapping.

Table 5 shows a mapping from the object model classes to VisualAge classes during the design. We explain the development process in more detail in the sections that follow.

Table 5. Mapping from object model classes to VisualAge Smalltalk and C++ classes			
Object model class	VisualAge part interface	Smalltalk class	C++ class
Attribute	Attribute	Attribute Instance variable Class variable	Attribute Attribute Static attribute
Object service operation	Action	Method Instance method Class method	Member function Member function Static member function
Messaging between associated classes (notification)	Event	Message #SignalEvent	Member function call Notification event

Defining the Public Interface

As mentioned, the public interface of a VisualAge part has three elements: attributes, actions, and events. In the following object model (OM) discussion, we use the terms *OM attributes, OM services,* and *OM associations* to refer to the corresponding elements defined in the object model.

The public interface for each nonvisual class is designed according to the following:

- OM attributes become VisualAge attributes, distinguishable as primary attributes, which can be read and set, or derived attributes, which can be read but not set. Derived attributes should not have set selectors when implemented in VisualAge.

- OM services become VisualAge actions, except for those that just provide requested information; such services can be better implemented as VisualAge attributes. An example of this kind of service is a list of depleted items in stock in our FCE application.

- OM associations map to VisualAge attributes.

Mapping Class Relationships

The design object model has three types of relationships: generalization, association, and aggregation. The following sections describe how these relationships can be implemented in the VisualAge environment.

Generalization

Generalization within the VisualAge environment is implemented by means of subclassing, that is, inheritance from superclasses. When a VisualAge class is created, we are asked which superclass to inherit from.

The design object model in the Currency subsystem (see Figure 59 on page 135) shows that BillType class is a subclass of the DenominationType class. When we create the BillType class, we specify the DenominationType class as the superclass to inherit from. By default, the VisualAge class inherits from the AbtAppBldrPart class. To inherit from a different superclass, we simply overtype or select from the drop-down list a superclass to inherit from. Figure 63 shows the creation of the BillType class with VisualAge Smalltalk.

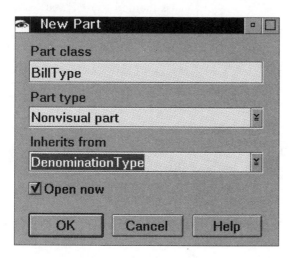

Figure 63. Creating a VisualAge Smalltalk class

Figure 64 on page 141 shows the creation of the BillType class with VisualAge C++.

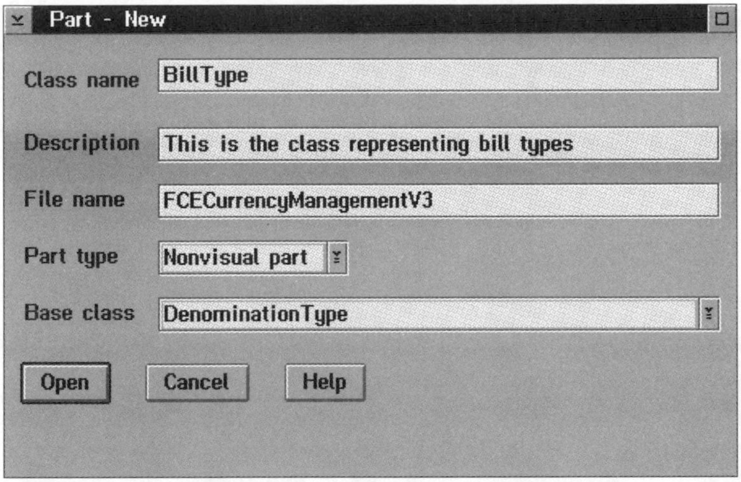

```
┌─────────────────────────────────────────────────────────┐
│ ⌄  Part - New                                         □  │
├─────────────────────────────────────────────────────────┤
│                                                          │
│  Class name  │ BillType                              │   │
│                                                          │
│  Description │ This is the class representing bill types │
│                                                          │
│  File name   │ FCECurrencyManagementV3               │   │
│                                                          │
│  Part type   │ Nonvisual part  ⌄│                        │
│                                                          │
│  Base class  │ DenominationType                   ⌄│    │
│                                                          │
│  ┌────────┐  ┌────────┐  ┌────────┐                     │
│  │  Open  │  │ Cancel │  │  Help  │                     │
│  └────────┘  └────────┘  └────────┘                     │
│                                                          │
└─────────────────────────────────────────────────────────┘
```

Figure 64. Creating a VisualAge C++ class

Association

Designing the implementation of associations involves four things:

- Analyzing and designing object pointers
- Choosing a data structure to implement cardinality
- Designing the implementation of aggregation
- Designing the implementation of the link attribute

An association between two classes is inherently directional. During analysis, this is manifested by defining the role each class plays in the association. During design, we can choose to implement either one-way traversal or two-way traversal for an association, depending on the required search criteria and efficiency, along with memory consumptions for implementing the association as design trade-offs.

Association with Cardinality of One-to-One In the Currency subsystem, Currency belongs to Country, and Country has Currency (see Figure 59 on page 135). This is a bidirectional one-to-one relationship. In this case, we add Country as an attribute in the Currency class, and add Currency as an attribute in the Country class. Figure 65 on page 142 shows the public interface of the Currency class; it contains Country as an attribute to point to the Country class.

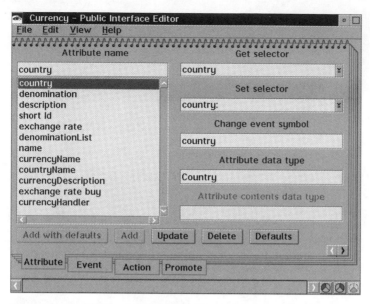

Figure 65. Public interface of the Currency class, showing an association with Country

Association with Cardinality of One-to-*n* In the FCE system, the bank trades a number of currencies. This is represented by the one-to-*n* association between the Bank class and the Currency class (see Figure 59 on page 135). We implement this one-to-*n* association by adding a currency attribute of the OrderedCollection class in the Bank class to establish the necessary traversal (see Figure 66).

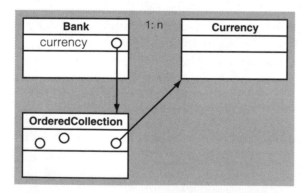

Figure 66. Bank's association with Currency

Figure 67 on page 143 shows the public interface for Bank; the currency attribute is specified to have OrderedCollection as its *instance variable class.*

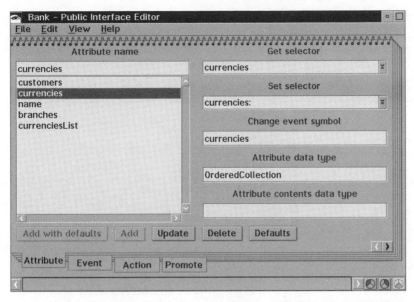

Figure 67. Using the OrderedCollection class for a one-to-*n* association

Similarly, a currency contains a number of denomination types. This is represented by the one-to-*n* association in the object model (see Figure 60 on page 137). Figure 68 shows the use of the Set class to implement this one-to-*n* association.

In general, collection classes can be used to implement associations with multiplicity. Later in this chapter we discuss how to choose and optimize the use of the various collection classes.

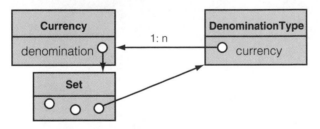

Figure 68. Using the Set collection class for a one-to-*n* association

Association with Cardinality of *n*-to-m Many bidirectional traversals can be implemented using a distinct association class, independent of either class, such as a Dictionary class, each element of which contains a pair of object IDs. Figure 69 shows the use of a distinct Dictionary class to implement the bidirectional association between the Currency class and the DenominationType class.

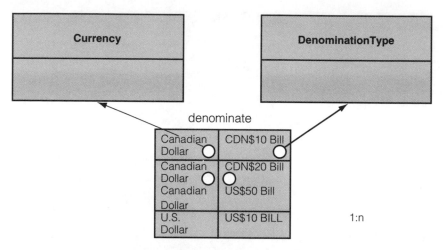

Figure 69. Association with an implementation class of Dictionary

Similarly, this technique can be applied to implement associations with *n*-to-*m* cardinality. For efficiency reasons, two Dictionary classes may be used in this case, one for traversing from each end of the association (see Figure 70).

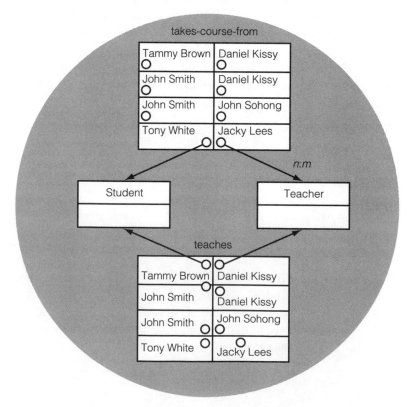

Figure 70. Implementing association with two Dictionary classes

Associations with Link Classes A link class is used to implement an *n*-to-*m* association. Figure 71 shows the OrderItem link class. Each instance of OrderItem specifies the ordered quantity for a link between CustomerOrder and DenominationType.

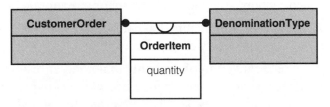

Figure 71. OrderItem link class

Because a link class is a distinct association class, it cannot be easily implemented by putting pointer attributes in the classes on either side of the association. However, by transforming the *n*-to-*m* link class association to a pair of one-to-*n* and *n*-to-one associations (see Figure 72), we can use the same techniques we used to implement the one-to-*n* associations to implement the link class association.

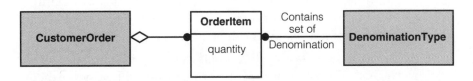

Figure 72. Implementation of a link class association

Optimizing the Use of a Collection Class We can implement associations with multiplicity by using a collection class; however, choosing the appropriate class to implement the collection has a significant impact on performance. There are several collection subclasses, and each has its distinct behavior.

Different terms are used for some of the subclasses of the Collection class in Smalltalk and C++, as shown in Table 6.

Table 6. Smalltalk and C++ collection class equivalents	
Smalltalk	**C++**
Dictionary	Map
OrderedCollection	IVSequence
SortedCollection	Sorted IVSequence
Note: Other collections have the same name	

The Collection class is perhaps one of the most powerful features of the C++ and Smalltalk environment. It is an abstract class; that is, it defines common characteristics of its subclasses but is never directly used. The Collection class comprises the following subclasses:

- Bag: keeps a collection of elements that may or may not be repeated.

- Set: keeps a collection of elements that cannot be repeated. Choose Set whenever Dictionary or Array cannot be used.

- Dictionary: keeps a collection of elements that are identified by a key. Choose Dictionary when fast access for a key value is required. Associative objects typically have a key. For example, the StockItems of a stock are keyed on the item.

- OrderedCollection: keeps a collection of elements that are identified by an index. OrderedCollection is used to build lists of objects to be shown to the user.

- SortedCollection: keeps a collection of elements that need to be kept in a sorted order. SortedCollection is used to build sorted lists.

- Array: keeps a finite-size collection of elements that are identified by an index. We use an Array when the association has a finite multiplicity. For example, a car can have at most five passengers, so a Passengers attribute for a Car class can be of type Array.

The Collection class and its subclasses are powerful but must be used with care because all instances must be brought into memory for them to work. In other words, the full set of the collection objects must be available in memory to use the Collection class and its subclasses. Sometimes the full set of collection objects is too big, and loading them into memory all at once may cause performance and resource problems.

For example, at first glance it seems that we could implement the association between Bank and Customer by adding an attribute Customers of the class Set in Bank. However, we will never be able to load the full Set of Customers into memory because it is too big. Therefore we cannot provide the user with a customer list that is built on an OrderedCollection derived from the Set class containing all Customers. A good technique in that case is to use a qualified association, where the qualifier is, for instance, the customer number.

Aggregation

In general, we implement aggregation the same way we implement associations. Using the VisualAge public interface editor, we can specify the aggregation relationship among the aggregate and its parts by defining the required attributes. This is a bottom-up process:

1. Start with the lowest aggregates and create base nonvisual parts as needed.

2. Traverse up the hierarchy and define each lower aggregate as an attribute.

3. Define the attribute's class instance variables as appropriate.

4. Implement cardinality with the appropriate collection class.

In this section, we use a series of screen shots to show the implementation details of the aggregation of the Car class shown in Figure 73.

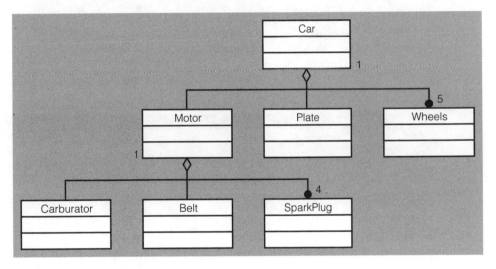

Figure 73. Aggregation of the Car class

On page 148, Figure 74 shows that the Motor class is aggregated from Belt, Carburetor, and a collection class called SparkPlug. Figure 75 shows how the Car class is aggregated.

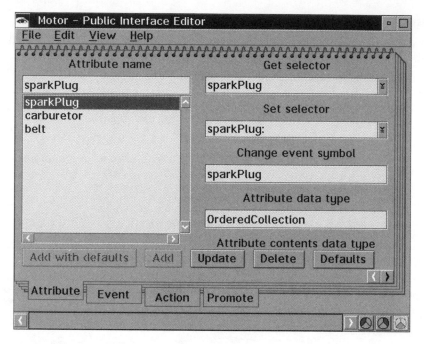

Figure 74. Aggregation of the Motor class

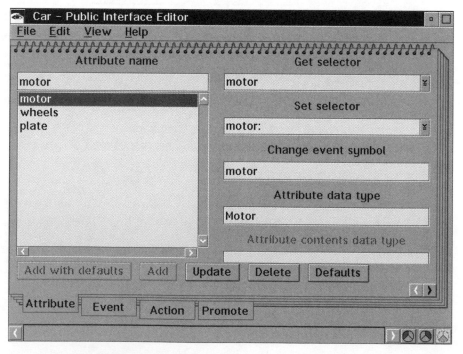

Figure 75. Aggregation of the Car class

Visual Representation of Aggregation for a Part VisualAge has a feature called Tear-off Attribute that is used to externalize the attributes of a composite part to allow access to the attribute values by other parts. It is analogous to peeling an onion: We peel off the outer layer to access the inner one.

The Tear-off Attribute feature also provides a visual representation of aggregation, which can be used to show model-to-code traceability. Using the Composition Editor, a tear-off diagram can be constructed by tearing off the composite parts to show the aggregation of each part. Figure 76 is a tear-off diagram of a car, which provides visual evidence of the car's aggregation hierarchy as shown in Figure 75.

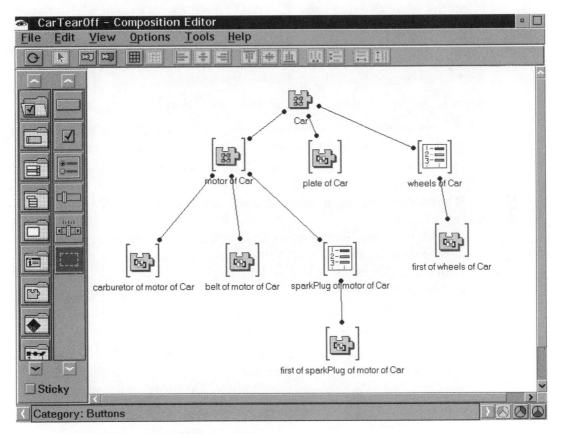

Figure 76. Tear-off diagram of a Car

6.2.3 Designing Methods and Instance Variables

We now discuss the design of Smalltalk methods and instance variables to support the public interface. Although the terminology used in C++ is different (see Table 4 on page 136), the design approaches described here are applicable to both Smalltalk and C++ implementation.

Designing a Derived Data Policy

Derived data is often required to build a usable application. For example, the user interface needs a list of ordered items to allow the cashier to modify the order; and the branch stock manager needs a list of depleted items from the cashiers' drawers to build a consolidated branch replenishment order. The problem can be seen as a client object needing to derive data from some primitive data known by a server object. Three decisions must be made to solve this problem.

The first decision involves who derives the data. Will the server provide the derived data directly, or will it provide just the base data and leave the client the job of deriving what it needs? Our approach, in general, is to assign the responsibility to derive data to the object that owns primitive data, that is, the server object. This enables us to obtain more information hiding (allowing for easier maintainability) and richer objects. A pragmatic decision should be made according to the following considerations:

- Is the derived data needed only by this client?

- Does the derived data depend on any server design decision that is likely to change in the future?

A VisualAge nonvisual class will have an external attribute declared for any piece of derived data required.

The second decision involves derived data that is saved. Two approaches can be followed:

- Each time the client requests derived data, the server obtains it from base data (for example, each time a client requests a total on an order, the order loops through all order items and recalculates it). This means that the derived data is up-to-date every time it is requested.

- Derived data is obtained and saved by the server object. Derived data can be obtained by the server object:

  —Each time the base data (that is, the data used to calculate the derived data) changes. This means that every time a client requests derived data, this data is up-to-date, but the server object must keep track of which derived attributes need to be updated for any base attribute.

  —When requested. This means that the server provides refresh services only if a client requests the value of a derived attribute whose base components have been updated. This policy can be appropriate if deriving data has a high overhead.

Which approach is used depends on storage space and response time constraints, and it usually implies a trade-off.

The third decision involves how derived data is obtained, by push or pull. VisualAge supports events; that is, a server object can signal to interested parties that a derived attribute is changed. This forces any attribute connected to another attribute to be refreshed (pushed). Alternatively, the server object can provide data only when required, and it is up to the client to require (pull) fresh data when needed.

Input Data Validation

Any interactive system must implement a complete validation of data entered by the end user. Some design decisions have to be made regarding who verifies data and when. The following are two alternative decision-making scenarios:

- The server object expects that data passed to it is correct, and the burden of verifying the correctness of the data is on the client. This approach complies with structured programming principles [WIR90] but violates the encapsulation principle because knowledge of the inner workings of the server object used outside that object.

- The server object verifies the correctness of the data when it is asked to make any modification to its state. This approach properly assigns the knowledge of which state is acceptable for an object to the object itself, but it also triggers verification when servers are modified in a friendly environment, and a lot of useless controls are produced.

However, most update messages cannot be verified one by one; the whole update operation must be verified. For example, if a client wants to change the minimum quantity allowed for an in-stock item from 10 to 100 and the maximum quantity from 30 to 300, we are not expected to raise an error saying "Minimum quantity greater than maximum quantity" when changing the minimum quantity before the maximum.

We suggest a compromise: It is the responsibility of any object to know whether a required update is acceptable, but it is a client's responsibility to trigger the verification logic. This responsibility assignment allows for different levels of verification enforcement:

- Server in a friendly environment (the update operation is surely correct and no verification is required). The client just updates the server object.

- Server in a hostile environment (the update operation must be verified; for example, the client is a user interface). The client asks the server whether the update it wants to do is acceptable; the server verifies the update request and asks the client to apply the change if everything is correct.

Figure 77 shows how the client/server update protocol can be designed logically. VisualAge has a DeferredUpdate object that provides the required function to implement this design.

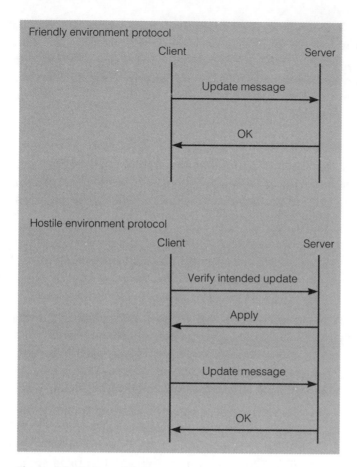

Figure 77. Data validation

6.3 Programming by Contract: Building Software from Parts

In the *programming-by-contract* discipline, the relationship between a class and its clients is viewed as a formal agreement expressing each party's rights and obligations [MEY88]. This approach can be extended to agreements between software parts or components, one considered as service providers and the other as service requesters. This agreement is established through certain expressions called *assertions,* which can be used to construct correct software systems, as well as document why they are correct.

As the name implies, an assertion is something that we say about the values of entities of the program. For instance, an assertion would be to specify that a certain number n has to be positive ($n > 0$).

Assertions can be used to specify the semantics of object methods. To that end, two types of assertions are associated with that method: a *precondition,* which expresses the properties that must be true when the method is invoked, and a *postcondition,* which describes the properties the method guarantees to hold at the end of its execution.

The presence of a precondition and a postcondition in a method should be viewed as a contract that binds the service requester and the service provider. [MEY88] dramatized the situation as the server saying to its clients "If you promise to invoke the method *m* with the precondition satisfied, then I, in return, promise to deliver a final state in which the postcondition is satisfied."

If a client's obligation is not fulfilled, that is, if the server method is invoked by the service requester without satisfying the precondition, the service provider ceases to be bound by the precondition and can do anything: crash, loop, or return strange values.

Programming by contract highly simplifies the programming style, since the programmer of the method does not have to check for the validity of the input to the method. This checking is supposed to occur elsewhere, and the programmer assumes that the input is correct without including the tests in the method's body.

6.3.1 A Framework to Provide Service Contracts

Figure 78 shows the framework for the implementation of service contracts within the VisualAge part framework. Under this framework, all the values in the public attribute are guaranteed. The framework consists of the following:

- All preconditions for a service are checked before the core business logic is invoked.

- All postconditions are checked before the public attribute is returned.

- The core business logic is hidden inside a private method and does not perform any validity checking.

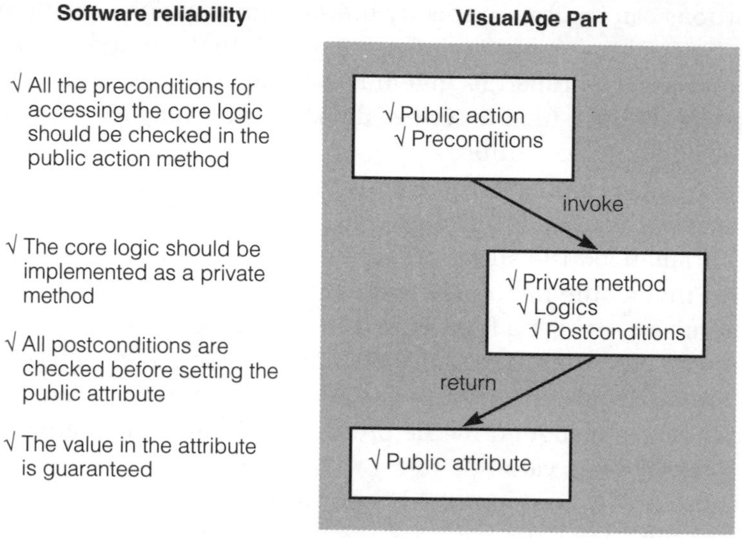

Software reliability   **VisualAge Part**

√ All the preconditions for
   accessing the core logic
   should be checked in the
   public action method   √ Public action
                                         √ Preconditions

                                                  invoke

√ The core logic should be
   implemented as a private
   method   √ Private method
                                              √ Logics
√ All postconditions are   √ Postconditions
   checked before setting the
   public attribute   return

√ The value in the attribute
   is guaranteed   √ Public attribute

Figure 78. Framework to provide service contracts

Let's look at an example from the FCE application that involves getting
money from the bank reserve. The BankReserve class implements the "pay-out-
money" service to satisfy this need. The BankReserve class contains, as part of
its public interface, a getMoney public action and a moneyPayOut public
attribute. The detailed implementation of the pay-out-money service is hidden
as a private method within the BankReserve class. This approach, an instantiation of the services contract framework, is shown in Figure 79.

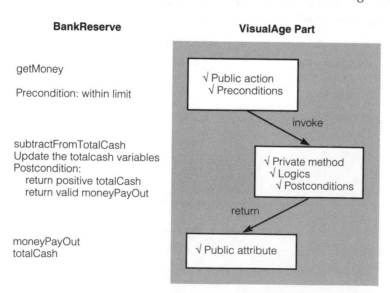

BankReserve   **VisualAge Part**

getMoney   √ Public action
                                          √ Preconditions
Precondition: within limit

                                                  invoke

subtractFromTotalCash
Update the totalcash variables   √ Private method
Postcondition: √ Logics
   return positive totalCash   √ Postconditions
   return valid moneyPayOut
                                          return

moneyPayOut
totalCash   √ Public attribute

Figure 79. Instantiation of the services contract framework

We show now how this instantiation of the services contract framework is implemented. First, we define getMoney as a public action using the public interface editor, as shown in Figure 80. This action has the responsibility of checking the preconditions to the subtractFromTotalCash private method.

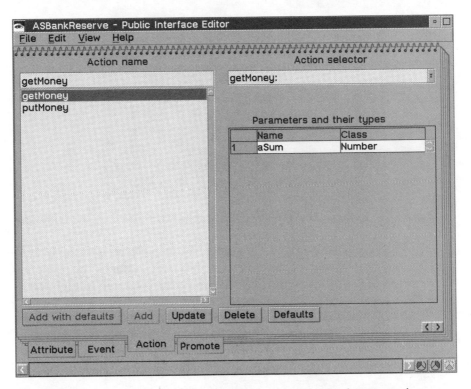

Figure 80. Defining the getMoney public action in the BankReserve class

The postconditions of this private method refer to the values it must leave after its execution. In our case, the postconditions are to return a positive value of the totalCash attribute and a valid value of the moneyPayOut attribute. The responsibility of returning the values complying with the postconditions lies in the private method; the values are returned in public attributes, and the client code does not need to check them.

Figure 81 on page 156 shows the creation of the moneyPayOut public attribute.

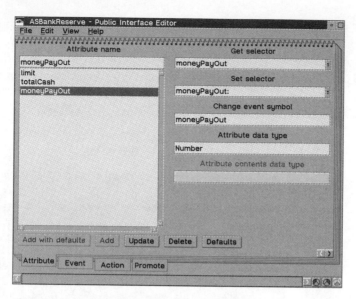

Figure 81. Defining the moneyPayOut public attribute in the BankReserve class

The action that verifies the precondition is triggered by an event external to the BankReserve part. The action executes code to check the preconditions. The creation of the action and its verification code is shown in Figure 82.

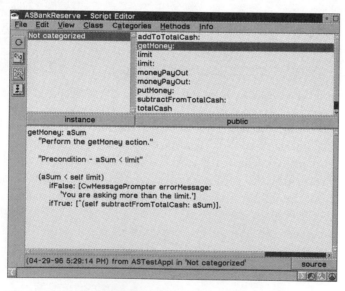

Figure 82. Implementing precondition checking of the requested amount

Once the code invoked by the action has finished checking the preconditions, it invokes the private method subtractFromTotalCash, which does the actual action of subtracting from the total cash available the money paid out. This method is shown in Figure 83.

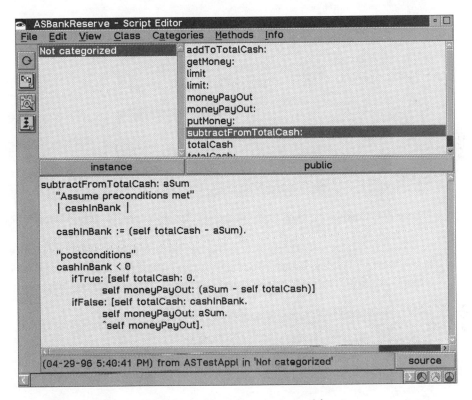

Figure 83. Private method for subtracting money paid out

The event external to the BankReserve part is raised in this application by a Cashier part. Visual programming of the application is straightforward. First, we program how the Cashier part invokes the getMoney action by establishing an event-to-action connection. This is shown in Figure 84 on page 158.

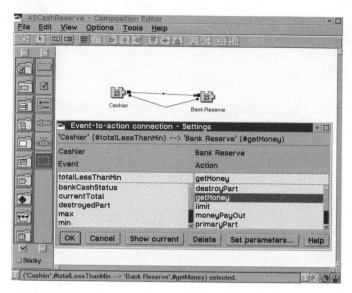

Figure 84. Cashier invokes getMoney through an event-to-action connection

We finish by returning the value of the totalCash attribute of the CashReserve part to the Cashier's bankCashStatus attribute. This is done by establishing an attribute-to-attribute connection, as shown in Figure 85.

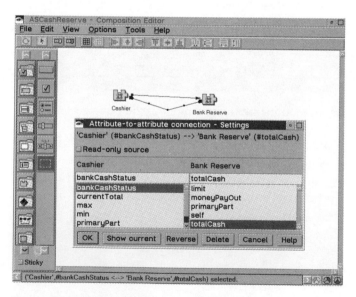

Figure 85. Result set through an attribute-to-attribute connection

The services contract framework is not limited to Smalltalk visual programming tools. For instance, the checking of the preconditions of the same example using VigualAge C++ is shown in Figure 86.

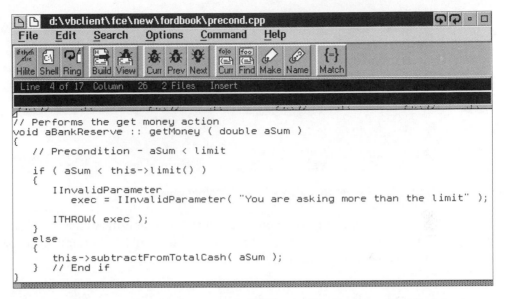

```
// Performs the get money action
void aBankReserve :: getMoney ( double aSum )
{
    // Precondition - aSum < limit

    if ( aSum < this->limit() )
    {
        IInvalidParameter
            exec = IInvalidParameter( "You are asking more than the limit" );

        ITHROW( exec );
    }
    else
    {
        this->subtractFromTotalCash( aSum );
    } // End if
}
```

Figure 86. Implementing the precondition of checking the requested limit in C++

6.4 Developing a GUI with Visual Components

Visual programming tools normally provide components for developing user interfaces. If the tool architecture supports the view-model-data segregation design approach, it facilitates reuse by allowing the construction of composite GUI parts from existing parts or by subclassing from base classes. The composite part provides encapsulation to all subparts, allowing user interfaces to be constructed with relatively simple connections.

User interface development can be developed in a bottom-up fashion, starting by building one or more elementary views for each base object (that is, each nonvisual class created previously). An elementary view is made up of only the basic nonvisual part and primitive GUI parts.

Once the elementary views have been created, they are used for building composite views. A *composite* view is a user interface part made up of one or more elementary views and other visual or nonvisual components. These elementary and composite views, called visual parts, are the building blocks for the final assembly of the user interface solution defined in the analysis prototype. The analysis prototype is used as a blueprint (specification) for identifying some of these reusable visual parts.

A visual class, or view, has at least one elementary view; some have alternative views. For example, the Customer object has one elementary view that displays all the attributes about the customer (see Figure 87).

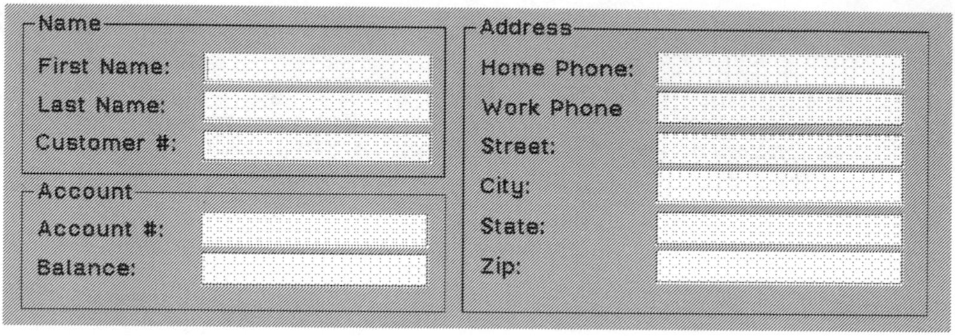

Figure 87. Elementary view of the Customer object

By adding controller components to the elementary display view, we can build edit and create views. These views allow entering of new or revised data. Figure 88 shows an example of a "create" view.

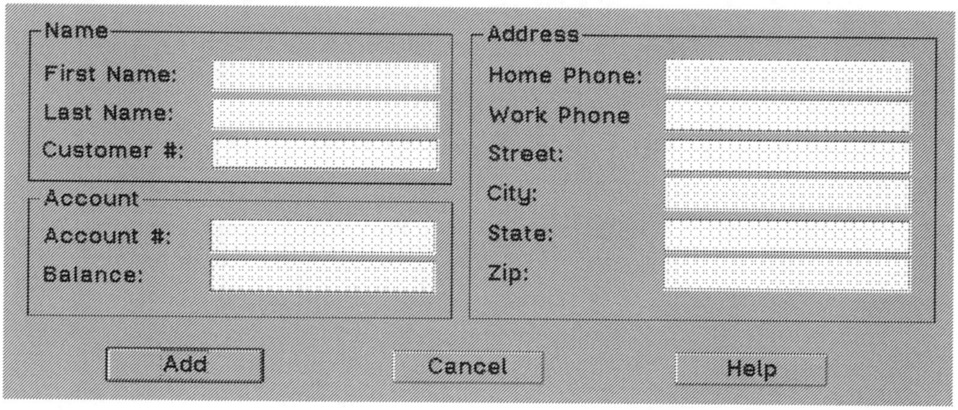

Figure 88. Composite view of the Customer object: the create view

As a final example of building a composite view, we consider list views. Assuming we have a view that displays a list of existing objects, the list view typically displays only a subset of the attributes for each object. The list view allows us to perform operations on any of the selected objects. The typical operations are

- Open: View all attributes of the object and, if required, update the object
- Delete: Remove the object from the list
- Add: Add a new object to the list
- Find: Find an existing object through a Find dialog

Figure 89 shows an example of a list view.

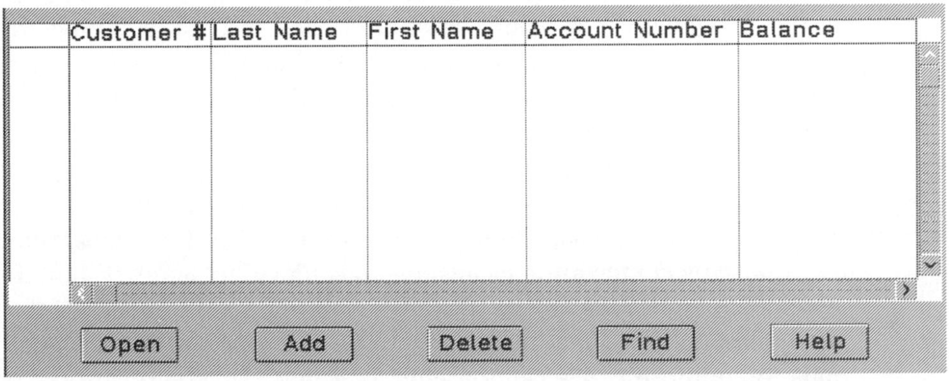

Customer #	Last Name	First Name	Account Number	Balance

Open   Add   Delete   Find   Help

Figure 89. List view of the Customer object

An application's GUI is constructed from a combination of such visual components. Figure 90 shows a final GUI developed for the FCE application.

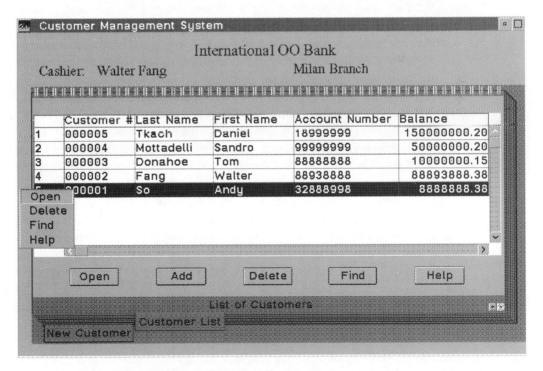

Figure 90. FCE application GUI: a list of customers

6.4.1 Reuse of Visual Classes

The object-oriented environment provides two ways for reuse of functionality at the design and code level: class inheritance and object composition.

The class inheritance mechanism is used to define the implementation of a class in terms of another [GAM95]; this entails using an extant class hierarchy and reusing the services provided by the superclasses. Reuse by subclasses can be called open reuse because the internal structure of the superclass is open and visible to the subclasses. In the literature, reuse by inheritance is frequently called white-box reuse, although *white* does not imply transparence.

Reuse by composition means that to achieve the required functionality, we assemble or compose objects that have well-defined interfaces. If the interfaces are adequately defined, the designer does not need to know the object internals to compose it. We can therefore call reuse by composition closed reuse. In the literature, reuse by composition is also known as black-box reuse.

Delegation is a way of using composition to achieve the same effect as inheritance, and in fact, it is an elegant way of avoiding the use of multiple inheritance. In delegation, two objects are involved in handling a request for services; the receiving object delegates the servicing of the request to the second object.

To show how delegation can replace multiple inheritance, assume that we want to build a model for university teaching assistant: a student who teaches. In a multiple inheritance design, there would be a class Teacher and a class Student, and the class TeachingAssistant would inherit from both. With delegation, TeachingAssistant can inherit from the most important source of functional characteristics, say Teacher, but acquire Student behavior by keeping a Student instance variable and delegating the student behavior to it. Therefore, instead of the TeachingAssistant being a Student (an Is-a relationship), it is a Teacher who has-a Student inside.

In a visual programming environment such as VisualAge, we can reuse a visual class by adding it as a subcomponent to the component. This is reuse by composition or delegation. When the subcomponent class is changed, the component will pick up all the changes, including any visual programming changes.

A visual class can also be created by subclassing it from another visual class, thus reusing the language-specific code by inheritance. Because the mechanism used is class inheritance, all instance data, such as attribute settings, are not inherited.

As a rule of thumb for visual classes, the visual programming environment encourages reuse by delegation, that is, adding the visual class as a subcomponent. Reuse by inheritance is more suitable for nonvisual classes.

6.5 Summary

In this chapter, we illustrated how VMT brings about a straightforward transformation from object model to code with the help of visual programming tools such as IBM VisualAge. VisualAge nonvisual parts represent object model classes and their relationship, whereas visual parts form necessary user interfaces. Furthermore, design decisions are easily verified in the working solution, and any necessary changes due to implementation can be directly updated in the design model. Such a consistent representation from modeling to coding satisfies user requirements better, reduces maintenance effort, provides greater extensibility, and facilitates reuse.

7

Case Study: Designing the Foreign Currency Exchange System

This chapter describes the design phase of the foreign currency exchange (FCE) application. It shows the creation of the work products of this phase of the application life cycle, including architectures, diagrams, and models. The implemented FCE solution is detailed in Appendix B.

7.1 System Design

Figure 91 shows the initial partitioning and layering of the FCE application as a result of decomposing the object model into five subsystems. They are then mapped to VisualAge applications when implementing with VisualAge for Smalltalk. The four subsystems—Currency Management, Stock Management, Customer Management, and Order Management—are the result of partitioning the object model based on functionality. All common support services, including data base accesses for persistent objects, are grouped in the Common Support Components subsystem. Although not shown here, we can apply the partitioning and layering technique to divide these initial subsystems further into fine-grain subsystems to accommodate various design considerations.

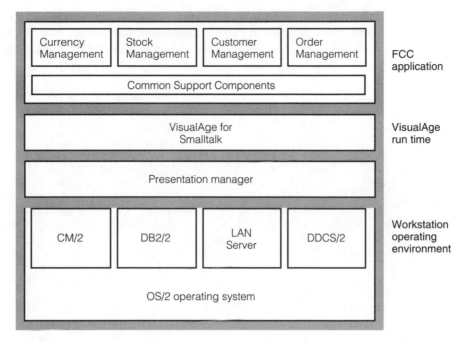

Figure 91. Application architecture

Figure 92 shows the high-level interactions among the five subsystems. These five subsystems represent the major functions of the FCE application.

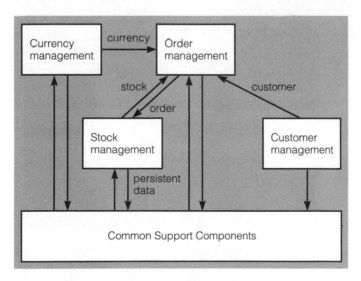

Figure 92. Subsystems interaction diagram

Figure 93 shows the system architecture of the FCE application. In this example, we use a simplified configuration that consists of two OS/2 workstations, one for the client workstation and one as the bank database server. The client and server workstations are connected in a LAN environment.

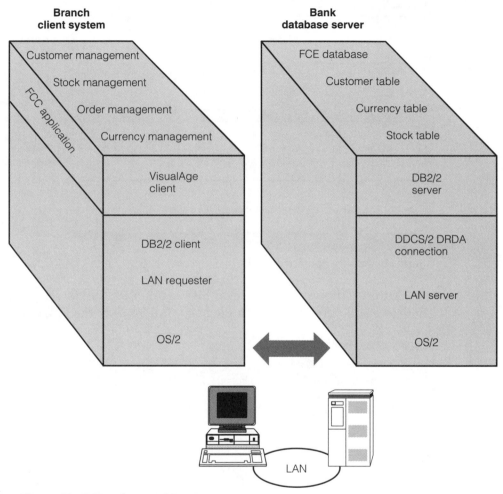

Figure 93. FCE system architecture

7.2 **Object Design**

Figure 94 presents the refined object model for the Order Management subsystem that was used as the blueprint for designing the VisualAge public interfaces for each object within the subsystem. In addition to the semantic objects we identified in the analysis phase, user interface objects, such as OrderManagementView, OrderNewView, and OrderItemView, as well as services objects, such as OrderHandler, were added in this design level object model.

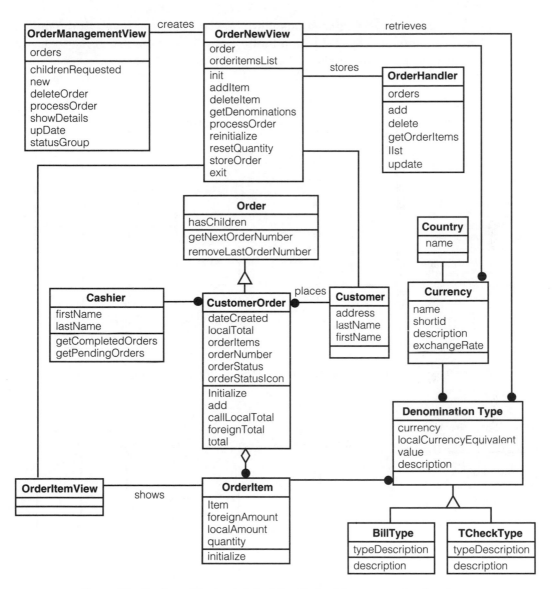

Figure 94. Design object model of the Order Management subsystem

As we explained earlier, one of the object design activities is to determine the derived attributes. As an example, refer to the object model, the localTotal is a primary attribute of the CustomerOrder class, while foreignTotal is a method used to derive the derived attribute of the same name.

To model the user interactions with the view objects as well as the model objects, we created object interaction diagrams for order entry of in-stock and out-of-stock scenarios, as shown in Figures 95 and 96.

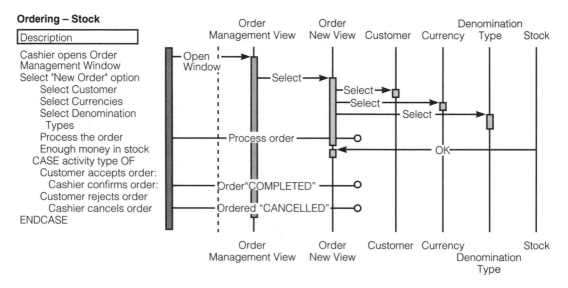

Figure 95. Object interaction diagram for the in-stock order entry scenario

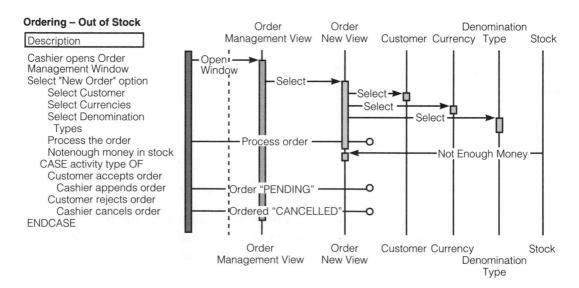

Figure 96. Object interaction diagram for the out-of-stock order entry scenario

Similarly, the refined object model for the Customer Management subsystem (Figure 97) contains the interface objects, model objects, and services objects for the Customer Management subsystem.

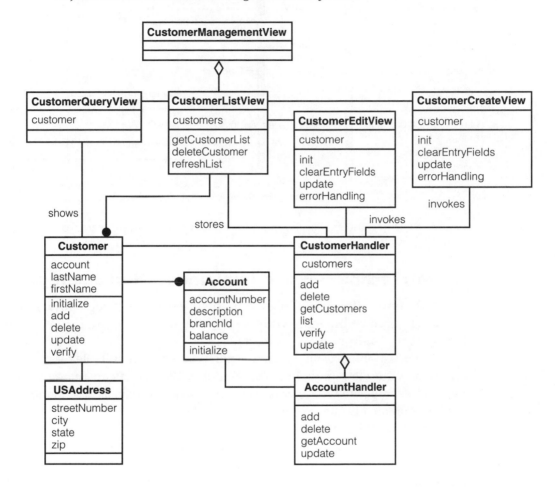

Figure 97. Design object model of the Customer Management subsystem

One of the design activities is to model the user interactions through the view objects. As an example, we show the customer information update scenario in Figure 98 on page 170. In this example, a cashier user invokes the CustomerManagementView, which will list all customers handled by this cashier in the contained CustomerListView. The cashier can then select a particular customer from the customer list to query the detail customer information, or to update information pertaining to the customer. The cashier can also invoke the CustomerCreateView, which is a template, to create a new customer.

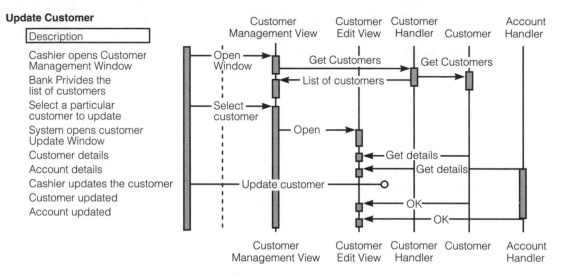

Figure 98. Object interaction diagram for the customer update scenario

7.3 Design Techniques and Implementation Strategies

The FCE application was designed following two key design guidelines: to adopt a layered architecture with view-model-data segregation, and to apply the construction-from-parts paradigm.

VisualAge supports model-view separation which is suitable for our design approach with view-model-data segregation. We can encapsulate the model objects in composite view components. All business logic and validation rules are implemented in the model (nonvisual) classes.

Let us examine the view-model-data segregation design approach we applied in the FCE application more closely. As it can be seen in Figure 97 on page 169, for the Customer management subsystem, the views include: CustomerManagementView, CustomerListView, CustomerQueryView, CustomerCreateView, and CustomerEditView. These views can then be implemented as VisualAge visual parts. The model objects include: Customer, Account, and USAddress. The data access objects are: CustomerHandler, and AccountHandler. The model and data access objects are implemented as VisualAge nonvisual parts. Separating the VisualAge parts this way helps to make the designed visual parts with fewer connections, and the resulting application more flexible to changes and easier to maintain. For example, future changes in the data base used would only affect the data access parts without affecting the view or model parts.

In Section 5.4, we discussed the design of data access parts. We now take a closer look at the CustomerHandler data access part as an example. Figure 99 shows how we use the VisualAge composition editor to compose the CustomerHandler. VisualAge enables us to construct a nonvisual part visually using its composition editor. By encapsulating the data base access behavior in this single part, we isolate potential changes that could affect the model object, Customer, from future data base changes.

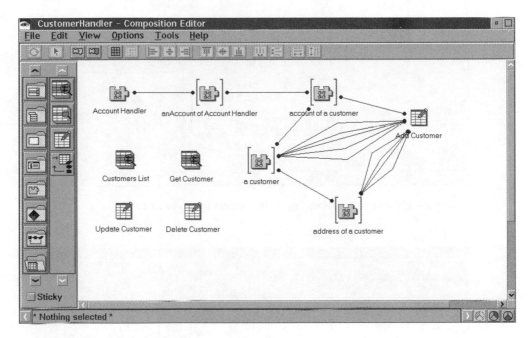

Figure 99. Compose the Customer Handler

Figure 100 on page 172 through Figure 102 on page 173 illustrate the public interface and the scripts for the CustomerHandler part.

In Section 6.4, page 159, we have illustrated the "construction from parts" approach. To apply this construction-from-parts design approach we made the following design decisions in the solution for the FCE application:

- Use the metaphor of containers and forms as the common user interface style.

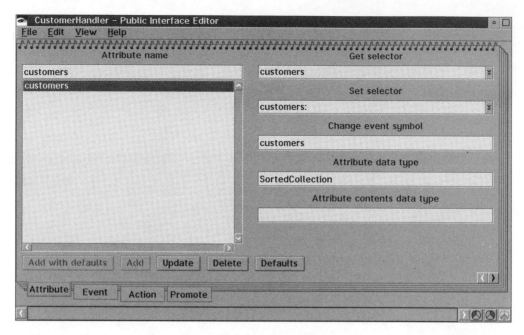

Figure 100. CustomerHandler public interface (one of two)

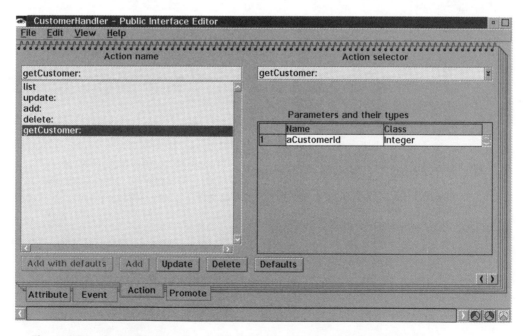

Figure 101. CustomerHandler public interface (two of two)

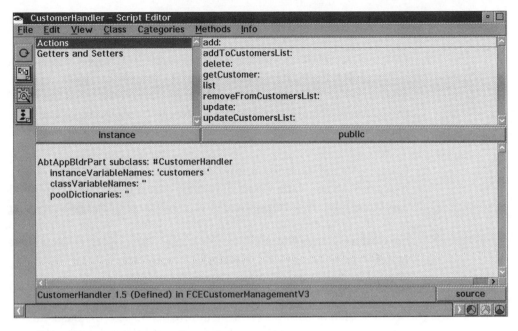

Figure 102. CustomerHandler scripts

- Use consistent selection styles across different subsystems to minimize relearning. Use the notebook control and notebook page to provide access to an object instead of the conventional pull-down menu. Use the context menu to choose an operation on an object. Use push buttons as an alternative.

- Design for maximum reuse and simplicity of connection. If, for instance, there are more than ten connections or ten subcomponents (or both) on the composition editor (that is, we have a complex component structure), it is advantageous to create a composite component to encapsulate some of the components and connections. The goal is to provide a public interface that should be easy and natural to use with visual programming.

The public interface for a part should be kept as simple as possible. As a rule of thumb, we try to have not more than three attributes, three events, and three actions in each VisualAge view part (not including the superclass external interfaces such as openWidget). For example, CustomerEditView would have only one attribute, aCustomer, and one event, CustomerChangeRequested. The actual editing of input data, updating of the customer record database, and so forth are encapsulated inside the component and transparent to the user of the component. The event is a postcondition event to be used to trigger other actions as a result of this event. Another example is CashierStockListView, which has two attributes, aCashier and selectedStockItem.

We then adopted the following implementation strategies to facilitate contruction-from-parts: For each nonvisual class (base object), we

- Create a visual class for displaying the object (primary display view) using Quick Form, or manually lay out the user interface. Look for any additional visual classes (alternative display views) that are required to assemble the final user interface. Add the nonvisual class as a variable subcomponent and add it as an attribute to the public interface of this visual class.

- Create a visual class for editing existing objects of the base class (primary edit view). This visual class may use the primary display view as a subcomponent or implement it as a subclass of the primary display view. To provide editing capability, the deferred update component can be used as a subcomponent in this class. The apply action will be triggered by a NoError event resulting from a verify action. Input data should be validated, and any necessary external events should be defined to the system.

- Create a visual class for creating a new object for this base class (primary create view). This may be identical to the primary edit view in some cases. Use the primary edit view as a subcomponent, or implement it as a subclass. In addition, use the object factory or our object cloner component to provide object template capability. (The ObjectFactory class creates new objects; it does not copy an object's attributes at any sublevel. We created our own ObjectCloner class that provides a DeepCopy capability.)

- Create a visual class for displaying a list of objects. Define any necessary external events.

For each subsystem, we create visual classes as defined in the analysis prototype and construct the view by using the various visual classes created in the first part as building blocks. These are the interfaces users will employ in the application. Define any necessary external interfaces that can then be used for the construction of the main application window.

Please refer to Section 6.4 on page 159 for the examples of the views created and reused in the Customer management subsystem. More examples can also be found in Appendix B at the end of this book.

7.4 Designing for Object Persistence Using a Relational Database

This section presents the process of transforming part of the object model into a data model in the form of an entity-relationship diagram (ERD). This ERD will later be the basis of implementing object persistence in a relational database.

Database design can start in parallel with object design when we have a fairly good understanding of the base objects in the system, the base attributes of those objects, and the services that the objects provide.

The following section describes how to map the object model to a relational database design.

7.4.1 Developing An ERD from the Object Model

We begin with the object model shown in Figure 26 on page 48. We perform the following tasks to map the object model to a relational database design:

1. Select an initial subsystem to design.

2. Identify the base entities from the object model.

3. Examine object relationships.

4. Map object relationships to entity relationships.

5. Add new entities and relationships.

6. Examine ERD and object model relationship types.

7. Make design decisions based on relationship types.

8. Translate the ERD to a database implementation model.

9. Review changes and validate the design.

Although the database design process is presented here as a sequence of steps, the process is actually iterative. The following sections give details on each step of the process.

Selecting A Subsystem

We choose a subsystem to work with for two reasons: to get a small and controllable start on the design process and to integrate database design with object design.

If possible, we want to start with an isolated subsystem that would lean toward a simplified test case implementation. Usually this simplifies the initial design effort. Also, a good understanding of the design basics can enhance discussions throughout later iterations as the object model becomes more complex. In database design terminology, consider the selected subsystem as the external schema for a single application.

We start with the Stock Management subsystem, which is shown in the lower portion of Figure 26 on page 48. This subsystem contains the group of classes that pertain to stock for our first database design iteration:

- Stock
- DenominationType
- CashierDrawer
- BranchReserve
- StockItem

Identifying Entities

Each class in the selected subsystem of the object model must map to an entity in the ERD, as shown in Figure 103. In the top part of the figure, both Stock and DenominationType map to an individual entity. The attributes for each class also map directly to the entity.

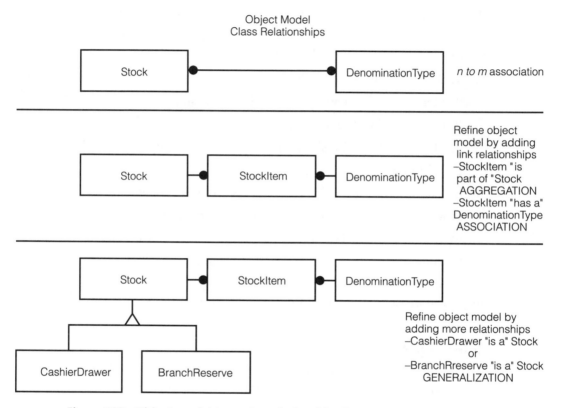

Figure 103. Object model to entity-relationship diagram

Examining Object Relationships

Objects in the object model are related to one another through aggregation (which implies a part-of or consists-of relationship), generalization (which implies an is-a relationship between the subclasses), or association (which implies a has-a relationship between objects), as shown in the middle portion of Figure 103.

The multiplicity of associations falls into the following categories:

- Zero-to-one
- One-to-one

- Zero-to-many
- One-to-many
- Many-to-many.

The inverses of these relationships are also considered valid.

Database design rules differ significantly based on the multiplicity of the association. This is key to understanding and properly transferring the object model into an ERD.

Mapping Object Relationships to Entity Relationships

The focus of relationship mapping is to accurately capture the object relationships and reflect them in the ERD. The relationship between Stock and DenominationType shown in Figure 26 on page 48 illustrates this point. Since the relationship described is many-to-many, database design rules dictate that we build a new entity. StockItem can be referred to as an associative entity because it reflects the many-to-many association between the classes. The middle section of Figure 103 on page 176 shows the creation of the new StockItem entity and the adjustment of the relationships among the entities. A single object model relationship has now been translated into multiple ERD relationships.

In some respects, mapping object relationships is similar to mapping basic entity model relationships.

Next we examine the ERD to be sure that we have captured the object model classes and relationships.

Adding New Entities and Relationships to the ERD

We have now added several new entities to our ERD. These are Stock, Denomination, and the new associative entity, StockItem. We have changed the relationship between Stock and Denomination. The many-to-many relationship is now one-to-many between both Stock and StockItem and Denomination and StockItem. In effect, we have completed the mapping of the class associations in the object model to the ERD.

Examining Relationship Types

All models are subject to scrutiny. At this point it is the designer's role to scrutinize the ERD, review the object model, and ensure that the classes and the underlying relationships are directly reflected in the ERD (see Figure 26 on page 48). We have not yet captured the relationship among CashierDrawer, BranchReserve, and Stock in the ERD. This is a generalization relationship that implies inheritance and is somewhat like a supertype and subtype in data modeling terms. In object modeling, however, generalization implies much more than a supertype and subtype relationship, it implies both attribute and behavioral inheritance.

Figure 104 shows the relationships among Stock, CashierDrawer, and BranchReserve that needs closer examination. Each branch has many cashier drawers and one branch reserve. Thus, the stock in a branch is made up of all the stocked currencies in the cashier drawers and the branch reserve stock. In addition, we can say that CashierDrawer is a kind of Stock, and BranchReserve is also a kind of Stock. Thus we have identified a generalization relationship. For relational database design, we can replicate the common attributes of the stock class in the CashDrawer and BranchStock subclasses and remove the Stock table.

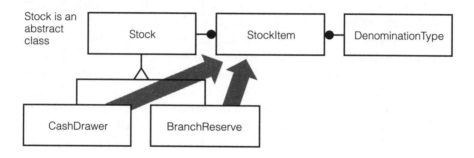

Assumed:
–exclusive or (XOR) relationship between CashierDrawer
  and BranchReserve
–replicated static attributes

Figure 104. Object Model to Table Mapping: Sample implementation of generation

An accurate ERD demands that we identify each class (Stock, Cashier-Drawer, and BranchReserve) as an entity. The ERD can also use supertype and subtype relations that capture the data relationship. As described in Chapter 4, we can identify basically four choices for physically implementing a generalization relationship:

- Each class is a table (Stock, CashierDrawer, BranchReserve).
- Only the subclasses are tables (CashierDrawer, BranchReserve)
- Only the superclass is a table (Stock).
- Each class is a table, and the relationship is a table.

From a theoretical point of view, the first choice is optimal. When each class is reflected as a table, normalization rules can be followed easily, and we know there are model extensibility advantages. From an implementation view, we may have added complexity to the data manipulation language (DML) for application developers.

From an implementation perspective, the second choice *may* be the best choice. However, there are disadvantages. Collapsing supertype attributes into subtypes can violate third normal form. Also, replicated data is introduced and can result in insert and update anomalies. We should look for opportunities to collapse supertype attributes, but this is a general-rule implementation.

Figure 103 on page 176 shows how we modeled and then implemented the generalization relationship. Although Stock was the superclass in the relationship, it was never instantiated. The data resided in the subtypes or subclasses, CashierDrawer and BranchReserve. Because of these factors, we eliminated this table from the physical design and replicated the attributes of stock in the subclass tables.

Implementing this generalization relationship broke a data-modeling design rule. The primary key of CashierDrawer and the primary key of BranchReserve serve as table identifiers *and* as identifiers of the subtype or subclass. Hence, we have added further meaning to the composite primary key of the StockItem table. This could cause problems, particularly in the extensibility of the preliminary design. However, for implementation elegance, the option was perceived as very attractive. As with all design decisions, there are trade-offs. The trade-off here was either to add meaning to the keys of a table or implement a redundant entity. We chose the former.

The third choice, collapsing the subtypes into the supertype, is a poor implementation alternative. This will usually break normalization rules and provide insert, update, and delete anomalies. As a result, entity modeling functions, data and relationship analysis, normalization, and domain integrity can be defeated.

Making Design Decisions

Our design decisions are based on the assumption that the case study application is the sole database user. Security and performance have not been directly addressed in this test environment.

Implementing the ERD

Converting an object model to an ERD and to the subsequent database implementation requires design rigor. The differences between an object-oriented environment and a relational environment are many. With a relational database implementation, the major difference is in designing and implementing generalization relationships. Although the relationship is new to database administrators, the design requirements are the same: concurrency, security, data integrity, recoverability, and performance.

Reviewing Changes and Validating the Design

In this step, we review modifications in the design according to requirement changes. The ability to reflect changes in object-oriented applications quickly is the greatest advantage of moving into object-oriented technology. The crucial information required to determine design and implementation adequacy lies in the implementation-specific results. Testing, with sound test case development and test case feedback, is a crucial source of information. But as practitioners know, there is no better feedback than production results. There is no "silver bullet" in object-oriented applications with relational databases. Analysis, design, and testing rigor are required. Tools to complete these functions should become more prevalent in the market as more and more organizations begin adopting and adapting to the object-oriented application development environment.

7.5 Refining the Object Model Using Design Patterns

After developing a working FCE application, we explore some design considerations to provide flexibility in future changes and subsystem placement, and to achieve better reuse through generalization.

Thus, in refining the object model, the focus is on

- Looking for class structure and potential reuse
- Building an expanded functional prototype
- Looking at system architecture alternatives

These design considerations suggest a refined object model, as shown in Figure 105. A comparison of this revised object model with the previous one, as shown in Figure 34 on page 71 indicates that a recursive aggregation pattern is used for the composite-component classes, StockComposite-StockComponent and BankComposite-BankComponent. This means that the BankComponent class is a new abstract class that represents the common data and behaviors of Cashier, Branch, and Bank. BankComposite is a subclass of BankComponent and represents common data and behaviors of Branch and Bank. BankComposite can contain many instances of BankComponent (recursive aggregation), so it is a general way to represent a composite class. This recursive aggregation generalizes the aggregation of many cashiers in a branch and many branches in a bank. In a similar way, we define a new composite-component subhierarchy to optimize the definition of stock and reserve.

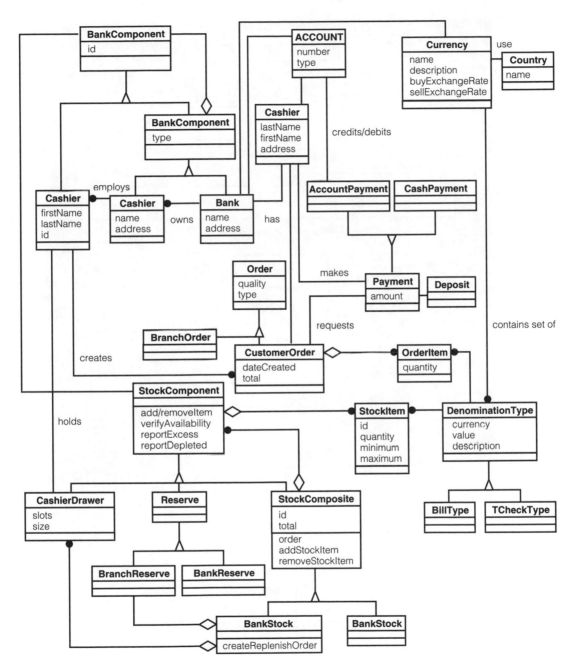

Figure 105. Refined FCE object model

Figure 106 on page 182 compares two subgraphs, one with recursive aggre-gation, as used in the new object model, and one with explicit aggregation, as defined earlier in the unrefined object model.

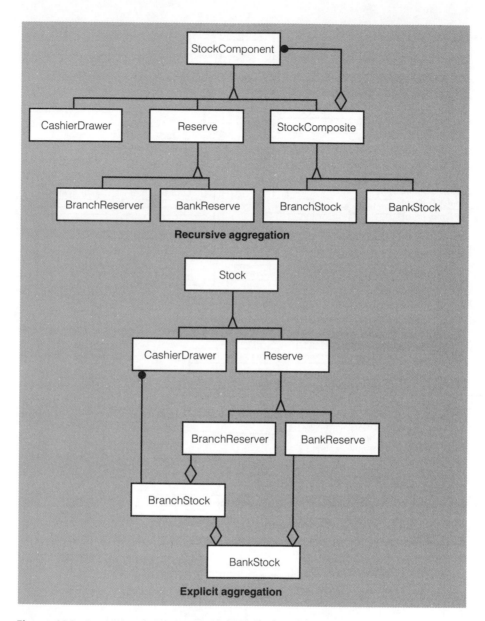

Figure 106. Recursive aggregation and explicit aggregation

The advantages of refining the object model with the recursive design pattern are

- Deeper inheritance: Less coding is needed for the methods of the lower-level classes.
- Flexibility: We can represent different object structures (a Branch that contains another Branch, for example) and easily arrange modification on the bank organization structure, as by adding a new subclass to Composite.

New abstract classes can be used in new contexts. However, overgeneralization can cause weakness in some semantic constraints (a Branch can contain a Bank), so some work is needed to create and manage object instances correctly at run time. This weakness is usually solved by adding new attributes to the classes to represent new associations, but that can make the object model structure too complex. In general, we can state that design optimization in the object model tends to produce a deeper hierarchy and to gain advantages from inheritance during implementation, but it often results in a more restrictive (and sometimes complex) object model.

7.6 Summary

This chapter describes aspects of the design of the FCE Application. It shows how design and implementation are interrelated. The design aspects described are applied to model and view components of a subsystem, as well as to the implementation of databases to store persistent object data. The use of a design pattern is also presented to exemplify design refinements.

VMT and Distributed Objects

8

Object Technology and Distributed Systems

The computing industry is embarking on one of the most drastic technological transformations of the decade: the transition from a traditional computing infrastructure to a new distributed object computing infrastructure. This shift must be taken into account in developing business applications.

This chapter reviews the main concepts used in distributed systems and client/server computing. We explain the benefits and challenges in developing distributed applications and how object technology can play a significant role in developing this new breed of distributed object applications.

8.1 Distributed Systems

A distributed system is a collection of autonomous computers connected by some type of network. Distributed systems offer a number of advantages over single-processor systems:

- Several computing elements are available in the system. If an application is decomposed into pieces that run concurrently, the application will run faster and yield more throughput.

- When several computers are used, fewer users are competing for resources on any one of them than when there is only a single computer. This reduces contention and minimizes the increase in response time during peak hours.

- Overall availability can be higher because the computers that constitute the distributed system have independent failure characteristics. By making redundant copies of hardware and software resources, it is possible to ensure that the failure of any single computer affects a reduced number of users. Availability of critical data can be ensured by replicating the data at server nodes.

- Distributed systems improve scalability. In addition, the total system can be configured with great flexibility. Nodes can be:

  —Added to or removed from the network.

  —Reconfigured to meet changing requirements. For example, disks can be moved from one node to another, data can be moved from one node to another, and data can be replicated at several nodes.

  —Made more or less powerful. For instance, a node can be replaced by a multiprocessor node to increase its processing power.

The flexibility offered by distributed systems is in sharp contrast to the limited change possibilities of traditional centralized computing.

The client/server computing model is widely used in a distributed system. The model defines two separate parts of a client/server application (see Figure 107 on page 188):

- The client (for example, an application running on a workstation) calls for services, such as data or processing services.

- The server performs these services on behalf of the calling client program.The server can be a program located on the same machine as the client, or it can run on a remote machine or even a different operating system from that of the client machine.

In the client/server computing model, the client application does not need to distinguish between local and remote services. The programming complexities of network distribution are transparent to the client application, regardless of whether they are handled by the called service or the calling mechanism. Thus the client application need not care about the location of services or the interconnection media.

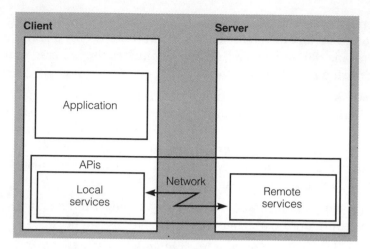

Figure 107. Client/server computing model

The client/server computing model facilitates resource sharing. A server can, for instance, provide access to data that resides on fast disks. It can improve data access further by using large cache buffers in memory. These expensive resources are made available to many client applications through client/server computing.

8.2 Approaches to Building Distributed Systems

Of the many approaches to building distributed systems, the following are the most common:

- Distributed operating system: A distributed operating system provides the programmer with a single-system image. A program running on top of a distributed operating system sees a collection of resources and services that it can use without any concern for whether the resources and services are actually available at the node at which the program is running. The advantage of this approach to writing distributed applications is that the effort of dealing with distribution has to be made only once, when the operating system is written. The disadvantage is that a distributed operating system requires the operating systems at different nodes to be homogeneous.

- Network operating system: In a network operating system, each node runs an independent operating system. Each operating system, however, provides a network interface, which application programs can use to communicate with other nodes. Because the network interface is supported "on top" of the operating system, this approach accommodates heterogeneous operating systems and processors. The IBM CICS product family is an example of a network operating system.

- Distributed file system: In a distributed file system, a node can mount a file system from another node at boot time or on request. In this way, the node has access to the remote file system. The disadvantage of this approach is that each application program has to deal with issues of distribution, indicating the node where the requested file resides.

- Distributed programming language: The programming language implementation of the run-time system is responsible for dealing with distribution issues. If the abstraction of nodes and remote resources is provided in the programming language, the application can access remote resources directly. Alternatively, the programming language can try to make the network transparent, much as a distributed operating system does. The advantage of this approach is that the language can be implemented on different operating systems and therefore can support a network of heterogeneous processors. The disadvantage is that it is complex to design such a language. Examples are IBM's Distributed Smalltalk, VisualAge Distributed Feature, and HP's Distributed Smalltalk.

- Distributed programming toolkit: The distributed programming toolkit approach is somewhere between a network operating system and a distributed programming language. It provides a library (toolkit) of routines that aid in writing distributed applications. These routines provide mechanisms for communication, synchronization, failure detection, and recovery. This approach is at a higher level of abstraction than the network operating system but below that of the distributed programming language approach. When there is no single appropriate abstraction for distributed programming, the toolkit approach is appealing. Examples are IBM's Distributed System Object Model (DSOM), Open System Foundation's (OSF) Distributed Computing Environment (DCE) Remote Procedure Call (RPC), and Sun's Network Computing System (NCS).

We focus mainly on the distributed programming toolkit and the distributed programming language approaches to distribution.

8.3 Challenges In Building Distributed Systems

Distributed systems present useful functional capabilities. However, their implementation presents many challenges, such as handling the following situations:

- Partial and independent failures: Because parts of an application run on different computers, it is possible that some parts will fail while others keep going, which leads to inconsistent states of the program. The application developer or administrator must be able to cope with such partial failures, possibly stopping the still-functioning parts of the application and undoing some of their earlier effects. A typical example occurs when money is debited from an account on one computer for deposit to an account on another computer. If the computer responsible for the deposit fails, what should be done with the money already removed from the source account?

- Concurrent and independent events: Many things that can be assumed in a single-processor environment do not apply to a distributed environment, where independent computing entities are active. A common way of ensuring atomicity of an action, such as updating shared data, is to apply a lock, make the update, and then release the lock to reenable the update possibility. This approach may lead to many performance problems in a distributed system. Overall, controlling access to shared resources is more difficult in a distributed computing environment.

- Site autonomy: There is a trade-off between making each node independent and integrating it into a single system. The advantage of having independent nodes is that users can continue to use the system even if other nodes fail. The disadvantage is that sharing and cooperation are harder to achieve. Integrating all nodes into one single system not only facilitates sharing and cooperation among users but allows one node to back up another. However, if too much interdependence is introduced, failure of one node may affect the rest of the system and its users. The extent of site autonomy can be determined by examining the impact on the rest of the system and its users when taking one machine off the network.

- Heterogeneity: The advantage of using distributed systems can be clearly recognized when the nodes on the network are different from one another, allowing applications to use the most appropriate nodes for each function they perform. However, integrating nodes with different system configurations, such as heterogeneous processors, operating systems, or programming languages, is challenging.

- Security: Application developers must recognize that the geographical distribution of nodes in a distributed system introduces security risks that do not exist with a single central system locked in a computer room. The OSF DCE is one approach to providing security for a distributed system environment.

8.4 Data and Function Placement

In designing distributed systems, a key consideration is the placement and distribution of data and processing functions. Another is how to share and manage data to ensure its integrity. A third, equally important consideration is the placement of the control and processing functions in the distributed systems to achieve optimal resource utilization and to maximize overall system performance.

We discuss the basic strategies for data and function distribution in the sections that follow.

8.4.1 Data Distribution

Data in a distributed environment can be managed through centralization, replication, or partitioning:

- Centralized data management: The data is placed at one node, and all access to that data is routed to that node.

- Replicated data management: Copies of data are made at various nodes. The nodes needing data can access the closest node.

- Partitioned data management: The data is partitioned into pieces that are placed at various nodes. Access to the data must be routed to the appropriate node according to which piece of the data is being accessed.

These three techniques of data management in a distributed environment apply equally well to the management of processing and control functions.

Centralized Data

Consider the case of workstations connected on a local area network, as shown in Figure 108. For authentication purposes, a list of users is kept at a central location, such as a server computer that all client workstations can access.

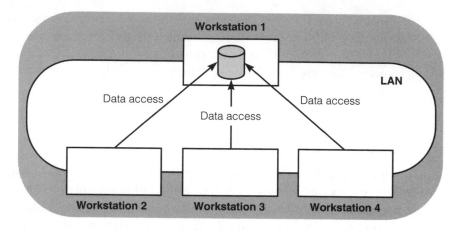

Figure 108. Centralized data management

The advantage of centralized data management is that, by maintaining a single copy of the data, changes to the data can be applied in one place. The disadvantage is that every access to the data from a client workstation requires a message between the client and the server; thus it may cause excess network traffic and performance bottleneck. Furthermore, if the server is nonoperational, all client workstations requiring the data are affected. Thus there are both performance and availability disadvantages in a centralized data approach.

Replicated Data

A circumvention of the problem of centralized data management is to have copies, or replicas, of the data files at multiple nodes, as shown in Figure 109.

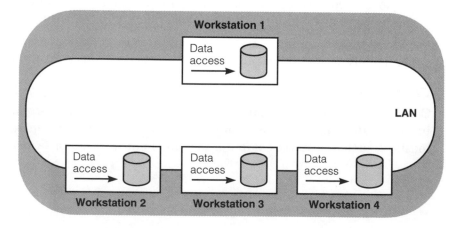

Figure 109. Replicated data management

Having multiple copies solves both the performance and availability problems. The performance problem is solved because access to the data file is made locally and not remotely. The availability problem is solved because it is easier to find an available copy of the required data file when several copies exist. In addition, concurrent accesses from multiple client workstations improve throughput.

The disadvantage of replicated copies is the new problem (and cost) of ensuring the consistency of the replicated data. There are many different ways of solving the consistency problem. The level of difficulty and the performance of the algorithm depend on the relative ratio of read operations to write operations against the replicated data.

One way to ensure consistency of replicated data is to lock all copies when an update is attempted. Only after all copies have been locked will an update to the file be allowed. The update is then propagated to the different copies. This approach decreases the amount of concurrency, however, because logins are not allowed during locking and propagating of the update. The basic trade-off in replication techniques is to support the highest amount of concurrency while providing the highest availability of up-to-date data.

Partitioned Data

Instead of replicating the data file, another approach to solving the performance and availability problems of centralized data management is to partition or distribute the contents of the file, as shown in Figure 110).

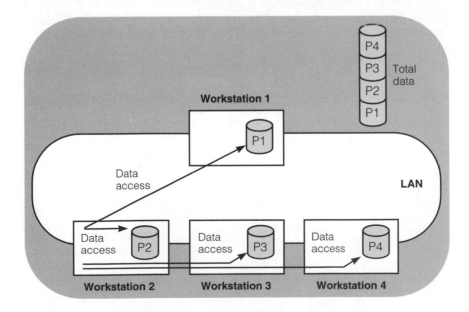

Figure 110. Partitioned data management

For a network of ten workstations, we could partition the data file into ten files, each *one-tenth of the total in size.* The collection would be "the data file." This solution provides some performance improvement because user authentication is likely to be distributed throughout the network rather than through a single node. This approach also improves availability because the unavailability of any single node prevents only a fraction of the users from accessing the data. As for data replication, there is some overhead at both data retrieval and update time. The correct partition to address data retrieval and update needs has to be determined. One possible way to partition the data is to have the data located near the nodes where it will be used most often. A typical example is a distributed database of bank accounts, where the account information database is partitioned according to the geographical location of the account owner.

When a database is used for storing partitioned data, one can distinguish between horizontal and vertical partitioning. Horizontal partitioning distributes data among tables. Vertical partitioning is distribution within tables (for instance, a customer table is divided into tables containing contiguous sets of customers).

8.4.2 Function Distribution

Control and processing functions can be centralized, replicated, or partitioned in much the same way as data.

Centralized Processing

Processing of user requests of a required function of a service is centralized at a single node, as shown in Figure 111.

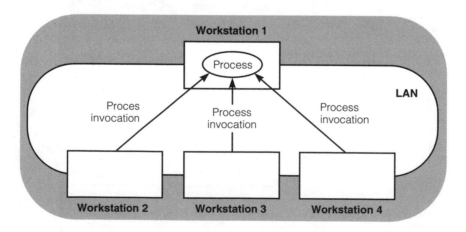

Figure 111. Centralized processing

Replicated Processing

In the replication approach to processing of user requests, a required service program is replicated in several nodes, as shown in Figure 112.

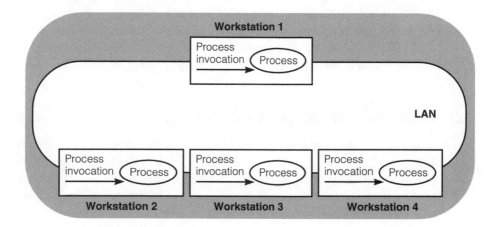

Figure 112. Replicated processing

Partitioned Processing

The processing of user requests of a required service is partitioned based on groupings of users or other criteria so that each node is capable of processing certain requests for services, as shown in Figure 113.

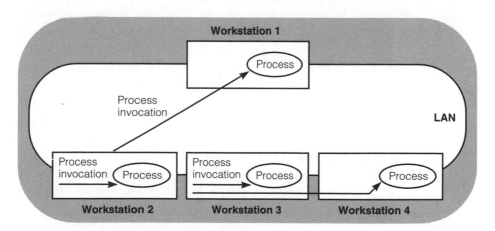

Figure 113. Partitioned processing

Process placement and data placement can be related. However, there are situations in which it is useful to consider replicating or partitioning processes independent of the data configurations. For example, in a database application, a single node could be designated to process all functions to minimize the problems of dealing with contention and locking; some nodes might be allowed to perform lookup requests while other nodes perform update requests. Also, we might consider replicating the function processing at several nodes to increase the concurrency handling capabilities of the system.

Functions and data are encapsulated in an object, therefore, the design considerations for object distribution are similar to those considerations in data and function distribution in traditional distributed systems.

8.5 Distributed Object Computing

Given the MIS trends toward distributed processing, developers must design their applications to run on networks of interconnected machines that share the processing load. Applications must make the best use of existing resources to meet the needs of business and to achieve performance, scalability, security, usability, and maintainability objectives.

MIS shops are also finding that the traditional client/server computing approach is inefficient. Typically, most of the application logic in a client/server environment is located on the client machines, with centralized or distributed database servers. This approach can lead to excessive network traffic and difficulty in maintenance. One solution to these problems is to put some of the application logic on the server, where it can access the data locally. This requires an approach that is much more flexible than the traditional client/server environment.

The new approach, called *distributed object computing,* has objects on the server as well as on the client machines. After all, object-oriented and client/server computing build on similar concepts: In client/server computing, the client requests a service, and the server fulfills that request; in object-oriented computing, the client (sender) object sends a message to request a service, and the server (receiver) object responds and acts on the message.

Distributed object computing allows developers to assemble applications from objects that run on disparate platforms distributed in a network. Objects communicate with each other through a message-passing mechanism. A given object may act as a server to some objects and, at the same time, as a client of other objects. Furthermore, these client and server objects may be on the same machine and even in the same business process.

Figure 114 shows the evolution of object-oriented implementation and indicates how it has moved into the client/server computing realm, primarily on the client side. Eventually, we will reach the situation represented by the rightmost configuration, in which objects are common to client and server alike.

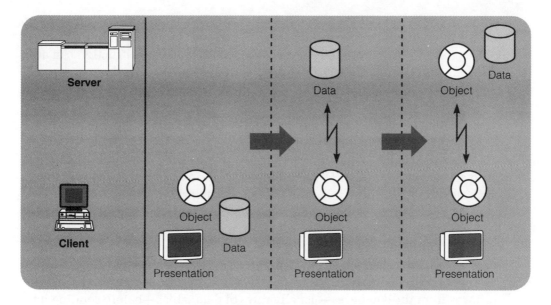

Figure 114. Evolution of object-oriented technology implementation

The benefits that object technology has brought to client programming can apply equally well to the server side. Perhaps most important is the ability to manage complexity and change. The multiuser requirements and available computing power on the server side introduce complexity, which can be handled with the help of object technology.

Encapsulation and reusability object technology also help to manage system changes. They enable server programmers to isolate changes and minimize maintenance costs. Close mapping between the problem and solution domains allows modeling the enterprise and then building of an implementation that ensures that changes are made quickly and correctly.

8.6 Distributed Object Applications

Three different types of applications are suitable for object distribution. These types of applications require the server to assume new roles as an *object server,* *active server,* or *peer application* in a distributed objects environment.

8.6.1 Object Server

As shown in Figure 115 on page 199, to avoid excessive network traffic, we could add processing functions in the server in addition to its traditional data access role. The server thus becomes an *object server.* Instead of using the SQL interface between the client and the server, the clients issue the request to the server objects. By constructing the requested objects at the server,[21] we can reduce the network traffic and improve the overall application performance. Letting the server perform the data massaging and object construction can also reduce the number of requests that the client needs to send to the server.

The most common client/server implementations use the *remote data access* style, in which all the business logic is on the client systems. These client systems become the so-called *fat* clients, accessing a remote relational database server.

Using distributed database approaches such as the Distributed Relational Database Architecture (DRDA), client workstations can access a centralized database through the SQL interface across the network. However, this approach can lead to excessive network traffic between the clients and the relational database server. This is especially true when we have to retrieve many intermediate results from the database server in order to accomplish one task on a client workstation.

In a fat client situation, the data server does not filter any information it retrieves from the databases—usually rows of data tables—before sending it to the client. Therefore it generates unnecessary network traffic.

One way to reduce the network traffic is to use *stored procedures* supported by many relational database products. A stored procedure is a named collection of SQL statements and procedural logic that is compiled, verified, and stored in the database server. Two problems with stored procedures is that they have no standard and they work for local databases only. Each relational database vendor has its own implementation. Therefore, if we want to use multiple databases from different vendors in a single client task, we cannot use stored procedures.

A side benefit of the object server model is that the relational database software does not have to be installed in the client workstations. In an operating environment with large numbers of clients, substantial savings can result from avoiding the database licensing cost for each client workstation.

8.6.2 Active Server

In a classical client/server computing model, it is always the client that originates requests. The server is *passive* in the sense that it only reacts to the client's requests. We can change the way the server behaves in this model so that the server is an active party in the system. The *active server* can process data by itself and initiate the communication with clients, for example, to notify a client of a change in the trading price of a common stock.

---

21 The client application objects send service requests to "proxy" or "surrogate" objects at the client side. The actual execution of the services takes place at the server, but the client application is not aware of this.

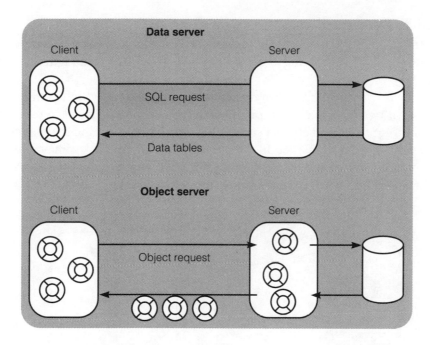

Figure 115. Object server application

Some database systems have programs that can be executed automatically. These programs are called *triggers*. Triggers are usually procedures that are stored on the server and are automatically executed based on data-related events. The difference between triggers and an active server is that triggers work on events originating from client actions; the server alone does not activate triggers.

One type of active server application is a publisher-subscriber scenario, in which the server publishes events, and clients subscribe to the events they are interested in. For example, in an active server environment, a stockbroker who is interested in the current prices of some specific shares asks the server for the available (published) share prices and then chooses (subscribes to) the stocks whose prices are needed.

Whenever the price for a subscribed stock changes, the subscribers are notified automatically. Figure 116 on page 200 shows this publisher-subscriber scenario.

Another example is an auction, in which the auctioneer is the active server that starts the event and keeps track of the bids. Clients can send their bids to the auctioneer server, which will hold the current highest bid price and the name of the client. All clients are notified whenever the situation changes.

8.6.3 Peer Application

In the peer application model, two client workstations communicate with each other directly, both acting as a server as well as a client (see Figure 117 on page 201).

In the classical client/server computing model, in which communication between two clients goes through the server, we would need to establish two concurrent sessions between each client and server, creating more overhead on the network and the server. In the peer application model, we have direct communication between the two clients. Clients are able to establish the connection whenever they want, without going through a server.

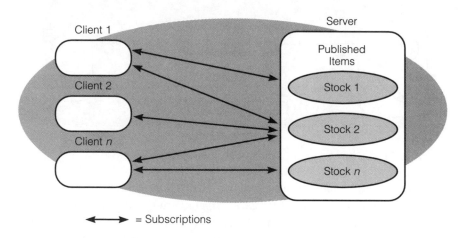

Figure 116. Publisher-subscriber scenario

Peer application design can be useful, for example, when two users on different client workstations need to establish a session for consultation or negotiation on a certain subject.

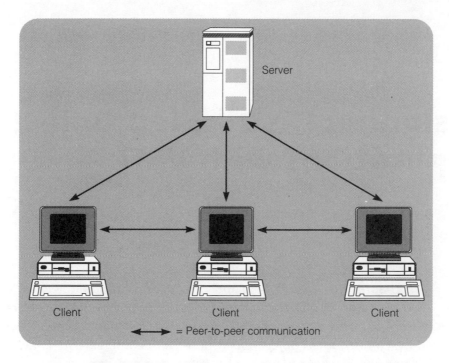

Figure 117. Peer application scenario

8.7 Summary

Object technology is especially suitable for building flexible distributed systems with high availability. Distributed programming languages such as IBM's Distributed Smalltalk, and distributed programming toolkits such as IBM's SOMobjects, can be used for building such a system. True distributed object computing enables an object to reside on the server instead of having to reside in the client, so that the server performs a portion of the business logic rather than only acting as the database server. A distributed system often requires different kinds of data management, control, and processing. Partition and replication are two common strategies to complement the traditional centralized approach.

9

Designing Distributed Object Applications with VMT

This chapter describes how to apply the VMT methodology when designing distributed object applications. It discusses general design considerations for distributed object applications and aspects of the development environment in which distributed object applications can be implemented, including considerations of what objects can be distributed and how.

To develop a distributed object application we start by developing and testing the application locally in nondistributed form. Once we have verified that the overall logic of the nondistributed application works correctly, we can then distribute the application and start testing and tuning the distributed version.

During the design of object distribution, several sources help to decide how to divide the classes among the different object spaces to which the application will be distributed. The following are some examples:

- Requirements specification: The customer may specify organizational or other requirements that affect the distribution of objects.

- Use cases: They may show the new locations of the actors and which use cases will run on which workstation types.

- Design: Includes system and application design. Defines how some subsystems should be mapped only into certain object spaces for organizational or other reasons. Also, the designer will require system environment information, such as the platform on which the server system (or systems) runs, LAN configurations, etc.

The work products of the design activity include high-level *system* and *application architectures* for the proposed solution. These include definitions of the major building blocks of the system, called subsystems; the allocation of these subsystems to processes and platforms; and their connectivity.

- Object design: Clusters of objects (that is, closely related objects with a high degree of interaction) should remain in the same object space to minimize the message traffic between object spaces. We also identify common server objects that are used by many different client workstations at the same time.

- Dynamic model: We identify interactions between similar kinds of objects within different machines that should be treated as peer applications.

- Persistent objects design: The databases and data storage devices should be on the same platform as the object servers, if possible.

9.1 System Design

During system design, we make initial decisions about the placement of the objects and the distribution of processes. We take a close look at the system environment in which the application is to run. Network-related topics include the following:

- What kind of network is or will be used?
- What is the estimated traffic rate between the clients and servers?
- Will the bandwidth of the network be able to handle this traffic load?

Geographical location topics include:

- How many different kinds of locations will there be for servers and clients?
- Will there be several layers of servers (department, company, enterprise)?

Security, reliability, and usability topics include:

- What are the security and reliability requirements for servers and clients?
- Who has the right to use an object, and how is verification accomplished?
- Which servers are responsible for maintaining persistent data?
- How does the system recover after a system crash?

We must also decide which client/server implementing technology to use and for what purpose. For example, we can use the VisualAge Distributed Feature to distribute some objects. Other objects are local to the client object space or use some distribution techniques of an Object Request Broker (ORB) as defined by the Object Management Group (OMG), such as an IBM SOM/DSOM.

9.1.1 Architectural Considerations

The first step in system design is the decomposition of the system to be built in subsystems. For instance, in decomposing the FCE application we can identify the Bank and Branch subsystems.

The subsystems have to be assigned to processors that have a physical location. The placement of object subsystems therefore forces the designer to consider design factors such as persistence of objects (which includes data integrity and consistency), concurrent access to objects, performance, and availability. Different design solutions can be achieved, depending on the facilities for managing distributed data and access concurrency. The distributed data represents in this case not only the application data files, but also the data base structure used to dematerialize and dematerialize objects (i.e., store the attributes of objects we want to persist until the next program execution and retrieve them during that execution to recreate the objects).

There are several possible architectural solutions. For instance, if we use a single server for objects and data, and a single process (i.e., a single program running in one address space), the concurrence access management has to be coded in the server objects. The client program accesses the server objects via proxy objects.

Another approach, maintaining a single server for objects and data, would be to have the replicated processes in the server containing all the objects' instances. In that case, the consistency among objects that participate in different processes is maintained by a replication framework. The shared data is stored in a database; the concurrency on the data is managed by the DBMS, which can handle the concurrent access from different processes. As before, the client accesses the process via proxy objects.

A better solution entails the use of multiple servers both for objects and data. The concurrency has to be handled by the objects, and special code to that end is required. The access by the client is also through proxy objects.

Other combinations can be considered for multiple server configurations, including the replication of processes and the use of distributed database management systems. The choice will depend on cost and performance considerations.

9.1.2 Choosing the Implementing Technology: An Example

VisualAge for Smalltalk, with its SOMsupport and its new Distributed Feature, is a versatile tool for developing distributed object applications. Appendix D describes SOM/DSOM, and Appendix E describes the VisualAge SOMsupport feature and Distributed Feature.

In this section, we list criteria for choosing between the VisualAge Distributed Feature and SOMsupport. The two features are based on different technologies and approaches:

- Pure Smalltalk programming for simplicity or language independence: If the aim is to develop an application with a single programming language, the Smalltalk distributed feature is the better choice. However, some designers may prefer to have classes implemented with language independence so that they can reuse the classes in different languages later on. In that case, SOM/DSOM is more suitable. In some cases, the legacy systems that customers have may dictate the language they choose. In other cases, there may be distinct advantages to choosing a particular language to use in the customer's environment. If a customer does not have interfering requirements, writing all of the code in plain Smalltalk seems the simplest and most straightforward way of developing object-oriented applications, and then distribute using the Distributed Feature.

- Cross-platform requirements: In the real world, most installations have more than one computer platform. Applications often have to be developed using various languages, and they often run on different platforms. To implement distributed cross-platform, cross-vendor applications, SOM/DSOM is a good choice. It is a proven technology for facilitating the communication of applications written in different languages. For example, a Smalltalk object application running on the client platform can communicate with C++ SOM objects running on the server. Currently SOM and DSOM are supported in OS/2, AIX, Microsoft Windows, MVS, and other environments.

- Availability of frameworks: SOM/DSOM provides a number of frameworks that are useful in developing distributed object applications. Currently VisualAge Distributed Feature provides a set of distribution tools instead of frameworks.

- Release-to-release binary compatibility: In a compilation language environment like C++, client program compilations are not required with SOM/DSOM, which the server method implementations change. Generally, if the changes to the SOM/DSOM objects do not require logic or source code changes in the client programs, those client programs will not have to be recompiled.

- Location transparency: Location transparency means that the client application objects running on one platform do not have to know where the server objects actually reside. What client objects have to do is communicate with the server objects by sending messages in the same way regardless of whether the server objects are local or remote.

Location transparency helps the distribution design for applications. VisualAge Distributed Feature and SOM/DSOM both provide a level of location transparency support. Using either implementing feature, we can initially develop both the client application and the server application on the same machine. After we finish developing and testing the applications locally, we simply move the server application to another machine.

It is important that if we have to make any changes to the implemented server environment, including moving it to another platform or rewriting it in another language, the client application would remain unchanged. This requires that the interface between them is not changed.

- Distributed tools: The VisualAge Distributed Feature has many tools that help the developer build distributed applications. Tools such as the distributed debugger and distributed event profiler help developers see which messages are going through the network and what is happening in the remote machine. None of these tools is available with VisualAge SOMsupport.

The SOM compiler provides a method-debug routine when it is generating the template functions. SOM class developers can use the method-debug routine for debugging how methods are invoked in a SOM/DSOM environment. However, the debugging of the business logic still relies on the debugger of the language of choice.

To debug an application that uses SOM objects, we must use the Smalltalk debugger for Smalltalk messages and the IBM Presentation Manager debugger (IPMD) for SOM messages. If we are using a DSOM object that exists in a remote machine, we have to use the IPMD in the other machine. As a result, debugging is much more complex with DSOM than with the VisualAge Distributed Feature.

9.1.3 Subsystem Design and Placement

The requirements for defining subsystems are that they should have clearly defined functions, be fairly independent, and have well-defined interfaces. Subsystems that meet these criteria become candidates for distribution. However, the placement of subsystems as well as some of their internal functions are influenced by nonfunctional requirements, such as the following:

- Data integrity: Managing data from places different from where the data are located is not easy. We must make the necessary trade-off between the level of data integrity dictated by the business requirement and the overhead costs and associated performance impact on the application, such as the time necessary to start up the application or to recover from a system failure.

- Data consistency: Data consistency ensures that data values are true values. Several different schemes are possible to ensure data consistancy, each with different consequences for the internal functioning and placement of subsystems.

- Performance: The placement of subsystems and the size and number of messages passing between subsystems are major factors determining the response time.

- Availability: The subsystems should be designed to have few dependencies on the other subsystems for most of their functions. Therefore the functions they provide can be available independent of the availability of other functions.

The VMT methodology system design begins with decomposing the analysis object model into subsystems and mapping the resulting subsystems to separate VisualAge applications. This is a design strategy for the initial application architecture structure and for developing work assignments among developers in a team. For example, if requirements analysis shows that three subsystems exist, the result of the mapping process is the simple structure shown in Figure 118 on page 208. Division of the business application into a number of VisualAge applications allows a team of developers to proceed with development work concurrently, each developer taking on at least one VisualAge application.

In partitioning the object model to subsystems, we will find some initial candidates for object space boundaries. We should minimize object references that cross object space boundaries, dividing into different object spaces only those subsystems that are loosely coupled and do not often interact.

9.1.4 Designing with the VisualAge Distributed Feature

The VisualAge Distributed Feature distribution matrix defines which application is to be loaded into which object space. That means that every analysis subsystem is actually further divided into multiple applications, each planned to be loaded into a dedicated object space.

Figure 119 on page 208 shows the resulting applications for the same problem domain shown in Figure 118 on page 208, but with three different kinds of object spaces.

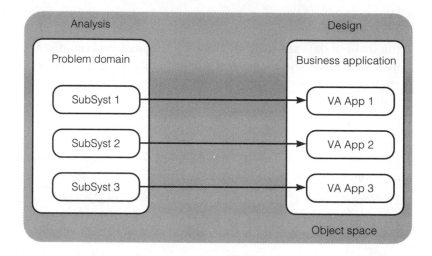

Figure 118. Defining VisualAge applications (nondistributed)

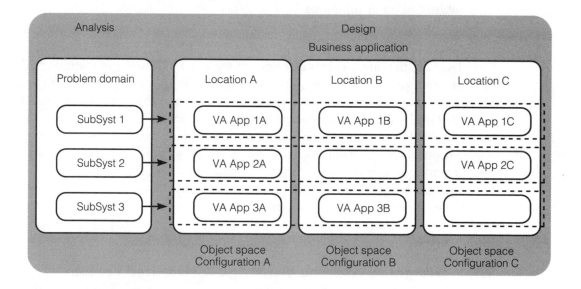

Figure 119. Defining VisualAge applications (distributed)

One design decision we must make is how to make references to remote objects. There are two techniques to make these references in VisualAge applications using the VisualAge Distributed Feature:

- Manually by using *reference-based distribution*
- Automatically by using *matrix-based distribution*

Reference-based distribution is used when we

- Want to build a completely new application and have a fair idea of what the distribution design will be
- Want explicit control over the creation and manipulation of references and shadows
- Have instances of the same classes on both the server object and the client object space

Matrix-based distribution is used when we

- Have a clear separation between server object space classes and client object space classes
- Don't know in advance in which object space the classes will reside
- Are not interested in controlling the creation of object references and shadows
- Have an existing application and want to distribute it without making any changes

The distribution technique used has an effect on the actual implementation of classes. Each approach has its advantages. If we decide to use reference-based distribution, then we must write some Smalltalk code: First we get the object reference from the NameServerList global dictionary, and then we send the *shadow* message to the object reference to get a shadow of the remote class. If we use matrix-based distribution, we get a shadow of an instance transparently whenever we need a new instance of the remote class. Also, the distribution matrix forces us to put server object space classes in a different application than client object space classes.

The unique aspects of designing with VisualAge SOMsupport are discussed in Section 9.2.2 on page 211.

9.2 Object Design

The initial design iteration focuses on designing the major functions of the application and not on distribution design issues. Distribution aspects are handled in later iterations.

The application usually consists of a larger set of classes than just those classes found during the analysis phase. Extra classes are needed in the solution to provide the concrete functions of the application. These classes can be categorized as either interface classes or service classes.

When designing the interface classes for a distributed application, one important factor to consider is using variables in the user interface classes (views) for those classes that will be in a remote object space. If we design using parts, we actually create instances of a class in our working image. If there are instances of a class in the image, we cannot simply unload that class if it is needed to move it to a different object space.

Service classes are used to provide database access and system services. We can use additional service classes as interfaces to remote objects in distributed applications. We may have a client object space service class for each remote server object space class. If we do not want to use service classes, the other way to improve application performance is to provide optimized public interfaces for those classes that will be distributed. This means that we must combine messages whenever possible to reduce the number of messages that will go through the network.

Location-independent data types for attributes that will be accessed and value returned over the network should be selected whenever possible.

If instances of server object space classes must be used concurrently from multiple clients, then we must provide a mechanism that can handle concurrent invocation of setter methods of these instances. We must make sure that a single update process of some attribute is not interrupted by another update process. Semaphores can be used to accomplish this task.

9.2.1 Designing for Performance

With object-oriented technology, configuration of data and the processing function are intimately related. Although function and data could be looked at separately from a logical point of view, an object is actually data and function combined. In a database that stores the state of the object, all data configurations—centralized, partitioned, and distributed—apply equally. An object could be constructed from state (data) residing at a different node. In the case of using proxy objects (stand-ins for another object), processing is partitioned. Process invocation and method dispatching are executed locally, and the actual execution of the method is done at a different node.

The two major factors that affect performance of a distributed object application are object distribution and data and object copy management. Object distribution affects the amount of network traffic and object messages across object space boundaries and hence affects the execution speed of the application. Copy management affects the amount of memory required and the execution speed.

As with every facet of object-oriented application development, several iterations are required until we find the optimum distribution design. Object space boundaries should be defined to minimize cross-space communication. We should avoid having every object communicate with every other object. Because designs tend to change during the implementation, it is necessary to refactor and optimize after the infrastructure is complete.

The following are some rules of thumb for designing for performance:

- Maximize local references: Local messages are generally faster than remote messages, and local debugging is faster than distributed debugging. To provide local references, we can

  —Make temporary copies when needed.

  —Cluster related objects and classes together in one object space.

  —Use location-independent data types such as dates, numbers, strings, times, and so on. Instances of these data types are always local regardless of what object space refers to them.

  —Introduce additional light objects when appropriate to avoid heavy network traffic. Light objects are classes that provide local copies of remote objects; they can be used as an interface between local views and remote objects.

- Minimize remote messages: The number of messages exchanged is much more critical for a good performance than the actual size of data objects. To minimize remote messages, we can

  —Create special methods to return collections of results.

  —Use wait commands only when required. User interface responsiveness is a true measure of performance. Parallel processing reduces wait time. Processing messages in parallel on different machines further reduces wait time.

  —Use object copy management. Object mobility can be used to select whether local or remote objects are sent or returned in remote messaging. Put the objects where they will be referenced the most.

9.2.2 Designing with VisualAge SOMsupport

In this section, we discuss the aspects of designing with VisualAge SOMsupport from both the client and the server perspectives: implementing the SOM classes to run in the server processes, and using the SOM objects in a client program.

As SOM class implementers, we first identify the SOM classes that are to be distributed. We must define the interface for the SOM classes using a standard Interface Definition Language (IDL). We then implement methods to add the desired behavior for the SOM classes with a programming language for which SOM bindings have been defined. (The current SOMobjects release provides bindings for C and C++). The SOM classes are then compiled into dynamic link libraries (DLLs). We must register their interface and implementation in the SOM Interface Repository (SOMIR), and we must also register them with DSOM before they can be used remotely by a client through DSOM.

To use the SOM classes from a VisualAge client program, we first generate SOM wrapper classes for them using the VisualAge SOMsupport feature. The SOM wrapper classes can then be used as other VisualAge for Smalltalk classes.

There are a number of design emphases when designing the interfaces for the SOM classes:

- Performance implications
- Object creation and destruction
- Exceptions handling
- Reuse considerations

Performance Implications

A properly designed interface for the distributed SOM objects can significantly improve their performance. To illustrate the performance-related design issues when creating the interface for SOM classes, consider the following IDL examples for SOMCustomer (SOMCust.idl) and SOMBank (SOMBank.idl):

```
/* SOMCust.idl */
    #include <somobj.idl>
    interface SOMAccount;
    interface SOMCustomer: SOMObject
{
    attribute string<10> id;
    attribute string<16> firstName;
    attribute string<24> lastName;
    attribute string<8> homePhone;
    attribute string<8> workPhone;
    attribute string<40> street;
    attribute string<16> city;
    attribute string<2> state;
    attribute string<5> zip;

    sequence<SOMAccount> accounts ();
    };
/* SOMBank.idl */

    #include <somobj.idl>

    interface SOMCustomer;
    typedef sequence<SOMCustomer> customers;
```

```
interface SOMBank: SOMObject
{
    attribute customers allCustomers;

    ..

    ..

    ..
};
```

In the example, the SOMCustomer interface contains a number of string attributes that belong to a customer (e.g., the customer's first name, last name, etc.) There is also a member function that SOMCustomer provides for a list of accounts that a customer owns. The SOMBank has an attribute of customers that contains a list of all customers for the bank.

While this represents a natural object-oriented thinking in writing the IDL and it works in a small-scale demo application such as our FCE case study, it imposes a number of performance considerations for use in a high volume, performance critical real-life application environment.

First, the attribute allCustomers of SOMBank is an unbounded sequence of customers. Every time this attribute is queried (a get method of this attribute is invoked) the whole list of customers will be returned. Consider if the bank has thousands of users, the link between the class users (clients) and the class implementer (server) will be flooded by data and will result in long response time.

One way to avoid this performance problem is to return only one attribute; that is, the customerIds of the customers, as shown in the following modified IDL:

```
/* SOMBank.idl */
    #include <somobj.idl>

    typedef sequence<string> customerIds;

    interface SOMBank: SOMObject
    {
    attribute customerIds allCustomerIds;

    ..

    ..

    ..
};
```

Here SOMBank just returns a list of customer ids instead of a list of the whole customer objects. This will greatly reduce the network traffic. An even better way is to add some intelligence to the SOMBank class and let it return only a small number of customers (or customer ids) according to some criteria or business rules. For example, a maximum of 20 customers will be returned each time a query or search by customer name.

```
/* SOMBank.idl */
   #include <somobj.idl>
   interface SOMBank: SOMObject
   {
      sequence <string> someCustomerIds(in string criteria);
      ..
      ..
      ..
   };
```

To further improve performance, we can change the attribute declarations for firstName, lastName, etc., to a structure containing all of them. The design trade-off is between the number of requests and the data traffic over the network per request (one query for the whole data structure versus a request for each of the attributes).[22]

Object Creation and Destruction

Objects are created and destroyed during the operation of an object application. There are a number of ways to allocate and deallocate objects. One has to be careful when defining the SOM IDL file, as the defined relationships between the class users and class implementers will affect the actual coding of the client and server programs, as well as the ownership of memory management for the created objects.

Another design issue is the actual creation and destruction of the SOM objects. In C++, we use the constructors and destructors to create and destroy an object. In DSOM, a factory interface should be defined to deal with the creation of new objects, as recommended by the CORBA Object Lifecycle service of the Common Object Services Specification (COSS). See the following example:

```
/* CustFact.idl */

   #include >somobj.idl>

   interface SOMAccount;
   interface SOMCustomerFactory: SOMObject
   {
     SOMCustomer create CustomerWithName( in string firstName );
     SOMCustomer create CustomerWithId( in string Id );
     SOMCustomer findCustomerWithName( in string firstName );
     ...etc...
   };
```

---

22 This is a compromise between a pure object-oriented design and performance over a network link.

VisualAge Smalltalk SOMSupport provides object creation and destruction support. By dropping a SOM wrapper onto the free form surface of the VisualAge Composition editor as a part, a SOM object will be created at runtime. VisualAge calls the newPart method of the SOM wrapper class, which creates an instance of the SOM class. Alternatively, the client program can also send a Smalltalk message somNew to the wrapper class directly to create an instance.

To destroy a SOM object, the client program sends the SOM wrapper object a Smalltalk message somFree, which then invokes the somFree method of the SOM object to destroy the object and reset the object reference of the wrapper object to nil. Note that the SOM object is actually residing outside of the Smalltalk image and thus it will not be garbage collected. When a client program no longer needs a SOM object, it has to explicitly destroy it.

To delete a SOM object using VisualAge visual programming, we can connect the closedWidget event of the main view to the somFree action of the SOM object. This will destroy the SOM object when the view closes at runtime.

Exceptions Handling

Another design consideration when designing SOM objects relates to the raising and capturing of exception information. The SOM exception handling capability is a powerful feature that allows a software designer to be explicit about the specific actions to take when an abnormal condition should occur.

By defining the exceptions and associating them with methods in the SOM IDL file, the class designer can easily show the client program designer exactly what will happen if abnormal situations occur when they invoke the method of the class. This helps to explicitly demonstrate the range of possible errors that a method might throw back and provides greater flexibility for properly describing each error condition.

The SOM Exception is declared in the SOM IDL file, as shown in the following example:

```
/* SOMBank.idl */
   #include <somobj.idl>

   exception noCustomer {
   string recommendedAction;
   }

   exception tooManyCustomers {
     sequence <string> customerIds;
     long numCustomerIds;
     }
   interface SOMBank: SOMObject
   {
```

```
          sequence <string> someCustomerIds (in string criteria)
          raises (tooManyCustomers, noCustomer);
          ..
          ..
          ..
    };
```

In VisualAge for Smalltalk, the SOMsupport maps SOM exceptions to the Smalltalk ExceptionalEvents, which extends the full power of Smalltalk exception handling to SOM exceptions.

By default, VisualAge Smalltalk will handle the exceptions raised by the SOM object. However, the default handling is designed for a development environment. Thus, it is better to override the default handling for production environment.

Reuse Considerations

When using an object-oriented language, we have three general ways of acquiring the services of other object classes: inheritance, aggregation, or delegation.

Inheritance: Obtaining services through inheritance is quite straightforward. A subclass inherits all the attributes and operations defined in its superclasses. Thus, all services of the superclasses are made available to the subclass as part of its public interface.

The drawback of this approach is that the subclasses are very dependent on the superclasses, which can cause a lot of recompilation in languages like C++, or force developers to include the complete class hierarchy in languages with late binding, like Smalltalk.

Aggregation: Services can be obtained through aggregation by creating a composite object class that contains the class with the desired services. In most object-oriented languages, the composite (aggregate) object usually contains a reference (object ID) to the contained object rather than to the object itself. The composite object and the contained object are coupled with this aggregation relationship. However, the coupling is not as tight as the inheritance relationship.

Providing the services to the client through aggregation enables one to define a cleaner interface between the server and the client. Creating an interface class using aggregation at the server provides even more flexibility. It can hide all functions that are not needed. It lessens the dependency on a superclass, therefore causing fewer recompiles, and does not force a lot of classes to be present during run-time for languages with late binding. The drawback is that all methods that are part of the interface must be coded in the composite class.

Delegation: Services can be obtained through delegation by invoking the desired service of another class—by sending it the proper message. A class can invoke the service of any classes with which it has an association relationship. This is the most flexible way in which classes can collaborate with each other with minimum coupling.

Effects of Inheritance and Aggregation

The effects of inheritance differ when the client is implemented in a programming language with static binding, such as C++, or with late binding, such as Smalltalk.

Another point worth noting is that, with SOM, there can be an inheritance relationship between a class written in one language with another class written in a different language. For example, with SOM, we can subclass a server class written in C++ in a *Smalltalk* environment.

Figure 120 shows the effect of using inheritance to extend and reuse the code of a DSOM server class by a client program developed with a static binding programming language.

In the figure, we have two server classes, **A** and **B,** where class **B** is a subclass of class **A.** On the client side we have class **C,** which is a subclass of the DSOM class **B.**

The methods of the classes are represented with a single letter. The bold letter is the method implemented for that class. The italic letter is an inherited method. An underscored letter is a method needed on the client side. The superclass **A** has a method **a,** the subclass **B** has a method **b.** Both methods are available on the client side, and class **C** adds the method **c.**

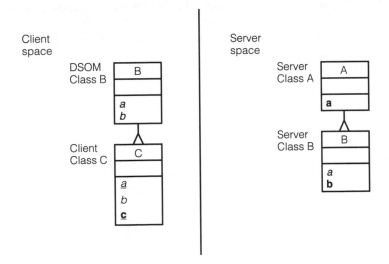

Figure 120. Effects of Inheritance for a client developed with static binding language

The presence of server Class **A** is not required in the client environment when the client is programmed with a static binding language.

Figure 121 shows the effects of inheritance when the client is developed with a late binding programming language, such as Smalltalk.

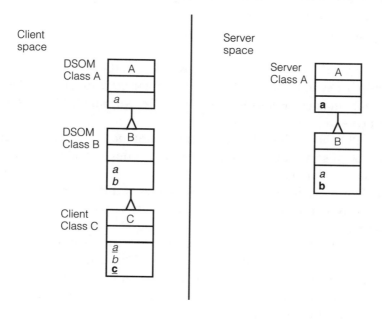

Figure 121. Effects of Inheritance for a client developed with late binding language

As the bindings are done at run time, in order for client class **C** to inherit and reuse code from server class **B,** all classes of the inheritance hierarchy tree on the server side must be present on the client side as well. In particular, if the client side is implemented with VisualAge for Smalltalk, we must generate SOM wrapper classes for not just the server class **B,** but all classes that it inherits from. In our example, this is server class **A.**

This means more effort during the development phase and also more overhead which affects the run time performance.

In conclusion, if the client environment is developed using a late binding language, such as Smalltalk, avoid inheritance relationship for a client class with a DSOM wrapper class that has a deep inheritance tree at the server side.

Now let us look at late binding with aggregation relationships. Figure 122 illustrates the effect of aggregation on the client side when the client program is developed with a late binding language.

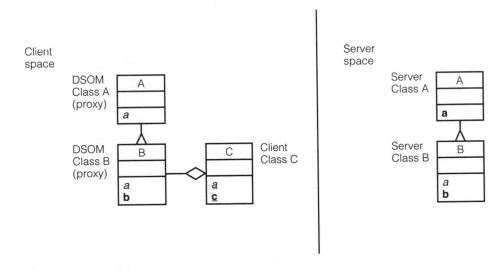

Figure 122. Effects of aggregation on client side developed with late binding language

With this option only the desired behavior of the class defined in the server is enabled. It requires fewer recompiles but has the same overhead on the client side as late binding with inheritance (see Figure 120 on page 217). It also provides more flexibility in creating instances and facilitates the coding of populating object structures.

Figure 123 on page 220 depicts the effects of aggregation on both the server and the client when the client is developed with a late binding language.

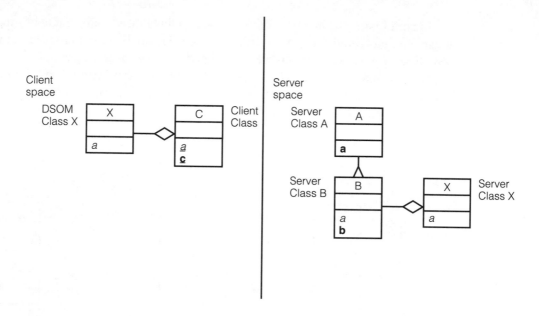

Figure 123. Effects of Aggregation on both the server and client sides client developed with late binding language

This is the *best* solution when the client side uses a language with late binding, such as VisualAge Smalltalk. It eliminates the need for a repeated inheritance structure on the client side, with all its associated problems. It is also the best solution for maintaining project library control in a project that uses different platforms.

Effects of Extending the SOM Wrapper Classes

This section examines the effects of directly extending the generated SOM wrapper classes in the VisualAge Smalltalk environment (see Figure 124 on page 221). We explored this approach in our case study. From the client application point of view, it only cares about the services that a customer class provides. Therefore, it does not matter how the customer class is actually implemented. Whether the customer class is a SOM-enabled class or native Smalltalk class should not affect the client application. Thus, any customer-specific methods or attributes could be added to the customer class.

If a SOM wrapping process is to occur in the future, the SOM wrapper in VisualAge will make only those modifications that are required. All methods, whether they were added in the Smalltalk environment or obtained from the previous SOM wrapping process, are kept untouched if they do not require changes.

Although directly extending SOM wrapper classes is possible, it should be done with caution and only in certain cases because the approach has some negative implications. For example, if you add instance data to a wrapper class, the instance data cannot be made persistent through SOM. Also, by directly extending the SOM wrapper classes, the explicit contract between the client and the server is broken, as represented by the IDL description of the server interface.

If we are adding real functions as opposed to minor auxiliary functions to assist in the Smalltalk environment, do not directly extend SOM wrapper classes.

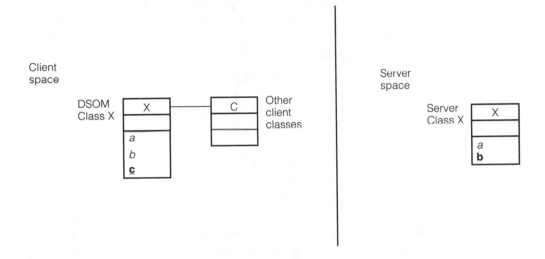

Figure 124. Extending the SOM wrapper classes on the client side

9.3 Object Persistence Design

Compared with the traditional design for a nondistributed solution, a distributed solution design involves trade-offs when objects are in server object spaces with local access to the database and when objects are in server object spaces without local access to the database. Obviously, when objects have local access, the corresponding persistence manager class should reside in the same object space. When objects do not have local access to the database, we can

- Place the corresponding persistence manager class into the object space that has local access to the database and use a shadow of the persistence manager to access its services. This approach places the object and data access within the same object space, but the complete object will be transferred between the object spaces over the network. Since the persistence manager uses instance methods to populate the object's data, the object class must also reside in that object space.

- Place the corresponding persistence manager class into the same server object space and use remote database access. This approach places the object class and its persistence manager class within the same object space, but the SQL query and results will be transferred over a network.

- Move the object class and the persistence manager into the object space that has local access to the database to minimize the SQL traffic; we use a shadow to access the object. This approach places the object class and its persistence manager class within the same object space with local SQL traffic, but every message to the object instances (and its return value) will be transferred over the network.

When designing distributed applications using SOM/DSOM, we can consider using SOM Persistence Object Service, which conforms to Object Management Group (OMG) CORBA specifications. The next section provides more details.

9.3.1 SOM Support for Persistence

The OMG has adopted a specification for the Persistence Object Service (POS) that provides an industry standard for writing data-store-independent code and for plugging existing data stores into an object storage framework. The adoption of the POS standard by this large industry consortium will likely have a major impact on the way object-oriented storage systems are designed and used in the next few years.

The POS specification ensures that the same client code can be used for storing objects, regardless of whether the object is stored in file systems, relational databases, object-oriented databases, or other data stores. For the first time, programmers have a well-defined interface for storing objects in existing corporate-centric data stores, such as relational databases.

The POS standard also defines the components that must be implemented by data store vendors to support the storage of objects. IBM is currently working on POS plug-in components for DB2, IMS, stream files, and other data stores. This will allow traditional IBM data stores to be used as full-fledged object storage facilities.

There are many advantages to using traditional data store products as object data stores, for both developers and users. Developers now have an industry-defined standard for accessing existing corporate-centric data and storing object data in a format compatible with existing multimillion-dollar software investments. Users can exploit mature data store technologies to ensure the reliability and integrity of their data.

The POS standard is designed to support object-oriented databases as well as traditional data store products. This offers application developers the best of all worlds: A single object interface to a multitude of data store products that encompass the best of the past, the present, and the future.

9.4 Summary

Object distribution provides the clearest implementation of the client/server computing paradigm. From an application modeling point-of-view, the location of an object at execution time is immaterial; from a resource utilization and optimization, it is crucial to achieve a good design, assigning objects properly to workspaces and processors.

The available underlying mechanisms for object distribution need to be carefully evaluated in the context of the deployment environment, including language, processor, and repository considerations. The main approaches include the use of an object request broker, such as IBM SOM/DSOM which allows for multi-language implementation, and language extension for distribution, such as those provided by IBM Smalltalk.

Distribution presents design, testing, and debugging challenges, It enables, however, a high degree of flexibility and adaptability for building systems and applications, which is invaluable in responding to today's dynamic business requirements.

10

Case Study: Extending the FCE System with Distributed Objects

In this chapter we extend the foreign currency exchange (FCE) application, to exemplify the development of distributed object applications with VMT.

10.1   Distributed FCE Application Scenarios

In Chapter 8, "Object Technology and Distributed Systems," we introduced the concepts of *object server, active server,* and *peer application*—new roles for the traditional data server in a distributed object application environment. We now look at how these new server roles can be applied to scenarios within the FCE application environment.

10.1.1   Customer Management with an Object Server

As described in the requirement specifications, assume that the bank maintains bank, customer, and account information in centralized databases located in the bank center system. The branches are remote from the location of the main bank.

Bank-specific operations, including certain customer management operations, are done in the central site, that is, the bank. However, the cashiers sitting in a branch also perform customer management functions, such as

- Adding a new customer to the list of bank customers
- Updating a customer's information
- Removing a customer from the list of bank customers

The required information to perform these functions includes

- The list of customers and related customer information
- The list of accounts and related account information
- Certain information about the bank (the bank name and so on)

Instead of accessing data from cashier-client workstations using a SQL database query, we can create objects locally in the database that access the bank server and still satisfy the client workstations for the required objects.

This approach has several benefits:

- Database access is required only on the server. Client workstations do not need to issue queries to access remote databases.
- Only a few objects (the customer and the account that reside in the server) have direct access to the data, thus simplifying data maintenance in the center.
- Network traffic can be reduced between the cashier-client workstations and the bank server, so that the cashiers experience an overall improvement in the FCE application.
- Database software is not required in each client machine, thus reducing the software license cost.

10.1.2   Exchange Rate Management with an Active Server

As described in Appendix A, "FCE Specifications," the bank maintains the exchange rate for each currency centrally. The exchange rates for all currencies are updated overnight and remain fixed during the day. The cashiers obtain the exchange rate for each currency to perform the foreign exchange transactions.

To allow the cashiers to use a fluctuating exchange rate for currency trading, a list of all currencies with their corresponding exchange rates is located on a bank server (a computer at the central site). All clients (the cashier workstations in the branches) have access to the currency information provided by the central site.

The bank server containing the list of currencies is an active server in the sense that it informs all the interested clients when a change has occurred. The clients can reflect that change on their corresponding views of the user interface.

10.1.3   Currency Trading Between Banks as Peer Applications

A *peer application* is a two-way client/server computing schema with direct communications between two client machines. For foreign currency exchange, a good example of a peer application scenario is currency trading between two different banks. In this scenario, each main bank center has to maintain the center currency stock trade with many banks around the world.

An external system offers the foreign currency trading facilities, for a fee, across a number of banks. The main duties of this system are:

- Maintain a list of the existing currencies and the rates each bank assigns to them. This helps each bank increase or decrease its own internal exchange rate.

- Maintain a list of all trading requests that the member banks send to the system. A trading request specifies the available currency and the amount, the requested currency, the requested exchange rate, and the bank that originated the request.

- Allow a bank to start a direct negotiation with another bank. Without intervention from the central system, a connection can be established between a bank and the bank that originally sent a trading request. In this way, the bank can negotiate the rate, the bulk transportation, date, time, and additional considerations.

This scenario is not implemented in the current example.

10.2   Design Considerations

In the distributed design example, the FCE application is split into two major subsystems: the bank subsystem and the branch subsystem. These subsystems were placed on separate platforms in a client/server computing environment.

Two design and implementation approaches are possible: DSOM and the Distributed Object Space technology. To illustrate these two approaches, we have implemented the various parts of the distributed FCE application using the VisualAge SOM/DSOM support features and the Distributed Feature. The first part of the example focuses on applying the SOM/DSOM technology through the SOM/DSOM support of IBM VisualAge and VisualAge C++ V3 to extend the application involving distributed objects. The second part illustrates the application of distributed objects using the VisualAge Distributed Feature to implement the fluctuating exchange rates of the foreign currencies. This part of the application consists of a list of currencies that is maintained at the bank server and can be accessed by all branch clients through object distribution. Each currency contains a country object. The currency has an ID, a description, and an exchange rate and can return the corresponding country name by asking its country component.

10.3   Application Development Iterations

Before developing the application extension to become an object server and active server, we revisited the requirement study, the object-oriented analysis, and the object-oriented design from the original FCE case study. This includes review of the following:

- The business application for additional requirements
- The object-oriented analysis and design
- The actual implementation, including system setup, code development, testing and packaging, and so on.

10.3.1   Incremental Development

To develop the distributed application, we use the incremental approach to building an object-oriented application. We have an existing nondistributed FCE application, and we want to add new functions to it using distributed objects. We must move object classes involved in distribution to a different object space and platform, and we can expect to redesign them. However, those parts of the existing application that are not to be distributed will remain much the same, with little or no change. The distributed portion of the application thus can be viewed as increments to the existing FCE.[23]

The VisualAge Distributed Feature provides distribution tools support to help the design and development of distributed object applications. This facilitates incremental development. Applications can be developed as local (nondistributed) and then modified to suit a distributed object space environment (see Figure 125 and Figure 126 on page 228).

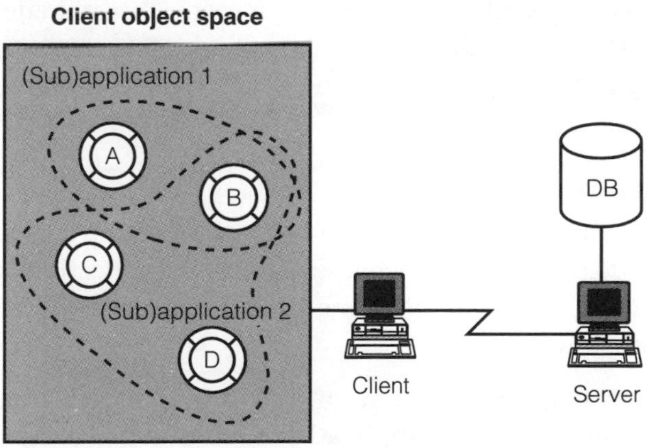

Client object space

Figure 125. Incremental development (nondistributed)

---

23 During the new case study, we developed the customer management object server and the currency management active server separately in two different subprojects. They use different technologies and can be viewed as increments to the original application.

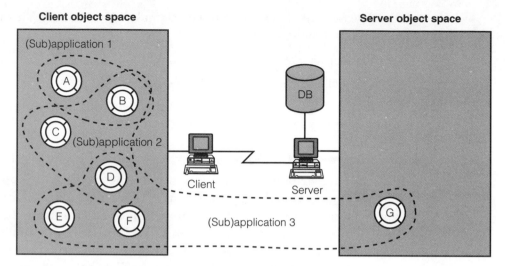

Figure 126. Incremental development (distributed)

10.4   Case Study: The FCE Application in a Distributed Object Environment

The following sections describe the implications of developing the FCE application in a distributed object environment. The analysis phase, including the original requirements as described by the use case model, are not affected by the distribution. However, new requirements may appear due to the criteria for distribution. The design of the application, however, changes reflecting the new distributed environment.

10.4.1   Case Study Requirements

The requirements for the distributed version of the application remain the same as in the original foreign currency exchange case study application (see Appendix A, "FCE Specifications"). The following list summarizes new assumptions made regarding the requirements:

- Now that the FCE application is running in a branch, we should retain the same look and feel of the application to minimize the impact on the user.
- The bank manages certain information centrally, including
    - A list of customers and customer-related information
    - A list of accounts and account-related information
    - Certain information about the bank (bank name and so on)

- Bank-specific operations are done in the central site (the main bank). These include customer management operations. However, the cashiers in the branch should also be able to perform certain customer management operations, including

  —Adding a person into the list of bank customers

  —Updating customer information

  —Removing a customer from the list of bank customers

- Other than customer management, the branch handles all other branch-specific transactions, such as order management and branch stock management. The requirements are the same as for the original FCE application.

- The bank has a policy that any FCE customer payment can only be made from a single account in the bank.

In the process of understanding the requirements, it becomes clear that we can reuse most of the analysis work from the original FCE case study, at least for the branch subsystem. The changes in implementation technology and platforms for the bank server have no effect on our analysis of the branch.

10.4.2   Use Cases

The use cases for the customer and currency management functions are repeated here for easy reference.

Customer Management

- Enter new Customer (Create Customer)

  1. Cashier requests to perform customer management function.

  2. System provides a form for the cashier to fill in.

  3. Cashier completes the customer information form.

  4. Cashier requests the system to perform the create job.

  5. System performs the customer create job.

  6. System notifies the cashier that the job is successful or not.

- Update Customer

  1. Cashier requests to perform customer management function.

  2. System provides a list of customers to the cashier.

  3. Cashier chooses the customer he/she wants to update.

  4. System informs cashier what customer he/she has selected.

  5. Cashier requests to perform customer management function on the selected customer.

6. System provides the cashier with a customer information form.

7. Cashier modifies the form with new information.

8. Cashier requests system to perform the update.

9. System performs the customer update job.

10. System notifies the cashier that job is successful or not.

- Delete Customer

  1. Cashier requests to perform customer management function.

  2. System provides the cashier with a list of customers.

  3. Cashier chooses the customer he/she wants to delete.

  4. System informs cashier which customer he/she has selected.

  5. Cashier tells the system that he/she wants to delete the selected customer.

  6. System deletes the customer from the bank customer list.

  7. System notifies the cashier that the job is successful or not.

Currency Management

- Browse Currency

  1. Cashier requests to browse currencies.

  2. System provides a list of currencies to the cashier.

  3. Cashier chooses a currency to view.

  4. System provides currency details, such as denominations, current exchange rates, and so on.

- Update Exchange Rate

  1. Rate administrator requests an update of currencies.

  2. System provides a list of currencies to the administrator.

  3. Administrator chooses a currency to update.

  4. System provides currency details, including the current exchange rates, and so on.

  5. Administrator updates the exchange rate of the currency.

  6. System confirms the update of the exchange rate.

10.4.3   User Interface

Because we want to retain the same look and feel for the application, there are no additions or modifications to the user interface design. We simply reuse the user interface from the existing FCE.

10.4.4   Object Model

After analyzing the use cases, we decide to use the same object model used in the original case study saving time and effort by reusing work products of the original application.

10.4.5   Dynamic Model

The event trace diagram for the update customer operation is shown in Figure 127. We show only the Customer Information Update use case here. Use cases, event trace diagrams, and state diagrams for other cases also need to be created.

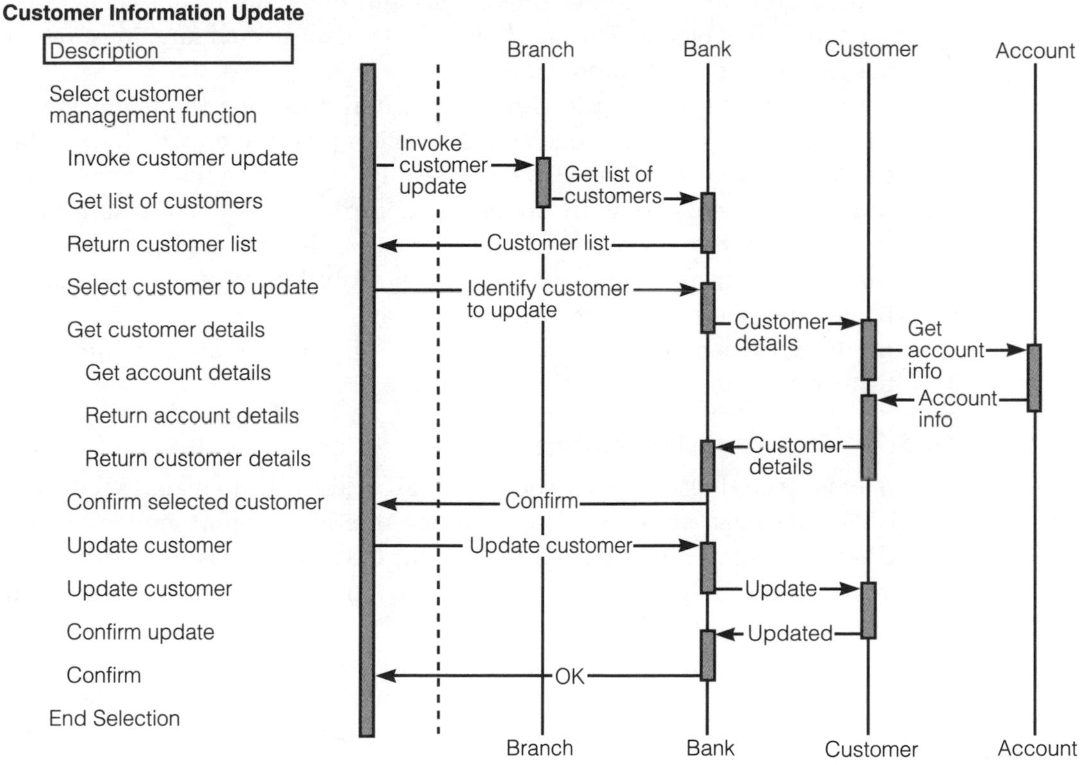

Figure 127. Event trace diagram of the Customer Information Update use case

10.5   Design

This section focuses on the activities involved in the design phase of developing a distributed object FCE application. We outline the steps necessary to transform the analysis work products into the required output. The VMT design stage encompasses iterations of the following three steps:

- System design
- Object design
- Object persistence design

10.5.1   System Design

During system design, we focus on decisions regarding enabling and implementing hardware and software platforms. We need to design a high-level architecture for the proposed solution that includes a definition of the major system building blocks and their high-level connectivity. An application architecture organizes the solution in subsystems and maps these subsystems into the system building blocks. The building blocks reflect system functions, rather than hardware or software products.

Another part of system design is making initial decisions on the placement of function and data as well as selecting the system platform on which the solution is to be implemented. The FCE system design runs in a client/server environment and presents us with numerous complex design considerations. Among the factors to be considered are the existing (legacy) systems, the capability of the chosen platform to implement the solution, performance issues, security requirements, and system integrity.

The design work products are system and application architectures and specifications.

10.5.2   Defining Subsystems

Subsystems, groupings of tightly coupled classes, allow us to manage the complexity of the design effort and also to divide the design effort among several teams. We can isolate specific design decisions that we can easily modify later. The grouping of subsystems also distinguishes different levels of abstraction in the services provided.

Figure 128 on page 233 shows how we divide the object model into two subsystems, the Bank subsystem and Branch subsystem. The Bank subsystem contains the bank, the customers, and the accounts. The Branch subsystems includes the cashier with the currency stock order details. The groupings match the case study requirements of putting branch functions locally in the branch and customer management functions remotely in the bank. Also, the two subsystems contain tightly coupled classes whose grouping produces a clear, well-defined external interface that helps us manage the design process.

The division into Bank and Branch subsystems is just the starting point. During the object distribution design, several factors can affect how classes are further divided and grouped into subsystems so that object classes can be distributed. For example, to have the SOM wrapper classes for Bank, Customer, and so on located on the client machine and the SOM objects on the server, we further divide the classes and group them in the Customer Management sub-

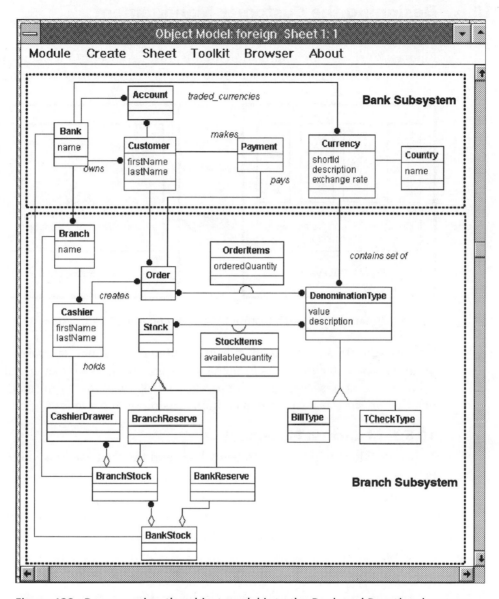

Figure 128. Decomposing the object model into the Bank and Branch subsystems

system. In addition, layering would also be employed to divide the classes further, which provides view-model separation, as shown later in the example using the VisualAge Distributed Feature.

10.6   Designing the Customer Management Application Using DSOM

Figure 129 shows the application architecture we use in our extension case study, and Figure 130, on page 235, shows the FCE system architecture.

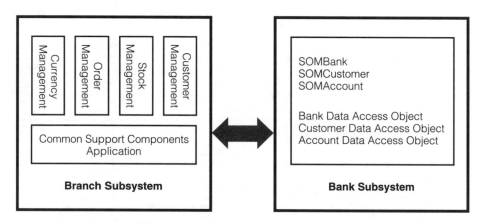

Figure 129. Application architecture for the extended FCE application

Both the Branch and Bank subsystems have relational databases resident on them. The database in the Branch subsystem contains branch-specific data, such as branch reserves, branch currency stock, and order information. The database in the Bank subsystem contains customer and account information.

10.6.1   Function Placement

To decide where to put the processing logic and the data, we look at these alternatives:

- We can have a branch client that performs most of the processing for the whole system (fat client). This leaves only the data-storing and retrieval functions to be done by the bank server.

- We can have a server that performs all the processing logic, leaving only the user interface handling be done on the client side (fat server).

Because the server (in our case, the bank) does not filter any information it obtains before sending it to the client, a fat client could cause excessive and unnecessary traffic between server and client. The problem is even more severe in a distributed object environment, where the attributes of an object can be another object (in an aggregate case) and that object's attributes can even contain other objects. As a result, a "get attribute" message sent to an object results in a number of database access requests to or from one or more tables. Performance can be seriously affected.

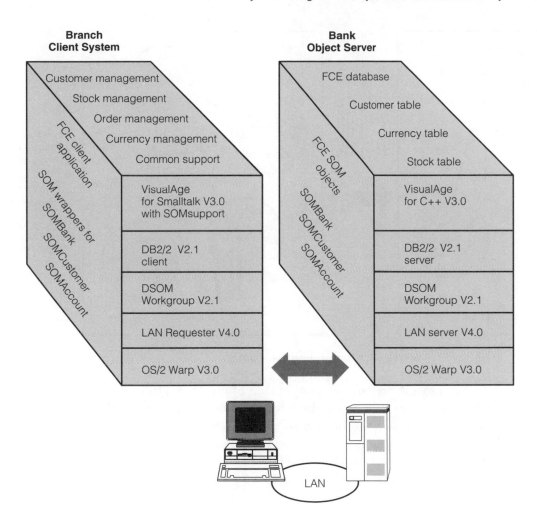

Figure 130. System architecture for the extended FCE application

Figure 131 shows how a fat client can cause excessive network traffic in a distributed object environment due to frequent data access requests and the amount of returned data. With a fat server, the client depends too much on the server. Again, we have a potential performance problem when clients try to access the server simultaneously.

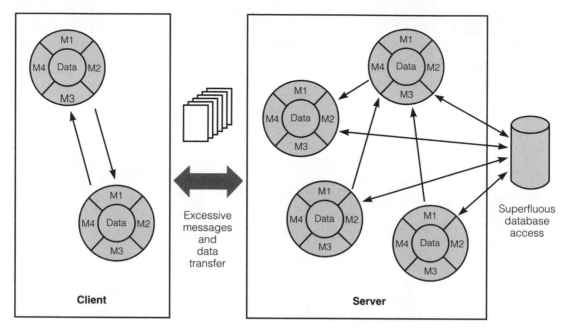

Figure 131. A fat client: an information glutton

As a result, we choose an approach of functional division processing that lies somewhere in between the two extremes. In our design, the branch functions are placed in the Branch subsystem, and the bank functions are placed in the Bank subsystem. The bank server performs shallow object data retrieval[24] in addition to object data retrieval that sends all actual data across the network. For example, when handling a request for a list of customers, the bank server returns only a list of customers with their account IDs. The actual content of the account is not retrieved until the cashier requests it. This eliminates potential performance problems and reduces network traffic loading. Figure 132, on page 237, shows our approach to maintain a balanced system

---

24 Some object-oriented design literature call this technique *lazy initialization*.

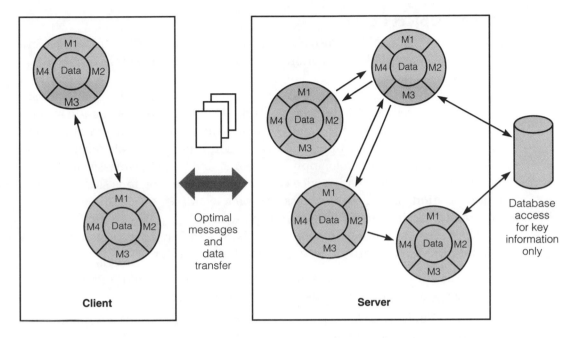

Figure 132. A balanced system in a distributed object environment

10.6.2 Data Placement

We put the branch-specific data into the Branch subsystem machine and the bank-specific data into the bank machine. Caching some local data obtained from the bank onto the branch client machine reduces the network traffic and the client's dependency on server availability. As a result, a list of customer objects is kept in the branch, and this list is obtained by requesting customers from the bank object.

These data placement and caching strategy raises a synchronization problem, however. When there are a number of branches, each with local data cache (such as account information), synchronization must be assured by using such mechanisms as the replication framework provided with SOMObjects Developer Toolkit.

10.6.3 Other Considerations

All database update requests done on the customer, bank, and account objects are followed immediately by "commit" statements; that is, all requests during customer management are committed immediately.

A transaction-based operation implemented during customer management allows us to use the rollback capability provided by generated data access objects. The rollback method of those data access objects can return the database to its original state if a problem occurs.

10.6.4   Object Design

The primary goal of object design is to map the semantic classes identified in the analysis object model into solution domain classes (for example, application classes and service classes).

The set of object classes that make up a running application is usually much larger than the set identified during analysis. The initial set of semantic application classes identified in the analysis object model represents only the core business behavior of the application. Other solution domain classes must be designed to provide concrete application functions. Interface classes that represent the user interface and service classes that provide functions such as input data validation and database access are some examples of additional classes required for the implementation of the application.

The design of solution domain classes is, as in other object-oriented development processes, iterative. We suggest the following steps:

1. Map the semantic classes, identified in the object model from analysis, to application classes; this is fairly straightforward.

2. Add interface and service classes to provide a user interface and additional required functions.

The object design phase involves the refinement and fleshing out of each object's internal structural and behavioral details, as well as the object interactions details.

In the FCE application, the semantic classes become the required SOM/DSOM and VisualAge classes. During object design, we iterate the following steps several times:

1. Refine the object interactions and message flows of the dynamic model.

   • Evolve event traces with detailed message passing and additional object interactions.

   • Prepare class specifications, methods, and message formats

2. Design the details of the SOM/DSOM classes. Define (and refine) their public interface (attributes, actions, and events) and methods, including the instance methods and variables, and devise the derived attribute policies. From these, we specify their interface using the IDL. The results are the IDL files produced.

3. Review the design of the VisualAge visual classes for the GUI of the FCE application to consider changes to the elementary visual class for each application class, additional composite visual classes required, input data validation, and deferred updates. In this distributed application, very little needs to be done because we reuse what we have from the original FCE application.

10.6.5   Object Design for the Server

Our initial server design uses the approach, shown in Figure 133, of acting as a simple server that handles data access and retrieval.

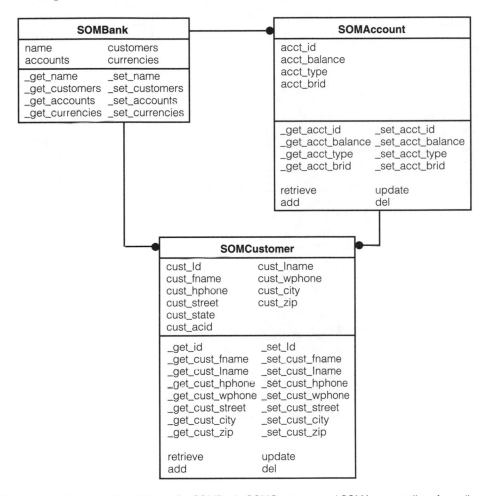

Note: The _gets and _sets to the attributes for SOMBank, SOMCustomer and SOMAccount all perform direct access to the database. No logic was added, and all codes are generated by the data access server.

Figure 133. Initial server design object model

We then refine the design for better traceability and maintainability. Instead of directly accessing the database, we create a SOM class that uses the data access objects to perform the data update and retrieval operations. We thus separate data access logic from business logic, which results in a more portable server. Also, the SOM classes we create can have attribute names that come close to matching those of the business world instead of the database tables. For example, the Customer object has an attribute of FirstName instead of Cust_Fname. Figure 134, on page 240 illustrates the object model for the refined design.

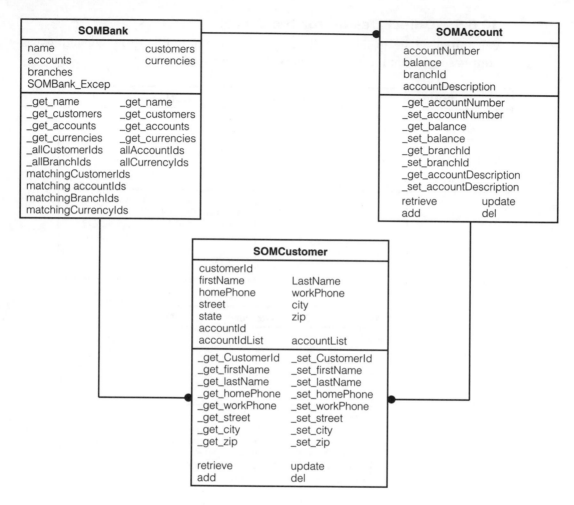

Note: (1) The_gets and_sets to the attributes for SOMBank, SOMCustomer, and SOMAccount all uses the corresponding data access server objects to access the database.
(2) Note all attribute names match the original, stand-alone, FCE application. This results in minimized changes in our client application.

Figure 134. Refined server design object model

10.6.6   Object Design for the Client

To extend the application, we take out the customer objects inside the original FCE application object design model and replace them with the SOM wrapper objects. The result is objects that talk with the SOM wrapper objects instead of interfacing with the original customer objects.

No additional work needs to be done because the SOM wrapper objects have the same public interface as the original objects. The only way other objects know that the wrapped objects are actually distributed across the network is that we name them deliberately SOMCustomer instead of Customer.

Figures 135 and 136 on page 242 show the object model diagram before and after use of SOM objects, such as SOMBank, SOMAccount, and SOMCustomer, respectively.

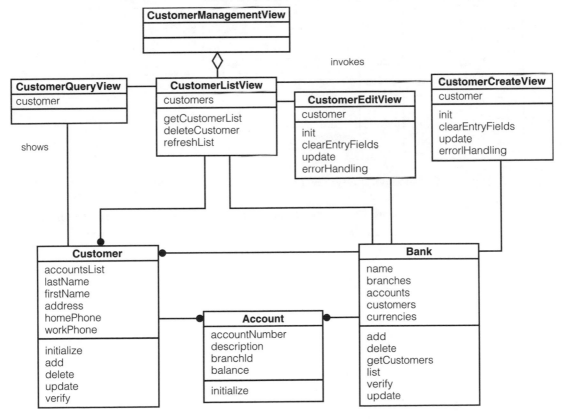

Figure 135. Original Customer application before SOMCustomer is used

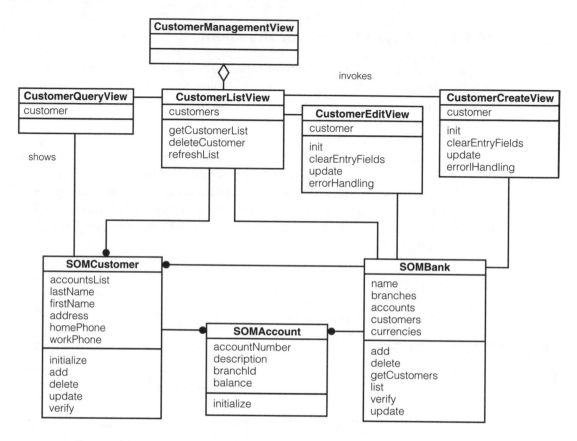

Figure 136. CustomerQueryView after SOMCustomer is used

Figure 137 and 138 on page 243 show how we implement the change in VisualAge for Smalltalk V.3 from using Customer to SOMCustomer.

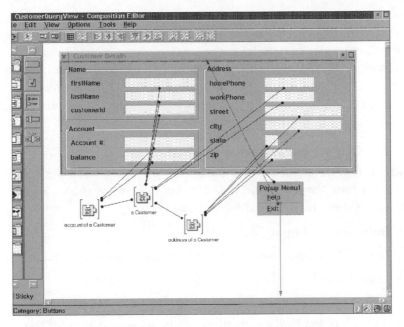

Figure 137. Original CustomerQueryView before SOMCustomer is used

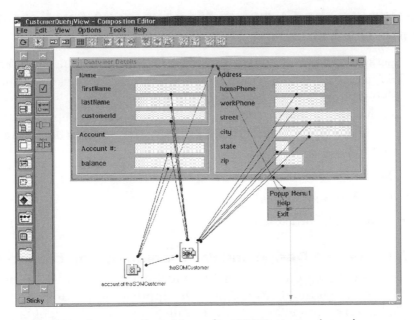

Figure 138. CustomerQueryView after SOMCustomer is used

We add a number of service classes for the SOM/DSOM support. As specified in the OMG Common Object Request Broker Architecture (CORBA), when the server object has difficulty handling a request from a client object, it raises an exception. The exception travels all the way back to the client application, and the client program handles the exception accordingly. For each DSOM class we create in the FCE application, we define an exception associated with it. In the branch machine, when we create the DSOM wrapper object, we also create a SOM exception-handling class, which is used to handle the exception coming back from the DSOM environment.

10.6.7   Object Persistence Design

When a relational database is used as data storage, object persistence design focuses on how the persistent data for the objects are stored and retrieved in the target system, including the following tasks:

- Build the relational data model.
- Define the interactions between database objects and model objects.
- Define the distribution of objects in user's images.
- Define access policies to retrieve and update shared data.

Not much in the FCE application needs to be modified for the extension.

10.7   Designing the Currency Management Application Using the VisualAge Distributed Feature

This section focuses on using the VisualAge for Smalltalk Distributed Feature to handle fluctuating exchange rates within the currency management subsystem. The analysis from the FCE case study still applies.

To optimize the performance of the distributed object application, developers using the VisualAge Distributed Feature should keep these three design rules in mind:

- Maximize local references.
- Minimize remote messages.
- Add parallel processing.

10.7.1   System Design and Partitioning of Object Spaces

We use the distribution matrix tool provided with the VisualAge Distributed Feature, to design the distribution of the application portions on the client (local), the server (remote), or both. The distribution matrix tool requires distributed classes to be grouped into VisualAge applications so they can be loaded selectively. We thus create these three different VisualAge applications for the distributed portions of the new Currency Management subsystem (the EMS prefix is arbitrary):

- EMSAFceClientApp for all classes on the client
- EMSAFceServerAoo for all classes on the server
- EMSAFceClientServerApp for all classes loaded on both the server and the client

Figure 139 shows the VisualAge applications and their classes.

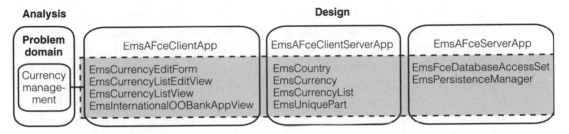

Figure 139. Defined VisualAge applications and classes

10.7.2   Object Design

The main consideration in object design is to optimize and improve performance. However, it is important to design in a natural way without emphasizing object distribution first, and then distribute the objects and the process. To help understand the message passing between the objects for the client portion of the application and the objects for the server portion, we develop event trace diagrams. The event trace diagram for the Exchange Rate Update use case is shown in Figure 140.

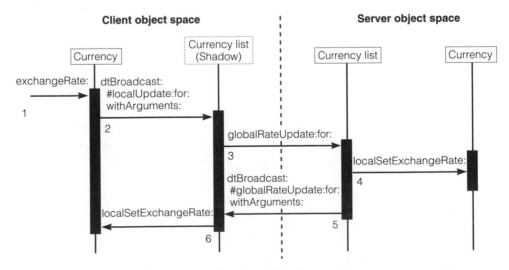

Figure 140. Event trace diagram for an exchange rate update

In considering the message flow when an exchange rate is modified, we use local copies of the EmsCurrencyList, EmsCurrency, and EmsCountry classes in the client object space instead of generating shadow objects. By creating these *light objects* that are local copies of the remote objects, we improve performance because we maximize local reference and minimize remote messages. The only shadow we create is that of the server's currency list instance. The resulting distribution matrix is shown in Figure 141 on page 247. When we put currency list objects in both the client and the server object spaces, we must take precautions to control the message flow when an exchange rate value is changed on a client machine. It is important to know whether code is being executed in the client object space or the server object space to be sure that only the server, not the client, broadcasts update messages to the server's dependents. The currency list has an instance variable serverCurrencyList. Its value is not nil for currency lists in client object spaces, but it is nil for the currency list object in the server object space. By testing this variable, we can provide correct method behavior in different object spaces, although the classes are actually identical in both locations. For example, in the code for the server CurrencyList, the server uses the retrieve method of its superclass. This in turn causes the data to be retrieved from the server's DB2/2 database.

When the client's view asks for the currencies from the local currency list the first time, the local currency in turn gets a local copy of the server's currency list. The server currency list adds the client currency list as a dependent at that time. The server currency list instance thus knows about all its dependents (subscribers) through the dependency mechanism and informs them about modified currency exchange rates.

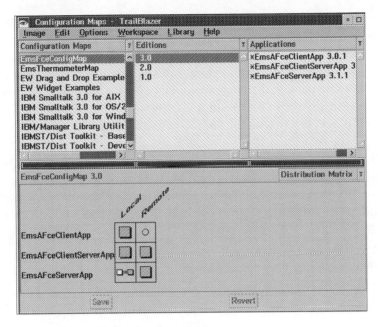

Figure 141. FCE distribution matrix

Figure 142 shows the client and server object spaces.

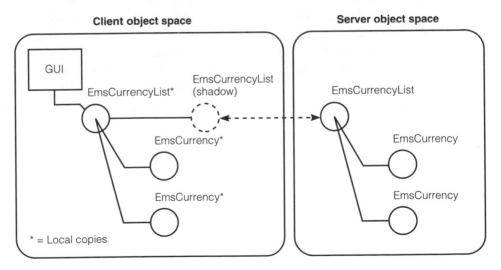

Figure 142. Object spaces for client and server

Using local copies instead of shadows minimizes the generation of remote messages. After copies of the instances are made in the client object space, only update messages are sent through the network to keep the local instances synchronized. Thus the view's table part would ask its attributes from the local instance each time the table needs to be refreshed instead of going over the network to the remote object.

Having local copies of remote objects in the client image means that we must have the classes EmsCurrencyList, EmsCurrency and EmsCountry in both the client object space and the server object space. Therefore, we cannot use the distribution matrix to make automatic remote object references. We must use explicit object references for remote objects. This is done by first defining a global object reference for the class EmsCurrencyList and then getting a shadow from that object reference. The object reference, named EmsServer-CurrencyList, points to the EmsCurrencyList of our server object space.

We get the shadow of the server's EmsCurrencyList class during the first invocation of the Currency's getter method. To get a local copy from a shadow, we used the method DSPerformWithLocalResult. This method creates a copy in the same object space as the sender of that message. Our currency list uses the retrieve method to initialize the currency list. This also includes making a copy of the server's currency list.

10.8 Summary

We have discussed the development of a distributed object application using IBM's SOM/DSOM and VisualAge SOMsupport through the example of a customer information management system for bank branches to trade foreign currencies.

The use of the VisualAge Distributed Feature distributed programming language has been discussed briefly in an exchange rate update scenario for currency management in the foreign exchange application.

Both the VisualAge SOMsupport and the Distributed Feature can be used for developing distributed object applications that enable the server to take the new role as object server, active server, or peer applications to the client.

Management Aspects

11

Managing Object-Oriented Development Projects

Object-oriented development is software development, and most of the considerations that pertain to good software management apply to object-oriented projects. Object technology, however, emphasizes three main aspects of development: fidelity to the real requirement (requirements), early fulfillment of user expectations, and productivity, which translate respectively into prototyping and iterations, incremental delivery, and reuse. None of these aspects can be left to happen by itself: All of them require process definitions and careful management. Visual programming is key to achieving productivity; on the other hand, it presents new management challenges.

The quality and the productivity of object-oriented software development can be far superior to those of any other approach. As a result, the reward is large enough to justify the investments needed to make it all happen.

The management aspects of object technology are the key factors to the success of the development of object application. These aspects transcend by far the education of programmers in an object-oriented programming language. Object technology is based on modeling, and the requirement-gathering process needed to build the models requires interaction with business users and domain experts as well as a hard look at the company's current processes and their possible enhancements. The use of object technology therefore has an impact on the whole enterprise.

The most profound changes introduced by object technology affect the way the enterprise builds applications and imposes a very clear discipline on the development teams. When a company adopts object technology and invests in the adoption process, it is not because of a whim to embrace the latest technology novelty but to reap benefits from its application.

The main benefits from object technology derive from the fidelity to user requirements, the flexibility to change, and the reuse of components already developed, in-house or by external vendors. The user requirements are captured and validated through an iterative and incremental process in which both analysis and design prototyping play an important role, facilitated by visual programming tools. Changes are accommodated in a process of similar characteristics but that can be vastly improved through the use of frameworks, which are adaptable, reusable components.

All these issues—iteration, change, and reuse—present formidable management challenges. None of these can be successful without proper management and infrastructure.

The application development process model is not a part of VMT. Each development team may have good reasons to choose its own process model. VMT, however, recommends constraints on the process model, such as the source of requirements, iterations, and prototyping. This part of the book presents the management considerations of addressing object application development productively under these constraints, as well as taking advantage of visual programming tools, and including testing, prototyping, and staffing aspects that are important to the success of the building and deployment of object applications.

11.1 VMT and Development Process Models

The object paradigm and the modeling, design, and implementation phases are independent of the chosen development process model [YOU92]. When developing applications with VMT, we could have chosen any development process model. However, some models are far more productive than others for a given paradigm.

The development process models that should be used with VMT obtain maximum advantage from the paradigm and the technology if they are both iterative and incremental. We consider the spiral [BOE88] and fountain [HEN93] models, as variations of this category.

There are a number of developmental iterations within the development stage of a product's life cycle. An iteration consists of a planning period for this iteration, followed by a producing period and an assessing period. Analysis, design, code, and test activities are carried out during the producing period of the development process. Because we learn from each iteration, the scope of the iterations change over time. The extent of each activity during each iteration varies depending on both the size of the project and the iteration objectives. During the early iterations, we may focus on the analysis of the problem, followed by iterations that focus on design and coding. The last few iterations involve performance tuning and final testing to get ready for packaging and delivering of the developed product.

While an iteration involves planned rework of a fixed set of functionalities, an increment involves dividing the application functionality into a number of increments to develop and deliver them in stages. The VMT development process accommodates this incremental development approach.

It is useful to group use cases to control the functionality provided in each iteration. For example, we can allocate core use cases for the initial iterations and then add secondary use cases to iterations to be developed later.

For large projects involving multiple development teams, it is also possible to have concurrent development iterations carried out by different teams, each being responsible for the development of a part of the target application.

Prototyping is part of the development process. Even early on, analysis prototyping is useful to solicit user feedback and validate user requirements. Design prototyping is used to build a partial working solution to be evolved to the final product. With visual programming tool support, prototyping is a seamless way to keep evolving the design and code at various levels, such as object classes, subsystems (categories), frameworks, and the like.

Reuse of components is built into this development process. During early iterations of the product development life cycle, there is an effort to find, match, and customize components from the reuse library to meet current development requirements. As development gets closer to completion, there are the "hardening" and "harvesting" activities to generalize and standardize. This is the point at which to organize the potential components produced from the project. The harvested components are then cataloged into a reuse library for future reuse within this project or for another project.

11.2 Prototyping

Visual programming makes prototyping much easier and faster than writing code. The goal of prototyping is to develop what is really wanted, not what is declared to be needed. Visual programming helps by quickly showing the result of implementing the requirement as stated, and encourages feedback because its effects can be visualized rapidly.

Prototyping is done interacting with users and domain experts. Users provide their preferred modalities of interaction. Experts provide a deeper vision of the application services and its future trends and possible modifications; experts also are a good source of knowledge about exceptions and exception handling.

Another use of prototyping is to show proof of concept and application feasibility. Two types of prototypes can be distinguished, as shown in Figure 143.

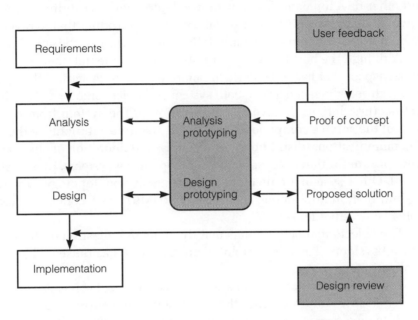

Figure 143. Prototyping in the VMT development process

- The analysis prototype is an aid for exploring the problem domain.
- The development prototype is an aid for incremental development of the solution.

11.2.1   Analysis Prototype

The analysis prototype is a tool to get feedback during requirements gathering and the analysis of the problem domain. It is used mainly as a proof of concept.

Using the model-view-controller paradigm, we can say that to build a prototype, we use visual programming tools to iterate the design of the model classes and to develop interaction techniques for the view classes. We also evaluate the feasibility of a project, often using existing components such as databases, communication managers, and object models and frameworks.

A golden rule in analysis prototyping is that it should be thrown away when finished. The developer should use the concepts exposed by it, not its code. A consequence of this rule is that an analysis prototype should not be evolved directly into a working application. The prototype was built to exhibit functionality; because it is neither robust nor scalable, evolving it into an application will produce poor results.

11.2.2   Development Prototype

The development prototype is a tool for staged delivery of subsystems to users and other development teams. It shows deployment feasibility; the emphasis, however, is on flexibility and scalability. It is a product that evolves through incremental development, usually following a variety of the spiral life cycle.

Although the building of the prototype is incremental, there is at least one global aspect that has to be defined before prototyping starts—the application architecture, which consists of both system and object architectures. The system architecture defines the overall organization of the system from the point of view of the service components and global resources; it includes the handling of communications, distribution of databases, and definition of client and server functions, definition of layers (hardware, operating systems, presentation, and so on). Other system architectural aspects are system topology, which defines the information flow among components [RUM91], task concurrency, and possible resource bottlenecks.

The object architecture refers mainly to the organization of the application into subsystems. The object architecture therefore has reuse and performance implications.

The criterion to define a subsystem is based on cohesiveness of its components and low coupling with other subsystems; concurrency aspects, such as multiple concurrent access to an object in a distributed system, must also be considered.

From a management point of view, a subsystem is usually developed by one team, which entails subsystem testing and integration considerations.

In the early stages of the development prototype, it is common to use scaffolding to keep the prototype runnable. For instance, flat files can be used to emulate a database. As the prototype grows, scaffolding is removed until it becomes a deliverable product. To that end, additional work is required, such as testing, documentation, code cleanup, and reviews.

11.2.3   Use of Prototyping: Pros and Cons

The appropriate use of prototyping has positive effects in application development. First of all, it shows concrete progress, which is very useful for user morale and managerial comfort. In the case of development by an external team, it provides milestones that can be related to partial payments. It also promotes interaction among different groups (users, domain experts, developers, planners, managers), which is very helpful in overcoming the roadblocks that every project encounters sooner or later.

Many times the application scope is not totally defined and its domain only partially explored. A prototype allows the exploration of fuzzy areas and gives room to experiment with implementation techniques, while the development team gains experience.

The main object problems associated with prototyping relate to scaling up the prototype, accessing the real environment resources, and servicing the required number of users with an adequate response time.

Developers may be perfectionists spending too much time not really solving user problems but iterating uncontrollably in what has been called "waltzing through the solution space" as all possible permutations are tried. When this happens, developments do not come to a proper closure. Because visual programming provides an environment where change is easy, the temptation to keep on prototyping may be strong.

Managers tend to underestimate the cost of the final product based on a linear extrapolation of the prototype. A consequence of that and the need to show results is that the pressure to ship a working prototype can become irresistible.

To be appropriate, prototyping must balance the development "meat" with the "sizzle." A hot-looking prototype with no decent model underneath is hard to evolve into a long-lasting product. On the other hand, a dull-looking prototype, even with a good model underpinning the design, is hard to sell to users and management.

The prototype should be built with both technical and business goals in mind: looking at only one of these goals may lead either to excessive costs (using a hot technology not especially required) or to basing a business solution on a technical environment that will soon be obsolete.

Finally, management of prototyping activities includes the requirement that developers set clear completion and evaluation criteria for the prototypes before they start building them, as well as for reviewing, refining, and documenting the prototypes before cut-over.

11.3   Rapid Application Development

The objective of rapid application development is to develop the right code quickly. To achieve this goal, we can build applications using existing components as well as generators and high-productivity tools. This includes maintaining control of the development process while managing user expectations.

One key decision is whether to build or buy components. This decision must be carefully weighed. A cost is associated with developing code in house, which also includes the cost of testing and documentation, and the cost of amassing domain and implementation expertise. Although the fastest way to develop code is not having to write it, there are costs associated with finding and evaluating components, as well as integrating the components in the application environment. Components often have to be adapted to fit specific requirements. The quality and ease of maintenance of the acquired components must also be considered.

For rapid application development, the most frequently acquired components are those that are domain independent, such as class libraries that include graphical user interface (GUI) frameworks, database components to materialize and dematerialize objects (that is, to store objects in and retrieve objects from a relational database, and communication components that support protocols such as TCP/IP or APPC. Domain- or business-oriented components require a more careful decision process based normally on their applicability and the cost of adapting them to the application to be developed.

When components must be generated in house, power tools and code generators can help. Although GUI builders and code template generators are available in the marketplace, visual programming tools that create and glue GUI and non-GUI components together, such as IBM VisualAge, provide the highest development productivity.

Rapid application development requires a clear control of the development process, but such control should not emphasize schedules and "administrivia." The main focus should be on deliverables, with a clear definition on their purpose, whether it is to prototype new functions or implement new areas, to implement or redesign well-defined services, or to produce code that will be shared with other teams. In addition, team dynamics are important, and an environment of confidence should be established: Managers must avoid making unrealistic commitments or overselling features, while programmers must live up to their promises and deliver their components on time. Coordination and trust must be developed among technical and managerial realms, among users and developers, and among the developers themselves. The not-invented-here syndrome is probably the deadliest disease that can affect object-oriented rapid application development.

The perceived success of a project is inversely proportional to the expectations of the recipients and directly proportional to the delivery time of the results. Managing user expectations is therefore important, especially with rapid development. A software development project with overblown budgets and missed schedules becomes a monster that cannot be tamed and must be destroyed. Object-oriented techniques are highly productive but not magic; there is no silver bullet [BRO87] that can replace effective management.

11.4 Supportive Development Environments

To show a payoff for the human investment in object-oriented technology, it is essential to have a development environment that supports the development effort in all its stages, starting with business process reengineering and continuing through the delivery of code. Assuming that the reengineering effort has been done already and a target "new real world" (the application to be) has been defined, the developing environment must include modeling, design, and code development tools. These tools should support the individual programmer as well as the team efforts.

Modeling tools have been in the marketplace for quite a while and usually have good drawing and documenting features, supporting one or more notations of published methodologies. The OMT notation is very popular, and most of these tools can be used to support modeling with VMT. Code generation is still rather elementary and is limited mostly to header files in C++-oriented tools and class structure in Smalltalk-oriented tools. No commercial tool in the marketplace handles frameworks and subsystem composition.

Tools are especially needed because of the iterative nature of object-oriented software development. If models must be constructed manually, there are likely to be too few iterations. In a real project, the number of iterations needed is not limited to the analysis and design phases but can span many development phases. Modification of the code affects the models, and systematic feedback on the effects is hard to obtain unless the process is supported by tools. In summary, we can achieve high levels of productivity and reuse if we can provide even small programmer teams with an integrated development environment that provides a seamless transition from requirements to code.

11.4.1   Configuration Management

For programmer teams, sharing of deliverables must be painless. These deliverables include models, designs, and code and can be held in module-based or subsystem-based library systems. The team should be able to maintain version control over developed deliverables, therefore managing configurations of versioned objects should be made easy.

The technology available in today's marketplace is focused on code configuration management, although the same concepts are being applied now to other development components in recently announced tool environments such as IBM Team Connection. A traditional code library system, such as CMVC or PVCS, is a module-based library system. It controls files that contain pieces of modules such as headers, definitions, and code. This type of library is managed via a mechanism that allows for check in and check out of individual pieces. These pieces can be modified in time by multiple developers. These modifications are incorporated through the file system, and the result is that many files may need to be changed when updating a single module.

Another approach is provided by subsystem-based library systems such as the one provided by the IBM VisualAge Smalltalk Team Environment and by OTI's ENVY/Developer. This type of library system controls objects that contain complete subsystems or "applications" that are managed via subsystem ownership: Each subsystem is an object that is controlled by its owner and modified through the development environment. The result is that only one object needs to be changed when a single subsystem is updated.

Ownership implies authority to change contents and release a new version. A version cannot be modified; an "open version" that is modifiable is called an *edition*. It becomes a version when the owner releases changes into it and gives it a version name (such as Version 1.2). Any developer can make local changes to anything in his or her edition, but only the owner of the subsystem (application) can take code from these so called *scratch* editions and release them into an official version. The owner remains the focus of control.

11.4.2   Configuration and Version Control

In a team development environment, two control disciplines are needed: configuration control and version control.

Configuration control keeps track of compatible sets of subsystem versions and manages prerequisites and dependencies on other subsystems. This allows subsystems to be built by different teams, and these subsystems can be handled as they evolve independently.

Version control maintains the development history and handles regression to prior versions. Version control also allows comparisons with previous approaches, which is essential for code maintenance, both during incremental development and after product shipment.

11.5   Development Approaches for Object-Oriented Projects

The development of an object-oriented project requires a process model, which we call the application development life cycle. The process model is the basis for decision support about activities, roles, work products, techniques and tools. Because it is a key factor in development productivity, reuse should be integrated into the development life cycle and not be a separate parallel activity.

We can consider two main types of reuse: domain-oriented reuse and cross-domain reuse.

11.5.1   Domain-Oriented Reuse: Architectures and Frameworks

Domain-oriented reuse can be considered at several levels of abstraction. The highest level is the architectural level: we can define reusable architectures that can be instantiated for a given enterprise or business.

Architectures

An architecture defines components and their relationships, without any reference to extensional component attributes. For instance, building architectures describe the relationships between the height and the width of the windows of a given style but do not prescribe any particular length or width; this allows us to recognize a Gothic style of architecture both in the cathedral of Notre Dame in Paris and in a miniature of the cathedral sold as a souvenir. An object architecture defines subsystems and their relationships and can be adopted (reused) at the same level in many projects.

A domain-oriented object architecture can be defined at an industry level, describing the processes that are typical of that industry, the subsystems usually found in the industry supporting systems, and the main objects and data structures supporting each process and subsystem and across processes and subsystems. Such architectures are built currently for the banking, insurance, and other industries.

There are many advantages of starting a development from an industry architecture: The global vision the architecture gives a coherence to the development of the individual business-supporting application. Also, object reuse is guided at a high level by the architectural definitions. Finally, the architecture provides a ground for understanding between developers, users, and business professionals.

When starting from an industry architecture, the next step is to build an enterprise model, which is an instantiation of the industry architecture to the corporation for which the support systems will be built. The criterion is to select the areas of the industry architecture that are relevant to the corporation, as well as to find out which corporate business areas are not covered by the selected industry architecture. If a business process reengineering activity is to take place at this corporation, the industry architecture may provide valuable guidance to that activity.

The next step is therefore to build a process model of the enterprise that will define which processes and jobs require automation support. This leads to the definition of application requirements by specifying the use cases and the problem statement that are the external inputs to the application development process.

The reuse perspective described, starting from industry architectures and going all the way to application development, vastly expands the scope of management of the object-oriented projects. Iterations now occur all the way. For instance, there may be several iterations between an industry architecture and a reengineered "to-be" process model, especially if the to-be model must be evolved from the current "as-is" model. The to-be model may require close scrutiny and validation, which can be achieved through simulation techniques. If so, additional iterations will be needed between the reengineering and the simulation activities, and only when a satisfactory result is achieved can the application development process rightly begin.

Object Frameworks

The construction and use of object frameworks has a definite impact on the application development productivity metrics. A framework is a collection of classes that work together, provide default behavior, and can be customized to address particular business needs, adapting the behavior accordingly.

From a business perspective, a framework encapsulates expertise about a problem domain. As such, its use may reduce development time significantly. An application can use one or more frameworks, and frameworks may use other frameworks, combining expertise in several domains. For instance a steel manufacturing framework may use an optimization framework for the production scheduling process.

Frameworks are valuable because they lead to easier programming development [WIL94]. Frameworks can be used by programmers who are not experts in that problem domain, but they save time for experts, too. In addition, a whole family of related programs can be built in a consistent manner based on a single framework.

Frameworks contribute to reduced maintenance because the applications that need to be written have fewer lines of code. Bugs in the framework need to be fixed in only one place.

There are, however, several costs involved in the use of frameworks. Framework development requires higher skills than program development. In addition, to encourage their use, frameworks must be "productized" by additional testing, documentation, and sample usage programs. Frameworks must also be maintained as circumstances, such as target platforms and problems solved, change over time. The cost of adding new features to the framework because of client requirements should also be considered.

11.5.2   Cross Domain Reuse: Frameworks and Patterns

[MAI91] suggests the existence of three knowledge components to describe software engineering problems: *domain knowledge,* which represents aspects of the problem domain, such as life insurance; *goal knowledge,* which describes the purpose of the application, such as to price insurance premiums based on life expectancies; and *solution knowledge,* which describes how to achieve the sought goal in the context of a certain domain, using for instance regression analysis to determine life expectancies for given populations.

Solution knowledge can be considered as a cross domain, or even more properly, an abstract domain knowledge structure that can be common to many problem domains. This abstract domain knowledge describes the causal relations between abstract objects and can be instantiated to a certain domain model to define causal relations between concrete objects. For instance, the knowledge involved in solving scheduling programs can be instantiated to different domains such as parcel scheduling, steel mill production scheduling, or car manufacturing scheduling. We might therefore build a scheduling framework that could eventually be reused in those domains.

Solution knowledge of a finer granularity than frameworks can be defined as *design patterns.* Each pattern describes a problem that occurs over and over again in the problem environments [ALE77]. The solution knowledge encapsulated by a pattern in object technology is described by four essential elements [GAM95]: a pattern name that describes the design problem; a description of the (abstract) problem to which the pattern applies; the solution to the design problem in terms of the elements that make up the design, their relationships, responsibilities and collaborations; and the consequences of applying the pattern, that is, the results and trade-offs. The goal of recording design patterns is to capture solution knowledge in a form that can be used effectively. Reusing a pattern, however, may affect the flexibility, extensibility, or portability of an application.

Other Reusable Components

Object technology fosters an "ecology of software," where most of the work products of each stage can be reused if properly designed, checked, and classified. In addition to paradigms, architectures, models, and code, test suites can be reused, including test cases and scenarios, and documentation describing problems, use cases, and documentation abstractions such as templates can be successfully reused in other projects.

If a reuse repository will be maintained for some or most of these reusable components, we have to decide what goes into the repository; that is, we need to have criteria to determine the reusability value of a component. We need to establish procedures for how components are checked in, to plan for browse and retrieval facilities, and to define check-out procedures as well. We also need to define a set of standards for the repository such as naming conventions, required descriptions, and documentation. To avoid having the repository become a write-only facility (one that nobody reads from), we need good management support and rewards not only for the creation of reusable components but also for their actual reuse.

11.5.3   The Reuse Process

The reuse of components must be defined as a process that can be established and managed. [GOL95] suggests a model for the reuse process that includes the following steps:

- Identify the need for a component that will be used repeatedly in a development project or that, even if used only once, has a clear and defined function, making it reasonable to expect that someone has built it already. For instance, a scheduling engine may be used more than once, or it may be complex enough to justify its acquisition.

- Acquire the component. This can be done by building it in house if the resources are available or buying it from a vendor if it has been built already. If the effort and cost of building it in house, including training, are higher than the contract fee, then its construction could be contracted out, depending on a set of factors such as availability of reliable vendors, confidentiality, and cost of maintenance.

- Certify the acquired component for safe use. We need to verify that the acquired component provides the required services, that it is reasonably bug-free, and that it can be integrated into the existing development as expected.

- Store the component in the repository through the established check-in procedure.

- Report the existence of the new component not only to the team that asked for it but to all the potential users and to the development community. The communication mechanism should provide enough information that prospective users can evaluate its usefulness. Recent trends are to use the World Wide Web as a communication mechanism, for example, the IBM Consulting Group uses IBM's AssetWeb. In that case, the Web is used both as a communication mechanism and as a repository from which components can be downloaded.

- Provide access to the component. This entails providing a facility to help the developers identify available components they were not aware of and that may meet their needs. This requires a rather sophisticated search mechanism as well as a thoughtful component classification schema, especially for searching cross-domain assets.

  Once the search mechanism has identified one or more assets that are potentially useful, the developer needs to look over these assets to have a better grasp of the way they fit the requirements. If their fit looks promising, they must be located, which may require a search of more that one repository, and retrieved.

- Once the component has been identified as potentially useful, we need to firmly assess its applicability and usability. A relational database handler written in Smalltalk, for instance, may or not be usable in a C++ environment, depending on the application architecture. A scheduling system used for building construction will probably not be usable for scheduling a steel mill but may be applicable in a shipyard.

- Integrate the component into the project and use it. This activity should be the responsibility of a skilled designer who understands both the current project and the component to be integrated.

- Maintain the component. Maintenance can be provided by the builders of the component or by the project team. The first option relieves the work of the project team, but successive improvements by the supplier of the component may require additional integration efforts. The second option provides more workload but more control, and it protects the team against surprises.

11.6   Staffing and Training

An object development project team should be composed of individuals with several required backgrounds. Good skills are needed in the following areas:

- Object-oriented analysis and design methodology
- Application and systems architecture
- End user interface design
- The chosen programming language and development environment
- Database design
- Client/server design
- Systems engineering
- Application systems implementation

11.6.1   Roles of Team Members

Traditional roles to be filled are

- Project manager
- Architect (or chief designer)
- Analyst (system or business)
- Developer (designer or programmer)
- Tester
- Technical support

New roles needed for object-oriented projects [GOL92] include

- Object-oriented architect
- Object-oriented mentor
- Development team
  - —Analysis prototyper
  - —Development builder
  - —Class librarian
  - —Tester
- Reuse team
  - —Reuse manager
  - —Reuse administrator

Some of these roles can be filled by existing members who gain the new skills.

11.6.2   Object-Oriented Architect

The object-oriented architect can be an expanded role played by an architect. The tasks include

- Set up architecture frameworks, policy, principles, and standards.
- Make design decisions and review the programming results.
- Explain to team members why design decisions are made.
- Work with developers to handle implementation issues.
- Ensure design style and programming consistency, adherence to standards, and naming conventions.

The qualifications needed are

- System design knowledge and programming background in organization's selected programming language and tools
- Communications and interpersonal skills

11.6.3   Object Mentor

The object-oriented mentor can be a new or expanded role played by a strong technical support person or an experienced object-oriented developer. For the first object-oriented project in an organization, this is the most important person in the team and is usually hired from outside. The mentor's tasks are

- Act as a general resource to answer questions about all technical aspects of the project (analysis, design, and implementation phases)
- Provide the core part of the analysis, design, and programming (hands-on)
- Assist the object-oriented architect in handling implementation issues

The mentor needs to have the following qualifications:

- Be a technical guru in object-oriented technology
- Explain clearly and have patience
- Be an excellent programmer in the organization's programming language and tools

11.6.4   Development Team

The analysis prototyper works with clients (end users) and with the systems or business analyst to program user interface prototypes. The qualifications needed are good programming ability in the selected visual programming and prototyping tools as well as strong communications and interpersonal skills.

The development builder works with the architect and designer to create the initial version of the solution, programs executable prototypes to prove design feasibility, and constructs final program deliverables. The builder must be an excellent programmer in the organization's selected programming language.

For smaller projects, the role of class librarian could be filled by the development builder. The class librarian must maintain configuration and version control and release management of the class structure for the project, and work closely with the reuse administrator. The only essential qualification is experience in a team programming environment.

The development team tester works with the object-oriented architect and mentor in designing the test strategy and plan, creates test cases for the different levels of testing, works with the development builders in carrying out unit (class) testing and integration testing, and works with clients (end user) in user acceptance testing. The two necessary qualifications for the tester are experience in testing and knowledge of the selected programming language.

11.6.5   Reuse Team

The reuse manager is responsible for identifying, evaluating, acquiring, and classifying new reusable components; for ensuring that the software components meet reuse guidelines, such as quality, style, documentation completion, and broad applicability; and for consulting with the prototyping team on available components. This role requires competence in object-oriented technology and the use of reusable components, programming background in the organization's selected programming language, and good communications and interpersonal skills.

The reuse administrator is required to classify, certify, and store new reusable components; communicate the availability of new components; assist the reuse manager in evaluating new components; and assist developers to locate or access reusable components on request. This role demands technical competence in object-oriented technology and the reusable components, as well as classification and abstraction skills.

11.6.6   Training

To achieve good teamwork, the whole development team should be trained in the new technology. The depth of training in each area will depend on the role of each team member, but it should be remembered that the learning curve is long and steep. The training plan should allow sufficient lead time for starting the project, especially if it is the first in object-oriented program development.

The following are the key areas of training:

- Object-oriented technology perspective
- Modeling methodologies and techniques
- Object-oriented design
- Object-oriented programming

- Implementation environment
- Project management

Different forms of training should be considered, according to project needs:

- Self-study (books and/or computer based training)
- Classes with instructors
- Residencies and internships
- Computer-based training
- Mentored apprenticeships

A variety of different training formats can be useful in helping developers and managers reach their target proficiency. Self-study provides a conceptual understanding of the subject matters. Traditional lecture classes usually provide an introductory level of instruction, even with hands-on workshops. Also, it is hard for a classroom instructor to provide meaningful instruction to 20 or more people, all with diverse backgrounds and learning styles.

Mentoring and apprenticeships offer a customized training program on a real-life project. The student has the opportunity to watch the instructor perform and then to work with the instructor, ending by performing all alone to demonstrate proficiency. Mentoring is practical and a very important element of an effective training plan, but it demands critical skills. A mentoring plan is not easy to establish. Residencies and internships often provide a viable real-world training alternative.

11.7 Estimating Project Cost and Duration

Good project management implies the need for an accurate estimate of project cost and duration and measurements that depend on the project size and complexity. Systems of measurement (such as number of lines of code) existed for a while, providing values with reasonable accuracy for function-based developments. Such metrics are usually based on project experience. Large projects using object-oriented technology are fairly recent, and their results are not publicly available because they represent a competitive advantage for the corporations that have run them. As a result, most of the work done on object-oriented development metrics is largely theory-based and relies on lengthy calculations using many subjective factors.

Detailed object metrics are described in [LOR94] and more recently in [HEN95]. In this section we describe the main factors that affect project cost and duration and the estimating and reporting pitfalls to avoid.

The first factors to consider are project size and complexity, since they will impact the analysis, design, coding, and testing. Two more factors need to be added: integration among the different subsystems and appropriate documentation.

The development environment weighs heavily in the productivity of application building. One of the environment elements, the programming language, is a factor that cannot be taken in isolation but must be considered together with the problem domain. For instance, it is well known that the trading corporations prefer developments in Smalltalk because of the productivity, flexibility, and extensibility it provides, while manufacturing enterprises prefer C++, which is closer to their extant C programs, is more effective for real-time applications, and interfaces with numerical control machines. A metric for project duration that does not take into account both the language and the problem domain may lead to gross estimation errors.

Size by itself is misleading. First of all, counting lines of code has no meaning because the objective of object-oriented development is to write as little code as possible to meet the application requirements. In addition, the different languages—Smalltalk, C++, Eiffel—have different computational power per average instruction; statistics show [GOL92] that programs written in C++ require about 27 source lines to provide one end-user function but can be written in 13 lines of Smalltalk. By emphasizing the strengths and weaknesses of each language in the test application, these numbers may be altered considerably.

Counting the number of classes is also misleading, because classes may exhibit different behaviors of varying complexity. Current approaches for estimating development costs calculate the required number of person-months based on an estimate of the number of behaviors to satisfy end-user requirements and on the estimated complexity of design of the defined class methods. As design patterns [GAM95] become more popular, they may be used to provide more accurate guidance to the program's complexity.

11.7.1   Cost of Reuse

Other cost drivers are related to the reuse policies of the corporation and to the availability of ready-to-reuse components. Reuse policies may mandate including in the project cost the additional cost of producing robust and error-free reusable project components. It is not difficult to identify project subsystems that can be used elsewhere; this is called *harvesting* components. Harvested components are not ready to be consumed as is; their characteristics are largely oriented toward the project they were developed for. To be useful in other areas of the project or in subsequent projects, harvested components require an additional process of generalization, quality control, debugging, and documentation called the *hardening process.* The cost of the hardening process can be charged to the originating project, to the projects that will reuse the component, or to a special reuse investment account that can help to manage the cost transitions from project to project.

In our experience, the additional cost of making something reusable is about 50 percent of the cost of developing it. This approximation comes very close to the values reported in [TRA95], where the following breakdown (qualified as "conservative") is presented:

Additional Reuse Costs

25% for additional generalization

15% for additional documentation

15% for additional testing

5% for library support and maintenance

_____

Total   60% additional cost for making something reusable

Our 50 percent incremental reuse cost would seem to imply that for every two developers on the project, one additional developer is needed for reuse. However, not everything in a project is reusable. Early computations of reusable code [BIG84] have shown that 40 percent to 60 percent of all code is reusable from one application to another. Our own estimate is that for domain-focused applications, 50 percent of the project deliverables are reusable. The 50 percent reuse cost is therefore applied to 50 percent of the project, which leads to a 25 percent cost increase, mostly translated into additional person-months. We do not favor, however, establishing a dedicated reuse team for a project—that is, a team that does only reuse. In our experience, it is far more productive, especially for domain-focused reuse, to have the same developing team (although not the same developers) do the hardening of the reusable components. Having the same team work on reuse means that the domain knowledge has been already acquired: An independent hardening team would have to spend time learning about the application domain. However, we do prefer to have the hardening done by a different developer from the one who produced the deliverable, because we want to externalize and make explicit and formal as much knowledge about the component as possible, and facets that are obvious for the developer may not be so for the hardener.

Developing reusable components has a cost, but hardening is not the only cost to consider. To reuse a component has an additional cost that depends heavily on the modifications that need to be done to the component in order to include it in the project. [TRA95] quotes, based on empirical studies, a ratio of 5 to 1; that is, five lines of reused code cost the same on the average as one line of developed code. He also refers to the findings in [SEL91], where it is reported that for black box (as-is) reuse, ratios of 20 to one or 25 to 1 are not uncommon. However, these ratios drop dramatically when 5 percent or more of the code has been modified.

Advanced visual development environments such as IBM VisualAge may yield even better reuse results. First, reuse of standard, cross domain components such as database managers, queries, and GUI elements is straightforward. Second, the system automatically builds a standard public interface for components, which allows for a systematic and repeatable software-building discipline. Third, to the trained eye, the relationships among components (expressed as colored connection lines on a display screen) provide a much faster understanding of the internals of the relationships than when the relationships must be derived from code.

11.8   The Transition to Object-Oriented Technology

The transition to object technology requires addressing several key questions at the corporate level, such as the opportunity for this kind of transition, the costs involved, resource allocation, and the preservation of existing systems [TKA93]. The new paradigm has to be internalized by the corporation, which cannot be done instantaneously; the transfer of technology that enables the paradigm shift is not a linear process. For any technology, four transfer phases have been identified from the point of view of the organization that is the target of the transfer:

- Awareness: The target organization knows about the existence of the new technology and understands the advantages and risks involved in embracing it.

- Exploration: The target organization sets up prototype projects using the new technology.

- Transition: The target organization decides to embrace the new technology, and the existing technology base is converted to the new one.

- Habit: The new technology becomes "business as usual" in the target organization. A mature stage of this phase would be characterized by the presence of process control, quality standards, and productivity measurements.

11.8.1   Defining Transition Projects

The transition to object technology can be considered in itself a reengineering activity. As such, current (as-is) and desired (to-be) situations need to be defined. [RUB95] describes a collection of transition projects that are typically involved in a successful transition to object technology:

Selecting a Business Architecture
The goal of this project is to obtain a business architecture that provides a framework for the construction and integration of business applications. The framework must capture the key business abstractions of a particular domain, such as retail banking, loan risk management, or transportation. Business frameworks are strategic, reusable assets that an organization uses to achieve its stated business values for software development.

Selecting a Technical Architecture

The goal is to develop a technical architecture that provides application programmers with an appropriate, well-defined, and consistent set of system-level services. Example services include security, transactions, printing, database access, and so on. These system services will be reused across an organization's portfolio of applications.

Selecting a Software Development Environment

The goal is to set up a development environment, for all team members, that enables the team to create, deliver, and maintain applications. This environment should include, but is not limited to, analysis and design tools, programming environment (language, library, and tools), configuration management tools, testing tools, and databases. Software development environments that support the construction of object-oriented software should consist of a fully integrated, interactive set of tools that support the incremental, rapid development of business models, databases, and visual presentations. An important aspect of the transition to object technology is to understand how the software development tools should support the incremental, rapid, and visual style of development common to the construction of object systems.

Defining a Development Process Model

The goal is to define the project management and software development processes that will be followed when developing systems using object-oriented technology. An effective development process model for use with such technology defines how to use different strategies such as iterative development, incremental development, prototyping, and producing and consuming reusable assets. In addition, the development process model must include strategies for quality assurance and integration. The resultant process model must be flexible enough to support the development of the different types of software systems that are created within an organization. A significant aspect of a successful transition to object-oriented technology is the ability to plan and control an object-oriented development project. The development process model must include strategies for creating project schedules and controlling execution. These strategies are used to build management trust and meet management development expectations.

Setting Up a Competence Development Plan

The goal is to develop a competence plan to give client team members the skills needed to use the object-oriented processes and technologies. The development of personnel competence is a critical issue when transitioning to the use of any new technology. Without the necessary skills, the transition will not be successful.

Selecting a Reuse Process Model

The goal is to set up a structure in which to plan and manage the process of acquiring, distributing and maintaining reusable assets throughout an organization. For many organizations, the expected value of using object-oriented technology is based on the prospect of high levels of effective reuse. A critical aspect of a transition management plan is then to define specifically how to address the steps of the reuse process model described earlier.

Selecting a Team Structure

The goal is to identify the purpose, roles, managerial style, and communication channels that build the teams needed to meet an organization's development goals and objectives. Interaction rules (within and between teams) must be determined. Finally, the proper personnel must be selected to fulfill the various team roles.

Setting Up a Software Measurement Program

The goal is to identify the required data, a means of collecting the data, and a way to use the results to meet goals. A successful transition to a new technology requires an ability to measure the improvements achieved by using the new technology. Without a measurement program, an organization will not be able to quantify (and justify) improvements. Furthermore, without a measurement program, an organization will not collect the necessary data to improve upon any new technology that it adopts. Long-term success with object-oriented technology, as with any technology, relies on an organization's ability to continuously improve its software development processes, resources, and products.

Selecting a Pilot Project

The goal is to choose and be successful with an initial first project that demonstrates the contributions object-oriented technology can make to an organization, and lays the foundation for making strategic decisions. The pilot project provides the opportunity to evaluate the selected development process model on a real project, to execute the competence development plan to train the pilot project personnel, to exercise the selected software development environment, and to exercise the technical architecture (and possibly a reusable business architecture).

To determine the success of the pilot project, the pilot project goals and objectives must be well-defined, and the software measurement process must be in place to assess the resulting outcomes.

11.9   Summary

Object-oriented technology has the potential to introduce high-productivity improvements in the application development process; however, it also introduces management complexities that should be handled in a systematic way, or the promised benefits will never be realized. The complexity mostly stems not from the technology itself but from the life cycle that makes better use of this technology. Controlled iterations, prototyping, and reuse can be either the key to success or the route to failure. Cost and duration estimates are still in a rather primitive state, and it is important not to overestimate results nor underestimate schedules—losing user credibility with a new technology can be very costly for the corporation, because the problems are now attributed to the technology itself, which blocks the transition to the new paradigm. Meanwhile, the transition may be happening at high speed at a competitor's site. To prevent such a result, technology transfer programs should include management and user education: Crises will arise, and the new technology must not be seen as the cause but rather as a part of the solution.

Finally, there can never be enough said about the need of skilled people, and a good team organization with high spirits. Technologies change; the key to success resides in the people who implement them.

12

Testing and Documentation

This chapter discusses testing and documentation in an object-oriented project. These two aspects, while important, usually receive too little attention. While object-oriented development facilitates construction of software systems, it adds to the complexity of testing. Some fundamental differences make the testing of object-oriented systems more difficult than the testing of traditional procedural systems. Usually testing is the last phase of the waterfall development model. It is important to incorporate testing in each iteration to validate the work products of the iterative development life cycle. A set of integrity rules is provided for validating VMT work products. We also show a way to create visual test data using encapsulation in the VisualAge nonvisual class. Finally, we list some of the documentation essential for maintaining an object-oriented system.

The more user-driven, iterative approach of the object oriented development life cycle does not mean eliminating (or even reducing) testing and documentation. Moreover, if object-oriented development is to handle the ever-changing needs of business, sound documentation and thorough testing are even more important than with the traditional approach.

Good documentation helps to manage user expectations, control user change requests, keep track of project status and resource utilization, and hence plan future projects. It also facilitates reuse and customization of prefabricated components. Sound testing guarantees software quality and facilitates future reuse of software components. Poor testing can not only retard the delivery of applications but also can threaten the overall stability of the system during run time.

12.1   Testing in Object-Oriented Development

Traditionally, testing has been an important element of software development. It has been said that "approximately 50% of the elapsed time and over 50% of the total cost are expended in testing a program or system being developed" [MYE79]. Bill Hetzel's *The Complete Guide to Software Testing* provides a good reference to software testing outside the object-oriented world. However, testing strategies and techniques specifically for object-oriented software are still being researched in the industry and are at an early stage of maturity.

Software development has made great advances with the recent success of object-oriented development and methodology. However, relatively little attention has been paid to the testing of object-oriented software, even though the key principles of object technology that provide benefits to software development also present new testing challenges.

Consider inheritance, for example. Each level in an inheritance hierarchy assumes both the testability and the reliability of higher-level classes. Otherwise inherited features and behaviors cannot be guaranteed at lower levels. This high dependency between objects causes a rapid increase of testing complexity.

For example, polymorphism with dynamic binding offers different challenges to testing because it increases the number of execution paths and its behavior cannot be determined through conventional source code inspection. It is difficult to have to go up and down the class hierarchy to analyze the system's behavior and determine the result of a message that may have been sent to the object itself. Also, because polymorphism hides the complexity of the code, we cannot see which code unit is actually invoked, not even in strongly typed languages.

Because objects encapsulate not only code but also data, testing in object-oriented systems cannot be limited to testing of code but must also include testing of data or the state of the object. Encapsulation becomes a hindrance in implementation in some cases because of the limited access to code and data.

The proper role of testing in object-oriented development raises other issues. Components offered for reuse should be highly reliable; extensive testing is warranted when reuse is intended. However, each reuse is a new context, and retesting is prudent. These are just a few fundamental differences that make the testing of object-oriented systems more difficult than that of traditional procedural systems.

12.1.1   Testing in the Development Cycle

A well-designed and well-managed testing process is essential to the production of quality software. Because of the inherited complexity of object-oriented software, testing should be started very early in the project. Early testing helps discover and prevent defects throughout the development life cycle, and it should be a component of the overall object-oriented development methodology.

In traditional software development, testing was a post-coding phase. Systems were designed and constructed, then tested and debugged. As practices matured, it has been recognized that early testing is important to identify problems in various later phases. If a misinterpretation of requirements in the requirement phase is not identified, it will be costly to fix when the system is built. This is even more true in object-oriented development, where the work products for each phase need to be fully tested or validated before moving to the next phase. A better practice is to have a complete testing life cycle embedded within the overall software life cycle, as shown in the following diagram:

Requirement	Analysis	Design	Code	Maintenance
Testing	Testing	Testing	Testing	Testing

That is, instead of being a discrete phase, testing in an object-oriented development should be an integral part of each phase.

12.1.2   Testing Methods and Techniques

As with analysis and design, it is necessary to define testing methods to be used in a project. Testing methods must address the following questions in each phase of the object-oriented development cycle:

- What should be tested? It is impossible to test all aspects of the work products in the phase. A strategy to identify a subset is important.

- When should testing start and stop? Criteria for the start and end of testing should be clearly defined, with clear criteria for success.

- Who does the testing? Who should carry out the testing work, and how should it be coordinated with the rest of the development process?

- How should testing be conducted? What techniques or tools are to be used in testing each phase?

The design of test cases is best performed in three increments:

- For the requirement or analysis phase, design tests from the use case and object models.

- For the design phase, take test cases from the architecture and class design.

- For the coding phase, design tests based on the coded logic and data structures.

Reviews, inspections, and walk-through are important tests of the early phases of object-oriented development. (Reviews are more important for preventing future errors than they are for discovering current defects, however.)

Here are some examples of useful tests:

- Requirements inspection
- Use-case walkthrough
- Architecture review
- GUI standards review
- System design inspection
- Object model review
- Test cases review
- Project plan inspection
- Class design inspection

The use cases that evolve with each refinement can become the user-acceptance criteria.

12.1.3   Testing Activities Within Phases

As an object-oriented iterative approach, VMT can be characterized as both top-down and bottom-up. During analysis, it is important to take a top-down view for the application to be built. During design, however, we must build the application bottom up: we construct the most primitive part first and gradually assemble the composite parts of the application, reusing those primitive parts built earlier. As a result, there are different testing approaches and activities within each phase of the development cycle.

Requirements/Planning

After the requirements are gathered, they should be reviewed with the target customers. All use cases should be reviewed with users as well as the project team to ensure correctness and completeness. Project plans should be inspected by all members of the project team and reviewed with the management team, not only to validate the business case but also to obtain resource approval for the project. Customers may need to be consulted to review the product release structure and plans.

Analysis

The work products of the analysis phase are the analysis prototype and the analysis object model. Simulation exercises should be carried out on the use cases to validate the prototype and the model. For example, various use scenarios associated with each use case can be reviewed with the target customers. With the aid of the analysis prototype of the proposed solution, the customers may test-drive the prototype to ensure the application look and feel are satisfactory.

Consistency checking can be done through manual inspection or automated when a supporting CASE tool is available.

The integrity rules listed below can be used as review guidelines to ensure that models produced during analysis are consistent. We can apply these rules as review guidelines during the assessment phase in each iteration:

- Object model (OM) versus CRC cards

    —OM class maps to a CRC card

    —OM role name maps to CRC collaborator

    —OM method name maps to CRC responsibility

- Event trace versus CRC cards

    —OM class maps to a CRC card

    —OM message from object A to B <—> CRC for A declares B as collaborator

    —OM message from object A to B <—> CRC for B declares that B has the responsibility to service message

Design

The system and application architectures, objects, and database design should be tested for limiting conditions using the design prototype. Any altered design should be investigated and validated through prototyping. Simulation or benchmarking of the application should be conducted to verify that it meets the performance criteria.

The rules listed below should be used to ensure that models produced during design are consistent with the implemented code. We applied these rules as review guidelines during the assessment phase in each iteration:

- Object model (OM) versus VisualAge design prototype

    —OM class maps to nonvisual VisualAge component

    —OM association role name maps to VisualAge component attribute

    —OM attribute name maps to VisualAge component attribute

    —OM method name maps to VisualAge action

Code/Implementation

Testing for the code can be carried out on the so-called white box and black box level. The functionality of each class and its associated methods can be unit tested. When an error is found, the developer may have to look inside the class and methods to examine the cause of the error—hence the name white box testing. An integration test is then perform at a use case level. At this level, the classes are treated as black boxes; only their behaviors are relevant to performing the required services.

It is important to understand that in an object-oriented project, we need to write code to test our own coding. The test code should be saved for regression tests during acceptance testing. Cases should be designed to test each method in a class. We suggest creating a class method that contains all the testing codes. Note that when we generate run-time code for the visual part of a class, it will generate a test method for us.

Similarly, test cases should be designed from use cases to test each subapplication. We create a class in the subapplication to contain all the testing code for each class in that subapplication as well as testing codes for the subapplication itself. At each application level, we create a class to contain all the testing codes for each of the subapplications as well as testing codes for the overall application. In this way, each component encapsulates all the testing codes for itself and its subcomponents. We are also building our testing code from the bottom up, so that each level reuses the test code from a lower level.

12.1.4   Testing Strategy in a Visual Programming Environment

Visual programming provides an opportunity to streamline testing for object-oriented software. In most visual programming environments, functions are available to test the application. However, not all visual programming tools are object-oriented. We focus here on object-oriented visual programming and use VisualAge as an example to illustrate the technique of testing component-based software.

Different levels of testing are involved:

- Primitive component testing—method and class testing
- Composite component testing—testing of nonvisual and visual components
- Subapplication testing
- Application integration testing
- System acceptance testing

Each component was individually validated before its integration in a higher level component (unit testing). During the unit test of each component, we treat each component as a white box: To perform integration testing, we follow the use cases as test scenarios to validate how the parts work together to provide the required functions. The individual parts are viewed as black boxes during the integration test. Only when we encounter unexpected results do we go to the suspected components and examine them again.

It is generally acknowledged that top-down testing is efficient, but it is often difficult in a traditional programming environment to provide test data to thoroughly verify the lower-level modules. In our environment, we provided test data through the relations of the objects in the object model, making a collection of business objects available for embedding in the components under development in order to verify their function.

Encapsulating Test Data in a VisualAge Nonvisual Class Figure 144 on page 280 shows the composition layout of the BankStubData class. The following explains our approach to devise the test data:

- The Bank class is embedded in a nonvisual component called BankStubData, which, as the name implies, represents the model containing the test data.
- The necessary business objects are created in the initializing method for the Bank class.
- External attributes of the Bank (customers, branches, currencies) are obtained through tear off of the appropriate parts and their addition to the interface.
- If external attributes are of the Collection class, a single test object is obtained by adding the first element of the collection to the interface.
- The previous procedure (tearing off and adding to the interface) is repeated until the lowest-level element is obtained.

The key benefit of this approach is that a single source of coherent and repeatable test data can be provided. For example, BankStubData can be added to the palette for reuse whenever testing is needed during the construction of the visual components. It allows the testing of the GUI before the databases are created. It facilitates the testing before using the database query parts or building the persistent data access classes to access the relational database. All the nonvisual subcomponents in the BankStubData class are variables and have been added as external attributes to the BankStubData class. It becomes a convenient way of supplying test data during development of the application; just add it as a subcomponent and connect the respective attributes.

BankStubData also provides a useful overview of the relations of the business objects in the object model and a hierarchical structure of the data. It serves as a good chart to show and document the high-level relationship among the different objects or classes.

As shown in Figure 144 on page 280, a set of test data has been created for the International OO Bank, which has a number of branches, including the San Jose Branch. The San Jose Branch has its branch currency stock, and a number of cashiers were created as part of the test data. Customer orders were created for one of the cashiers. The cashier has stocked some currencies in the cashier drawer. The same procedure is used for the rest of the test data scenarios shown in Figure 144.

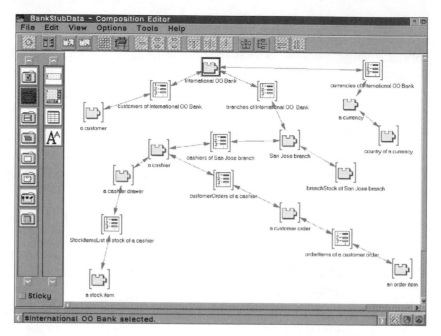

Figure 144. Tear-off attribute diagram for the VisualAge nonvisual Bank StubData part

12.2 Documentation

Different stages in the project life cycle have different documentation needs. Also, the varieties of project documentation have different target audience or users and serve different purposes. For example, we can provide documentation to

- Communicate among the project team members, or with the clients or sponsors
- Educate or provide references for the end users of the system
- Track and report project progress status to management
- Provide information for the maintenance and reuse of the system

Documentation may be textual, graphical (diagramming), or both. Documentation for end users may even be in multimedia format, including sound and video.

Finally, different software components require different levels of documentation.

We concentrate here on the necessary documentation during the development stage of the product life cycle. The following are the work products for the model and the code that needs to be captured for the development, maintenance, and future reuse of the application:

- Class specification
- Method specification
- Data or attribute types
- Program modules
- Configuration maps
- Release notes
- Database design
- Project plan
- Application and systems architectures
- Metrics and performance data
- Status reports with resource utilization
- Change requests and issues tracking

12.2.1 Guidelines for Good Documentation

[STE95] suggests the following basic principles for documenting object-oriented software components:

- Conceptual integrity: Documentation should be on the same conceptual level as the software component.
- Accuracy: Documentation should consistently and accurately describe the software component.
- Accessibility: Documentation should be accessible to the creators and users of the system.
- Measurability: Documentation should include measurements of components both quantitative and qualitative.

It is important to consider that:

- There is never too much documentation.
- Outdated documentation is useless.
- Project managers should start documenting early in the project—from Day 1, if possible.

12.3 Summary

While object-oriented development facilitates design and construction of software systems, it adds to the complexity of testing.

The benefits of object oriented application development cannot be fully realized without robust and complete testing. The iterative development life cycle requires testing to begin right at the start of the project. Testing for each iteration must be completed before the team moves to the next iterations. Also, testing is not limited to the coding and implementation; it should include the requirement and planning as well as analysis and design.

For the coding and implementation phase, it is useful to write test cases for each method for different classes. Top-down testing using stub data is the most efficient way, but lower-level components should be fully tested before they are integrated into higher-level components.

A single source of coherent and repeatable test data is necessary for well-planned, controlled, and reproducible testing. This is not easy in any programming environment. Object-oriented visual programming tools such as VisualAge facilitate such testing.

Business Process Reengineering and Object Technology

13

Business Process Reengineering

The Holy Grail of today's information technology is to be able to model the corporation. The implicit assumption is that building an enterprise model leads to a better understanding of the business and the ability to predict corporate behavior. Furthermore, predicting changes in business conditions means we can build systems to support the business operations we plan for the future.

Such a model would be a simulation model. Simulation, however, has a scope problem: It must simulate the enterprise at different but coherent levels of abstraction to satisfy operational, evaluation, and strategic planning needs. With current technology, this approach is beyond the scope of one tool and is not even supported by one unified methodology.

Enterprise modeling is not entirely successful because it puts too much emphasis on the technology aspects of the model and not enough on user needs. Also, enterprise modeling cannot be successful when it reflects only the executive view of the business functions.

Because datacentric models provide a higher level of abstraction, they seem more stable. However, by themselves, they are not good enterprise models because they cannot model corporate business processes, which span many business functions.

Object modeling is another approach to business modeling. Object models are not restricted to a given business area. Indeed, the objects in an object analysis model—built only with business objects, not with implementation constructs—may belong to different domains. However, object models do not constitute enterprise models per se. Although objects encapsulate behavior, today's object technology does not define the behavior of a model, and although this technology has a simulation inheritance, most current implementations lack simulation capabilities.

The advantage of object models is that they are built by modeling the real world. In most cases, object models represent elements or concepts that users and domain experts recognize as pertaining to the business problem domain. Techniques such as use case analysis, coupled with rapid prototyping disciplines and tools, ensure fidelity to user requirements. Encapsulation provides modularity and therefore the flexibility required to address changes.

Object technology by itself, however, still does not provide the complete desired enterprise-modeling capabilities desired. The reason is that object technology usually models only that portion of the business processes that will be supported by computers, which makes up only a fraction of the total business environment. The complete environment includes such elements as human service encounters with the customer; workflows involving manual processes; paper documents; and goods, facilities, and agents external to the enterprise. Overall corporate activity must be modeled to help see where to change corporate processes and thus better address challenges such as flexibility, cost reduction, and less time to market.

We need, therefore, a different model of the enterprise, a model that helps us describe the whole corporation by describing its business processes and enables us to decide for each process what must be changed, what organizational structures have to be modified to support that change, and what portion of the business processes can be improved through automation. We need a modeling approach that supports the reengineering of business processes.

Reengineering business processes requires two phases of model building: the model of the enterprise with business processes as they are today (the as-is state of the enterprise), and the model of the enterprise after the processes have been reengineered (the to-be state). This kind of process reengineering capability profoundly impacts on the enterprise data model, because reengineering can require a new definition of the business functions and the data needed to support them, as well as new business objects and even the need to model completely new problem domains.

Modeling a corporation therefore entails (1) the definition of an enterprise architecture defined by corporate processes, (2) the object models of the automated business solutions of the problem domains, and (3) the data models required to support the automated business solutions (possibly relational data models).[25]

We need to describe this architecture as is, and how it is to be after reengineering. The architectural constructs should show the relationship between

---

25 The constructs (2) and (3) are the basis for defining the Information Technology architecture of the corporation.

these two models, enabling the reengineering changes to drive the changes in the corporate information systems rapidly and effectively.

A further extension of the enterprise architecture is the concept of an industry architecture. An industry architecture is a high-level description of the to-be processes, object models, and data structures applicable to all enterprises of a certain type of industry, such as banking, insurance, or manufacturing. Industry architectures are valuable because they can be used for building, benchmarking, or reengineering current business processes and their automation support.

This chapter describes an approach for business process reengineering and enterprise modeling using the Line of Visibility Engineering Methodology (LOVEM), a business processes charting discipline developed by IBM Canada, and sets the stage for its integration with the development of object technology applications supporting the business processes, using VMT, which will be discussed in Chapter 14.

LOVEM is a business process modeling methodology that supports business process reengineering and business process management. It is a role-oriented methodology that uses an integrated set of graphics called Line of Visibility Charts (LOVCs) to document and evaluate business process flows between functions, departments, or jobs.

LOVCs help to identify the *service encounters* with the customer. An LOVC highlights each contact an organization, department, or individual has with its customer, known as a *moment of truth* of the business. It fosters an understanding of how the customer sees the company's structure and processes, and focuses the business process designer on areas to improve. Process redesigners generally look for opportunities to improve customer services, reduce cycle time, improve resource use, reduce costs, improve employee morale and foster teamwork.

The following sections provide details of LOVEM, its major components, and its uses.

13.1   The LOVEM Approach for Process Mapping

LOVEM is a business process reengineering methodology designed for business and systems professionals. The focus is on

- Evaluating the service encounter with the customer
- Satisfying customer needs by providing quality service in the service encounters
- Improving employee productivity by focusing on individual jobs
- Reducing cost by optimizing process path or workflow steps

Evaluation is accomplished by analyzing the business processes with these types of questions:

- What needs to be done and why?
- Who is involved?

- How does work get done?

- How long does it take?

- How much does it cost?

- What are the roles and responsibilities of everybody involved?

- What is the maturity level of the process?

LOVEM is based on the process path management concept and uses a pictorial language to demonstrate the processes of an enterprise. Symbols represent logical and physical processes and data components arranged in the sequence of a process path or workflow. In this way, each service encounter, process or data component, problem, or opportunity can be examined in the appropriate context of a process path or workflow, and the maturity level for the overall process or process path can be established. LOVEM produces a set of maps of the business, charting the processes and providing guidelines to help create and read the charts. This methodology shows all the elements of the business in relationship to one another—similar to maps showing the relationship between cities and countries.

LOVEM is also built on the realization that business and systems professionals are jointly responsible for process design and management. Business process design and ongoing business process management, according to services marketing principles, must be shared between business and systems professionals. LOVEM provides a *common specification language* that lets business and systems professionals document, analyze, evaluate, rate, and manage business processes and systems functions.

13.2   Line of Visibility Charts

A line of visibility chart (LOVC) is a pictorial representation of the business processes and their relationships, and the data that flow among them. LOVCs are derived from the analysis and design of the sequential and parallel business processes.

Often the process of creating a LOVC is called *blueprinting* or *modeling,* because these charts are blueprints or models of the overall business process operations and the jobs within each operation. Blueprinting allows us to graphically depict a company's process design, whereas modeling is part of the design process. By modeling, we create several alternatives in the design before committing to the final blueprint.

An LOVC can identify the following elements:

- The aspects of the business that directly affect the customers or clients—the *service encounters* that are shown at the *line of visibility*

- The functions, processes, and jobs that make up the business

- The opportunities, problem areas, and critical measurement points

- Employee skills, education, and training requirements
- Hand-offs and dependencies
- Possible solutions that often become obvious through the process of creating the LOVCs

Figure 146 shows a generic LOVC. In this example, a customer establishes a relationship by making contact with the first business area, department, or job. The first business area must seek support from the second business area which, in turn, seeks support from the fourth business area. The fourth business area completes the relationship with the customer. The line separating the internal business areas from the customer is the *line of visibility* (*LOV*). Any interaction between the customer and the enterprise takes place at the LOV and is called a *service encounter*.

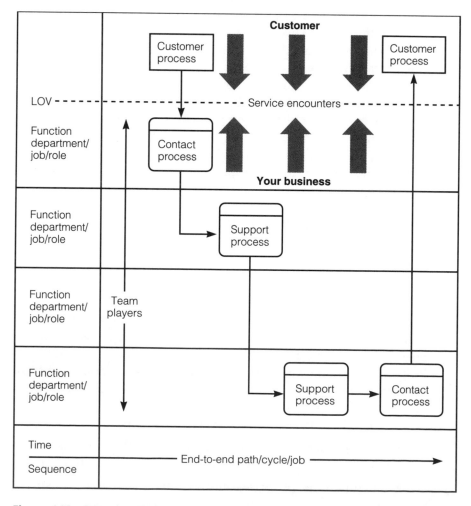

Figure 146. Generic LOVC

13.3   The Family of Line of Visibility Charts

The family of LOVCs is an integrated set of graphical representations of the business processes from the customer's point of view. LOVCs show the relationship between an organization and its customers for any given business unit, *line of business* (LOB), or any job. The key features are

- Service encounters that occur at the LOV
- Internal interfaces, hand-offs, dependencies, and organizational considerations
- Processes, activities, and procedures that the business performs, with special emphasis on those that deal directly with the customer
- Major data entities and data flows that are required for a business
- Upstream and downstream data dependencies, especially for those contact processes that deal directly with the customer
- Manual/automated interfaces, which are especially important since, in most modern businesses, the majority of business processes are performed by systems
- Process cycle time and critical measurement points to provide benchmarks and comparisons to best-of-breed competitors
- Other business factors that a business person deals with, such as process path costing, skills requirements, and problem or opportunity areas

The family of LOVCs consists of

- Architecture LOVC (ALOVC)
- Logical LOVC (LLOVC)
- Physical LOVC (PLOVC)
- Job LOVC (JLOVC)

We can create and use any or all of these types of charts to represent process paths or jobs for an enterprise or LOB. The charts use a predefined set of symbols and techniques that can be understood by people not involved in the process.

The following sections briefly define the four types of LOVCs.

13.3.1   Architecture LOVC (ALOVC)

The ALOVC has a predefined structure. It focuses on

- The main customer processes
- The main enterprise processes and key data components
- Critical measurement points and critical success factors

The normal procedure of charting the processes is to create a high-level ALOVC process architecture chart and then divide the enterprise into its business units or lines of business. The ALOVC is logical and unconstrained, and it shows the sequential nature of enterprise processes.

13.3.2 Logical LOVC (LLOVC)

The LLOVC is the starting point for creating a design of the individual lines of the business. At this stage, we assess the business at a high level—first, as it is today and then as it could or should be in the future. Often the charts that describe the current processes are referred to as the as-is blueprints, and the charts that describe the processes after reengineering are called to-be models or blueprints.

When working with an LLOVC, we concentrate on *what* makes up the business. We do not include any physical constraints, like systems, geographic locations, or organizational units; we rather identify the logical business areas and processes as they currently exist or as we would like them to exist. This results in a stable model or blueprint of the business.

When creating an LLOVC, we focus on the following:

- Customers

- Service encounters with customers

- Interactions between logical business areas

- What the business does

- Maturity levels of the processes or process paths

13.3.3 Physical LOVC (PLOVC)

A PLOVC deals with the constraints of the business processes. We now ask the following questions:

- Who performs a process?

- How is a process performed?

- Where is a process performed?

- When does a process take place?

- How much does it cost to perform a process?

- How long does it take to perform a process?

- Where do the hand-offs occur?

- What systems or tools are used?

- What is the maturity level of the process?

On a PLOVC, we identify the manual activities and their interfaces to customers, internal or external organizations, and systems. A PLOVC can represent either as-is processes or to-be models or blueprints of a physical process path.

13.3.4   Job LOVC (JLOVC)

The JLOVC focuses on the people who perform the tasks within the business. A JLOVC shows the activities and tasks of a job and their relationships with customers, other jobs, internal or external organizations, and systems. As with the LLOVC and PLOVC, we can create as-is blueprints when assessing the jobs that make up the business and to-be models and blueprints when redesigning the jobs.

Although the JLOVC is the lowest level of the LOVCs, it is also the most important. It is from the JLOVC blueprints that the new business process design will be implemented. The JLOVC is used to

- Implement new procedures
- Improve existing procedures
- Define skills requirements
- Define systems requirements
- Define tool requirements
- Provide education for improving efficiency
- Consider all aspects of jobs that affect customer service and internal efficiency and effectiveness
- Define the maturity level of individual jobs

13.4   Processes

A process is a particular method of doing something, generally involving a number of steps or operations. [HAM 93] defines a business process as "a collection of activities that takes one or more kinds of input and creates an output that is of value to the customer."

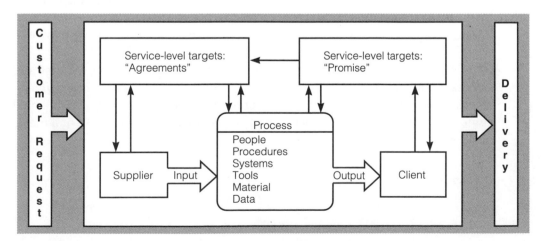

Figure 147. Definition of a process

According to these definitions, a process can span an entire LOB, such as the mortgage LOB of a bank; but a process can also be the smallest unit of work, such as entering data into a data processing system or informing the customer that the mortgage application is approved.

The term *process* in LOVEM means a *logical process,* that is, a logical view of the business that can be transformed into several manual activities and systems functions. A *process path,* on the other hand, can be defined at both the logical and physical levels. At the logical level, it is a sequence of processes and, at the physical level, a sequence of manual activities and systems functions.

This provides the flexibility to analyze and design business processes at various levels of complexity and detail (see Section 13.6). It also allows moving from the more abstract and static concept of process to the concept of a multi-dimensional and dynamic *customer-oriented process path.* This allows us to analyze and design processes as they are interacting with customers. It also allows us to reengineer the end-to-end processes for optimum results.

Because a process is dependent on one or more inputs, there are multiple dependencies within an end-to-end process path that can be analyzed for problem areas at the various interface points and subsequently redesigned with clearly defined interfaces.

13.5   Process Path Management

Businesses were, and often still are, organized into vertical process structures. For example, in Figure 148 on page 293 the sell, order, supply, distribute, settle, and support processes are organized vertically. The compensation and reward systems are also structured vertically. While this created internal excellence, the customer, who experiences the contact points, or service encounters, with the business, generally remains outside the system. As businesses recognize the importance of customer satisfaction, the customer becomes the focus—and the final arbiter—of business processes.

This attention and focus calls for a new way of looking at business processes: management *across* the vertical processes, or *process path management.* A process path is a sequence of processes that start and end with a customer service encounter. A process path can be aligned with an LOB or a major business unit of a company.

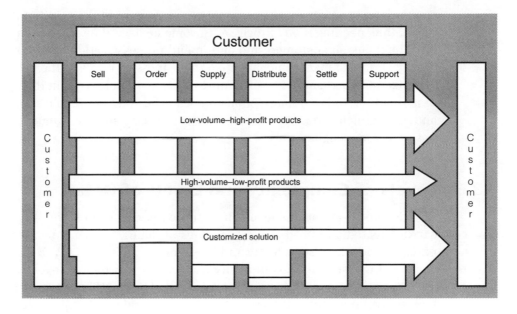

Figure 148. Process path management

13.5.1   Customer-Oriented Process Path

Orienting the process path design through the eyes of the customer is an important concept in business process reengineering. Figure 148 illustrates this concept, showing the following three horizontal process paths crossing the vertical processes:

- Low-volume–high-profit products path
- High-volume–low-profit products path
- Customized solutions path.

The starting point for each of these process paths is the customer with a need; for example, the customer can ask for a product, a price, a contract, or other information. At the end of the process path, the customer receives the product, pays the bill, and gets support. The execution of all the vertical processes along the process path determines the level of customer satisfaction. Throughout the process path, there are many different service encounters. For example, customers may inquire about the product, price, and delivery or may request a change in the delivery schedule or an address.

Each process path has different process characteristics; for example, a *high-profit* LOB usually has many processes aimed at helping the operation of the business. On the other hand, a *low-profit* LOB has to manage expenses cautiously and tightly with fewer processes. Many modern businesses offer highly customized products and services that cross several of the traditional process paths, thus needing many processes in some areas and fewer in others.

The focus on customers and end-to-end processes adds complexity to the organization and management of modern businesses. While in the past a simple organization chart and a few procedures were enough to explain the operations of a business, today's complex businesses need new approaches for defining and managing business processes, such as process path management and business process reengineering.

13.6   Levels of Complexity and Levels of Detail

LOVCs appear at various levels of complexity, and each level of complexity can be created and used at various levels of detail. Figure 149 shows a comparison of levels of complexity and levels of detail. The ALOVC, for example, is at the highest level of complexity because, at this logical level, it provides the most unconstrained view of the business. The JLOVC, in contrast, is at the lowest level of complexity because, at this physical level, it provides the most constrained view of the business.

All types of LOVCs can be used at any level of detail.

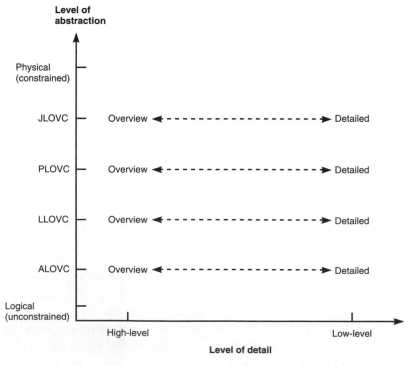

Figure 149. Comparison of levels of complexity and levels of detail

13.7 Comparison of Logical and Physical Representations

Different business process reengineering activities can be carried out at various levels of complexity, for example:

- At the enterprise architecture level, as expressed by the ALOVC
- At the logical and physical process path levels, as expressed by the LLOVC and PLOVC
- At the job level, as expressed by the JLOVC

Figure 150, on page 296, outlines the characteristics of the four different types of LOVCs.

13.7.1 Logical—Unconstrained

The starting point is usually to draw a logical representation of the business processes to get a stable framework for the design work. This would be the equivalent of drawing a map of a continent showing only the borders of countries with capitals, mountains, and rivers but without railroads, roads, or other constraining elements. Figure 151 on page 296 illustrates a logical process.

At this logical level, the focus is on *why* the process is needed and *what* the process does, not *how* it is done. At this stage, we do not add any constraints such as organization, time, people, tools, and so on, to the process. To represent the *logical process path* views graphically, we can use

- The ALOVC for the enterprise architecture process path view
- The LLOVC for the process path view for one line of business

13.7.2 Physical—Constrained

Once we have a stable enterprise architecture and a logical process path design, we can start to add the various constraining factors to the design, such as organizations, people, information and goods flows, EDI (Electronic Data Interchange) transactions, documents and forms, systems, means of transportation, timing parameters, or any other real-life items that contribute to a process or process path. This is like adding all the roads, mountains, airports, or other specifics to a map of a country. Figure 151 illustrates of the physical constraints for a process.

At this physical design stage, we can start by experimenting with various alternative models before committing to a detailed design.

To represent the physical process path views graphically, we can use

- The PLOVC for modeling the physical constraints of the process path
- The JLOVC for modeling the physical constraints of individual jobs and systems functions

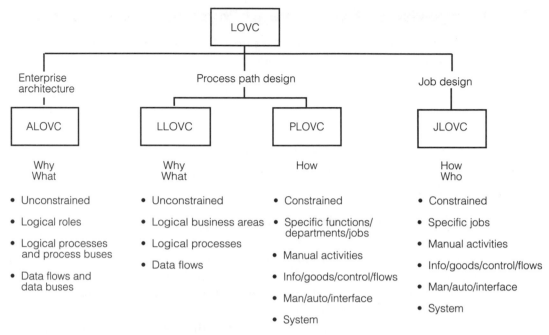

Figure 150. Characteristics of the four types of LOVCs

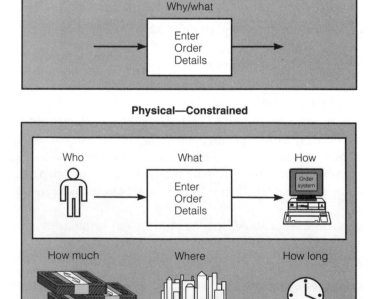

Figure 151. Comparison of logical and physical representations

13.8   Views of a Business

We can portray the processes of a business in five different views, four of which can be expressed by LOVCs, as shown in Figure 152. At the highest level are the processes, process paths, and jobs of an enterprise. This matrix can be used as the first step to understanding the scope and language of an enterprise. It can also help to set the boundaries for the project. It is a view of the business that is useful to senior management for committing resources to a major business process reengineering project.

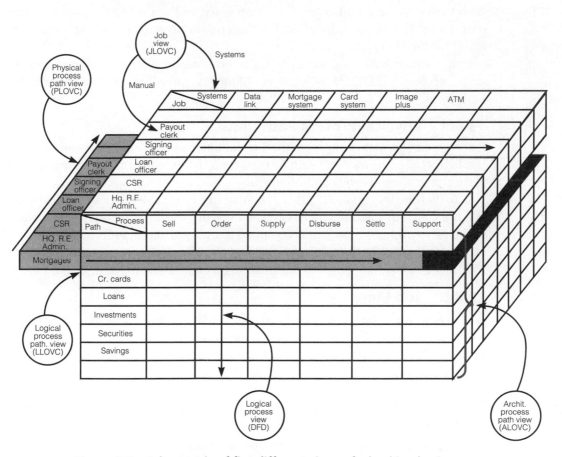

Figure 152. Cube matrix of five different views of a banking business

13.8.1   Logical Process View

The vertical columns of the front face of the cube matrix represent the major logical processes that a bank performs; this logical view can be expressed through a decomposition technique like a hierarchical structure diagram (HSD). In Figure 152, the logical processes are Sell, Order, Supply, Disburse, Settle, and Support.

13.8.2   Logical Process Path View

The horizontal rows on the front face of the cube matrix show the various logical process paths. In this example, Mortgages, Credit Cards, Loans, Investments, Securities, and Savings are the major lines of business for a bank. This view of the business is expressed by the LLOVC. Through this view, we first see the service encounters with the customer.

13.8.3   Enterprise Architecture View

The enterprise architecture view encompasses all logical process and process path views, but at a higher level of complexity. In Figure 152 on page 297, the entire front face of the cube illustrates the enterprise architecture which is captured in the ALOVC.

Note that the ALOVC lets us build an end-to-end architecture of the enterprise, while the LLOVC is a design technique for individual process paths at the LOB level.

13.8.4   Physical Process Path View

Once we have a stable model of the logical business processes (at one or all of the logical views), we can begin to transform these logical models into physically constrained models and blueprints.

To do this, we use the PLOVC as shown in Figure 152 (refer to the arrow on the right face of the cube matrix in the horizontal plane). A physical process path, as expressed by a PLOVC, consists of a series of individual jobs, as expressed by the JLOVCs. We can think of the physical process path view as a linking of individual jobs that are fulfilling a customer's request.

13.8.5   Job View

At the top face of the cube matrix, we can see that the physical process path is a succession of individual jobs in the business. These jobs are supported by systems. In the banking example in Figure 152, these jobs include

- Payout clerk
- Signing officer
- Loan officer

The systems that support these jobs, include

- Data link
- Mortgage system
- Card system

To focus on an individual job, we use the JLOVC. Because most of today's jobs are partly manual and partly automated, the JLOVC shows a clear boundary between manual activities and automated systems. We can also show this manual/automation boundary on the PLOVC at a higher level of complexity.

13.9   Summary

The Line of Visibility Engineering Method (LOVEM) is a business process modeling methodology that provides a common specification language for business and system professionals to document, analyze, evaluate, rate, and manage business process and system functions. It allows them to carry out business process reengineering and business process management.

Line of visibility charts (LOVC) are an efficient tool for LOVEM. Different types of LOVCs represent different views of the business process model in different levels of complexity and details.

This classification addresses the needs of different business process reengineering activities that require different levels of complexity. In some cases, we focus on the unconstrained logical level (why the process is needed and what the process does without adding physical constraints), while in other cases we focus on the constrained physical level (how the process is done, with consideration given to constraints such as people, information, and time).

Integrating Business Process Reengineering with Object-Oriented Modeling

This chapter looks at the link between business processing reengineering (BPR) and object-oriented modeling. We discuss the relationship between the two disciplines, and when and how to start object-oriented modeling during the BPR cycle.

14.1 Object-Oriented Modeling in the BPR Cycle

It is the stability of domain objects relative to use cases that suggests the feasibility of starting object modeling in parallel with BPR. We can assume that part of the object model will not change with radical reengineering of the business processes. Object-oriented modeling can be applied at two different levels: modeling a domain and modeling an application within the domain. Applying domain knowledge, we can develop high-level domain models as part of the BPR effort. The complete object model for the application includes objects found both in use case analysis and in domain analysis. Many times the objects derived from the two sources have the same semantics and provide some overlapping and complementary services; sometimes the objects found are rather different.

As the business processes are reengineered, new LOVCs are created, and lines of automation are defined and documented by way of use cases. From these new use cases, the object model can be revised, although a large percentage of the analysis for the existing domain should be reusable for the new "to-be" business model, despite the radical changes in the reengineered processes. The following sections describe the two levels of object-oriented modeling, domain modeling and application modeling.

14.1.1   Domain Modeling

Domain knowledge is a primary source for object modeling.

Domain analysis can start during the assessment of lines of visibility, near the start of BPR. Modeling of current processes is done to understand the current business and to scope and prioritize the redesign. Developing a domain model can help us understand and capture the important domain knowledge.

Domain knowledge can be derived from problem specifications or domain experts and from formalized domain knowledge frameworks called *architectures.* Domain knowledge analysis yields a set of classes that best describes the static or structural aspects of the domain. In most cases, these classes are independent of the enterprise processes and are therefore not related to a prior BPR.

Occasionally, however, domain knowledge and process knowledge are related. This is the case when the domain knowledge is expressed as an architecture. Architectures can have varying scopes: Application architectures, enterprise architectures, and industry architectures are defined more or less explicitly by the processes they support. In our case, we define an enterprise architecture centered around enterprise processes.

When using an industry architecture to build an enterprise model for a corporation, the architecture, which is an abstraction, has to be instantiated to conform to the processes and domain objects of the enterprise. Thus BPR and domain knowledge are closely related.

The domain model derived from analysis of domain knowledge that is not formalized as an architecture contains the static class structure of the business objects involved and their relationships, and should be relatively independent of business process reengineering. The problem with a domain model is that its boundary is not very clear. A domain model can help us understand the real-world situation, as statements of the facts to capture domain knowledge, but it is not a model of an application.

14.1.2   Application Modeling

When applying VMT, we model an application by first developing a use case model. A use case model consists of actors, which represent user roles, and use cases, which describe the interaction between the actors and the information system that will provide automation support to the business processes. There is a clear system boundary for the use case model. Use cases are therefore highly dependent not only on the dynamics of business processes but also on decisions regarding automating some parts of these processes. As the business processes are expected to change radically after reengineering, it is clear that use cases are highly dependent on BPR.

Since use cases are one of the sources for classes and relationships that define the object model, and we expect the object models to be as stable as possible, there are two points when it is productive to define a use case model:

- After BPR has taken place: This approach is fairly straightforward, and it provides a well-defined and loosely coupled interface between BPR and object modeling. It ensures coordination between both activities, but it does not provide cross-fertilization opportunities between them.

- As part of the BPR activities: This approach is iterative and stepwise. It starts with a BPR step using reengineering heuristics and enterprise policies and constraints. One of the deliverables of this step, as defined by the LOVEM methodology, is a set of process charts with a line of automation that defines the points of interaction of users with the automation support to be provided by the information system. The line of automation provides input to the next step.

For the next step, we apply use case modeling techniques. We define the use cases for interactions with the systems as described by VMT. We can then refine them by prototyping the application and receiving feedback from users based on a working prototype rather than on a symbolic description or chart. This early prototyping activity may result in a redefinition of part or all of the business processes, which leads to the next step, and so on. This iteration can converge quickly: Two iterations are usually enough to reap the benefits of the mixed approach.

The advantage of this approach is a better understanding of user needs and working conditions. The disadvantages stem from a lengthier interaction with users and experts, who can be confused by processes that appear and disappear and who may refuse to cooperate if they perceive the modeling activity as threatening their jobs.

14.2   An Integrated Approach Using LOVEM and VMT

This section describes an approach to integrate business process engineering using LOVEM and application development using the VMT object-oriented methodology.

BPR aims at designing the business, while application development aims at automating the reengineered business processes. It makes sense that object-oriented modeling of the business application that supports the new business processes should take place after the "to-be" business processes are designed. We believe that LOVCs and use cases can together establish the link between BPR and the application development. Figure 153 illustrates this integrated approach.

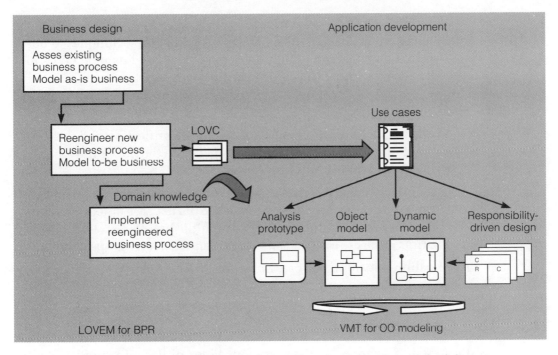

Figure 153. **Integrated approach to BPR and object-oriented modeling**

At a high level, we can describe three main phases of the BPR process, each of which has substeps:

1. Assess the existing business organization and processes.

   a. Model the architecture of the as-is reality of the enterprise using ALOVCs. The ALOVC data buses define the initial enterprise domain objects.

   b. Model the high-level functions and processes of the as-is reality of the enterprise using LLOVCs and/or high-level PLOVCs.

   c. Using problem domain analysis techniques, develop the as-is domain model from the as-is LOVCs.

   d. Integrate the as-is ALOVCs generated in step 1a with the data models to obtain the initial to-be architecture in ALOVCs. Use hierarchical structure diagramming on the ALOVC data buses (corporate objects) to obtain the initial to-be object/class hierarchy.

2. Reengineer the new business processes.

   a. Iteratively generate the to-be processes using LLOVCs or PLOVCs.

   b. Complete the to-be process path design using line of visibility techniques.

3. Implement the redesigned business processes.

    a. Iteratively define the to-be process by using JAD techniques to blueprint initial use cases. To-be jobs must be defined using JLOVCs to balance the initial use case blueprints.

    b. Iteratively generate the to-be object model and class model as the to-be processes are engineered or reengineered using lines of visibility. This integration will improve the classification and development of the class model. Iteratively generate the object interaction diagram in line of visibility format.

    c. Iteratively refine the use cases by VisualAge prototyping. Balance prototype changes and refinements back to the use case blueprints, Two sets of use cases should be defined as initial line of visibility blueprints of the use case scenarios and completed use case prototypes.

Application development continues, following the VMT methodology described earlier in this book.

14.3 Use Cases and JLOVCs

As discussed in Chapter 13, there are four types of line of visibility charts: architectural, logical, physical, and job. The job line of visibility chart (JLOVC) most resembles a use case. The physical line of visibility chart (PLOVC) and JLOVC together set the context for a well-scoped set of use cases.

The following use case examples are reverse-engineered into line of visibility format to show their similarity.

14.3.1 Use Case Example: FCE Customer Order Management

Let us consider a user interaction with the foreign currency exchange (FCE) system, where the user is a bank cashier and the scenario describes the FCE interfaces when a customer buys (orders) foreign currency from a branch cashier. The use case is documented as follows:

1. The cashier creates a new order.

2. The cashier fills out the order form (currency type, amount, amount type, (cash/check), type of payment, customer information).

System internal interactions not described in the use case:

- The system determines currency type based on country.
- The order can handle multiple currencies and checks.
- The system can determine country restrictions.

3. The system tells the cashier about stock availability—in-stock case.

4. The system determines payment and exchange rate.

5. The system prints a tab.

6. The cashier notifies the system; the customer accepts (signs) the order.

7. The cashier handles customer payment—points to another use case.

   System internal interactions not described in the use case:

   - The system reduces the stock level of the currency type and the amount of the order.

   - The system generates an accounting entry.

8. The system notifies the cashier that the order is OK.

9. The cashier completes the order.

14.3.2   Representing the Use Case by a Partial JLOVC

The use case for buying foreign currency is represented by the partial JLOVC shown in Figure 154 on page 308. To aid in the description of the mapping of object-oriented techniques to LOVEM, specific line of visibility terms used in the following discussion are shown in *italics.*

The line of visibility modeling technique uses the *banding* formalism. The branch cashier and the FCE application are represented by *horizontal bands.* The two *bands* are separated by the *line of automation,* which represents the cashier's interface with the FCE application. Above the *line of automation* are the cashier's *manual activities.* On the *line of automation* are the FCE user interfaces. Below the *line of automation* are the FCE functions not visible to the user. Each system interface (eight transactions in this use case example) is represented by a cashier's *manual activity,* the FCE *system,* and at least one *information/ goods/control flow* that connects the *manual activity* with the FCE *system.*

The *manual activity symbol* is a rectangle with rounded corners and a dashed line separating the *manual activity identifier* from the *manual activity description. Manual activity identifiers* in this example are a sequence number prefixed with CA, for cashier. *Manual activity descriptions* should be singular verb/object descriptions in the language of the business domain. The sequence of *manual activities* is left to right.

The *system symbol* is a rectangle with rounded corners and a solid line separating the *system identifier* from the *system description. System identifiers* in this example are sequence numbers prefixed with UI, for user interface, or FCE, for foreign currency exchange. *System symbols* labeled UI are on the *line of automation. System symbols* labeled FCE are below the *line of automation.* Optionally, the *screen symbol* can be used to represent the user interface. *System descriptions* should be singular verb/object descriptions in the language of the application domain.

The *information/goods/control flow* is shown as an arrow pointing in the direction of the predominant flow of information, goods, or control. If information is being entered into the FCE, the *information/goods/control flow* points from the cashier *manual activity* to the FCE *system.* Job line of visibility flows represent any combination of information, goods, and/or control.

Since each user interface requires the user to perform a *manual activity* in accessing or invoking a *system,* the cashier *manual activity* and FCE *system* can have the same description across any given interface. Figure 154 on page 308 shows the cashier *manual activity* Create New Order (CA1.1) as enabled by the FCE *system* Create New Order (UI1.1). Information entered into the FCE application by the cashier is labeled New Order Info.

Step 2 of the example use case, represented by Prompt Order Entry (UI1.2), invokes FCE functions that are system internal interactions, meaning that they are hidden from the user and are shown below the *line of automation.* System internal interactions are represented with the *system symbol* having the *system identifier* prefixed with FCE, for foreign currency exchange. Figure 154 shows that the following FCE functions are invoked by Prompt Order Entry (UI1.2):

- Determine Currency Type (FCE1.2)
- Handle Multiple Currencies (FCE1.3)
- Determine Country Restrictions (FCE1.4).

System internal interactions are *system functions* grouped with an optional *boundary symbol* to show that they are invoked or executed as a cluster.

Step 3 of the use case, Display Stock Availability (UI1.3), points to another use case to handle out-of-stock conditions. This is represented on the job line of visibility chart with the *JLOVC symbol,* which points to another use case labeled USECASE2A Order Management System: Out of Stock. The use case scenario continues until the purchase of foreign currency is fulfilled.

Graphical representation of the use case, with components of the job line of visibility is complete from the perspective of object-oriented analysis, in which the cashier's interface with the FCE coincides with the *line of automation.* However, accepted line of visibility modeling should always include the customer *service encounters,* if they occur with the system user.

14.3.3 Representing the Use Case by a Complete JLOVC

The use case example for the customer purchase of foreign currency is augmented to include assumed customer *service encounters,* as shown in Figure 155 on page 309. Line of visibility components added include

- *Line of visibility:* a dotted line between the customer and bank
- *Customer activities* above the *line of visibility*
- *Information/goods/control flow* between the cashier and customer
- *Media of the service encounter* (that is, in person or over the phone)

- *Cycle time:* how long it takes to conduct the scenario

- *Critical measurement points* denoting metrics

- *Skills* required by cashiers to perform their function

Details of what happens in an organization in supporting a customer are hidden from the customer and are shown below the *line of visibility.*

The *customer activities* touch the bank organization at *moments of truth,* or *service encounters.* By definition, a *service encounter* is a *customer activity* in contact with an organization via an *information/goods/control flow.* Figure 155 shows that the first *customer service encounter* occurs with the *customer activity* Purchase Foreign Currency sending the *information/goods/control* Purchase Request to the cashier *manual activity* Create New Order (CA1.1).

Icons may be added to the *service encounters* to show exactly how they occur and/or what conditions are created for the customer. *Moments of truth* that occur over the phone or in person (face to face) are shown with the telephone icon and person icon, respectively. The happy face icon is used to show a happy customer as displayed at *customer activity* Receive Cash or Check.

The *time line* shows *cycle time* at the bottom of the chart. *Time marks* can be added at any number of points on the *time line* in units of minutes, days, months, and so on.

Critical measure points (*CMPs*) and *skills symbols* are included to describe metrics and human resource skills. Figure 155 shows that the important critical measurements are standard fulfillment (fill rates, defect rates, time duration) and quality (cashier accuracy, courtesy, and politeness). The critical skills required to enable the critical metrics are customer relationship skills.

Although the object-oriented analyst may not be overly concerned about the added process engineering information, the object-oriented analysis and systems design should be fully aligned with the customer's line of service. For example, Figure 155 shows that the most important, most critical customer moment of truth is when the customer receives cash or a check. This moment of truth, not having an FCE interface, is excluded from the use case representation.

In business scenarios involving the customer directly interfacing with a system, such as a customer executing bank transactions with an ATM machine, the use case and the JLOVC may be synonymous. In these scenarios, the *line of automation* is concomitant with the *line of visibility.*

The visualization of use case analysis along the system interface or line of automation, driven by the visualization of customer moments of truth along the line of visibility, can enrich the system's enabling of reengineered business designs.

The JLOVC in Figure 154 has the internal/external band excluded for clarity. If empty, a band can be excluded.

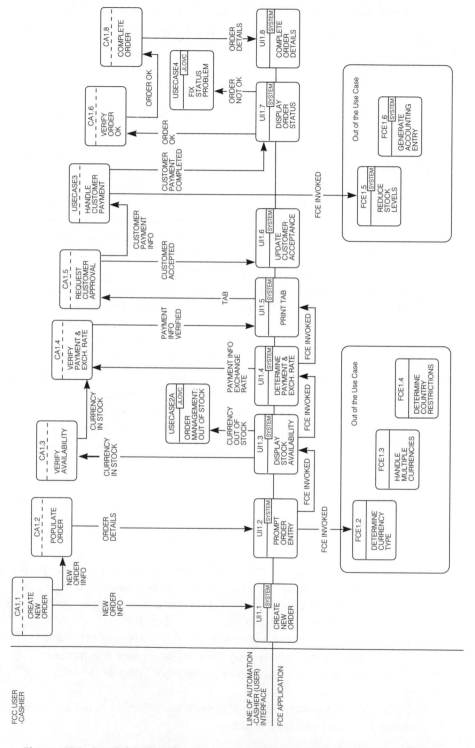

Figure 154. Partial JLOVC for the use case Customer Order Management

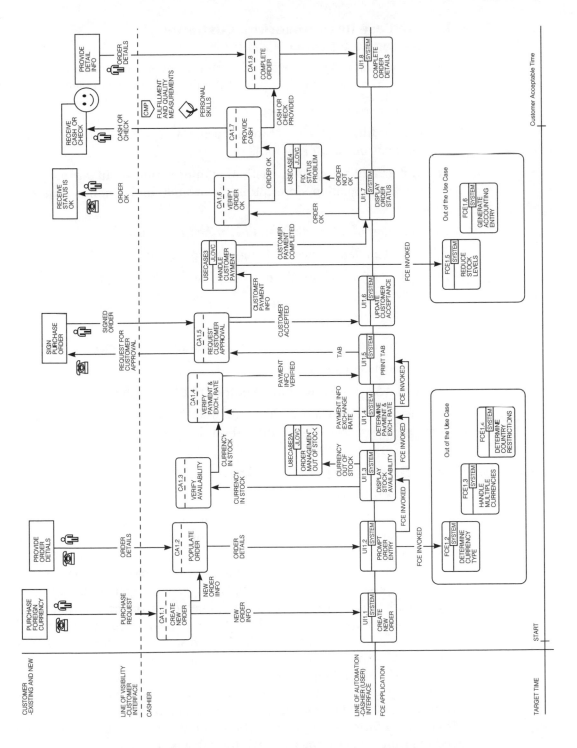

Figure 155. Complete JLOVC for the use case Customer Order Management

14.3.4   Use Case Reengineering: Customer Selling to a Branch Cashier

The following is an example use case describing the scenario of a customer selling to a branch cashier, which is part of the FCE management system.

1. The cashier creates a sell order.

2. The cashier fills out the order form (currency type, amount, denomination, and customer information).

3. The system tells the cashier qualitative information about currency, country, denomination, description of currency, and common forgery errors.

   System internal interactions not described in the use case:

   • The system determines exchange rate, payment.

4. The system prints tab for the customer and a bank receipt.

5. The cashier examines currency.

6. The cashier accepts the order.

   System internal interactions not described in the use case:

   • The system adds stock to stock totals.

   • The system passes accounting entries to the branch or bank.

Figure 154 on page 308 shows the partial JLOVC for this use case, and Figure 155 on page 309 shows the complete JLOVC.

14.4   Business Engineering Enabled by Process Visualization

The use case and job line of visibility for a customer selling currency to the branch are similar to the use case and job line of visibility for the scenario of the customer purchasing foreign currency.

However a comparison of the JLOVCs for the two use cases (see Figures 155 and 157) should prompt the object-oriented analyst and/or business engineering analyst to ask why it appears more complicated for the cashier (and system) to sell foreign currency than to buy. There appear to be twice as many cashier activities and system interfaces for branch selling than for branch buying. There may be valid business reasons why selling to the customer is more complicated, such as checking availability, having the customer sign the order, and verifying payment. On the other hand, if the possibility of counterfeit currency is introduced, buying may turn out to be the more complex process.

Perhaps the information system for branch buying and selling should be enhanced to enable the customer to have the same ease of use in both foreign currency transactions. These suggestions can come from the systems analysts if they have the same visualization of the business as the business engineering analysts using line of visibility.

14.4.1   Modeling Business Rules

Business rules can be modeled as a sequence of interactions of transactions, event triggers, and rules. For example, the event of a customer requesting foreign currency requires the cashier to check availability of the supply of foreign currency. If the cashier's drawer and local branch do not have sufficient foreign funds, then a business rule is invoked transferring the customer's request to the bank head office. In process engineering terms, the rule to transfer to the bank is viewed as a poor customer moment of truth, handing off the customer to another bank location.

14.4.2   Reengineering Paradigm to Shift Business Rules

Business process engineering and reengineering adopt the concept of asking why business is conducted in certain ways. Are there rules, guidelines, or other inherited ideals from previous generations that are obsolete? "It is done this way because that is the way it was done 100 years ago, and no one questions the rules."

In the foreign currency use case example, rather than referring customers to another bank department for situations of insufficient funds, information systems technology can be used to enable the new business rule of not handing off the customer. The system is enhanced to provide the cashier immediate foreign currency cash balances of the cashier's drawer, branch, bank and other locations. The customer request is, in the worst case, an immediate partial fulfillment of requested funds, with an automated invocation of a courier delivery of the unfulfilled balance to the customer's destination of choice, at the expense of the bank. The paradigm shifts from the customer being inconvenienced by insufficient branch funds to the bank being inconvenienced. Information technology enables the bank to manage conditions of insufficient funds, thus meeting and surpassing customer expectations. Visibility is the key to understanding a business's opportunities for improvement.

14.5   Forward Reengineering Methods with PLOVCs, JLOVCs, and Use Cases

Seamless BPR with object-oriented application development is aided by the use of use cases in partial job line of visibility format (see Figures 154 and 156) generated from the physical line of visibility modeling sessions. Called use case line of visibility blueprints, they are initially identified with a use case line of visibility chart (ULOVC) symbol added to the PLOVC. Like the JLOVC, the ULOVC relates to the PLOVC and is detailed to the blueprint level using JAD techniques. ULOVCs are used as input to system prototyping using VisualAge.

Completion of prototyped ULOVCs must be balanced to the PLOVCs blueprints. Done iteratively, use case scenarios are fully aligned in support of customer production lines of service along the customer line of visibility.

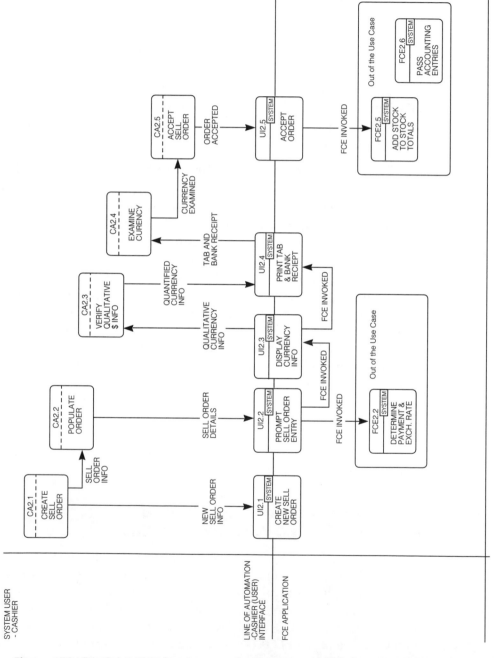

Figure 156. Partial JLOVC for the use case Customer Sells to Branch Cashier (ULOVC)

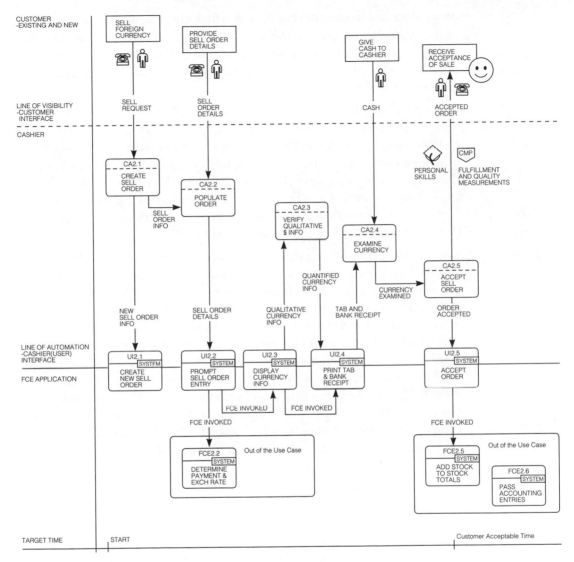

Figure 157. Complete JLOVC for the use case Customer Sells to Branch Cashier

14.6   Identifying Business Objects

Analyzing the domain knowledge related to a process can yield a wide collection of classes. Some of them are relevant to the process and can be used to build the object model. The following premises apply with LOVEM charting techniques:

- Line of visibility charts help to identify relevant classes. When the object model related to a business process is being built, the LOVCs can be used to understand the context in which the domain is analyzed, helping thereby to identify the relevant objects and discard the others. Because vague objects with weak semantics (such as the system or the organization) can remain, the analyst must use sound criteria and common sense to identify and prune them.

- The line of visibility method has a generic fulfillment model that can quick-start object modeling. The LLOVC and ALOVC contain this generic model, which can be related to an equivalent object-interaction diagram. The object-interaction diagram can be reused to help clarify the requirements for application development. More specifically, event trace diagrams and object-interaction diagrams, which are commonly used in object-oriented analysis and design to depict object interactions, can be represented using modified LOVCS.

- The physical line of visibility can be modified to represent object-interaction diagrams. Object interactions can be mapped to the concepts of line of visibility as follows (line of visibility techniques are in *italics*): Object methods can be considered similar to either *manual activities* or *automated activities.* Since the objects of our concern are those that will evolve into information systems, their methods are most similar to *automated activities.* Therefore, the process activities help us to identify the interaction among the objects included in the object model. These objects are real-world objects because their responsibilities are business activities. Messages are, in this case, mapped to *info/goods/control flow.* Events may be mapped into lines of visibility but are usually excluded from the object-interaction diagrams.

In Figure 158 on page 315 the objects are shown in *horizontal bands,* with methods shown in PLOVC *system symbols.* Messages are represented by *info/goods/control flows.* In this example, the *line of visibility* is synonymous with the *line of automation.*

The advantage of mapping object interaction into a modified physical line of visibility is that the systems implementation of object interaction can be fully aligned with the production line of the service expected by customers. The visualization of object interactions in the line of visibility formalism results in clearer requirements from the business domain. End users, business domain experts, actors, and customers can visualize object interaction and system behavior, normally hidden below the *line of automation,* thus providing for aligned business requirements.

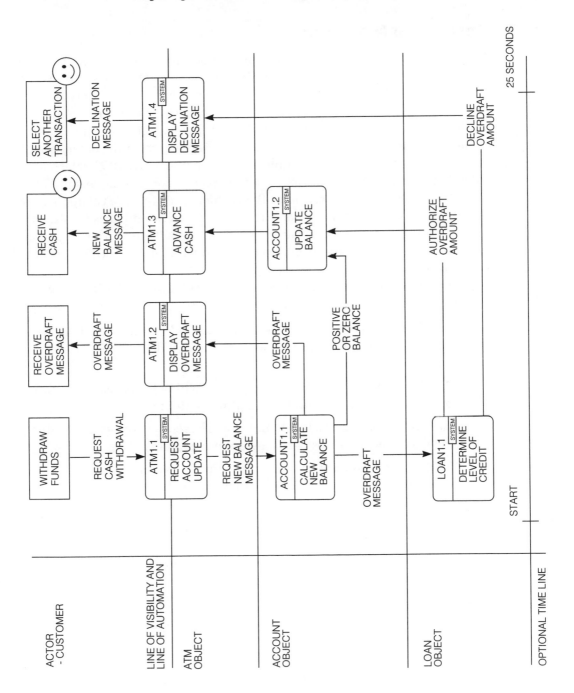

Figure 158. Object-interaction diagram

14.7   Enterprise Modeling

LOVEM charts can be used for enterprise modeling in several ways. Initial object models can be generated from line of visibility. ALOVCs and LLOVCs contain horizontal bands of roles and functions, respectively. ALOVCs model the generic roles of marketer, fulfiller, and settler across the enterprise. LLOVCs model the functions of sell, order, supply, distribute, settle, and support within a line of business of the enterprise. Mortgage services with the enterprise of a financial institution is an example line of business. ALOVC roles can be extended to include actor roles and institutional roles. For example, the ALOVC role of fulfiller can be described as the cashier actor in the FCE application. Institutional roles, such as the bank and branch, can be added as bands. Other objects such as account, customer order, stock, stock items, currency, and currency type can be represented as object buses to parallel the ALOVC concept of data buses.

An enterprise, including processes and objects, can be built by augmenting the ALOVCs with object buses:

- Replacing data buses with object buses can add to the line of visibility but may be of little value to object-oriented modeling unless better objects can be found earlier.

- ALOVCs contain the notion of sequence, which is not required for the object model but is useful for workflow modeling.

- Hierarchies within the bands and object buses may be needed to find the major relationships of has, owns, and contains.

- Customer moments of truth along the line of visibility need to be mapped to the object model's relationships between the customer object and other objects contained within the object domain.

- The ALOVC data buses may be encapsulated objects that are shared across the enterprise. The ALOVC can be used to help develop the enterprise (corporate) object model. The corporate object model provides corporatewide reuse of objects.

14.8   Industry Architectures

Industry architectures enable a coherent and productive approach to application development in an enterprise of that industry. In this section we define a model for an industry architecture based on the processes and objects common to the enterprises of a given industry, and we show a path for integration with data-modeling-based approaches:

- Enterprises of an industry share common processes and objects. An enterprise model can be built by instantiating and extending an existing industry model. This provides a very productive approach to enterprise modeling based on formalized industry knowledge.

- An extended line of visibility can integrate industry architecture models with object-oriented development. Implementing industry architectures is a two-step process: The first step is to generate generic, reusable domain and process models by industry—for instance insurance, finance, or retail marketing. These generic models at the industry level can be reused by specific companies and organizations within each industry segment. The second step is to tailor the generic models to the specific processes, culture, and systems requirements of each organization within the industry segment.

Line of visibility methods are used to implement reengineered business processes, culture changes, organizational and skills gap analysis, and automated workflow. VMT object-oriented techniques are used to implement the reengineered processes requiring new information systems and interfaces to legacy systems.

14.9 Components of Industry and Implementation Models

The generic models, reusable by industry, can be generated from the existing architecture models to include the industry domain object model and the industry process model built with ALOVCs and LLOVCs at the business-actor level.

The generic model of each industry can be iteratively refined to include the following:

- Company-specific domain models, such as the object model, object interaction, state diagrams, and so on.

- Company-specific process models, including

  —All levels of line of visibility models. Figure 159 on page 318 is an example of a PLOVC that is a component of the implementation model of an insurance industry architecture. Modified LOVCs support or replace use cases, state diagrams, and object interaction diagrams; these are optional, however.

  —Migration plans to implement new business processes.

  —Organizational gap analysis (how to migrate the company organization).

  —Staff/skills gap analysis (how to migrate the company staff and skills).

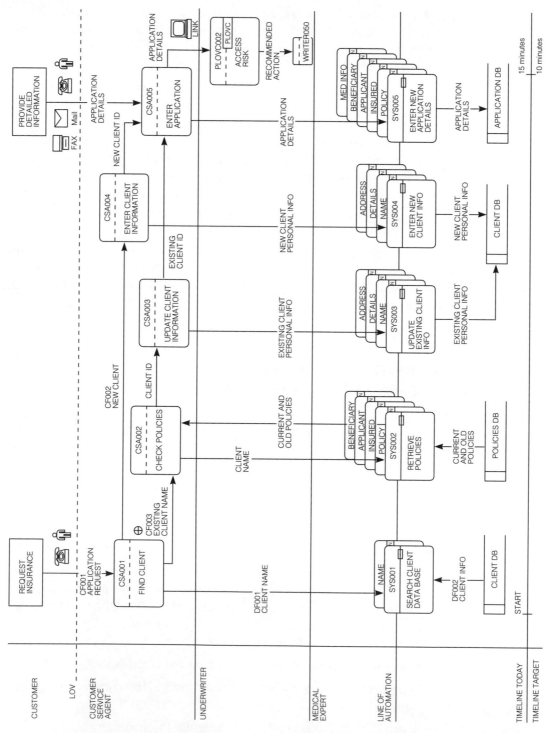

Figure 159.   Example PLOVC implementation of the life insurance industry architecture

14.10 Charting Industry Architectures Using Objects

ALOVCs can be modified to represent an industry architecture that describes the industry processes, the problem domains of the processes, and the main object models used by the processes pertaining to their domains. Combining the industry processes with the objects they use provides a powerful representation of an industry architecture. We call the new charts object ALOVCs (or OALOVCs).

The following paragraphs describe how object modifications are integrated into new OALOVCs. New terms unique to OALOVCs are highlighted in *italics*.

The ALOVC data buses are now called *domain buses* and represent object-oriented problem domains. The ALOVC data group connectors (circles) that connect to the object buses are now called *object group connectors* and represent models of the objects that participate in the associated processes. These processes are referenced by connecting the process (or logical process) to the object bus with arrows. The arrows that in LOVEM terms are called data flows are called *object flows* in the OALOVCs.

For example, Figure 160 on page 320 shows that the ALOVC domain buses representing problem domains are claims, policy and payments, products, and quotes. The logical process called P&C Claim Payments (LLOVC022) connects to the Claims domain bus; the connecting point (the object group connector) represents the object model of the P&C Claim Payments process; the objects of this model pertain to the Claims domain.

14.11 Further Trends in Integration

The integration of object technology and business process reengineering we have presented can be considered as a loose coupling of the domains of both disciplines. This type of coupling has several advantages, not the least of which is it can be applied immediately in an organization that has practitioners of both disciplines, because it does not require many additional skills nor does it substantially modify the underlying theories. Current tools can still be used, and existing notations retain similar semantics, except for the architecture charts that allow defining an enterprise architecture in terms of processes and objects.

In this section, we examine two additions to the methodologies that tighten the coupling of BPR and object technology with the purpose of improving the productivity of translating business requirements into object applications.

- The use of process objects in object modeling and their relationship with workflow management.
- The use of business rules both for requirements gathering and process modeling. This is discussed in Chapter 15.

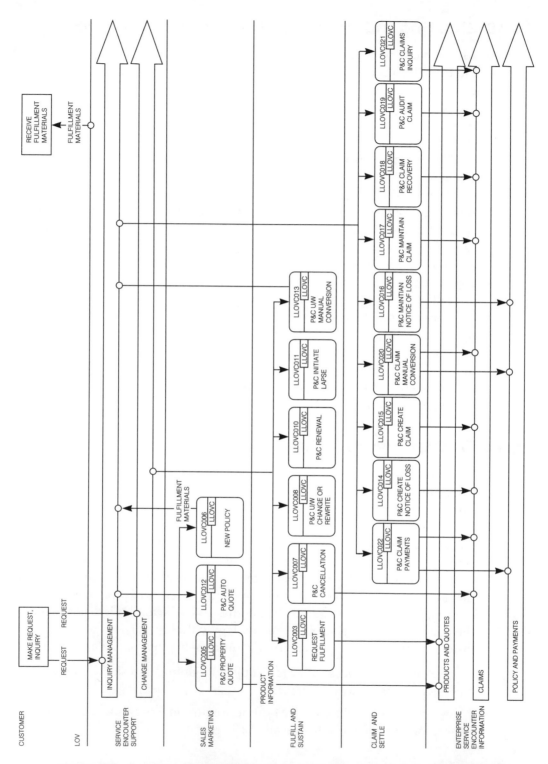

Figure 160. Example of an OALOVC implementation of industry architecture for property and casualty insurance

These additions fulfill the following conditions:

- The business user or business professional should deal only with business concepts. Some authors have suggested that the business world can deal with the anthropomorphic view of objects, that is, the description of objects as entities that have responsibilities and exhibit behavior. In our experience, the validity of this assertion is limited to real-world objects, and it is, for instance, hard for users to visualize a process or business operation as an entity with behavior and responsibilities.

- The classical object paradigm should not be modified; any addition should be expressed in terms of objects, classes, procedural methods, events, messages, and so on.

14.11.1 Process Objects

In many cases, the business process follows a complex path with many branching conditions. Several objects in the business process can interact in many ways, depending on events, the completion of previous tasks, and the fulfillment of certain conditions, such as the availability of required resources. Handling such processes with traditional object-design approaches, such as Responsibility-Driven Design, is rather awkward. For instance, an object can perform different roles in a complex process, and each role can have an associated set of responsibilities that we want to be active in a given role but not others. [TAY95] proposes that in these cases we define *process objects,* which are objects that cannot be derived directly from either use cases or domain knowledge but are derived from reengineering charts.

If a business process is defined as a sequence of tasks that is started by an event, we can visualize a process object as an entity that receives an event (external event or internal message) and has the responsibility of ensuring that the process-related tasks will be performed in a prescribed order for a given set of conditions. When all the tasks are completed, the process object first determines the next process in the chain and then sends a message to have it start.

A task is a responsibility of a certain object. This responsibility can be implicit in the nature of an object for an elementary task. For instance, determining if a withdrawal is legal and updating the account balance are natural tasks for an object of the class Account. Many times, however, a task is actually a subprocess and can be handled in a recursive way, which suggests the existence of a process or composite task pattern such as this:

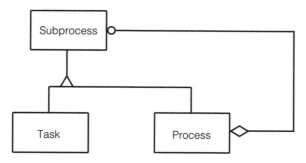

Figure 160a

A process can be decomposed into subprocesses, and a subprocess can be either a task (an elementary process) or a composite process. The figure below highlights relationships that can be used for efficient object design and code reuse. It does not, however, show the sequence of tasks executed in the process, which can vary with the conditions of the environment and the result of the execution of the previous task. This is a dynamic aspect of the process and can be made explicit in an event trace diagram such as the one in the following figure:

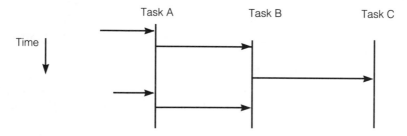

Figure 160b

Process objects by themselves are a weak attack on the complexity of processes for two reasons: First, in standard object-oriented implementation environments using procedural methods, the designer must provide deterministic algorithms that take care of all the possible branches; that is, the designer must solve the task-scheduling problem beforehand. The second is that since the process object must be aware of all the events and conditions in the system, it can become a message bottleneck that grows rapidly worse with the complexity of the process.

Process objects with procedural methods are therefore a useful solution for problems of medium complexity. More complex problems can be handled using programming environments that allow for nondeterministic methods, such as inference rules or logic theorem provers. In such environments, the process object has knowledge about task handling and finds the solution on the spot by mechanical reasoning constrained by the task-completion conditions, resource availability, and environment variables.

Using inference methods with process objects does not reduce the message bottleneck. This problem can be solved if the objects involved in the process are built as intelligent, cooperative agents. There are many advantages to this approach, such as

- An intelligent agent can fulfill distinct roles in the most appropriate way

- A cooperative environment allows us to share needed information and optimize the process, for instance, based on available resources

Agent technology is not broadly available today for business applications. Intelligent objects or knowledge objects, which can use both procedural and inference methods, are available, although in most implementations encapsulation is not enforced. Extending current object languages such as C++ by adding rules and an inference engine has been demonstrated in software labs. An industrial-strength fully object-oriented development software product allowing the construction of systems with intelligent objects—both domain and process objects—will be a key factor in enabling true object-oriented enterprise modeling.

14.12 Summary

LOVC and use cases bridge BPR and object-oriented application development. Use cases can be derived from PLOVC and JLOVC. The process visualization using JLOVC clarifies the business rules to be modeled and gives insights on how a process can be reengineered to make it more customer driven. Object models and object interaction diagrams can then be identified readily.

ALOVC and LLOVC lead to enterprise modeling. Moreover, due to the commonalities that often exist among the business processes and objects of different enterprises in the same industry, industry-specific reusable architectures can be established. Software development can shift from the traditional labor-based paradigm to one based on assets, constructing applications based on prefabricated, industry-specific components. The whole framework can be represented by the object ALOVC.

Future trends in integrating BPR and object technology call for a closer coupling between the two business requirements can be translated into object applications with higher productivity. The use of process objects simplifies the representation of a business process, which follows complex paths with many branching conditions.

15

Augmenting VMT Requirements Modeling with Business Rules

Problem statements, domain knowledge, and use cases are the elements that are used in object-oriented technology to convey user requirements in a way that is descriptive enough to build object-oriented applications. From a business point of view, however, there is a need for an additional component to express requirements in the proper context: the explicit statement of the policies of the enterprise for handling business situations. Understanding the business policies allows for effective business process reengineering; being able to trace them to the design and code of applications provides software flexibility, enables effective change management, and helps align the requirements with the corporate goals in an effective way. This chapter describes how requirements modeling can be enhanced by augmenting use case specifications with business rules, and shows how visual requirements modeling is done productively using a visual requirement specification tool.

15.1   Requirements

To develop applications that support the result of a business reengineering effort requires the specification of context-related aspects. The problem statement, the domain description, and the interactions with the user provide part of the context. These elements, however, should be stated together with the specification of the purpose of the application and of its goals, that is, the benefits we intend to receive from its implementation.

The specification of requirements is achieved with the desirable degree of precision and completeness only after a certain number of iterations. Methodologies such as Concurrent Knowledge System Engineering (CKSE) [KUN89] recommend working on several specification aspects concurrently, jumping from one to the other in an opportunistic fashion as one aspect triggers new questions about the other. In this section we consider the four specification aspects: identifying the purposes of the application, describing the domain knowledge, specifying the uses interface, and defining test procedures.

15.1.1   Identifying the Purposes of the Application

In building an object-oriented application (or any type of application), a question to ask is, what are the purposes of the application, both from the perspective of the end user and the business professional or domain expert. Writing down a statement of purpose seems deceptively straightforward. It stops looking so when a development team tries to agree on its content. Making the purpose explicit and precise is key to successful reengineering.

The following is an example of a statement of purpose:

The purpose of the proposed banking application is to enable the customer to purchase foreign currency from a set of currency denominations, charging the amount of the transaction either to the customer checking or savings account.

This description of the purpose may be sufficient from a user's point of view. Users usually deal with one case at a time. Other bank departments, however, may be interested in analyzing multiple related cases, such as "What currencies are most required during January?" and the statement of purpose should include the additional purposes as well.

The development team will arrive at a precise statement of purpose only after multiple tries, integrating input from different sources. This statement may also be modified after prototyping, since it will be influenced by the implementation of the use cases describing, for instance, how users handle simple as well as complex transactions.

The process can be enhanced by using tools that enable the users to visualize the input-gathering process and help the convergence toward an adequate purpose specification. A desirable characteristic for such a tool is ease of change to encourage the repetition of iterations.

15.1.2   Describing the Domain Knowledge

The knowledge about a domain can be formulated as a set of facts and criteria for decision making. The facts can be structured as objects, each of which represents a concept of the domain with its facets or traits described by attributes. The decision-making criteria are defined at the business level as business rules, describing desired patterns of business behavior. These business rules are mapped at the object level to one or more object behaviors, implemented as procedural methods.

From a traceability of requirements viewpoint, making this mapping explicit is extremely important, since if this relationship is not recorded, the business rules will be hard to recognize, whether in the method's code, the object model, or even the use case model.

Decision-making criteria can be seen in a more general sense as reasoning activities within the given domain. Reasoning defines the actions that objects can perform. The reasoning processes will reference certain attributes of particular objects to determine the state of the object, and will make conclusions about objects or change the value of some attributes. Reasoning within a problem domain can be represented declaratively as rules or as algorithms in a procedural language. In any case, the reasoning process must specify a strategy to determine the derived values that are not explicitly represented within the domain model.

15.1.3 Specifying the User Interface

The user interface is a key requirements component and should be specified in conjunction with the user while prototyping the use cases. The user interaction is therefore defined by the business rules that govern each transaction of the use cases, and so is the user interface because it has to service this interaction.

15.1.4 Defining Test Procedures

Systems must be tested repeatedly during their development to verify their validity. The validity of a system resides mainly in the way it obeys the business rules the design was based upon. The test suites should therefore be defined based on the business rules and should be rerun each time a change is made to the system to ensure that the system is built to satisfy both the old and new requirements.

The purpose of the application, the domain representation and reasoning, the definition of the user interface, and the validation through test procedures, are distinct perspectives that are mutually supportive [KUN89]. That means that the effectiveness in one of these areas needs to be evaluated with respect to its contribution to the other areas. For instance, the effectiveness of an object model cannot be determined solely by examining the model in more detail; we need to determine how this model serves the purposes of the system, how difficult it is to traverse the model to obtain derived data, and how well it represents the concepts exposed by the use case model as defined by users and business professionals in the real world. The environment in which the application will be deployed will also determine the feasibility and effectiveness of the proposed testing plan.

15.2   Business Rules in Reengineering

Processes and process paths are governed by business rules. Process reengineering efforts focus on business rules to understand the processes' constraints and as an indicator of the value each process adds to the process path. This reasoning can be applied at multiple levels of abstraction, from the logical process path to the individual transaction between an actor and the information system.

Business rules are explicit statements of constraints placed on the business [LOU91, MOR93]. The concept of constraints can be extended to include the procedures under which a system operates [GOT94b]. From a different perspective, a business rule is an assertion that describes an essential concept, relationship, or constraint about the business [MOR94].

Although the rules can be written using formal expressions, they are frequently stated using the specialized natural language of the business user. Making business rules explicit in natural language has many advantages: Rules provide a direct link between business needs and information modeling while serving as an opportunity to uncover suboptimal business practices [SAN91]. They also evolve information and knowledge into a business asset.

Business rules are the real invariants to be considered when modeling a system with the object-oriented paradigm or any other information-analysis approach. Therefore they withstand information technology paradigm shifts but may be modified due to change of company policies, external factors, or as a result of business process reengineering efforts.

15.2.1   The Classification of Business Rules

Business rules can be classified from either a formal or a business semantics perspective. From a formal semantics, such as the one defined by the Conceptual Rule Language [LOU91], the following types of rules are distinguished:

Constraint rules are concerned with the integrity of the object model components. There are two types of constraint rules:

- Static constraint rules are expressions that hold in any valid state of the object model; for instance, "A cashier should never have more than $5,000 in the drawer."

- Transition constraint rules are expressions that allow for valid object state transitions; for example, "The interest of this mortgage can never be increased."

Constraint rules can require enforcement or can be expressed merely as a test. A rule that has an enforcement power must always yield true. A test rule may yield either false or true and can be used to enforce other rules when (and while) the test rule yields true.

Derivation rules define or modify derived components of the model (that is, they define business information) in terms of other model components that can themselves be primitive or derived. Derivation rules are also constraint rules because there can be only one derivation rule per component, thereby establishing a constraint on the way the component is derived. There are two types of derivation rules:

- Static derivation rules are time independent; for instance: "A bank note is unacceptable if more than a third of it is missing or if the bank note number is illegible."

- Transition derivation rules depend on a time stamp on a model component; for instance: "A currency that had maximum demand during the last week is a preferred currency."

  Action rules invoke transactions if their preconditions are satisfied; for example: "When the stock of a currency falls below the reorder quantity level specified for that currency, then start the reorder transaction."

15.2.2   A Business-Oriented Classification

Another classification, made from a business point of view [GOT94b] allows for an organized and focused approach on discovery and recording of the rules, and on the completeness (closure) of the rule analysis. The rules can be grouped by their effect on business objects and processes:

- Rules that change the state of a business object, including actions such as Make (such as build, create), Move (such as transfer, receive), Keep History, and the like.

- Rules that track/control business objects and processes, such as Schedule (such as dispatch, allocate), Monitor (such as measure, evaluate), Keep Summarized History, and so on.

- Rules involved in the planning and accounting of processes, such as Develop Estimates (such as Standards, Targets), and Budgeting (such as billing, paying).

- Rules that refer to the enterprise strategy and policy, such as those for decision making and modeling.

15.2.3   Business Transactions, Use Cases, and Rules

Business transactions are interactions between the system under considerations and its users [GOT94a]. Input transactions (stimuli) are initiated by users and output transactions (responses) are created by the system. The system connects certain input transactions to certain output transactions, thus providing a natural grouping that helps in their study and management.

Use cases have been defined as a sequence of transactions between the user and the system to achieve a business objective. For each use case, the user is an actor, playing a given role in a script. For instance, the same user plays the role of a different actor when depositing money (hero) than when withdrawing money (villain).

A use case can be seen from the system's perspective as follows: a transaction is coming in (input transaction) to which the system may respond with one of a set of transactions (output transaction) if the input transaction is a recognized stimulus. (If not, the system may answer with no transaction at all.) For instance, if the input transaction is caused by the user by inserting a card in an ATM slot, the output transaction may be the request for a PIN if the user inserted a valid card; it may also be a message telling the user that an invalid card was inserted. But inserting a card is a valid transaction in both cases. If instead the user starts by punching a PIN number (which is a perfectly valid input transaction in another phase of the use case), in most cases the system will not recognize the transaction, and no response (output transaction) will be sent to the user.

If the input transaction is a valid transaction, which of the possible output transactions started as a consequence of that input depends on decisions to be made based on input parameters and bank policies. The decision-making mechanism can be made explicit through the formulation of business rules.

15.2.4   The Structure of Business Rules

Business rules relate transactions to the state of the system. This state, from a business point of view, is a composite of business information. In an object model, business information is kept in objects. Business rules therefore provide a bridge between transactions and objects.

When an input transaction occurs, business rules indicate what will happen. An incoming transaction triggers one or more rules in sequence. Rules contain behavioral specifications that can be expressed through logic expressions, using natural language or any combination that will ensure that the business user is comfortable reading them.

[GOT94a] suggests the following syntax for a business rule:

- A condition that defines the business information interrogated by the rule

- A section indicating the names of other business rules expected to be satisfied

- A main body, describing the actions (that is, the modifications) to be performed on one or more business information elements

- A list of transactions initiated by the rule (such as reports)

- Definitions of transactions by establishing relationship constraints on the primitive and derived business elements affected by the transactions

- An indicator showing whether the rule should be continued or stopped

A rule can be read as follows: take a condition and, if satisfied, execute the corresponding action. If not satisfied, skip to the next action and test the corresponding condition. When the condition is true, execute the actions indicated in the rule body. When done with an action, test the indicator to see if we need it to proceed to the next action or we should stop reading the rule. If the indicator is set to *continue,* we proceed to the next action. If it is set to *stop* or if all conditions are read, the rule execution has ended.

For example, for the use case describing the the purchase of foreign currency at a bank branch office, the following business rule can be established:

If there is not enough stock of foreign currency to complete the transaction at this branch, then the purchase must be denied, and the branch manager should be notified about the need of replenishing the stock of that currency. If there is enough stock, however, then update the currency stock and the cashier drawer, accept the purchase, print a tab, and notify accounting of the purchase.

Each *then* clause usually invokes another transaction.

This example shows clearly why making business rules explicit is key to reengineering. We could, for instance, examine the purchase process and come to the conclusion that no business value is added by notifying the branch manager about the need for replenishing stock: This operation could be started by the cashier with proper system support or just by making a telephone call to the bank's main office.

This approach to business rule syntax complies with the requirements that allow for a practical and effective use, such as the ones described, for instance, in [ROS94]. It is extensible, allowing for the construction of compound rules based on simpler rules. It is expansive, in the sense of providing a consistent solution to the widest possible variety of cases. It is expressive, due to the use of natural language, allowing for the capture and communication of business rules at a high level—that is, independently of any specific implementation strategy, software, hardware, or architecture. It could also be made executable by the use of a variable names schema and an adequate inference engine, providing diagnostics and explanations about the handling of situations, from business cases to transactions.

15.3   Visual Modeling of Requirements with Business Rules

Use case prototyping and domain models are part of the visual modeling approach in VMT. At a different level of granularity, the visual modeling of business transaction and business rules provide a better understanding of the enterprise business needs. As always, the use of a visual modeling tool is key. We provide an example of visual modeling of requirements using the IBM VisualAge

Requirements Tool, developed at the IBM Santa Teresa Laboratories. This tool provides visual modeling facilities and a consistent notation as well as integrity checking.

15.3.1 Requirement Modeling Elements

Figure 161 shows the relationships between business rules, transactions, business information and facts, business operations or processes, and the user.

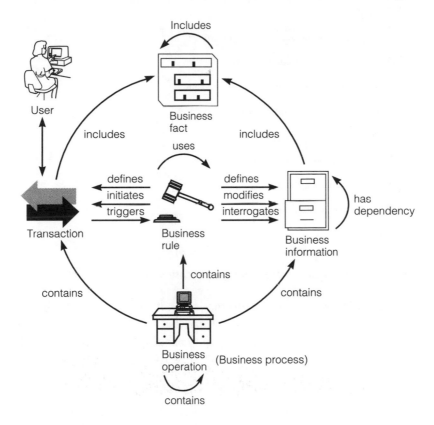

Figure 161. Business rules and business elements

A business rule is triggered by a transaction. A transaction can be initiated by a user, an event, or a business rule.

Transactions are formal interactions between business agents—that is, those who carry out the business work. The agent originates a transaction by creating a business event.

Transactions include facts made up of data. A structural perspective on business transactions is to consider them as business slots that have slots for facts. These slots can be filled-in by the actor or by the system when sent or received, and they represent the data exchanged through the transaction.

A use case is a sequence of transactions that is geared toward accomplishing a certain business goal. Figure 162 shows a use case structured as a set of input and output transactions indicating the role of the use case actors.

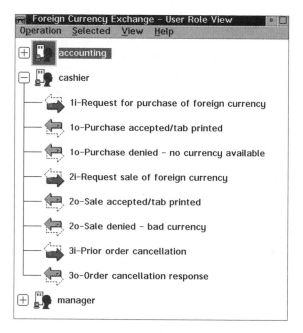

Figure 162. Foreign currency exchange use case showing transactions and actors

A formal interaction is an interaction that follows an established business behavior defined by business rules. Business rules can define aspects of transactions or business information. In that case these aspects are constraints that are assumed to be true at all times. These rules have no active action: They merely state the relationships expressed by these constraints and can therefore be categorized as static rules.

Rules that can be triggered by transactions, can initiate output transactions, and can interrogate or modify information are categorized as dynamic rules.

Business rules can also use other rules; this allows for the reuse of rules under different contexts defined by distinct transactions.

Figure 163 on page 333 shows the relationship between an input transaction requesting the purchase of foreign currency, the foreign exchange rule described above, and the effect of this rule on business information and output transactions.

The rule is expressed in structured natural language, indicating the condition that must evaluate to true to yield the result. The result can define transactions or information, initiate transactions, modify information, and indicate whether to stop, that is, not to proceed, with the remainder of the rule.

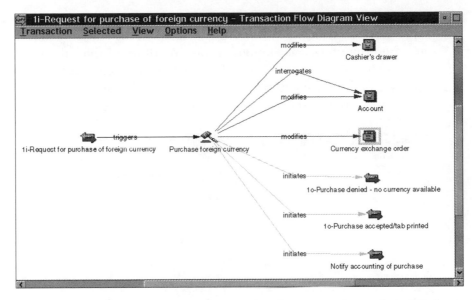

Figure 163. Purchase of foreign currency showing transaction, rule, and information

In the IBM VisualAge Requirements Tool, the rules are stored in a notebook. Figure 164 shows the page of a notebook indicating the first action of the purchase-of-foreign-currency rule.

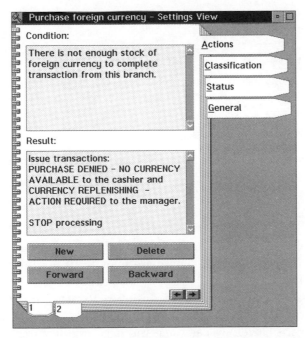

Figure 164. Foreign currency exchange showing the first action of a rule

The rule indicates that if there is not enough stock of foreign currency, a set of transactions related to the replenishment of the currency stock is initiated, and then the process is stopped. If the condition of the rule is not true, and there is enough foreign currency, then the purchase must be accepted, the stock updated, and the accounting department notified. This is shown as the second action of the purchase-of-foreign-currency rule, in Figure 165.

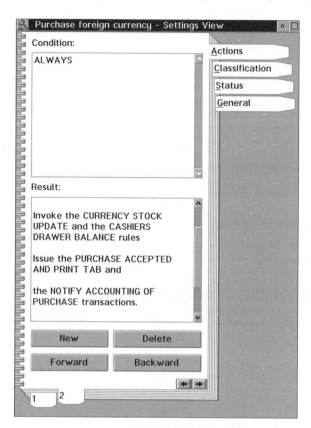

Figure 165. Foreign currency exchange showing the second action of a rule

15.4 Business Rules and Reuse

The application development productivity can be enhanced through a systematic reuse process properly managed. There are many reuse opportunities in the life cycle of an information system: We can reuse experiences, paradigms or approaches, business and domain models, design patterns, frameworks and libraries, code, test procedures, user information, tools, and development environments. At an enterprise level, we can reuse industry architectures that apply to that enterprise.

All the named reusable elements can be described in a broader sense as knowledge structures. From the developers' point of view, the most important mental process in the job is understanding. An important part of what we mean by understanding is accessing existing knowledge structures to which we can map our current experiences [SCH86]. These knowledge structures can be internal, that is, in the developers' minds, or external, structured as reusable components. Understanding is a process in which a relationship is established for related experiences, accessible through memory and expressible through analogy. Indeed, the depth of understanding will increase if there are many available relevant personal experiences in whose terms inputs can be processed.

To understand an enterprise, we need to understand the goals, beliefs, and prior business experiences of that enterprise. The more this knowledge is shared with the developers,[26] the more complete the level of understanding that can take place. This is a different level of understanding than just gathering facts, finding out what events took place, and relating them to a perception of the world that can be quite different from that in the mind of the actor in those events.

The explicit statement of business rules enhances the developers' understanding of the enterprise they are building applications for because the business rules, at different levels of abstraction, record the goals and beliefs of the enterprise and are capsules of distilled knowledge that come from previous business experiences. [ROS94] presents a vision for information systems as a "set of clever compounds of business rules that are known only to few people in the enterprise, all based on a relatively small set of basic or *atomic* rule types, known to many."

Explicit statements of business rules are therefore one of the most effective vehicles for knowledge reuse in the development of applications for an enterprise. At the proper level of abstraction, many of the rules are valid throughout the enterprise organization. A subset of these rules will be proprietary and applicable only to the enterprise; others will be related to the industry in a given environment (for instance, the retail banking modalities in Brazil), others will be applicable to a given industry worldwide (for instance, the steel industry), and others, finally, apply to business in general.

Understanding the proprietary business rules of an enterprise allows for the proper implementation of an industry architecture that encompasses business rules of a more generic nature. Architecture-driven information systems development is one of the most effective reuse-based development approaches. To ensure success, the developers should understand the company rules that, together, describe the company's goals and beliefs. Business process reengineering may modify or nullify some of these rules, but they can never be ignored.

---

26 The term *developers* is used here in its broadest sense and it is not restricted to designers or coders. It may encompass the whole development organization, whether an enterprise MIS department or a consulting and services organization.

15.5 **Summary**

The traditional approach to use cases can be enhanced by determining the explicit business rules that determine a sequence of input and output transactions. This enhancement has several advantages: It extends the traceability of requirements to the processes, facts, goals, and organizational beliefs that motivated the creation and enforcement of those rules; it facilitates business process reengineering by providing focal points to examine the up-to-dateness of processes and the value they add; and it offers a powerful construct to avoid the common pitfall of building heaps of use case instances instead of the selected number of use cases. The value of the use of rules is further enhanced by the use of a visual requirement gathering tool that provides a fast and comprehensive way to visualize and manipulate the use cases, transactions, data, and the rules that relate these elements and govern the enterprise businesses.

16

Conclusion: Trends and Perspectives

Object-oriented technology has come a long way from the time when it was considered mainly an interesting programming approach, materializing formal language concepts such as abstract data types and enforcing well-known principles of modularization and information hiding. Once the domain of individual hackers, objects are now mainstream components of information technology, and the MIS departments of most large corporations have already started major object-oriented projects. In most cases, these projects are new implementations, while the legacy systems still follow their life cycle; many extant systems, however, have already been rewritten to meet the imperatives of the market.

The question with objects is no longer why, but when. The answer is usually driven by business opportunities and financial considerations, where the cost is just one factor, albeit an important one. Customer satisfaction, time to market, and competitive pressure, among other factors, impose service demands on MIS departments that are under budget and headcount constraints. Object technology can help corporations build the information technology support they need to achieve their goals; it can also change the way corporations look and how they describe themselves.

Object technology has entered maturity by proving its applicability to very large projects. There is, however still plenty of room for refinement, evolution, and usability improvements.

Object methodologies are both evolving and being refined; for instance, Syntropy and the Unified Method are evolutions and refinements of both OMT and the Booch method; VMT is an evolution and refinement of OMT and OOSE, with ideas from RDD. If we look at these examples, we see some clear evolution trends.

First, there is evolution toward design rigor. The specification of correctness of classes and methods through the use of assertions, advocated by Bertrand Meyer, has been incorporated in most modern approaches in practical ways. There is also an evolution from tactical to positional design, borrowing terminology from chess: Designers are starting to recognize known patterns in their designs and to build new ones. We are still missing a true graphic pattern language that should allow designers to iconize and connect patterns as components and build software through pattern black box reuse. Conversely, we need program and model browsers of industrial strength that should recognize known patterns in extant models and code. Such browsers would speed object software engineering by orders of magnitude.

Second, we can expect an evolution driven by a development environment. An iterative approach can be successful on sizable projects only if it is supported by proper tools. Current object application development support tools allow for iterations in the modeling and design phases and one or two aspects of the requirements phase, and most generate header files for C++ or class templates for Smalltalk. Some can reverse-engineer C++ or Smalltalk code to a certain extent. But an object developer's wish list includes an integrated object application development environment, from requirements to code. This environment should include the following:

- A facility for capturing requirements in text or graphic form. This facility could be fed by the output of a business processes modeling tool and by input from users and domain experts.

- A text and graphical syntax parser that would analyze problem statements and use cases and would come up with a set of candidate objects, attributes, and relationships that the developer would validate, prune, or augment.

- A facility to feed these objects directly to the modeling tool. The developer would then accept, refine, or discard the object model structure proposed by the tool. A pattern recognition facility would suggest possible patterns in the model.

- A facility for dynamic model animation or execution, to allow testing at the model and requirement level.

- A facility for generating executable code from the dynamic model that could be fed into a visual programming prototyping tool. The combination of requirements gathering and prototyping facilities in a seamless environment would greatly enhance the developer's productivity. This code would not be used for the final application because of its lack of architectural and performance-related characteristics. However, a reverse engineering facility would allow for building the design and object models from the final code for a subsystem, including the dynamic model.

It is easy to envision how such an environment would benefit from a methodology geared toward optimal utilization of the environment facilities.

Third, as further abstractions are formalized, we can expect that more object frameworks will be available off the shelf. Today we have no agreed way to define, document, and reuse frameworks, but there is a trend toward definition by functionality, documentation by sample applications, and reuse by framework composition with user object code (black box reuse). As with patterns, a framework language, framework iconic representation, and visual code composition would represent a productive realization of the software factory model. The frameworks and other components could be available everywhere, using, for instance, the World Wide Web as a new repository containing hyperlinked application components.

Another methodological evolution will be fostered by the appearance of industry architectures. These architectures describe the main objects and processes of an industry and are derived by abstraction and generalization of the objects and processes of many real enterprises of that industry that often participate in industry architecture consortiums. Once industry architectures are defined and mature, they will be customized to build enterprise architectures for corporations, thus enhancing cross-organizational reuse and providing guidance for process reengineering. The correctness of the reengineering work done will be verified by using simulation systems that allow for reengineering iterations. Once the reengineered processes become fairly optimized and stable, the object modeling activity can follow. Methodologies will have to provide road maps to address this architecture trend in a systematic way.

Technology is modifying not only the way we build applications but also the environment in which these applications are deployed, and perhaps even the meaning of the word *application.* Client/server computing is evolving into network-centric computing, where the network becomes the computer. And many home and office appliances are candidates to become user access terminals.

There is, however, one thing that will not change: Applications are developed by people. Skills, understanding, motivation and teamwork have been, are, and will continue to be the critical factors of success in application development and deployment.

FCE Specifications

This appendix describes the specifications of the foreign currency exchange (FCE) application.

A.1 Branch Functions

Because small branches do not maintain their own stocks of foreign currency and traveler's checks, they can satisfy demand only by ordering from the center on the customer's behalf. Large branches do maintain stocks, and customer sales and purchases are handled by cashiers allocated to a foreign currency exchange "bureau" within the branch.

The following sections describe the functions performed at the branch.

Customer Order Management

- Customer Purchases from Branch Cashier

  This is the most frequently performed function in the FCE application. Purchases are usually made for one currency and one type of check. Payment for the purchase can be made in cash, by credit card, or with a local check, or a debit can be raised against the customer's account in the bank. Stock levels are reduced, a customer tab is printed, and accounting entries are passed to the accounting system.

  Subfunctions of this function include

—Check stock levels

—Reduce branch stock levels

—Determine currency and/or check denominations

—Obtain exchange rate

—Print tab (duplicate for the signature)

—Generate accounting entries (debit currency code and credit dollar branch account)

—Handle multiple currencies and checks

—Handle country restrictions, warnings, general information

- Customer Sells to Branch Cashier (Note: This function is not implemented in the application)

Customers are able to sell unwanted foreign currency, traveler's checks, or checks made out against foreign banks to the bank. Bank notes and checks are checked for forgeries by referencing to the textual information on legitimate denominations, descriptions, and known forgery defects.

Subfunctions of this function include

—Obtain exchange rates

—Increase branch stock level

—Print tab (duplicate for the customer's signature)

—Handle multiple currencies and checks

—Pass accounting entries (debit currency code(s) and credit dollars branch account)

- Customer Order Form Cannot Be Satisfied (Note: This function is not implemented in the application)

Not all branches may have the requested stock currencies and checks. Very few branches stock the whole range of currency denominations. All orders that cannot be satisfied by the branch are routed to the bank main office. If payment has been made or the customer has an account with the bank, the currencies and/or checks will be sent to the customer's address; otherwise, they will be sent to the branch for later collection.

Subfunctions of this function include

—Handle country restrictions/warnings/general information

—Handle currency and/or check denominations (small, mix, large, or specified)

—Handle multiple currencies and checks

—Obtain exchange rate

—Take deposit if noncustomer

—Print tab (duplicate for the customer's signature)

—Pass accounting entries (debit currency code and credit dollar branch account)

Cashier Management

- Cashier Stock Reconciliation

At the end of each day, or more frequently if required, each cashier must verify that the checks and foreign currency in her or his drawer are equal to the totals held in the system. This is done by viewing the values held for each denomination within each currency or check. If these totals cannot be reconciled, the difference is passed to InExcess or Depleted accounts, and the totals are amended accordingly. These operations must be confirmed by the branch manager.

Subfunctions of this function include

—Obtain exchange rate for each currency or check

—Display each currency or check total and local currency equivalent

—Display each currency or check denomination total and local currency equivalent

—Order replenishment stock if minimum stock quantity reached

—Send excess stock to center if maximum stock quantity exceeded

—Display total local currency equivalent

—Raise compensating accounting entries for small losses or gains

—Archive reconciliation

Branch Management (Note: This function is not implemented in the application)

- Branch Stock Replenishment

At the end of each day, cashier requests are consolidated. Each request can be an order either to replenish stock or to return excess stock. A consolidated branch order is then sent to the center.

Subfunctions of this function include

—General inquiry as to branch stocks

This function is similar to the Customer Order (branch) function but does not include update intent.

—General inquiry as to central stocks

This function is similar to the Customer Order (center) function but does not include update intent.

—Forgery recognition (computer image)

This function is for inquiry only (compare a computer image to the real note and verify descriptive information on what faults to look for).

A.2   Center Functions

The center bank is responsible for supplying foreign currency and travelers checks to the branches (outlets) and for selling excess foreign currency received from branches. It is done by dealing on the foreign currency markets and arranging bulk shipments at favorable exchange rates.

The following describe the functions performed at the center:

- Bank Management (Note: This function is not implemented in the application)
- Branch Order

Orders from branches are usually for several currencies and/or checks. All orders are processed in batch mode, bulk quantities are picked, delivery arrangements are made, postal charges are set, stock levels are reduced and accounting entries are passed between the branch and the center.

Subfunctions of this function include

—Currency and/or check denominations (small, mixed, large, specified).

—Check stock levels (single currency, single checks, multiple currencies, multiple checks, multiple currencies and checks).

—Print picking lists

—Reduce center stock level

—Obtain exchange rate

—Weigh packages and establish postal charges

—Print branch documents

—Pass accounting entries (debit currency code, credit dollars center account)

- Customer Order

Where branches have been unable to satisfy any part of the customer order, the whole order is supplied by the center. Purchases are normally for one currency and one check for the destination country.

If payment for this service has been made at the branch, then the foreign currency and traveler's checks are mailed to the customer; otherwise, they are mailed to the branch for collection. Stock levels are reduced, a customer tab is printed, and accounting entries are passed to the accounts application.

Subfunctions of this function include

—Handle country restrictions, warnings, and general information

—Handle currency and check denominations (small, mix, large, or specified)

—Handle check stock levels

—Handle one currency

—Handle one check

—Handle several currencies

—Handle several checks

—Handle multiple currencies and checks

—Print packing lists

—Reduce center stock levels

—Weigh packages and establish postal charges

—Obtain exchange rate

—Print customer tab

—Pass accounting entries (debit currency code credit dollar center account)

- Branch Excess

Excess foreign currency received from the branches is counted, reconciled with the branch delivery record, and added to central stocks. If the customer does not accept an order sent by the center to the branch for collection, the accounting entries are reversed for this cancellation.

Subfunctions of this function include

—Add to central stock

—Match value to branch file

—Pass accounting entries

— Reverse entries for cancellations/returns

- Central Stock Reconciliation

At the end of each day, or more frequently if desired, the center verifies the checks and foreign currency for equality to the totals held in the system. This is done by viewing the values held for each denomination within each currency or check and counting the actual stock. If the totals cannot be reconciled, the difference is passed to InExcess or Depleted accounts, and the totals are amended accordingly. Authority can only be granted by the senior manager.

Subfunctions of this function include

—Obtain exchange rate for each currency and/or check

—Display each currency and/or check total and local currency equivalent

—Display each currency and/or check denomination totals and local currency equivalent

—Order replenishment, if minimum stock quantity is reached from other banks via the foreign note dealers

—Sell excess, if maximum stock quantity is exceeded, to other banks via the foreign note dealers

—Display total local currency equivalent

—Raise compensating accounting entries for small losses/gains

—Archive reconciliation

- Maintain Branch Stock Limits

Periodically, the stock held at each branch is reviewed to check whether the stock minimum and maximum levels are still appropriate. A number of "what-if" conditions are used to establish a revised set of limits, including seasonal, period-on-period, and general demand conditions.

Subfunctions of this function include

—Inquire if stock levels still valid (season change, period-on-period demand change, abnormal condition, etc.)

—Change stock level minimum or maximum

—Add or remove stock type or denomination

- Maintain Center Stock Limits

This function is similar to the Maintain Branch Stock Limits function but includes issues of bulk transport, international availability, and capacity.

- Maintain Exchange Rates

Dealers maintain the rates for each currency and check by comparing with other banks' rates and general market rates and by checking general availability. A different rate may be applied for small and large denominations.

- Miscellaneous Transactions

    Subfunctions of this function include

    —Maintain forgery images

    —Create, amend, and delete currency images

    —Produce customer labels/envelopes/documents

    —Produce branch sack labels and documents

FCE Implementation Details

This appendix contains the implementation details for the FCE case study. The application was developed using VisualAge for Smalltalk for OS/2, with DB2/2 as a database server.

B.1 FCE Application Components

Figure 166 shows the VisualAge Organizer view of the FCE application for the case study project. It describes the VisualAge applications that make up the FCE application and the classes under each VisualAge application.

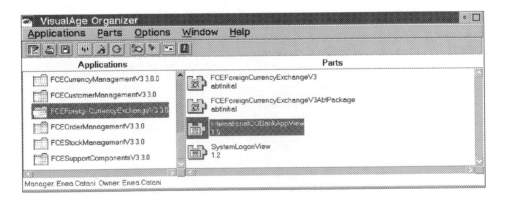

Figure 166. VisualAge Organizer view of the FCE applications

B.2 Base Objects: VisualAge Nonvisual Classes

Base objects are used later as building blocks of other composite objects. The FCE application has base objects in both the visual and the nonvisual class hierarchies. Figure 167 shows the attributes of the Bank class, which is a base object, as presented by the Public Interface Editor. The attributes and their corresponding classes are shown in Table 7, which also indicates whether or not each attribute is derived.

Derived attributes are derived from other basic attributes. They are normally read-only fields and do not need a set selector. Also, since these attributes do not have a set selector, we cannot use Quick Form to lay out the screen.

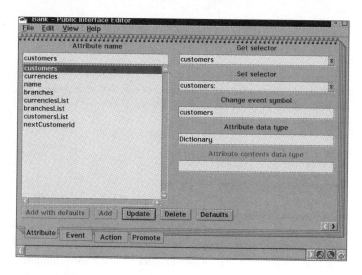

Figure 167. Base object: Bank

Table 7.	Base nonvisual class: Bank	
Attributes	**Instance Variable Class**	**Derived Attribute**
customers	Dictionary	No
currencies	Set	No
currenciesList	OrderedCollection	Yes
customersList	OrderedCollection	Yes
name	String	No
branches	Dictionary	No
branchesList	OrderedCollection	Yes
nextCustomerId	Number	No

Figure 168 shows the attributes of the class Country. Table 8, on page 350, describes the attributes of this class. The Currency attribute is used to maintain the association of the Currency objects with the Country objects.

Associations are bidirectional. We used a Currency attribute in the Country class, and now we need a Country attribute in the Currency class. This is shown in Figure 169 and in Table 9 on page 351.

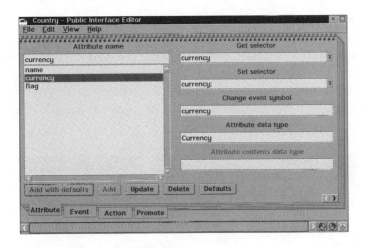

Figure 168. Base object: Country

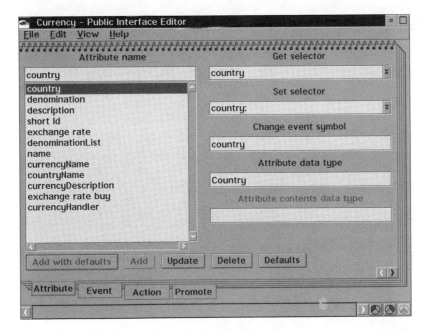

Figure 169. Base object: Currency

Table 8. Base nonvisual class: Country		
Attributes	**Instance Variable Class**	**Derived Attribute**
currency	Currency	No
name	String	No

The DenominationList attribute is a derived attribute. The Country attribute is of class Country and is used to maintain the association with Currency.

DenominationType is a class that represents the unit of currency in a given country. Figure 170 and Table 10 on page 351 show the characteristics of this class, which uses the Bitmap attribute of the AbtBitmapDescriptor class to display the bitmap of the denomination, that is, to show the sample of an HK$100 bill (as shown in Figure 171 on page 351.)

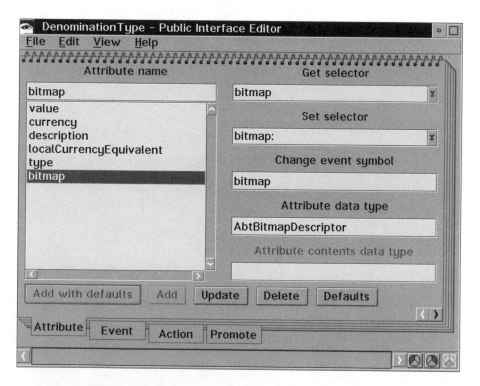

Figure 170. Base object: DenominationType

Table 9. Base nonvisual class: Currency

Attributes	Instance Variable Class	Derived Attribute
country	Country	No
description	String	No
short Id	String	No
exchange rate	Number	No
denomination	Set	No
denominationList	OrderedCollection	Yes

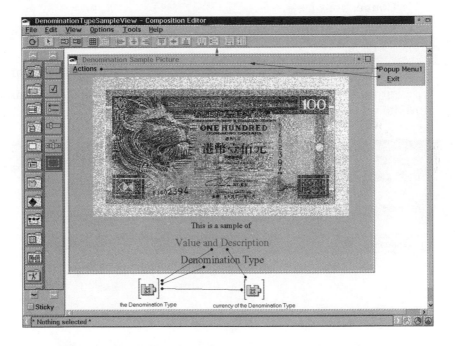

Figure 171. Base visual class: DenominationTypeSampleView

Table 10. Base nonvisual class: DenominationType

Attributes	Instance Variable Class	Derived Attribute
localCurrencyEquivalent	Number	Yes
value	Number	No
currency	Currency	No
description	String	Yes
bitmap	AbtBitmapDescriptor	No

B.3   Base Visual Classes

This section presents a sample of visual classes. We will use the Currency-Management subsystem as an example. The attributes of these visual classes are implemented by using the VisualAge variable part and adding it to the public interface.

Figure 171 on page 351 shows a primary view for DenominationType. It is used to display, in this case, a picture of the denomination. It has the following external interfaces and connections:

- External interfaces
    —The denomination type a (DenominationType variable instance)
- Connections
    —A bitmap of the denomination type <—> GraphicsDescriptor of Label
    —A description of the denomination type <—> LabelString of Label

Figure 172 shows the composite view of DenominationList. It has a public attribute variable instance called the DenominationList. We reuse the Denomin-

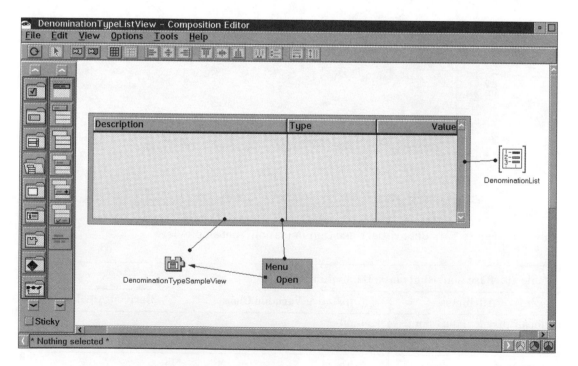

Figure 172. Base visual class: DenominationTypeListView

ationTypeSampleView components shown in Figure 171 on page 351. The selectedItem attribute of the container is connected to the denominationType attribute of the DenominationTypeSampleView subcomponent. Therefore, when the menu item Open is selected, it opens the DenominationTypeSampleView to show the picture of the selected currency.

The DenominationTypeListView component has the following external interfaces and connections:

- External interfaces
  - — The denomination list: an OrderedCollection variable instance
- Connections
  - — Attribute self of menu <—> menu of Table
  - — Attribute self of the DenominationList <—> items of Container
  - — The denominationType of DenominationTypeSampleView <—> selectedItemsOfContainer
  - — Click Open push button <—> openWidget of DenominationTypeSampleView

Figure 173 shows the composite view of CurrencyView. It has a public attribute variable instance of Currency. We reuse the Denomination TypeListView, shown as a view wrapper (Denomination Types) in the figure as a subcomponent.

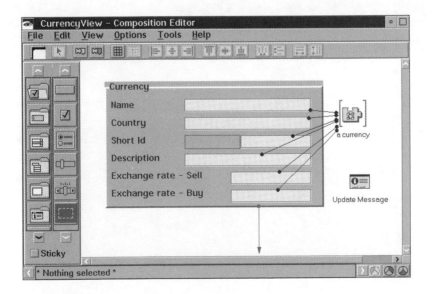

Figure 173. Base visual class: CurrencyView

Figure 174 shows the composite view of CurrencyCreateView. This is the first view that has a primary window, which is one of the windows defined by the user in the analyst prototype. As an example of how to use subclassing, we will create this view by subclassing CurrencyCreateView. The differences between the two views are

- The edit window has a Change button instead of an Add button.
- The edit window has a primary window.
- The event is changeCurrencyRequested instead of newCurrencyCreated.

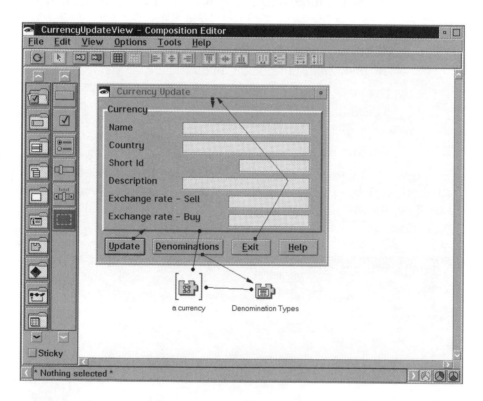

Figure 174. Base visual class: CurrencyUpdateView

Figure 175 shows the composite view of CurrencyCreateView. This view consists of a reusable component, CurrencyView, shown in Figure 173 on page 353 as a subcomponent.

The public interfaces for this view are

- The currency attribute

- The newCurrencyCreated event

We use an event-to-script connection to signal the NewCurrencyCreated event when the Add push button is clicked. The method of SignalAddButton-Pushed is shown below:

```
signalAddButtonPushed
^self signalEvent: #newCurrencyCreated.
```

Figure 176 on page 356 shows the composite view of CurrencyListView. It has a public interface attribute variable named Bank. The list of currencies the Bank trades is created by the CurrencyHandler, which contains the attribute currencyList in its public interface. We reuse the CurrencyListForm component shown in Figure 177 on page 356.

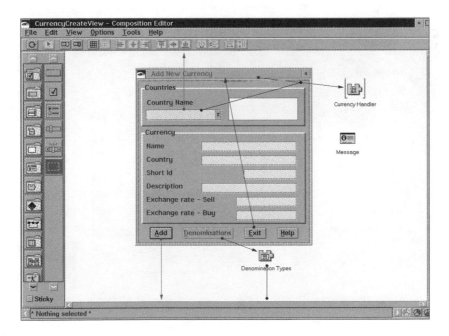

Figure 175. Base visual class: CurrencyCreateView

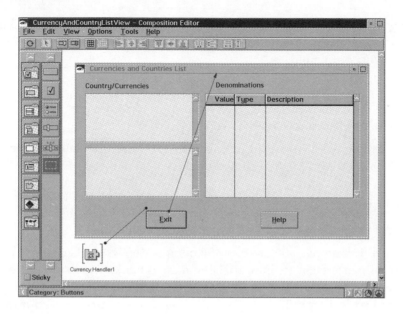

Figure 176. Base visual class: CurrencyAndCountryListView

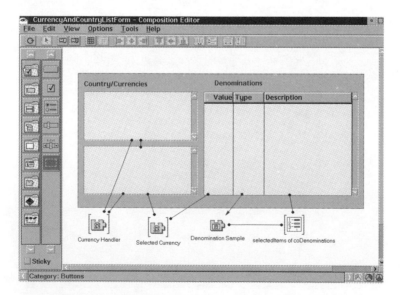

Figure 177. Base visual class: CurrencyAndCountryListForm

B.4   Stock Management Subsystem: A Component Reuse Example

The figures in this section show how we built some of the parts of the currency stock management application. They also illustrate how an application can be built from basic or previously developed components.

Figure 178 show the Cashier Drawer main screen. The notebook is connected to the nonvisual objects that represent the drawer and the bank's currency stock, respectively.

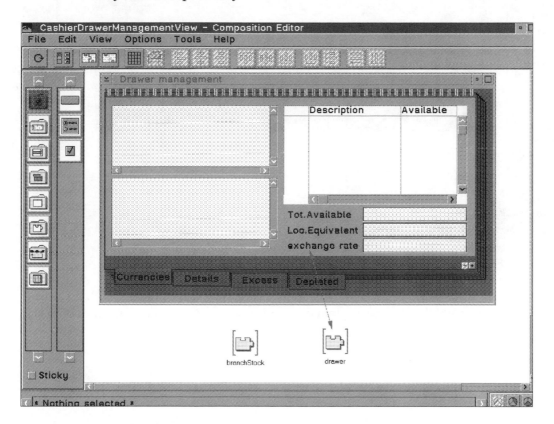

Figure 178. Base visual class: Cashier Drawer main screen

Figure 179 on page 358 shows the Excess currency page of the Cashier Drawer notebook. The transfer to Reserve button is connected to both the Drawer object and the BranchStock object.

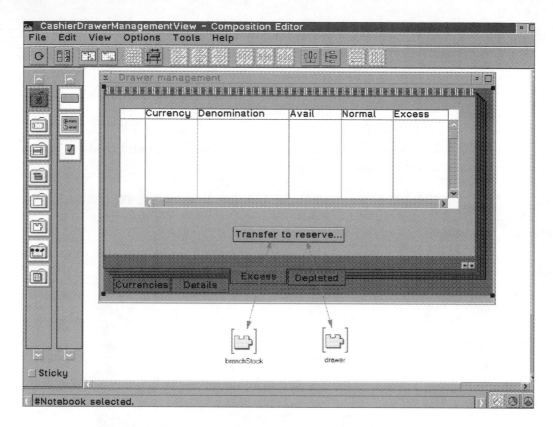

Figure 179. Excess currency page

Figure 180 on page 359 shows the Depleted currency page of the Cashier Drawer notebook. The Replenish from Reserve button is connected to both the Drawer object and the BranchStock object.

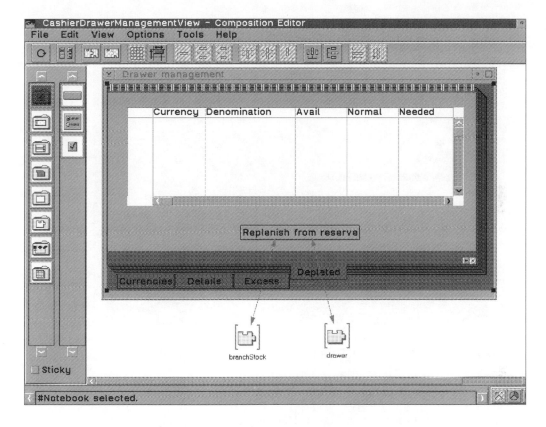

Figure 180. Depleted currency page

Figures 181 through 184 describe aspects of the development of StockItem model class, together with its respective view classes. The StockItem class represents the items in the bank's stock. Figure 181 on page 360 shows the Public Interface Editor that generates the get and set methods for the Stock instance variable of the StockItem class.

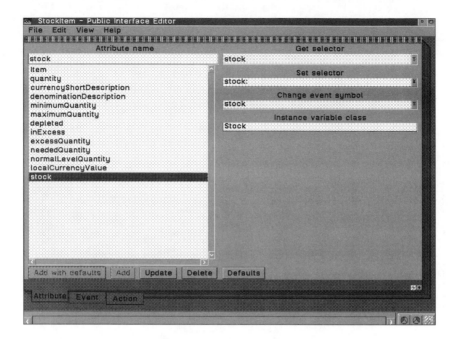

Figure 181. Public Interface Editor used to develop the StockItem class

The figures that follow show the construction-from-parts mechanism: Figure 182 contains the parts shown in Figure 183 on page 361, while Figure 183 reused the parts shown in Figure 184 on page 361.

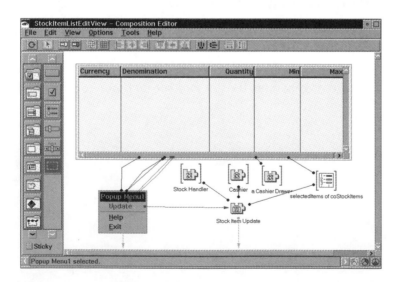

Figure 182. StockItemListEditView

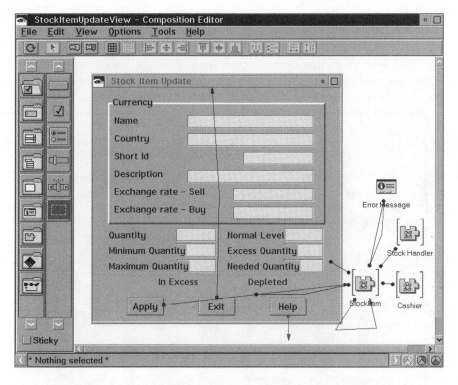

Figure 183. StockItemUpdateView

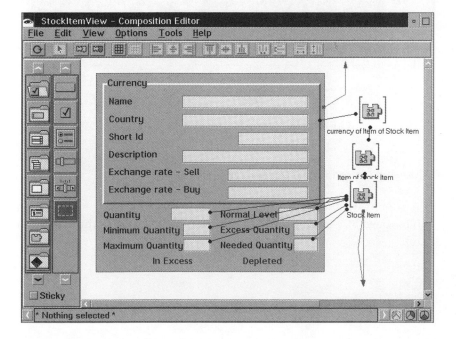

Figure 184. StockItemView Component

B.5   Running the FCE Application

This section illustrates the operational aspects of the FCE application using a series of screen images captured from a running FCE application. The first screen seen by the user when starting the application is shown in Figure 185.

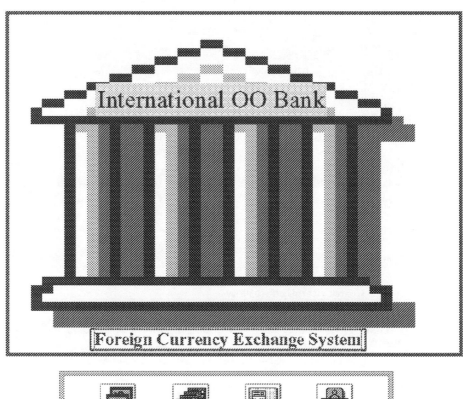

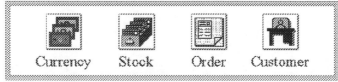

Figure 185. International OO Bank main screen

After system initialization, the bank organization screen is shown as Figure 186 on page 363 to prompt the user (cashier) to identify the branch and cashier name.

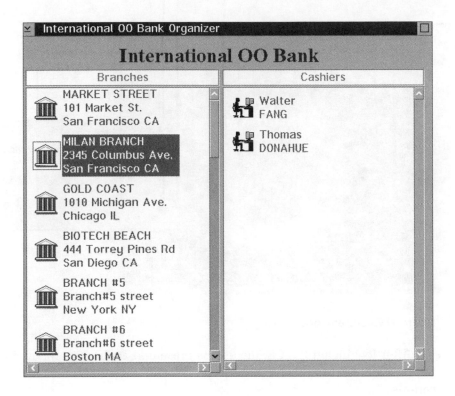

Figure 186. International OO Bank organization screen

The user is then presented with the logon screen shown in Figure 187 on page 364.

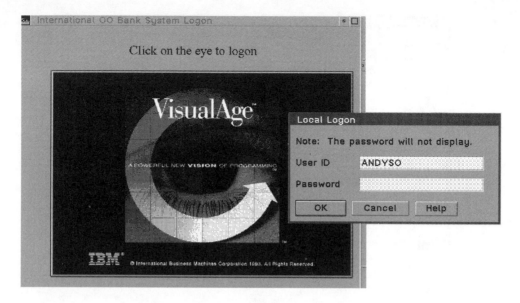

Figure 187. System logon view

After logging on to FCE, the user is presented again with the main screen, which includes four icons that can be selected to start the respective applications.

Currency Management Subsystem

- Assuming the user selected the Currency icon, the currency list screen will appear which lists all the currencies that the bank trades (see Figure 188 on page 365).

Figure 188. Currency Management system: currency list

- The user double clicks on a currency listed in the currency screen to display currency details as shown in Figure 189 on page 366. This screen displays the names of the country and the currency, the current exchange rate, as well as the denominations of the currency.

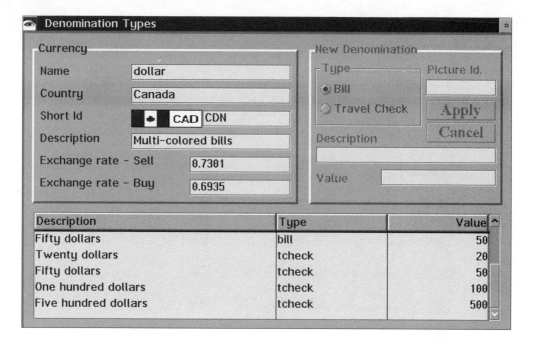

Figure 189. Currency Management system: currency details

- The user can also use the right mouse button to bring up the context manual to select more options, such as looking at the countries and currencies at a glance (see Figure 190 on page 367), or the exchange rates for all currencies (see Figure 191 on page 367).

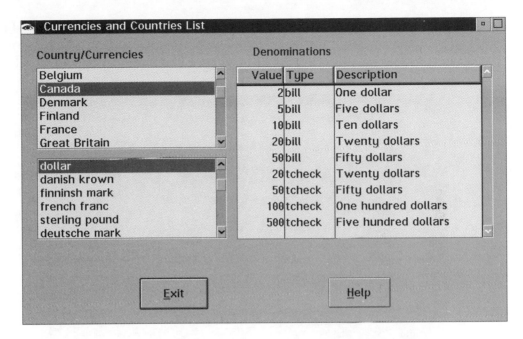

Figure 190. Currency Management system: currencies and countries list

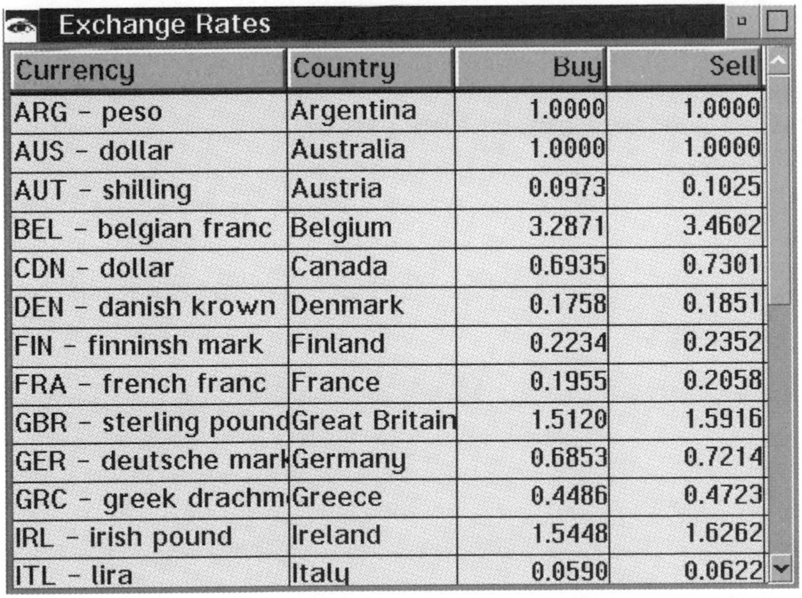

Currency	Country	Buy	Sell
ARG – peso	Argentina	1.0000	1.0000
AUS – dollar	Australia	1.0000	1.0000
AUT – shilling	Austria	0.0973	0.1025
BEL – belgian franc	Belgium	3.2871	3.4602
CDN – dollar	Canada	0.6935	0.7301
DEN – danish krown	Denmark	0.1758	0.1851
FIN – finninsh mark	Finland	0.2234	0.2352
FRA – french franc	France	0.1955	0.2058
GBR – sterling pound	Great Britain	1.5120	1.5916
GER – deutsche mark	Germany	0.6853	0.7214
GRC – greek drachm	Greece	0.4486	0.4723
IRL – irish pound	Ireland	1.5448	1.6262
ITL – lira	Italy	0.0590	0.0622

Figure 191. Currency Management system: exchange rates display

- The currency application allows the user to display the image of a given denomination type, that is, a bill of a valid currency of a certain value. Figure 192 shows the display of a sample denomination type.

Figure 192. Denomination sample display

Customer Management Subsystem

The user can query or update the customer information by double-clicking the customer icon. The following screens display the customer list and customer details:

- The screen shown in Figure 193 on page 369 displays the list of customers.

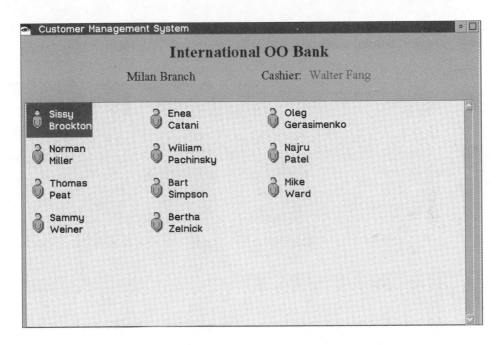

Figure 193. Customer Management system: a customer list

- From the list of customers, selecting a customer and right-clicking brings up the icon's context menu, as shown in Figure 194.

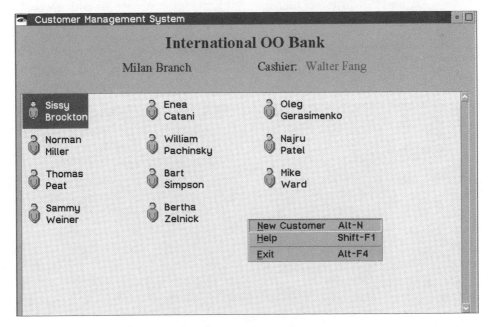

Figure 194. Customer Management system: a customer list with an icon's Context menu

- Right-clicking outside the customer icon brings up the view's Context menu, as shown in Figure 195.

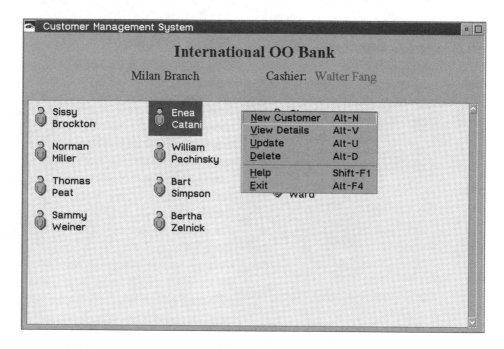

Figure 195. Customer Management system: a customer list with a view Context menu

- Double-clicking on a customer icon brings up the customer's detail information menu, as shown in Figure 196.

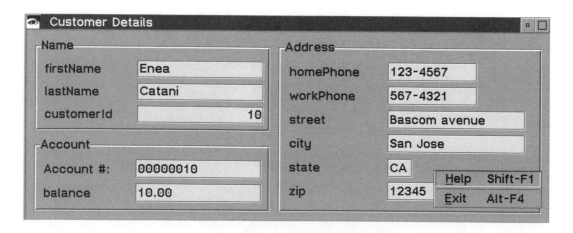

Figure 196. Customer Management system: customer details

Order Management Subsystem

The following screen images illustrate the aspects of the FCE Order management subsystem:

- Figure 197 shows the list of orders handled by a cashier when the order management system is selected.

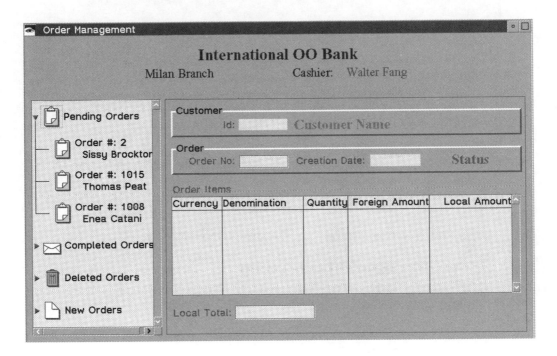

Figure 197. Order Management system: order list view

- Double click on a particular order shown the details of the order as shown in Figure 198 on page 372.

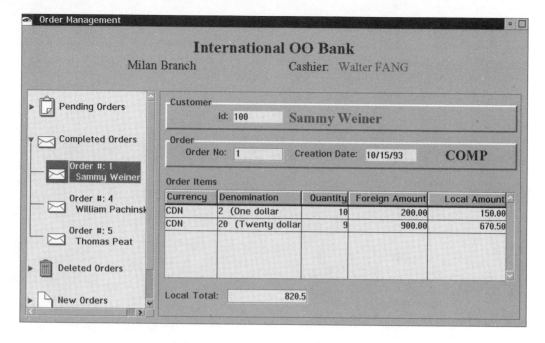

Figure 198. Order Management system: order details view

Stock Management Subsystem

The screens in Figures 199 through 202 illustrate the aspects of the FCE Stock management subsystem:

- Figure 199 shows the display of money available at a certain moment in a cashier's drawer.

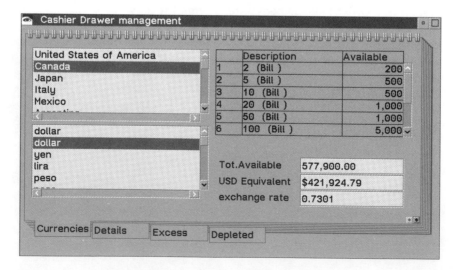

Figure 199. Cashier drawer contents

- When the user selects the notebook entry Details of the Drawer Management screen, the screen shown in Figure 200 is displayed.

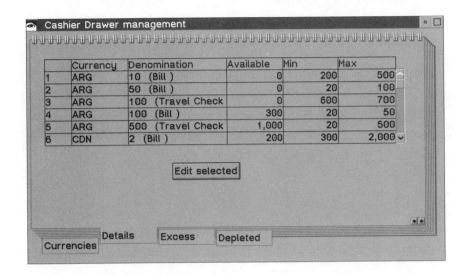

Figure 200. Cashier drawer details

- Figure 201 displays that the money in the cashier drawer has exceeded the normal limit for a given currency, and the cashier can transfer the excessive money to the branch's reserve.

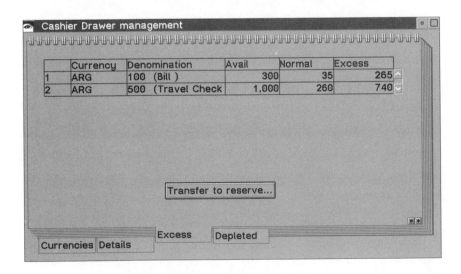

Figure 201. Transferring excessive currency to reserves

- Figure 202 displays the money in the cashier drawer has reached a value below normal for a given currency and must be replenished from the branch's reserve.

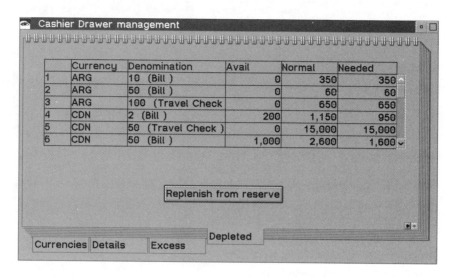

Figure 202. Replenishing of currency from reserves

The Common Object Request Broker Architecture (CORBA)

In this appendix, we review the emerging standards and architectures for object-to-object communication and interoperability in a heterogeneous environment.

As with any new technology, common standards are required for object technology to move into the mainstream; such standards are increasingly evident.

The industry consortium known as the Object Management Group (OMG) has developed the Common Object Request Broker Architecture (CORBA), which provides the specifications that define the interfaces for sending messages from one object to another. This common standard should assist application designers in object-oriented application integration over multiple platforms and operating system environments. The standard also provides the basis for the Object Transaction Service (OTS) Distributed Object Architecture. In addition, two distributed transaction standards with object-oriented implications are widely recognized: the X/Open Distributed Transaction Processing (DTP) model and the ISO/OSI-TP standard.

Standardization of programming languages is equally essential. In recent years the industry has begun to converge on C++, Smalltalk, and Object COBOL as standard object-oriented languages.

Standards can help ensure that objects developed using the tools of different vendors are mutually compatible. As software vendors develop object-oriented components that conform to these standards for the server, customer confidence will continue to grow, and customers will increasingly adopt this new technology. Thus the OMG CORBA standard will facilitate the delivery of off-the-shelf object-oriented solutions for distributed systems.

C.1   The CORBA Standard

OMG is an industrywide, nonprofit consortium of over 600 members, including Apple, AT&T, Hewlett-Packard, IBM, and Sun, to name a few.

The mission of OMG is to create a standard that realizes interoperability between independently developed applications across heterogeneous networks of computers. Furthermore, a single architecture and set of specifications, based on commercially available object technology, will be developed to enable the integration of distributed applications. The goal is to achieve reusability of components, interoperability among heterogeneous platforms, and portability of applications. To that end, OMG has defined the architecture of an object request broker (ORB) that makes interoperability possible. This architecture, known as CORBA, defines object distribution (the distribution mechanisms and services available to applications) and object services (a collection of services that define object interfaces that provide basic functions for realizing and maintaining objects). Object services provide the following functions:

- Class management: Maintain (create, delete, and copy) definitions of classes, interfaces of classes, and the relationships among them

- Instance management: Maintain (create, delete, and copy) objects, and the relationships among them

- Storage: Provide permanent or transient storage for objects

- Integrity: Ensure the consistency and integrity both within objects (through locks) to allow for concurrent object access and among objects (through transactions)

- Security: Provide access constraints for objects

- Query: Select objects from collections based on a specified predicate

- Versions: Store, correlate, and manage object versions

A variety of subcomponents, such as object-oriented database management systems, transaction managers, query facilities, directory services, and file services, can be used to implement object services.

CORBA defines a framework that allows different implementations to provide common ORB interfaces and services, thus supporting interoperability of systems with object-oriented applications. Its intent is to allow for the integration of a large variety of object systems.

CORBA is based on an abstract object model. The object model describes concepts such as how to create objects; how to issue requests and operations; and how to define types, signatures, methods, server processes, and object activation. The object model is very specific in its client aspects and less specific in its object implementation aspects, to allow maximum implementation freedom. The model describes objects, object semantics, requests, object creation and destruction, types, interfaces, operations, parameters, return results, exceptions, contexts, execution semantics, and attributes. The object implementation part of the model describes how to perform services and construct a model, but leaves it up to the developer to define a functioning object system that can execute requests (services) on behalf of clients.

Not included in the object model are some aspects of the application architecture and the specific domains to which the object technology is applied, such as compound objects, links, copying of objects, and transactions.

C.1.1   Object Management Architecture (OMA)

To support heterogeneous, distributed, networked environments, the Object Management Architecture (OMA), defined by the OMG, combines distributed processing with object-oriented computing. It provides a standard method for creating, preserving, locating, and communicating with objects, which can be anything from complete application systems to parts of applications. The OMA defines a layer above existing operating systems and communication transports that support standard RPCs.

In OMA's generalized object model, requests for object services are sent to the ORB (see Figure 203). The requester can specify providers or alternative providers or leave the selection of a provider to the ORB. The model provides a common interface for objects of different origins. All client requests are issued in a standard format, improving modularity and decreasing coupling among modules.

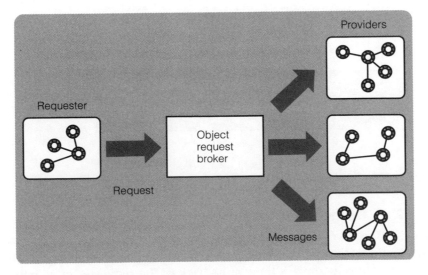

Figure 203. OMA generalized object model

The OMA defines the mechanism that allows client objects to issue requests to and receive responses from OMA-conforming objects.

The OMA reference model can be divided into four components (see Figure 204):

- Application Objects: Correspond to the traditional notion of an application, representing related functions, such as the electronic office or CAD systems. Application objects are the business objects that provide the application logic (for example, a payroll system).

- Object Services: Provide standard functions that objects require to support their existence, for example, integrity, storage, instantiation.

- Common Facilities: Provide more standard functions but at the level of generic application functions, such as database access, printing facilities, security, and error reporting.

- Object Request Broker: Provides an infrastructure allowing objects to communicate, independent of the specific platforms and techniques used to implement the objects.

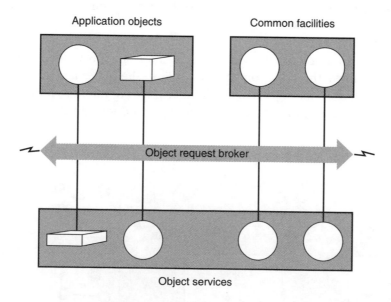

Figure 204. OMA components

C.1.2   **Object Request Broker**

The ORB receives a request for a specific operation, finds the appropriate object and methods to process the request, and passes the parameters specified in the request. Then it conveys the results back to the requester or somewhere else. The ORB must execute many functions to support this simple operation consistently and effectively, but they are hidden from the user. Thus, the ORB provides a framework for cross-system communication between objects. The ORB is the first technical step toward interoperability of object systems. The goal of the ORB is to move from point to point, providing local communication to hubs. Everyone can talk to everyone through some common syntax and traffic systems, without the need to understand anything about their partners except for their external interfaces. Thus encapsulation is maintained.

The ORB should address

- Name services
- Request dispatch
- Parameter encoding
- Delivery
- Synchronization
- Activation
- Exception handling
- Security mechanisms

The ORB provides the basic mechanism for transparently making requests to and receiving responses from local or remote objects, without the client needing to be aware of the mechanisms used to communicate with, activate, or store the objects. As such, it forms the foundation for building applications constructed from distributed objects and for interoperability between applications in both homogeneous and heterogeneous environments.

Using an ORB, we can request an object's services without regard for the location or implementation of the object providing the service; that is, without regard for the mechanisms used to represent, store, manage, invoke, or communicate with the object. Objects made available through an ORB publish their interfaces using the interface definition language (IDL), which provides a way of specifying an object's operations and attributes that is independent of the programming language.

The ORB is a specification for a system (see Figure 205 on page 380) that manages the communications among objects: location transparency, naming and delivery services, activation and deactivation of remote objects, method invocation, parameter encoding, synchronization, exception handling, and security. It sits on top of a network or RPC mechanism but does not get involved in the applications or the structure, form, or capabilities of the objects themselves. However, this is not enough on its own to guarantee interoperability.

Two object systems cannot exchange messages successfully unless their object brokers can communicate physically. Also, the ORB addresses the syntax, not the semantics, of interobject communications. We may not need to know the details of an implementation if we are addressing an object, but we do need to know the details of the behavior the object will exhibit when a message is sent to it and the parameters the message needs. The ORB is just a standard for a component; it cannot overcome incompatibilities in the rest of the world.

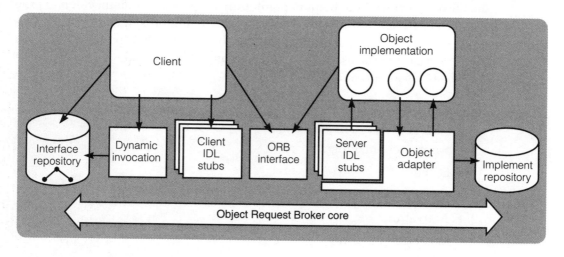

Figure 205. The structure of a CORBA ORB

Figure 206 on page 381 shows the client and server components of an ORB. On the client side,

- Client IDL stubs define how clients invoke services on the servers.
- Services are declared using IDL, and client stubs are generated by the IDL compiler.
- The dynamic invocation interface APIs allow the discovery of classes and their function at run time.
- The interface repository APIs allow the acquisition of descriptions of registered classes and the methods they support with their respective parameters.
- The ORB interface consists of APIs to local services that may be of interest to an application.

On the server or object implementation side,

- Server IDL stubs provide interfaces to each service exported by the server. They are generated by the IDL compiler, in much the same way as the client IDL stubs.
- The object adapter interfaces with the ORB's core and accepts requests for service on behalf of the server's objects.
- The implementation repository provides run-time directory information about the classes a server supports.

Communication between the client and server is accomplished through the ORB core, which is not defined by CORBA but is implementation specific (see Figure 206).

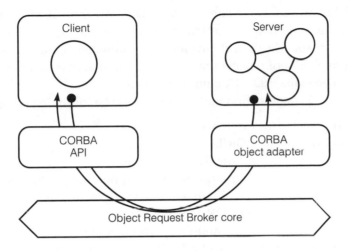

Figure 206. Relationships among the client, the server, and the ORB

The ORB establishes the client/server relationship between objects. It intercepts the call from the client object and it is responsible for

- Finding an object that can answer the call
- Passing all parameters to the server object
- Invoking its method
- Returning the results to the client

C.1.3   CORBA 2.0 Specification

CORBA 2.0, adopted in December 1994, defines true interoperability by specifying how ORBs from different vendors can interoperate. The CORBA 2.0 interoperability architecture, also known as Universal Networked Objects (UNO), specifies a simple, streamlined TCP/IP-based object-messaging protocol. The OMG also allowed vendors to provide ORBs that support additional protocols to provide higher-function, distributed object services. This opens the door to IBM, HP, DEC, and others to build CORBA 2.0 ORBs based on the Distributed Computing Environmental (DCE) protocols and services.

Beside the interoperability issues, CORBA 2.0 clarifies some topics that were left open in the CORBA 1.2 specification. For example, the interface repository specification now defines the support for interface-type equivalence checking, type codes, and IDL attributes.

The specification is a merged version of two responses to the OMG ORB 2.0 Interoperability and Initialization Request for Proposal. The first response to this RFP was submitted by BNR, Expersoft, IBM, ICL, IONA, and SunSoft. The interoperability of the first response was based on TCP/IP. A specification based on the DCE-CIOP protocol was submitted by DEC, HP, and IBM. OMG asked both groups to merge their specification and come back with a unified version. Therefore the final specification stands for a comprehensive, flexible approach to supporting networks of objects that are distributed across and managed by multiple, heterogeneous, CORBA-compliant ORBs.

The CORBA 2.0 specification currently defines the following components:

Component	Contents
CORBA2/CORE	CORBA1.2
	minus IDL C mapping
	plus extensions to support some object services
	plus interface repository extensions
	plus ORB initialization
	plus inter-ORB bridge support
CORBA2/Interoperable	CORBA2.0/CORE as defined above
	plus CORBA2.0/Internet Inter-ORB Protocol (IIOP)
CORBA2/C	IDL C language mapping, defined as a stand-alone specification
CORBA2/C++	IDL C++ language mapping, defined as a stand-alone specification
CORBA2/Smalltalk	IDL Smalltalk language mapping, defined as a stand-alone specification

Note that each language mapping is defined as a single component.

The System Object Model (SOM)

IBM's System Object Model (SOM) is a CORBA-compliant software technology developed to ensure the portability of objects across platforms and programming languages.

One of the main advantages of the System Object Model (SOM) is its ability to describe the interface for a class of objects in a language-independent manner through the IDL. A SOM class can be implemented in C++, for instance, whereas a client program using this class can be implemented using C.

Since SOM is language neutral, it preserves the key object-oriented programming characteristics of encapsulation, inheritance, and polymorphism. The user of a SOM class and the implementor of a SOM class are not forced to use the same programming language.

SOM includes a run-time library, which provides a set of classes, methods, and procedures used to create objects and invoke methods on them. To use this library, a programming language must be able to

- Call external procedures
- Store a pointer to a procedure and subsequently invoke that procedure
- Map IDL types onto the programming language's native types

These requirements indicate that the programming language that uses or implements a SOM class does not even have to be an object-oriented language.

In addition to its programming interface, SOM provides *language bindings* as a more convenient way to use and implement SOM classes. Language bindings tailor the SOM programming interface to a particular programming language. They make SOM classes appear like ordinary constructs of the programming language as much as possible.

D.1   The IBM SOMobjects Toolkit

The IBM SOMobjects Toolkit comprises a set of object-oriented application development frameworks. The frameworks support such tasks as remote access to objects (DSOM framework), making and synchronizing copies of objects in different address spaces (replication framework), saving and retrieving objects in and from data stores, and organizing objects into base data structures such as queues, lists, and sequences (collection class framework).

The SOMobjects Toolkit frameworks are described briefly below. Particular attention is given to DSOM, which is IBM's CORBA-compliant ORB.

D.1.1 Replication Framework

The replication framework enables multiparty applications where the requirement is for each user to have access to his or her own copy of an object; that is, a single object with multiple shadows spread throughout the system or network.

The framework provides all of the necessary functions for serializing the updates to the master object as well as selecting a new master if the original master unexpectedly goes away.

Figure 207 illustrates the basic facts about the replication framework, which are as follows:

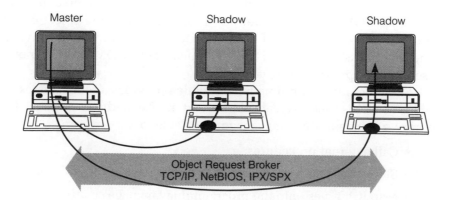

Figure 207. Replication framework

- The replication framework is the first implementation of replicas using objects. Replicas of data (and databases) are a well-known problem to analysts. For the first time, replicas are implemented for objects with the SOM replication framework.

- The replication framework synchronizes multiple copies of a single object in the address spaces of several distributed processes, thus providing the foundation for collaborative online activities such as distributed whiteboards, group editing, and games.

- Updates are communicated in real time, without the use of a secondary store.

- None of the participants knows how many replicas exist or where they are located, because replicas are totally transparent. In addition, any participant is free to join or leave the replica group at any time.

- Replica support is made possible through multiple inheritance: All replicable classes must be derived from the SOMRReplicbl class.

D.1.2   Persistence Framework

The persistence framework is a series of classes that allows the state of an object to be easily stored and available after termination of the process that created it.

This framework provides a generic interface so that the actual data store for object is independent of the method calls used to make an object persistent. SOM provides a default facility using the standard file system. However, one can easily extend this to use object-oriented databases or other facilities based on the application requirements.

Figure 208 on page 386 shows the basic facts about the persistence framework:

- The persistence framework stores complex objects in files.

- Objects contain persistent pointers to other objects.

- The persistent store uses standard files. Objects can be grouped together in files or stored individually. Grouped objects are said to be near each other. Although the persistence framework uses a standard file system, persistent framework classes managing the store can be overridden to make them work with an object or SQL database.

- Any IDL-supported data type can be declared persistent.

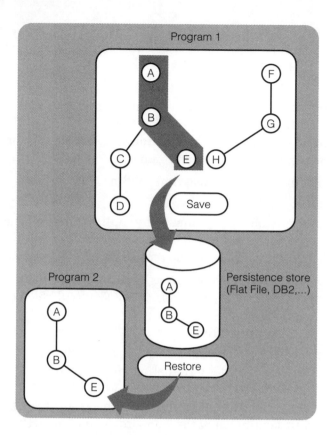

Figure 208. Persistence framework

D.1.3   Event Manager Framework

The event manager framework, also known as EMan, is a set of classes that handles the sending and receiving of asynchronous events. It is particularly useful in a single-threaded environment, where an application would like to be notified when a particular event occurs elsewhere in the system.

The EMan designed is similar to many typical GUI environments, where applications need to respond to messages generated by external events or by other components of the application:

- EMan loops forever to handle events and distribute them to the callback methods. It is similar to the presentation manager event loop, except that events can be routed across the network.

- EMan currently supports four event types:

    —Timer events

    —Sink events, such as socket calls

—Client (for application-specific) events

—Work procedure events, which are background tasks that can be executed when the event loop is idle

- EMan is extensible. Any special event can be managed by the application, if the EMan classes are subclassed and personalized.

D.1.4   Emitter Framework

The emitter framework is a collection of SOM classes that allows programmers to customize the operation of the SOM compiler. The SOM compiler processes IDL files, which define class interfaces. The emitter framework simplifies the process of creating an emitter to generate language-specific bindings from an IDL file.

Bindings are not the only thing that can be emitted. For example, using the emitter framework, we can create an emitter for generating skeleton documentation files, based on the contents of an IDL file.

D.1.5   Collection Class Framework

The SOMObjects Developer Toolkit provides a set of commonly required collection classes, including the following:

- Hash table: A table of key/value pairs providing fast access by hashing on the key
- Dictionary: A table of key/value pairs similar to the hash table, however, objects with equal keys can appear only once in the dictionary
- Set: An unordered collection of objects in which each object can appear only once
- Queue: A list of objects that are inserted and removed in first-in-first-out order
- Dequeue: A double-ended queue in which insertion and removal can occur at either end
- Stack: A list of objects that are inserted and removed in last-in-first-out order
- Linked list: A list of objects in which each object is linked to the object in front of it and the object behind it
- Sorted sequence: A collection of objects whose order is determined by how the objects relate to each other
- Priority queue: A special case of the sorted sequence in which ordering is based on priority

Other classes are designed to assist in the use and mixing of any of the above classes.

D.1.6 Distributed SOM Framework

Distributed SOM (DSOM), part of the SOMobjects Developer Toolkit, is a framework that provides the ability to make calls on SOM objects across processes (see Figure 209 on page 389). The interprocess communication (IPC) is totally hidden from the programmer.

DSOM can be viewed in two ways:

- As an extension to SOM, allowing one process to invoke methods on objects in other processes
- As a CORBA-compliant ORB

DSOM was developed to meet three basic goals:

- Extend SOM to provide support for accessing remote objects
- Comply with the OMG's CORBA specification
- Enable existing SOM classes and SOM applications to be used in multiple-process environment

DSOM is extensible. With a socket interface for communication services, it now supports TCP/IP on AIX and TCP/IP, NetBios, and Netware on OS/2. In the future it will support large-scale distributed environments on the basis of OSF's Proxy Object (DCE).

Distributed Computing Environment Protocol

A proxy is an object that is a local representative for a remote target object. A proxy inherits the target object's interface, so it responds to the same methods as the target object.

DSOM users and applications access objects via a direct reference called a handle. If the object is local, the handle maps to the actual object. If the object is remote, the handle maps to a proxy object. The proxy object takes the request and delivers it to the remote object. Remote objects are managed by an object adapter.

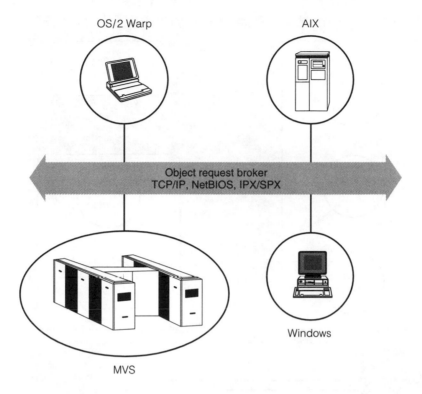

Figure 209. DSOM workgroup environment

While SOM separates clients from the object implementation, DSOM adds location separation A DSOM workstation supports client/server object interactions among processes on the same machine, using existing interprocess communication (IPC) facilities. A DSOM workgroup supports client/server object exchanges across networks of Windows, OS/2, and AIX machines. It uses socket-based TCP/IP, IPX/SPX, and NetBIOS stacks, and it can be customized to other stacks.

Simplified DSOM Environment

Figure 210 on page 390 shows a high-level view of some of the components in a DSOM environment. Actually, the DSOM environment has more classes than shown, but this simplified view provides a starting point for a basic understanding of DSOM. The following sections summarize the parts of this simplified DSOM environment.

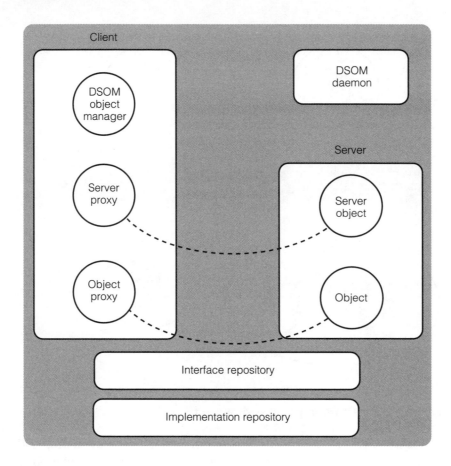

Figure 210. Simplified DSOM environment

DSOM Object Manager This object assists the client application with locating object servers. An object server, simply called a server in DSOM, is the program (process) running on the remote machine (or, if a DSOM workstation is used on the same machine, in a different process). The server is the entry point into the application; it accepts requests on the objects it controls. We could imagine the server to be a large program housing a large number of objects on behalf of many clients. The server waits within a request loop and executes requests on behalf of the various clients. It also provides high-level methods for creating and destroying remote objects.

Server Proxy and Object Proxy The client contains proxies for real objects located in the server. The local client makes method calls on these proxies as if they were the target object. DSOM then passes the method call to the server, where the method call is invoked on the actual objects and the results are returned.

Operations invoked on the proxy are not executed locally but are forwarded to the real target object for execution. The DSOM run-time environment creates proxy objects automatically whenever an object is returned as the result of a remote operation. A client program always has a proxy for each remote object on which it operates.

Daemon On any system that acts as a server, a separate daemon process called SOMDD must be active. This process is instrumental in initializing server processes and in creating the binding between the client process and the server process.

Interface Repository The interface repository provides a mechanism for storing interface definitions. Class interface definitions or signatures (a method's parameters and return value) are registered with the interface repository. This is accomplished by compiling the IDL file with the ir emitter and the -u (update) option.

DSOM makes extensive use of information stored in the interface repository. Before an object can be accessed remotely by DSOM, it is necessary to register the class interface and implementation (from the IDL) in the interface repository. DSOM uses the interface information to drive the generic remote dispatch routine. Based on the parameter type descriptions in the interface definition, the remote dispatcher traverses the method call parameter list and copies the parameter data into a message buffer. A receiving process performs the symmetric operation when extracting parameter data from a message buffer.

Implementation Repository A server's implementation definition must be registered in the implementation repository before a server can be used. The implementation definition contains server information that includes the name of the server program, the name of the host machine for the server, and the classes that are associated with this server. When a client wants to use any of the methods, the DSOM object manager consults the implementation repository to find a server that can satisfy the request.

D.1.7   Server

In a DSOM environment, client programs can access one or more distributed objects that reside on DSOM servers. The following list gives a rough definition of what a server is and does:

- A DSOM server is a process that manages target objects on behalf of a client.

- A server manages objects of a set of classes. In particular, it takes care of creation and destruction of instances of those classes. The server handles messages passed to it from clients and passes them to the proper method of a target object.

The classes supported by a server usually implement business logic; that is, they represent a part of the application's problem domain. Also, they usually have to access data held in databases or files.

- One or more class libraries provide implementation for classes the server manages. They are built as dynamically linked libraries that can be loaded by the server on demand.

- A default server implementation somdsrv) provided by DSOM can be used as a generic server program. The generic server receives request messages, executes them synchronously, and passes back the results to the client.

- The DSOM server must be registered with DSOM in the implementation repository before it can be used.

- A DSOM server does not have to run on a different machine than the client program; it can run on the same system in a separate process.

Server Object

There is one server object per server process. Each server process has the following responsibilities for managing objects in the server:

- Provide an interface to client applications for basic object creation and destruction services, as well as any other application-specific object-management services that may be required by clients.

- Provide an interface to the SOM object adapter for support in the creation and management of DSOM object references (which are used to identify an object in the server) and for dispatching requests.

Object Adapter

The SOM object adapter (SOMOA) is the main interface between the server application and the DSOM run-time environment. In particular, the SOMOA handles all communications and interpretation of inbound requests and outbound results. When clients send requests to a server, the requests are received and processed by the SOMOA.

The SOMOA works with the server object to create and resolve DSOM references to local objects and to dispatch methods on those objects.

Figure 211 on page 393 depicts the DSOM components as a CORBA compliant Object Request Broker (ORB) implementation.

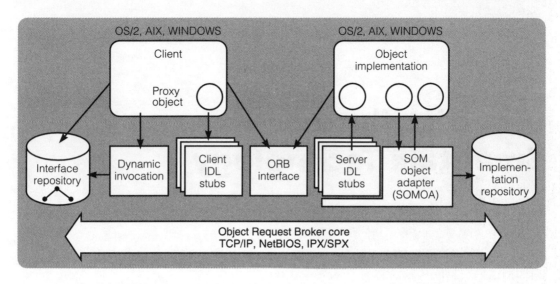

Figure 211. DSOM as a CORBA ORB

IBM Distributed Smalltalk Technology

IBM's Distributed Smalltalk technology provides a set of Smalltalk classes and tools designed to support the development of distributed applications in an IBM VisualAge Smalltalk environment. The IBM Smalltalk language is powerful, easy-to-learn, and well suited to short development cycles. It lends itself to the development of GUIs as well as application business logic. IBM VisualAge for Smalltalk provides visual programming capabilities for the Smalltalk environment to further enhance programmer productivity.

Distributed Smalltalk technology provides a two-level solution for distributed programming that is available for both the VisualAge for Smalltalk and IBM Smalltalk environments (see Figure 212 on page 395):

- Distributed object space: Takes advantage of "Smalltalk everywhere" applications to provide true local and remote transparency. Distributed object space technology is provided through the Distributed Feature available for both the IBM VisualAge for Smalltalk and IBM Smalltalk products.

- Support for IBM's CORBA-compliant SOM and DSOM: Provided through the SOMsupport feature in VisualAge for Smalltalk and IBM Smalltalk as part of the base products.

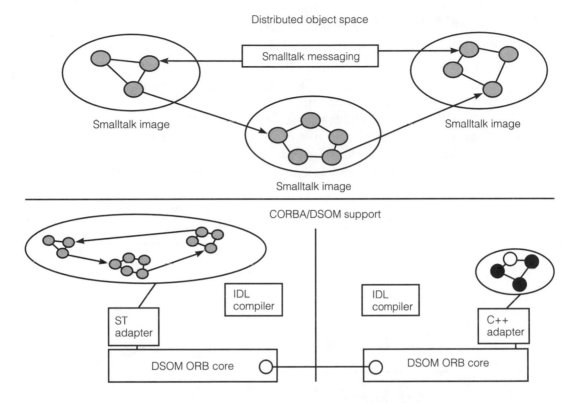

Figure 212. IBM Distributed Smalltalk solution for distributed programming

The Distributed Feature extends the basic Smalltalk model to support distribution of objects in different object spaces. These objects can send standard Smalltalk messages to one another, regardless of their physical location. They can also freely send other Smalltalk objects as arguments and receive objects as results. The different parts of an application can be located on any computer in the network that is running IBM Distributed Smalltalk.

The VisualAge Smalltalk SOMsupport feature provides a mechanism for distributed programming in heterogeneous environments where some parts of an application are written in languages other than Smalltalk. The SOMsupport feature is intended for distributed applications that are built with multiple programming languages for which SOM bindings exist. Currently, this includes C, C++, and IBM Smalltalk.

IBM's Distributed Smalltalk technology offers flexible development alternatives that ease the transition to object-oriented, distributed application development.

E.1   VisualAge SOM/DSOM Support

The VisualAge SOMsupport feature provides an interface through which VisualAge applications can use objects implemented with SOM. These SOM objects can be developed in any language that has SOM bindings. With this interface, VisualAge applications can create instances of SOM objects and send messages to them. This capability extends to the classes that make up the SOM kernel; VisualAge applications can interact with the SOM run-time environment.

SOMsupport is implemented through the use of Smalltalk wrapper classes that represent SOM classes, as shown in Figure 213.

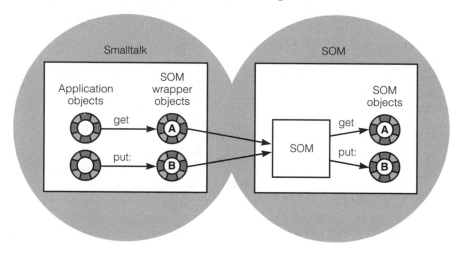

Figure 213. VisualAge SOMsupport overview

Interaction with these wrapper classes is the same as direct use of the SOM classes they represent. When an instance of a wrapper class is created, an instance of the associated SOM class is also created. Interaction with the instance of the Smalltalk wrapper is the same as with any Smalltalk class. The attributes and methods of the SOM class are represented by methods of the Smalltalk class.

SOM Smalltalk wrapper classes can also be used visually in the VisualAge Composition Editor. A wrapper object added to the Composition Editor appears as a nonvisual part. Attributes and actions on the part's public interface represent the attributes and methods of the SOM object.

E.1.1   New In VisualAge Version 3.0 SOMsupport

VisualAge Version 3.0 SOMsupport includes a subset of the SOMobjects Base Toolkit, so no additional software is needed to create Smalltalk bindings in order to use SOM objects. The SOMsupport is delivered with complete pregenerated bindings for all SOMobjects base components to simplify setup. The SOMsupport provides both an API and a visual interface for creating SOM bindings.

Enhancements in version 3.0 include:

- Conformance to OMG Smalltalk language mappings. This affects some of the SOM data representations in Smalltalk.

- Improved exception handling. SOM exceptions are now mapped to Smalltalk exceptions, thus providing complete user control of exception handling with default behavior.

- Support for SOM character output, such as somPrintf. Users can redirect SOM print output to a Smalltalk stream, such as the Transcript.

- Support for all SOM data types, including float and pointer data types.

- Improved data marshaling and demarshaling. Deep nested, constructed data types are now supported.

- Availability of all SOM global information in Smalltalk environment.

- Automatic memory management for SOM parameters. Users do not have to free memory themselves.

- Automatic environment management, removing the need for users to supply setup code.

E.1.2   Expected Benefits

By integrating the strengths of the VisualAge development environment with IBM's SOM and DSOM technology, VisualAge developers and users of the resulting applications will benefit from the following enhancements:

- Cross-language object classes: Using currently available development tools, object classes developed in one language environment cannot be effectively reused in another language environment.

SOMsupport enables VisualAge Smalltalk developers to reuse and subclass object classes developed in other languages. This possibility of cross-language reuse of classes significantly increases the availability of object classes in VisualAge and other development environments, such as C or C++. In all, the support of SOM by VisualAge enables developers to reuse more code, thus resulting in less costly and risky development.

- Support for CORBA distributed objects: Client/server computing is quickly becoming a normal requirement for the development and deployment of new applications. The OMG's CORBA standard (fully implemented in IBM's SOM/DSOM technology) was designed to provide a productive, flexible, and dynamic client/server solution by exploiting the power of distributed object services. IBM's DSOM is a scalable extension of SOM that provides local and remote distributed object services across a heterogeneous network.

VisualAge SOMsupport enables the development of CORBA-based distributed objects. VisualAge SOMsupport can significantly reduce the costs and risk associated with developing, deploying, and adapting client/server applications while enhancing the migration path from local objects to distributed objects.

- Support for SOM-based operating system services: Over time, an increasing number of operating system services will be packaged as SOM object classes and frameworks. The first of these frameworks was the OS/2 Workplace Shell, which enables developers to customize, extend, and integrate into the Workplace Shell desktop as well as inherit behavior and characteristics (such as drag/drop) to develop new applications. OpenDoc, a compound document architecture supported by IBM, Apple, Novell, WordPerfect, and others, will be packaged as a framework of SOM classes that can be used in developing document-centric applications.

VisualAge SOMsupport is positioned to exploit these frameworks, which will help automate the design and development of a new wave of document-centric, collaborative, distributed object applications.

- Industry standard class definitions: The SOM IDL and interface repository, which provides run-time access to class information and definitions, fully conform to the OMG's CORBA standard.

The VisualAge Version 3.0 SOMsupport Smalltalk bindings comply with OMG standards as defined in CORBA 2.0 Smalltalk mapping specifications. VisualAge SOMsupport classes therefore will adhere to industry standards (CORBA IDL), enabling customers to retain investments in skills and code, while providing a mechanism for interoperability with other CORBA-compliant object ORBs (such as Hewlett-Packard's HP ORB).

In summary, SOM, when integrated with the VisualAge development environment, can result in a more productive and powerful set of application development capabilities.

E.2 **VisualAge Distributed Feature**

VisualAge Distributed Feature provides distributed object space support. When all parts of a distributed application are written in Smalltalk, IBM Distributed Smalltalk takes advantage of this situation with a technology called the distributed object space. In effect, the distributed object space extends the Smalltalk model across a network. The following highlight some features of Distributed Smalltalk:

- IBM Smalltalk Base: IBM's Distributed Smalltalk technology is based on IBM Smalltalk, an object-oriented development environment. The industry-standard Smalltalk language provides a smooth transition to object-oriented development. IBM Smalltalk provides an open and extensible programming environment that supports large-scale team development with version control.

IBM Smalltalk is the foundation of IBM's VisualAge, an object-oriented visual programming environment. IBM Smalltalk applications are portable to any platform on which IBM Smalltalk runs. With VisualAge and IBM Distributed Smalltalk, Smalltalk programmers can quickly begin to build portable distributed applications.

- Smalltalk Development Model: Using IBM's Distributed Smalltalk technology, programmers can quickly develop applications that span networks, without having to learn the details of network communications, distributed application programming, or specialized interfaces. IBM Distributed Smalltalk extends the familiar Smalltalk tools—browsers, inspectors, debuggers, and workspaces—to the distributed environment.

- Flexible Distribution Approach: The IBM Distributed Smalltalk model supports much more than a simple client/server approach. Applications can be split in many different ways, supporting both client/server and true peer-to-peer designs. The distribution of an application can be dynamically changed throughout the development cycle.

- Security: IBM Distributed Smalltalk uses the industry-standard Generic Security Service API (GSS-API) and currently supports Network Security Program (NetSP) Version 1.2. Used with NetSP, IBM Distributed Smalltalk provides transparent support for client authentication, message verification, and message encryption.

- True Server Programming: IBM Distributed Smalltalk provides full support for true server programming:

  —It is scalable to accommodate the demands of your business.

  —Its security support provides for authentication of clients and servers.

  —It supports concurrent execution of multiple client requests within a single server Smalltalk image.

E.2.1   Distributed Object Space

Distributed object space is made up of multiple, individual object spaces. An object space is a single instance of a running Smalltalk image, and it can exist on any computer attached to a network and running IBM Distributed Smalltalk. With this technology, objects can

- Send standard Smalltalk messages to one another regardless of physical location.

- Send and receive other Smalltalk objects as arguments and results—even across the network—without having to "flatten" them into serialized data.

- Reside in different physical locations from one application version to the next, without requiring any change to the Smalltalk code.

Distributed object space enables developers to use the full power of the Smalltalk language, including high-performance messaging and efficient storage management through automatic garbage collection.

Because distributed object space is based on Smalltalk, you can send Smalltalk objects as arguments to remote objects just as you would pass them locally, without any conversion necessary. The Smalltalk code used to send messages to remote objects is the same standard syntax used to communicate with local objects. Therefore, at development time, the programmer need not be concerned with the physical location of the objects in the application. In fact, the physical location of the application modules can be dynamically changed throughout the development process, without any change to the Smalltalk code.

E.2.2　Distributed Object Space Run-Time Environment

The distributed object space run-time environment provides all of the support necessary to implement distributed execution of Smalltalk applications with true local and remote transparency. The run-time environment provides an additional layer on top of IBM Smalltalk (see Figure 214 on page 401). It provides the following distribution services:

- Messaging: IBM Distributed Smalltalk provides all of the communications logic necessary to send Smalltalk messages between object spaces. Once configured with the necessary location information, IBM Distributed Smalltalk handles the low-level task of passing Smalltalk objects across a network connection.

- Distributed Garbage Collection: IBM Distributed Smalltalk extends Smalltalk garbage collection so that it is distribution-aware. Unused memory is freed when it is no longer being used by other local or remote objects.

- Activation Support: IBM Distributed Smalltalk provides the necessary support to start any remote Smalltalk images that are required by the application. If an object in one object space sends a message to an object space whose image is not currently running, the IBM Distributed Smalltalk activator automatically starts it.

- Name Server Support: A name server is a directory of objects in a network. A name server contains object references, which provide information on the physical location of objects used by an application. By changing the object references, developers can update the location information for the objects without having to change the Smalltalk code.

If the name server cannot resolve a particular object name, it has the ability to relay the request to a second-level name server. The IBM Distributed Smalltalk name server is designed to comply with the industry-standard OMG Naming Service specification. The name server is also designed to be adaptable to other naming services, such as the OSF DCE directory service.

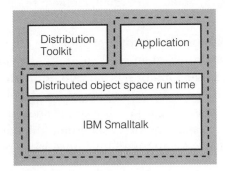

Figure 214. Distributed object space run-time environment

E.2.3   Distribution Toolkit

The IBM Distributed Smalltalk Distribution Toolkit is delivered as a set of tools to help developers and administrators design, develop, debug, optimize, and configure distributed applications from a single physical location. The Distribution Toolkit is a set of applications that run on top of the Distributed Object Space run-time environment (see Figure 214). The toolkit includes the following tools:

- **Remote Transcript and workspace windows.** A remote Transcript window is a local window that mirrors the System Transcript window of a remote object space, enabling developers to interact with a remote Smalltalk image as if it were local. Likewise, a remote workspace is a standard Smalltalk workspace from which objects in a remote object space are addressable.

- **Remote inspectors and browsers**. IBM Distributed Smalltalk extends the IBM Smalltalk inspectors and browsers to enable browsing and editing of remote objects and classes. Using these tools, we can browse other object spaces on the network; add, delete, and edit the classes that reside in those object spaces, provided we have authority to do so; and inspect and modify the contents of remote objects.

- **Distributed debugger**. IBM Distributed Smalltalk provides an enhanced Smalltalk debugger that shows distributed program execution as a single call stack. The debugger allows you to trace program execution that spans a network just as you would with an entirely local application. It is also possible to make changes to remote code from within the debugger.

- **Name server GUI**. IBM Distributed Smalltalk provides a graphical user interface that can be used to browse and update the contents of the name server. Thus we can add, delete, and change object references and other named objects.

- **Distribution configuration editor.** This editor enables the developer to partition and distribute the modules of an application to the various object spaces on the network. Each module is a group of Smalltalk classes.[27] Using the distribution configuration editor, the developer can specify into which object spaces (images) each module should be loaded. After the location for each module is specified, the developer can also use this editor to automatically load the appropriate modules into the remote images.

The distribution design of an application—the designation of which applications are loaded into which object spaces—is saved along with each version of the application. Developers can dynamically change the locations of the different modules of the distributed application to fine tune performance.

The distribution design of an application is always kept in synchronization with any corresponding code changes. The developer can freely modify the design of the application to use a different distribution design without having to keep track of which versions of the code belong with each design. Each version's code and distribution are stored together.

- **Remote message probe.** This tool profiles all messages traveling between object spaces. It shows you a stack containing every message sent from a particular object space. Thus the developer can analyze the message traffic and evaluate the efficiency of a design.

- **Event profiler.** The event profiler is used to analyze the message traffic among the objects in the application. Such analysis helps in deciding

---

27   Each group of classes is actually called an *application* in IBM Smalltalk terms, although in fact it may be only a part of a complete distrubted business application. This is based on the terminology of the IBM Smalltalk Team environment.

the best way to split your application. For example, if two objects have a lot of traffic between them, they should probably be in the same object space, whereas two objects that seldom interact can generally be remote from one another.

- **Runtime configuration tool**. This tool is used to set up the components of a distributed application on the system upon which it will run. When an administrator installs a distributed application, the runtime configuration tool ensures that the IBM Distributed Smalltalk runtime environment can find all of the object spaces and objects that make up the application. Using this tool, the administrator configures the name server information to reflect the physical locations of the object spaces that make up the application.

Bibliography

[Ale77]   C. Alexander, et al., *A Pattern Language: Towns, Building, Construction,* Oxford University Press, New York, 1977.

[Ara89]   Guillermo Arango, "Domain Analysis: From Art Form to Engineering Discipline," *SIGSOFT Engineering Notes,* Vol. 14, No. 2, pp. 152–159, May 1989.

[Bar91]   Barnett et al., Iterative Development Process Guide, IBM Cary Development Laboratory, April 1991. Internal document.

[Bea90]   S. Bear, P. Allen, D. Coleman, and F. Hayes. "Graphical Specification of Object Oriented Systems," *OOPSLA '90 Proceedings,* pp. 28–37, 1990.

[Bec89]   K. Beck and W. Cunningham, "A Laboratory for Teaching Object-Oriented Thinking," *OOPSLA '89 Proceedings,* 1989.

[Bec93]   K. Beck, "CRC: Finding Objects the Easy Way," *Object Magazine,* Nov-Dec 1993.

[Big89]   Ted Biggestaff, *Software Reusability,* ACM Press, 1989.

[Bin94]   R. Binder, "Testing Object-Oriented Systems: A Status Report," *American Programmer,* April 1994, pp. 22–28.

[Bla92]   M. Blaha, "Models of Models," *Journal of Object-Oriented Programming,* September 1992.

[Boe88]   B. Boehm, "A Spiral Model of Software Development and Enhancement," *Computer,* Vol. 21, No. 5, pp. 61–72, May 1988.

[Boo86]   G. Booch, "Object-Oriented Development," *IEEE Transactions on Software Engineering,* Vol. SE-12, No. 2, February 1986.

[Boo91]   G. Booch and M. Vilot, "Object-Oriented analysis and design," *The C++ Report,* Vol. 3, No. 8, September 1991.

[Boo94]   G. Booch, *Object-Oriented Analysis and Design with Applications,* Benjamin/Cummings, 1994.

[Boo95]   Grady Booch, *Object Solutions,* Addison-Wesley, 1995. ISBN 0-8053-0594-7.

[Bro84]   Mel Bordie, *Databases and Programming Languages,* Springer-Verlag, 1984.

[Bro87]   F. Brooks, No Silver Bullet, *IEEE Software,* August, 1987.

[Cat91]   R.G.G. Cattell, *Object Data Management: Object-Oriented and Extended Relational Database Systems,* Addison-Wesley Publishing Co., 1991. ISBN 0-201-53092-9.

[Col95]   Dave Collins, *Designing Object-Oriented User Interfaces,* Benjamin/Cummings, 1995. ISBN 0-8053-5350-X.

[Coo94]   Steve Cook and John Daniels, *Designing Object Systems,* Prentice Hall, 1994. ISBN 0-13-203-860-9.

[Dav93]   Alan Davis, *Software Requirements: Objects, Functions and States,* Prentice-Hall, Englewood Cliffs, NJ, 1993. ISBN 0-13-805763-X.

[Ech94]   Dennis D. King, Carol A. Jones, Randall P. Echhoff, "Multimedia Parts for VisualAge," *IBM Technical Reports,* Jan 1984 1994.

[Elm93]   Ramez Elmasri, et al., Entity-Relationship Approach-Er'93: 12th International Conference on Entity-Relationship Approach, Arlington, Texas, Dec. 15–17, 1993.

[Fan96]   W. Fang, S. Guyet, R. Haven, et. al., *VisualAge for Smalltalk Distributed: Developing Distributed Object Applications,* Prentice-Hall, 1996. ISBN 0-13-570813-3. IBM ITSO (SG24-4521-1).

[Fan96a]   W. Fang, R. Chu, and M. Wegerhäuser, *VisualAge for Smalltalk and SOMobjects: Developing Distributed Object Applications,* Prentice Hall, 1996. ISBN 0-13-570805-2, IBM ITSO (SG24-4390-1).

[Fan96b]   W. Fang, A. So, and J. Kreindler, "The Visual Modeling Technique: An Introduction and Overview," *Journal of Object-Oriented Programming,* Volume 9, No. 4. July/August, 1996.

[Fau93]   Gregory Faust, "Using a Visual Framework to Optimize O-O Development," *Object Magazine,* pp. 50–52, July-August 1993.

[Fow91]   Martin Fowler, "Which OO Analysis and Design Method," *SCOOP* Europe, September 1991.

[Gam95]   Eric Gamma, Richard Helm, Ralph Johnson, and John Vissides, *Design Patterns: Element of Object-Oriented Software Architecture,* Addison-Wesley, 1995.

[Gib90]   E. Gibson, "Objects—Born and Bred," *BYTE,* October 1990.

[Gol92] Adele Goldberg, presentation on Object Behavior Analysis, 1992. At the OBJECT EXPO.

[Gol95] Adele Goldberg and Kenneth R. Rubin, *Succeeding with Objects,* Addison-Wesley, 1995. ISBN 0-201-62878-3.

[Got94a] Goti, J. Carlos, *Business Rules: Their Role in Systems Requirements,* IBM Technical Report TR03.587, October 1994.

[Got94b] Goti, J. Carlos, *A Business Classification for Business Rules,* Database Newsletter, Vol. 22, Num. 5, Sept/Oct 1994.

[Ham93] Michael Hammer, James Champy, *Reengineering the Corporation: A Manifesto for Business Revolution,* Harper Collins, 1993. ISBN 0-887306-40-3.

[Har92] Paul Harmon, "CASE, Object-Oriented Programming, & Expert Systems," *American Programmer,* October 1992.

[Hay90] F. Hayes and D. Coleman, "Coherent Models for Object-Oriented Analysis," *OOPSLA '91 Proceedings,* pp. 171–183, 1990.

[Hek88] S. Hekmatpour and D. Ince, *Software Prototyping, Formal Methods and VDM,* Addison-Wesley, 1988.

[Hen93] Brian Henderson-Sellers, *A Book of Object-Oriented Knowledge: An Introduction to Object-Oriented Software Engineering,* Prentice-Hall, 1993. (2nd Edition, 1996). ISBN 0-135688-90-6.

[Hen94] Henderson-Sellers, B. and Edwards, J.H., *Book Two of the Object-Oriented Knowledge, The Working Object,* Prentice Hall, 1994. ISBN 0-13-093980-3.

[Het88] Bill Hetzel, *The Complete Guide to Software Testing,* John Wiley & Sons, 1988.

[Jac92] I. Jacobson, M. Christerson, et al., *Object-Oriented Software Engineering: A Use Case Driven Approach,* Addison-Wesley, 1992. ISBN 0-201-54435-0.

[Jac94] Ivar Jacobson: *Basic Use-Case Modeling, Report on Object Analysis & Design,* Volume 1, No. 2, 1994.

[Jac94a] Ivar Jacobson, *Systems of Interconnected Systems Report on Object Analysis & Design (ROAD)* Volume 2, No. 1, May-June 1994.

[Jac95] I. Jacobson, et al., *The Object Advantage, Business Process Reengineering with Object Technology,* Addison-Wesley, 1995.

[Jac95a] Ivar Jacobson: *Use Cases in Large-Scale Systems, Report on Object Analysis & Design,* Volume 1, No. 6, 1995.

[Jac95b] Ivar Jacobson et al., "Using Contracts and Use Cases to Build Plugable Architectures," *Journal of Object-Oriented Programming (JOOP),* May 1995.

[Kim92] Won Kim, *Introduction to Object-Oriented Databases,* Cambridge, Massachusetts: The MIT Press, 1992. ISBN 0-262-11124-1.

[Kun89]   Kunz, John, *Concurrent Knowledge Systems Engineering*, CIFE Working Paper Num. 5, Stanford University, 1989.

[Lal96]   Wilf Lalonde and John Pugh, "Preparing To Use the Distributed Facility in IBM Smalltalk," *Journal of Object-Oriented Programming*, May 1996.

[Lin94]   Robert Lindsay, "VisualAge Wrappers," *OS/2 Developers Magazine*, September/October 1994.

[Loo92]   M. Loomis, "Client-Server Architecture," *Journal of Object-Oriented Programming*, February 1992.

[Lor92]   M. Lorenz, *Object-Oriented Software Development: A Practical Guide*, Englewood Cliffs, NJ: Prentice Hall, 1992.

[Lor93]   M. Lorenz, *Object-Oriented Analysis and Design Methodologies: Object-Oriented Technology Center (OOTC)*, IBM PRGS Cary Laboratory, February 1993. Internal document.

[Lor94]   Mark Lorenz, *Object-Oriented Software Metrics: A Practical Guide*, Prentice Hall, 1995. ISBN 0-1317292-X.

[Lou91]   Loucopoulos, P., et al., *Business Rules Modelling: Conceptual Modelling and Object-Oriented Specifications*, Proceedings of the IFIP TC8/WG8.1 Working Conference, 1991.

[Mar93]   A. Margaroli, "Visual Programming & Visual Languages," *Sistemi Software*, pp. 40–66, May 1993.

[Mar94]   Xavier March, "Testing of Object-Oriented Methods, Classes and Systems: A Practitioner Guide, " *IBM Consulting Group*, June 1994.

[McG92]   J.D. McGregor and D.A. Sykes, *Object-Oriented Software Development: Engineering Software for Reuse*, Van Nostrand Reinhold, 1992. ISBN 0-442-00157-6.

[McL91]   D. McLeod, "Perspective on Object Databases," *Information and Software Technology*, Vol. 33, No. 1, pp. 13–21, January/February 1991.

[Mey88]   Bertrand Meyer, *Object-Oriented Software Construction*, Prentice-Hall, Englewood Cliffs, NJ, 1988. ISBN 0-13-629049-3.

[Mey95]   Bertrand Meyer, *Object Success*, Prentice-Hall, 1995. Englewood Cliffs, NJ, 1995. ISBN 0-13-1928333.

[Moc92]   M. Mock and L. Hodge, "An Exercise to Prototype the Object-Oriented Development Process," *Software Engineering Journal*, March 1992.

[Mon91]   Stephen Montgomery, *AD/Cycle*, Van Nostrand Reinhold, 1991. ISBN 0-442-30825-6.

[Mor93]   Moriatry, Terry, *The Next Paradigm, Database Programming and Design*, February 1993.

[Mor94] Moriatry, Terry, *Database Newsletter*, May/June 1994.

[Mye79] Glenford Myers, *Art of Software Testing*, John Wiley & Sons, New York, 1979. ISBN 0-47-104328-1.

[Ner92] J.M. Nerson, "Applying Object-Oriented Analysis and Design," *Communications of the ACM*, Vol. 35, No. 9, pp. 63–67, September 1992.

[Ner91] Kim Walden and Jean-Marc Nerson, *Seamless Object-Oriented Software Architecture*, Prentice Hall, 1991. ISBN 0-13-031303-3.

[Nor91] R. J. Norman, "Object-Oriented System Analysis: A Methodology for the 1990s," *Journal of System Management*, Vol. 42, No. 7, July 1991.

[Ode92a] J. Odell, "Dynamic and Multiple Classification," *Journal of Object-Oriented Programming*, January 1992.

[Ode92b] J. Odell, "Managing Object Complexity, Part I: Abstraction and Generalization," *Journal of Object-Oriented Programming*, September 1992.

[Orf96] R. Orfali, D. Harkey, and J. Edwards, *The Essential Distributed Objects Survival Guide*, John Wiley & Sons, Inc., 1996. ISBN 0471-12993-3.

[Pac92] Isabelle Borne and Pracois Pachet, "From Object-Oriented Design to Visual Programming," *European Journal of Engineering Education*, Vol. 17, No. 2, pp. 195–201, 1992.

[Pau91] M.C. Paul, B. Curtis, and N.B., Chrissis, et al., *Capability Maturity Model for Software*, Software Engineering Institute, August 1991. CMU/SEI-91-TR-24.

[Pri87] R. Prieto-Díaz and P. Freeman, "Classifying Software for Reusability," *IEEE Software*, January 1987.

[Puh92] David E. Monarchi and Gretchen I. Puhr, "A Research Typology for Object-Oriented Analysis and Design," *Communications of the ACM*, Vol. 35, No. 9, pp. 35–47, 1992.

{Rad85] Radice, Hardin, Munnis, and Ciarfell, "A Programming Process Study," *IBM Systems Journal*, Vol. 24, No. 2, 1985.

[Ros93] Doug Rosenberg, "Using the Object Modeling Technique with Objectory for Client/Server Development," *Object Magazine*, pp. 54–57, November-December 1993.

[Ros94] Ronald Ross, *The Business Rules Book*, Database Research Group Inc., 1994.

[Rub92] K.S. Rubin and A. Goldberg, "Object Behavior Analysis," *Communications of the ACM*, Vol. 35, No. 9, pp. 48–62, September 1992.

[Rub95] Ken Rubin, "Object-Oriented Transition Management," IBM North America Object Technology Practice document.

[Rum91] J. Rumbaugh, M. Blaha, W. Premerlani, F. Eddy, and W. Lorenson, *Object-Oriented Modeling and Design*, Prentice Hall, 1991. ISBN 0-13-630054-5.

[Rum92a]   J. Rumbaugh, "Derived Information," *Journal of Object-Oriented Programming,* January 1992.

[Rum92b]   J. Rumbaugh, "Over the Waterfall and Into the Whirlpool," *Journal of Object-Oriented Programming,* May 1992.

[Rum94]   J. Rumbaugh, "Getting Started, Using Use Cases to Capture Requirements," *Journal of Object-Oriented Programming,* September 1994.

[San91]   Sandifer A., Van Halle, B., *A Rule, by Any Other Name,* Database Programming and Design, February 1991.

[Sch86]   Roger Schank, *Explanation Patterns,* Lawrence Erlbaum Assoc., 1986.

[Sha95]   Yen-Ping Shan, Ralph Earle, and Skip McGaughey, "Rounding Out the Picture: Objects Across the Client/Server Spectrum," *IEEE Software,* October 1995.

[Shl88]   S. Shlaer and S.J. Mellor, *Object-Oriented Systems Analysis: Modeling the World in Data,* Englewood Cliffs, NJ: Yourdon Press, 1988.

[Shl92]   S. Shlaer and S.J. Mellor, *Object Lifecycles: Modeling the World in States,* Englewood Cliffs, NJ: Yourdon Press, 1992.

[Sta95]   Jean Stanford, "Enterprise Modeling with Use Cases," Workshop on Semantic Intergration in Complex Systems: OOPSLA '95.

[Ste95]   Jan Steinman and Barbara Yates, "Managing Project Documents," *Smalltalk Report,* June 1995.

[Str87]   B. Stroustrup, *The C+ + Programming Language,* Addison-Wesley Publishing Company, 1987.

[Sum89]   R. Summersgill and D.P. Browne, "Human Factors: Its Place in System Development Methods," *ACM,* pp. 227–234, 1989.

[Tay90]   David Taylor, *Object-Oriented Technology: A Manager's Guide,* Addison-Wesley, 1990. ISBN 0-201-5638-4.

[Tay92]   David Taylor, *Object-Oriented Information Systems: Planning and Implementation,* New York: John Wiley & Sons, Inc., 1992. ISBN 0-471-54364-0.

[Tay93]   David Taylor, "Finding Good Objects," *Object Magazine,* Sept. 1993.

[Tay95]   *Business Engineering with Object Technology,* John Wiley & Son, 1996. ISBN 0-471-04521-7.

[Tka92a]   D. Tkach, "Knowledge Engineering with Object-Oriented Technology," IBM ITL Conference on Expert Systems, 1992.

[Tka92b]   D. Tkach, and R. Puttick, *Object-Oriented Technology in the Application Development Environment,* IBM ITSO (GG24-3859), 1992.

[Tka93]   D. Tkach, R. Kegelmann, R. Singh, and R. Tsuyuki, *Object-Oriented Applications using Relational Databases,* IBM ITSO, 1993.

[Tka96]   D. Tkach, and R. Puttick, *Object Technology in Application Development,* 2nd Ed., Addison-Wesley, 1996.

[Tka96]   Tkach, D., Puttick, R., *Object Technology in Application Development,* Addison-Wesley, 1996.

[Tra95]   Will Tracz, *Confession of a Used Salesman,* ACM Press, 1995.

[Ven95]   Michele Vening, "Writing Cross-Platform User Documentation," *Cross-Platform Strategies,* Fall 1995.

[Was91]   A.I. Wasserman and P.A. Pircher, "The Spiral Model of Object-Oriented Software Development," *Hotline on Object-Oriented Technology,* Vol. 2, No. 1, pp. 8–12, 1991.

[Weg90]   P. Wegner, "Concepts and Paradigms of Object-Oriented Programming," *OOPS Messenger,* Vol. 1, No. 1, ACM Press, August 1990.

[Weg91]   P. Wegner, *Perspectives on Object-Oriented Design,* Brown University, January 1991, Technical Report No. CS-91-01.

[Wil90]   David A. Wilson, "Class Diagrams, A Tool for Design, Documentation and Teaching," *Journal of Object-Oriented Programming,* Vol. 2, No. 5, January/February 1990.

[Wil94]   David A. Wilson and Stephen D. Wilson, *Tutorial on Designing Object-Oriented Frameworks,* 1994. At the 77th IBM Conference on Object-Oriented Software Development, Santa Clara, California.

[Wir89]   Rebecca Wirfs-Brock and Brian Wilkerson, "Object-Oriented Design: A Responsibility-Driven Approach," *OOPSLA '89 Proceedings,* 1989.

[Wir90]   R. Wirfs-Brock, B. Wilkerson, and L. Wierner, *Designing Object-Oriented Software,* Prentice Hall, 1990.

[Wir93]   Rebecca Wirfs-Brock, "Characterizing Your Objects," *The Smalltalk Report,* February 1993.

[Wir94a]   Rebecca Wirfs-Brock, "What's Important about Responsibility-Driven Design," Report on Object Analysis & Design, Volume 1, No. 2, 1994.

[Wir94b]   Rebecca Wirfs-Brock, "Characterizing Your Application's Control Style," Report on Object Analysis & Design, Volume 1, No. 3, 1994.

[You92]   Edward Yourdon, *Decline & Fall of the American Programmer,* New Jersey: Yourdon Press, 1992.

[You95]   Edward Yourdon, et al., *Mainstream Objects: An Analysis and Design Approach for Business,* Yourdon Press, 1995. ISBN 0-13-209156-9.

Index